Land Records
of
SUSSEX COUNTY DELAWARE

1769-1782

Deed Books
L No. 11 & M No. 12

F. Edward Wright

Indexed by
Charlotte Meldrum

HERITAGE BOOKS
2008

HERITAGE BOOKS
AN IMPRINT OF HERITAGE BOOKS, INC.

Books, CDs, and more—Worldwide

For our listing of thousands of titles see our website
at
www.HeritageBooks.com

Published 2008 by
HERITAGE BOOKS, INC.
Publishing Division
100 Railroad Ave. #104
Westminster, Maryland 21157

Copyright © 1994 F. Edward Wright

All rights reserved. No part of this book may be reproduced or transmitted in any form or by any means, electronic or mechanical, including photocopying, recording or by any information storage and retrieval system without written permission from the author, except for the inclusion of brief quotations in a review.

International Standard Book Numbers
Paperbound: 978-1-58549-298-5
Clothbound: 978-0-7884-7245-9

INTRODUCTION

Sometime ago Elaine Hastings Mason and I compiled the land records of Sussex County for the period, 1782-1789 comprising the Deed Book N, No. 13. You are invited to read the excellent introduction written by Ms. Mason. I have included the maps with this introduction.

This book represents the compilation of land records for the prior period, 1769-1782. These are records of deeds, mortgages, agreements, bonds and other transactions found in the deed books, Liber L, No. 11 and Liber M, No. 12. I have omitted the commissions given to the justices of Sussex County from the provincial government and I have also omitted the names of individual attorneys appointed by the grantors and grantees - considering these data of no genealogical significance.

The first number in the entry is the page of the original volume. The first date given is the date the transaction took place. The recorded date or acknowledged date is usually given at the end of the entry. Full description of the land is not given, only references to adjoining land owners and significant land marks. The term "more or less" when applied to acreage has been omitted.

F. Edward Wright
Westminster, Maryland
1994

Abbreviations:
ackn = acknowledged
dec'd. deceased
wit: = witnesses

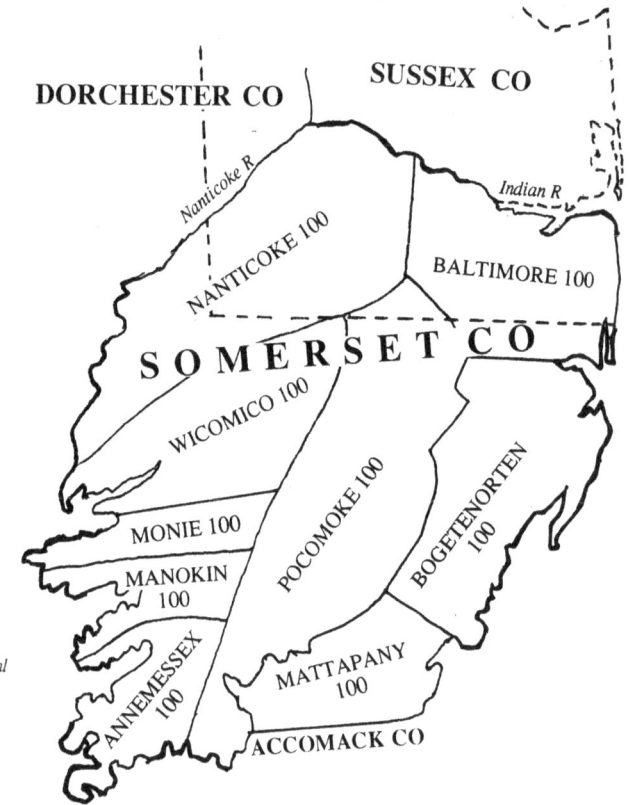

Somerset County MD in 1724, based on a map from *The National Genealogical Society Quarterly*.

IN 1742, WORCESTER COUNTY, MD, WAS CREATED FROM SOMERSET COUNTY. In setting the northern boundary at 'Broad Creek Bridge', site of present day Laurel, Lord Baltimore reaffirmed his claim to Sussex County lands even though, in 1732, he had signed an agreement in which he ceded them to Wm Penn. *A word of caution: information derived from the above map should be interpreted very broadly, based as it is on vague descriptions of Lord Baltimore's boundaries which often conflict with maps from the period. Surviving maps, in fact, often conflict with one another, and even bear obvious inaccuracies like the transposition of Somerset and Worcester Counties.*

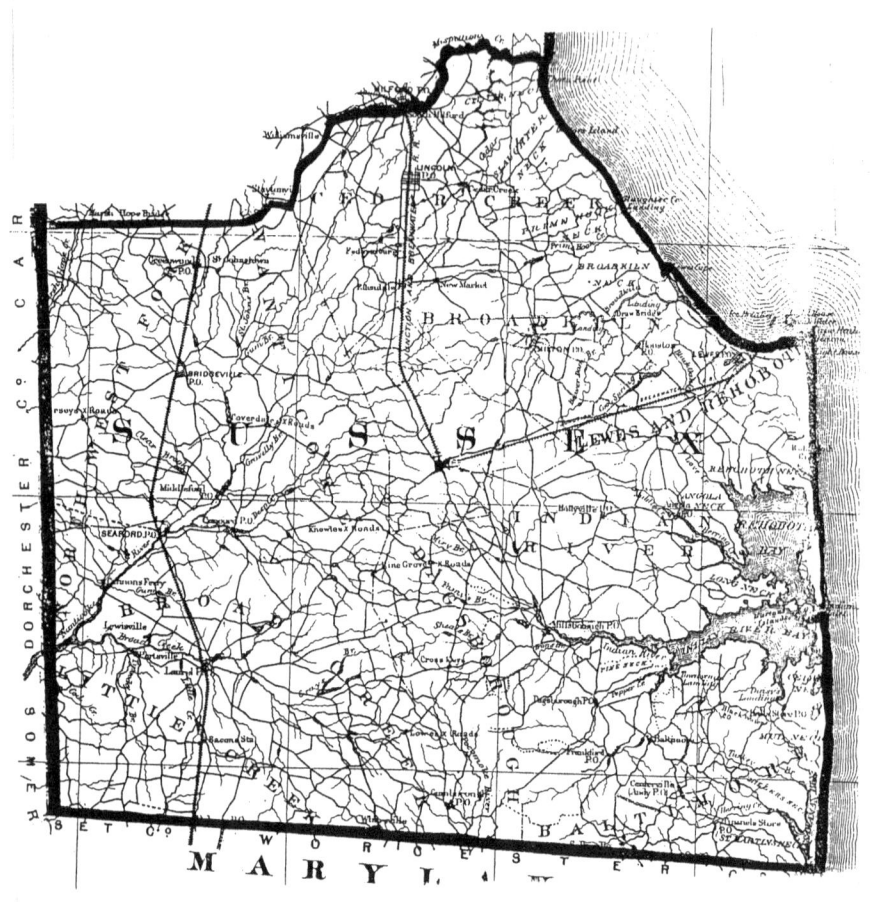

SUSSEX COUNTY, DELAWARE, FROM AN 1868 PROPERTY MAP. The various hundreds are located approximately as they were in 1780-86.

Liber L No. 11

1. William Bell of Sussex Co., planter, from Benjamin Wynkoop of City of Phila. for 5 shillings. Deed of release. As described in the deed of sale from Benjamin Wynkoop and his wife Sarah Wooddrop dated 9 Oct 1767, recorded in Liber K. No. 10., folio 305. Clear of claim of Absalom Hart. 7 Feb 1760. Ackn: 7 Feb 1769.

1. Nehemiah Field, from Henry Fisher and Abraham Wiltbank, all pilots. 1 Jan 1769. Lot in town of Lewes with 60 feet on 2nd Street, adjoining on the southeast the lot now in possession of William West and on the northwest the lot now in possession of Frances Cahoon, which said lot said Henry Fisher and Abraham Wiltbank purchased of Samuel Davis, pilot, and Samuel Davis purchased of John Jones and Anne Jones his wife and Comfort Poor who were heirs to Thomas Mershall who died intestate, as appears in a deed from said John Jones and wife Ann Jones and Comfort Poor unto Samuel Davis in Liber I No. 9, folio 301, 16 Jan 1762. For £17.7.6. Wit: Daniel Nunez, Purnal Johnson. Ackn: 9 Feb 1769.

2. Rhoads Shankland from John Wiltbank, Sussex Co., Esqr. 7 Feb 1769. Part of a tract of said Wiltbank purchased of Nehemiah Field and adjoining said Rhoads Shankland's 6-acre lot on the northwest end of corner of the tract bounded by corner post of Jacob Kollock's land standing on the southeast edge of market Street of town of Lewes with line intersecting the run of Pagan Creek, containing 2 acres. For £3. Wit: Nehemiah Field, Lewis West. Ackn: 9 Feb 1769.

2. Prettyman Stockley, Sussex Co., weaver, from Rece Woolf, Junr., Sussex Co., planter. 6 Feb 1769. Parcel of land in town of Lewes, beginning at the corner stone of land of John Hall, blacksmith, dec'd., on the southeast side of the southernmost street of town of Lewes ... land formerly of Thomas Cale ... corner stone of lot of heirs of Thomas Clifton. 6 acres. For £70. Wit: John Clowes, Junr., Ephraim Darby. Ackn: 8 Feb 1769.

3. Deed of release. Moses Allin from William and Joseph Allin, yeoman. 500 acres which formerly belonged to John Allin, senr., dec'd., who by his will left me afsd. land to his two grandchildren, Moses Allin and above said William Allin who have consented, with the consent of afsd. Joseph Allin, exr. of John Allin, dec'd. to the division of the above land, being part of a larger parcel surveyed for Richard Bundick for 1200 acres, 13 Dec 1681, called Arcada, on the south side of Long Love Branch in Indian River Hundred and afterward a warrant of resurvey was granted for afsd. tract to John Allin, John Coulter, Charles Prat, Paynter Stockley and Robert McIvain, dated 1 March 1755 and resurveyed on 12 Feb 1760. Beginning at the corner of the tract of Cord Hazzard ... to corner stake of land of Robert McIlvain. Wit: John Shankland, William Little. Ackn: 10 Feb 1769.

4. William Allen son of John Allen Junr., late of Sussex Co., from Joseph and Moses Allen, exr. of John Allen, late of Sussex

Co. 10 Feb 1769. Whereas there was in 1753 a bill filed by Joseph Hazzard and his wife Mary, William Allen and Elizabeth Allen, minors of John Allen, Junr. afsd, in the Chancery Court of Sussex Co. against John Allen, Senr. afsd. in his lifetime begging release. The court hath decreed that John Allen the Elder, should convey 250 acres mentioned in said bill to afsd. Mary as widow of John Allen, Junr., and afsd William Allen and Elizabeth Allen, that is, 1/3 to Mary during her natural life and then to William and Elizabeth and the other 2/3 immediately to William and Elizabeth and before the deed was executed William Allen purchased of afsd Joseph Hazzard and Mary his wife all their right to the afsd. land. Elizabeth died before she arrived to the age of 21, without issue, and her part fell to the afsd. William. John Allen, Senr. died before he executed the deed and exrs., Joseph and Moses Allen, have remised, released and forever quit claimed unto afsd. William Allen a parcel of land in Indian River Hundred and on the south side of Long Loved Branch, being part of a larger tract laid out for Richard Bundick called Arcadia bounded by ... Hazzard's Resurvey ... corner stake of Coulter's ..., containing 242 1/2 acres. Wit: John Shankland, William Little. 10 Feb 1769. Deed of release ackn. 10 Feb 1769.

5. John Wiltbank, yeoman, from John Prettyman, yeoman, Sussex Co. 8 Feb 1769. For £50. Land being part of a tract and marsh willed to him by his father John Prettyman which land and marsh was formerly taken up by Francis Cornwell. Beginning at a corner post of the land adjoining land whereon Wrixam White, Junr., now dwells and at a corner of land John Prettyman now owns ... through the eastern most of the two island known as Hawks Nest Gutt, 22 1/2 acres. Within deed of sale ackn. 8 Feb 1769.

6. Jonathan Tilney from Absolom Little. For £382. Tract called Swan Point originally patented by Bryant Rolls, lying on the north side of Broad Kiln Creek, beginning at a corner post near Isaac Jones' fence, containing 360 acres. Deed ackn. 7 Feb 1769.

6. Isaac Watson, Esqr., Sussex Co. from Cornelius Stockley, blacksmith, Sussex Co. 9 Feb 1769. Tract in Slaughter Neck Forrest in Cedar Creek Hundred, being part of a tract of Robert Lee, Junr., beginning at a corner stake on the line of said Isaac Watson's land called The Orphans Portion ... corner tree of land called Lebanon, containing 48 1/2 acres. Wit: John Wiltbank, Rhoads Shankland. Deed ackn. 8 Feb 1769.

7. Joseph Cord, yeoman, Sussex Co., from Joshua Fisher, City of Philadelphia, merchant. 22 April 1768. For £35. Tract bounded to the eastward by Woolf Branch or Woolf Pit ... to the northward by marsh formerly of Abraham Potter, westward and southward by other land of said Joseph Cord, 18 acres, being part of a tract called Sw---, granted by patent to John Street conveyed by said John Street to William Clark who conveyed same to Thomas Fisher who by his last will to devised same to Joshua Fisher, party to these presents, containing 300 acres. Wit: Thomas Fisher, Miers Fisher. Deed of sale ackn. 9 Feb 1769.

7. Nathan Spencer, yeoman, from William Blocksom, yeoman. 9 Feb 1769. William Blocksom of Accomack Co., Virginia, by Power of Attorney dated 25 Aug 1767 hath given William Blocksom of Sussex Co. afsd. full power to convey parcel of land to Nathaniel Spencer. Whereas a warrant granted to David Smith of county afsd. for 200 acres dated 24 April 1702 in forrest of Cedar Creek Hundred called Thompsons Ridge which land was surveyed unto David Smith by Deputy Surveyor on 25 Jan 1742. For consideration of £13.2.6. 35 acres. ---, John Walton(?). Within deed of sale ackn. 9 Feb 1769.

8. Mary Craig, widow and extrx. of John Craig, from John Wiltbank, Esqr. For £25 paid by John Craig, dec'd., for tract and swamp called Hawks Nest Gutt. Beginning at a corner post of afsd. John Wiltbanks ... to a corner post of John Prettyman. 11 1/4 acres.

9. George and John Rickards from Abraham Wynkoop, exrs. 7 Feb 1769. Between Mary Wynkoop, John Vining and Phebe his wife and Benjamin Wynkoop, surviving executors of Abraham Wynkoop, Sussex Co., dec'd. of the one part and George Rickards and John Rickards of the same county of the other part. Whereas there is a parcel of land in Cedar Creek Hundred being part of a tract that was willed to Susanna Jouns wife of James Jouns by her father Edmond Mills and the same afterwards sold by John Spencer, John Polk and Thomas Wynkoop to afsd. Abraham Wynkoop, dated 14 Sep 1753 and by sd. deed recorded in Book H No. 7, folio 379. For £20. Wit: William Molleston, Daniel Nunez, Junr. Deed ackn. 8 Feb 1769.

9. Charity Turner from Boaz Manlove, Sheriff. 9 Feb 1769. The chattels of Ephraim Turner were to be levied a sum of money which Francis Murray in the Court of Common Pleas recovered against him and the sheriff seized the right of said Ephraim Turner in a tract that his father, Humphrey Turner died possessed of and intestate of and then in the possession of Charity Turner which said land is adjoining the land of Wrixam White and the land of John Wiltbank, Esqr. and part of a tract that William Clark, Esqr. took up by virtue of a warrant and the Sheriff caused a valuation to be made of the undivided right of said land and the two freeholders appointed returned that the share of Ephraim Turner would not rent to pay the debt and the land was sold to Cornelius Turner who purchased it for afsd. Charity Turner and requested that it be conveyed to her for £6. Wit: Jacob Kollock, Junr., Jno. Russell. Deed of sale ackn. 7 Feb 1769.

10. Ebenezer Spencer from Isaac Townsend, Sussex Co., yeoman. 8 Dec 1768. For £100+. Parcel of land and marsh being part of a tract formerly granted to Alexander Draper and the marsh part of a warrant granted to Coston Townsend, lying in Slaughter Neck on the southeast side of Cedar Creek. 71 acres. Wit: Nathan Young, Dormon Lofland. Within deed ackn. 8 Feb 1769.

11. Wrixam Lewis, shipwright, of Sussex Co., from Simon Kollock, Sussex Co., cooper. 11 Jan 1769. For £50. Part of a tract called [blank] about 3 miles from the town of Lewes and on the

south side of the county road that leads from Lewes Town to Coolspring or to the upper end of the county. Beginning near the road that leads out of said road to Parkers Mill or Drawbridge ... Craigs land ... 39 3/4 acres. Wit: Hercules Kollock, John Lewis. "The recitals and conveyances may be had by applying to the Rolls Office for Sussex afsd. in a deed Charles Dingee to Charles Perry who willed and bequeathed the afsd land to his daughter Cathrine who intermarried with the said Simon Kollock and afterwards died leaving one child who also died in its minority and the afsd. land fell to the afsd Simon Kollock party to these presents he being heir at law. Within deed ackn. 8 Feb 1769.

12. John Little, Sussex Co., from John Lockwood, Worcester Co. 7 March 1769. Land in Angola and Indian River Hundred being part of a larger tract called Arcada granted by patent to Richard Bundick. For £95 paid by Josiah Martin of Sussex Co. Wit: Sacker Wyatt, Wm. Peery. Within deed ackn. 9 March 1769.

12. John Little, Sussex Co., from Josiah Martin, Sussex Co. 7 March 1769. Tract in Angola and Indian River Hundred known as Watsons Choice. Beginning at the southeast corner of Watsons Patent. 77 acres, for £40. Wit: Wm. Peery, Sacker Wyatt. Within deed ackn. 9 March 1769.

13. Peter Riggs, Sussex Co., from Boaz Manlove, Esqr., Sussex Co. 13 Feb 1769. For £25. Land in Cedar Creek adjoining said Riggs' land ... to a hickory of Mary Borough's field. Wit: Isaac Smith, Manuel Manlove. Within deed ackn. 7 March 1769. Know that Magdalon Manlove of Sussex Co., widow, was bound to Peter Riggs, planter, in the sum of £100 on 25 Jan 1769. For the quit claim to the above named tract.

14. Peter Marsh, Junr., Sussex Co., from Elon Roads, Sussex Co., admr. of John Roads, dec'd. 7 March 1769. Whereas John Roads in his lifetime by a bond of conveyance bound himself to said Peter Marsh, Junr., for the remainder reversion of land called Timber Neck in Rehoboth Hundred which land is part of the patent granted by Edmond Andross to Andrew Deprey, dec'd., dated 20 Aug 1769 as by a deed of indenture dated 6 Aug 1735 from John Deprey to Richard Henmon (grandfather to the afsd. John Roads). 160 acres. The consideration money for the said land was fully paid to John Roads in his lifetime. Wit: Boaz Manlove, Alexander Shankland. Within deed ackn. 7 March 1769.

14. Bond of conveyance. John Roads, Sussex Co., yeoman, bound to Peter Marsh, Junr. for £500. 24 Nov 1768. To convey land called Timber Neck near Rehoboth Bay. Wit: William Shankland, James Newbold, Richard Little.

15. Petition of Elon Roads, widow and admx. of John Roads to execute a deed of conveyance [for above mentioned land]. 7 March 1769.

15. Jacob Kollock, Esqr. from Hercules Kollock. 7 March 1769.

Part of a tract in Lewes and Rehoboth Hundred adjoining land of afsd. Jacob Kollock and land of John Russel and the land of Gilbert Marriner. 40 acres. Part of a tract that Shepard Kollock and Mary his wife died possessed of and was allotted to afsd Hercules Kollock as his part of said dec'd. land by 5 freeholders appointed by the court of Orphans. For £100. Solomon Stockley, Daniel Nunez. Within deed ackn. 8 March 1769.

15. Francis Bagwell from William Bagwell. William Bagwell, Esqr. son and legatee by last will of his father Thomas Bagwell, late of Accomack, Virginia, dec'd., for divers good reasons ... "and preventing future contests and troubles that may arise between myself, my heirs, exrs., admrs. or assigns and my brother Francis Bagwell, his heirs, exrs. admrs. and assigns, release to said Francis Bagwell to land called Long Neck in the Indian River Hundred, the half part of 500 acres purchased by my father of William Burton, late of Accomack afsd., yeoman, dec'd." Wit: Philip Russel, Cornelius Wiltbank, Thos. Fisher. Above deed ackn. 1 Aug 1710.

16. A lease from Josias Martin to John Hopkins and James Martin in Trust. Whereas a number of inhabitants near Cool Spring have agreed to build a house for the edification of youth and have subscribed several sums of money for the same and have appointed John Hopkins and James Marton as Trustees to impower workmen to build said school house in proportion to said money, know that Josias Martin has leased one acre on the southeast corner of his dwelling plantation for 99 years or as long as the house shall be kept in repair. 2 Dec 1768. Wit: William Shankland, Charles Rawlins. N. B. The house is to be built on the southeast corner of John Kiphaven's and Alexander Molleston's patent of 1000 acres.

17. Jeremiah Warder, City of Philadelphia, merchant, from Robert Talbert and wife, Sarah, Sussex Co. 4 Sep 1769. Tract of 280 acres adjoining the north side of Pembertons Branch being the northwest fork of Broadkill Creek, beginning at a corner oak on the north side of said branch on the head of Peerys Mill Pond. 224 acres of above 280 acres was granted by patent to Thomas Pemberton who at his decease left the same to his daughter Elizabeth who afterwards married Zachariah Goforth of Kent Co., Delaware and by deed of sale with her husband dated 1 Nov 1729 conveyed said 224 acres to Samuel Stuart who by his deed of sale dated 3 Feb 1729 conveyed same to Robert Cravins and said Robert Cravins by his attorney James Hood his deed of sale dated 3 Feb 1747/8 conveyed same to Robert Talbert, father of the present Robert, party to these presents and the other 56 acres by legal conveyances from Charles Spooner the original taker up, became the property of afsd Robert Talbert the Elder who deceased intestate. There is also one acre lying on the south end of the mill dam on Pembertons Branch afsd. which became the property of John Talbert, brother to the first above mentioned Robert which said John Talbert also dec'd. intestate. Therefore all the above real estate of the above descendants became the joint property of the first mentioned Robert Talbert and his sister Elizabeth

Talbert who afterwards married Robert Stephenson, to be equally
divided between them and they chose John Clowes, David Hall,
Gilbelcher Parker, William Fowler and Samuel Tam to partition
their land. Wit: Thos. Robinson, Peter Robinson. Sarah Tolbert
acknowledged she executed the deed freely. Within deed ackn. 5
Sep 1769.

18. Charles Draper, Sussex Co., Innholder, from Isaac Townsend,
Sussex Co. 13 April 1769. A tract adjoining the lands of
Ebenezer Spencer in Slaughter Neck being part of the same which
formerly belonged to Coston Townsend, dec'd., called Little
Britten, containing 101 1/2 acres. ... till it comes to David
Watsons bounder one perch to the eastward of the wharf called
Isaac Townsend's Wharf ... For £41.2.3. Wit: David Wattson,
Ephraim Holcager. Within deed ackn. 3 May 1769.

19. George Kollock, ship joyner, from Boaz Manlove, High Sheriff
of Sussex Co. 4 May 1769. Simon Kollock, Esqr., late of Sussex
Co., died intestate, and 2/3 of his tract fell to Shepard
Kollock, eldest son, admr. of his late father who left and
bequeathed by his last will the afsd. land amongst his several
heirs, which heirs exhibited a petition to the Court of Common
Pleas for a division of the land and the above land was allotted
to Alice Henderson wife of John Henderson, shopkeeper, being one
of the heirs of Shepard Kollock, land in the suburbs of the town
of Lewes, on the southeast side of the main county road that
leadeth from the town of Lewes to Rehoboth and on the northeast
side and adjoining David Hall's land which he bought of Simon
Kollock, one of the afsd. heirs and joining the afsd. George
Kollock's land on the southwest side of his land, being part of
the afsd. dividend or tract surveyed and divided of 42 1/4 acres,
which John Henderson as above mentioned by a certain obligation
became indebted to John White and Samuel Coldwell of
Philadelphia, merchants and sometime afterwards said White and
Coldwell recovered a judgement against afsd. Henderson for the
sum of the afsd. obligation and whereas his land was seized and
sold by public sale to George Kollock for 40 shillings. Wit: John
Russel, William Prettyman. Within deed ackn. 4 May 1769.

19. Power of attorney. John Paynter, late of Sussex Co.,
blacksmith, appoints John Rodney his attorney to deliver to his
brother Samuel Paynter, the younger, any conveyances and
assurances regarding the lands, tenements, etc. which Samuel
Paynter the Elder, dec'd. by his last will devised to him, John
Paynter. Wit: Alexr. Shankland, Obediah Dinge. 26 Aug 1768.

20. John Paynter late of Sussex Co., blacksmith, for £70, paid
by Samuel Paynter, his brother, releases his right to land and
marsh near Lewes Town called Marsh Pasture, 30 acres, between the
marsh pastures of Jacob Kollock, Esqr. and Comfort Jenkens, which
piece of land was devised to him by the last will of his father
dated 11 Oct 1767. This deed of release was ackn. 5 May 1769.

20. John Paynter, blacksmith, for £150, paid by his brother,
Samuel Paynter, releases possession of tract in Lewes and

Rehoboth Hundred, containing 74 acres and 157 square perches, being the same land which William Shankland, John Niel, Elizabeth Niel, Robert Shankland and Alexander Shankland by deed dated 3 March 1756 released to Samuel Paynter, the elder, dec'd. who by his last will devised to his son John Paynter. Wit: John Wiltbanck, Hercules Kollock. Within deed of release ackn. 5 May 1769.

21. William Delany, Sussex Co., from Major Warren, Sussex Co. 3 May 1769. Land in Broadkill Hundred, granted by warrant to Joseph Rotten for 700 acres by indenture dated 7 Nov 1758 who conveyed to David Rotten 300 acres, part of the afsd tract and David Rotten conveyed said 300 acres to Nehemiah Reed and he conveyed it the above Major Warren who conveys it to William Delany for £45. Bounds to a corner oak standing by John Pridex(?) field ... to a sapling on a small island in the swamp ... containing 150 acres. Wit: Wm. Peery, William Kiphaven. Within deed of sale ackn. 3 May 1769.

22. James Gordon, farmer, Sussex Co., from Mary Collings, Sussex Co., widow and admx of George Collings, farmer, dec'd. 3 May 1769. Whereas George by bond dated 9 May 1764 obliged himself to convey to afsd. James Gorden a tract of 110 acres on the north side of Cowbridge Branch in Rosmery Neck near the head of Indian River being part of a larger tract formerly surveyed for Robert West, surveyed 9 Jan 1717 commonly known as Robert West's Plantation, ... to a line dividing the land from Richard Tomplin's land. George Collings died intestate before any conveyance was executed to James Gordon. Wit: Robert Prettyman, Samuel Darby. Within deed ackn. 3 May 1769.

22. James Gordon from George Collins, a bond. 9 May 1764. George Collins of Sussex Co., yeoman, bound to James Gordon of the same place, innholder, for £120, re land bounded on said Gordon's mill pond and some land of Richard Tomplin's containing 110 acres, being the land that Wrixam Christopher now lives upon, said land from the heirs of Gilbert Mariner whose widow sold sd. land by order of court. Wit: John Gordon, Jemima Lacey. ackn. 3 May 1769.

23. George Kollock, Sussex Co., joyner, from Alice Henderson, Sussex Co., spinster. 4 May 1769. For £87. Parcel of land being part of a larger tract granted by patent to Alexander Molleston, late of afsd co., dec'd. and by sundry deeds of conveyances became the property of Simon Kollock, Esqr. late of the county afsd., died intestate and Shepard Kollock admr. of afsd. Simon Kollock and the land became the property of Shepard Kollock and the land fell to the heirs of afsd. Shepard Kollock and a parcel was allotted to Alice Henderson, one of the daughters of afsd. Shepard Kollock. Land being in the suburbs of the town of Lewes joining land of David Hall and George Kollock. 41 1/4 acres. Wit: Benjamin Miflin, John Heverlo. Within deed of sale ackn. 5 May 1769.

24. James Thompson, town of Lewes, Gentleman, from John Heaverlo

and wife Hannah. 20 May 1769. Bounded to the north by Lewes Creek, to the southeast by land of Jacob Wiltbanck, to the southwest by Pagan Creek and to the northwest by land late of Peter and David Hall, containing 33 acres and 11 square perches which by deed of sale from Serjeant Smythers and Mary his wife conveyed to Nathaniel Naws who died intestate leaving a son which said son died in infancy whereupon the land descended to afsd. Hannah the sister of the afsd. Nathaniel and only heir at law. And whereas John Cord and Hannah his wife now the wife of John Heavelo one of the parties thereof conveyed by deed to Stephen Green of Sussex Co., shipwright, dated 4 May 1748 the land and premisses afsd. with an exception or reserve of one acre on the front or ? which acres is deducted out of the afsd quantity of acres which lies to the west adjoining the burying ground leaving on the front to Prettyman Green 15 perches, 11 1/2 feet. For £12. Wit: Jacob Kollock, Junr., John Adams. Within deed ackn. 20 May 1769.

24. John Fisher, yeoman, Sussex Co., from Benjamin Carpenter, Sussex Co., cordwinder. 3 May 1769. Tract in Broadkill Hundred of 200 acres bound on the land of Purnal Johnson, on the south on land of the Quaker Meeting house and east on the Cool Spring Creek. Wit: Benjamin Stockley, Joseph Hall. Within deed ackn. 5 May 1769. On 6 May 1772 Peter Fretwell Wright, exr., one of the heirs of the mortgager(?), recorded full satisfaction from Benjamin Carpenter and released the land from the heirs of John Fisher.

25. Mary or William Peery from Isaac Straton, Kent Co. and wife Ann. 4 May 1769. For £10. Tract in Broadkill Hundred being part of a larger tract called Coolspring Tract being a tract James Campbell died seized of and intestate. The tract was divided amongst his several heirs and 100 acres thereof became the property of Dorthia, the daughter of afsd. James Campbell and Dorthea dying intestate 1/4 of the said 100 acres became the property of afsd. Ann Straton, sister to the afsd. Dorthea and another daughter of afsd. James Campbell. Wit: John Harmonson, Jos. Shankland. Within deed ackn. 4 May 1769.

26. Bethual Watson from William Walton. 6 May 1769. Indenture between Boaz Manlove, High Sheriff of Sussex Co., and Bethual Wattson, Sussex Co., yeoman. Tract in Cedar Creek Hundred of 200 acres, being entered by John Walton, dec'd. father to the afsd. William Walton on 7 May 1724. And whereas Cornelius Stockley assignee of Levi Robens at a certain term recovered judgment against William Walton and John Walton of said county in 1767 whereby the land was seized along with certain household goods and the land was sold to Bethual Watson for £25.1.6. Wit: John Shankland, Rhoads Shankland. Within deed ackn. 6 May 1769.

26. Robert Jones, farmer, Sussex Co., from John Musterd, yeoman, Sussex Co. 3 May 1769. For £65. Tract in Broadkill Hundred being part of a larger tract which was conveyed to Thomas Staton, Senr., dec'd., by William Shankland then sheriff of sd. county by indenture dated 3 Feb 1746 which being part of a larger tract

left by will to his son Thomas Staton and conveyed by him to afsd. John Mustard by deed of sale dated 1 Sep 1761, 100 acres. Beginning at Mill Creek. Wit: Nathaniel Gordon, Samuel Darby. Within deed ackn. 5 May 1769.

27. Spencer Chance, planter, Sussex Co., from Ebenezar Spencer, Sussex Co., planter. 20 May 1769. For £120. Parcel of land and marsh in Cedar Creek Neck on the south side of Mispillion Creek called Gravelly Landing which by the last will of Samuel Spencer became the right of said Ebenezar Spencer. Boundary intersects Paynters Gutt. 100 acres. Wit: Thomas Eavan, Wm. Chance, Junr. Within deed ackn. 20 May 1769.

28. James Richardson, late of Maryland, yeoman, from Joseph English, Sussex Co., yeoman. 21 Sep 1762. Land in forrest of Broadkill Hundred called Good Luck, granted to Joseph English by proprietary warrant. Boundary intersects Keneys Branch. 260 acres, for £60. Wit: Jacob Dewson, Rhoads Shankland. Within deed of sale ackn. 5 May 1769.

28. Robert Prettyman, Sussex Co., from John Futcher, Sussex Co. 4 May 1769. Tract in Indian River Hundred being part of a tract called Strife, whereof John Prettyman of Sussex Co. was seized and by his last will devised to his son Thomas Prettyman and he dying intestate it became the property of afsd. John Futcher. 58 acres for £43.10. Wit: Wm. Peery, Robert Burton. Within deed ackn. 4 May 1769.

29. John Crippen to Noble Cordry. 3rd of 2nd month 1769. Indenture made between John Crippen, Joseph Crippen, Mary Crippen and Catharine Crippen of Sussex Co. and Noble Cordry of Kent Co., Delaware, yeoman. By virtue of a warrant there was surveyed and laid out for John Murphy, a tract in the forrest of Cedar Creek Hundred and on each side of Bowman Branch beginning at a marked oak of a tract called Cotland Land. 200 acres. Surveyed and laid out on 21st day of the 11th month 1719. And said Murphy by his last will devised same to Nehemiah Tindley which Tindley died intestate and without issue leaving three sisters, Mary, Bridget and Thamer(?). Said Mary married Thomas Crippen and Mary died leaving issue the above said John Crippen, Joseph Crippen, Mary Crippen and Catharine Crippen to whom 1/3 of the land descended. Wit: Jane Maxfield, Jonathan Manlove, Saml. Merideth. Within deed ackn. 4 May 1769.

30. David Wattson, Innholder, Sussex Co., from Isaac Townsend, Sussex Co. 13 April 1769. Land in Slaughter Neck on the east side of Cedar Creek being part of a tract formerly known as Little Button being part of the same which belonged to Costin Townsend, dec'd., containing 2 acres and 5 perches, laid off and surveyed 1 April 1769. Below Isaac Townsend's wharf ... to a line of the land which formerly belonged to Thomas Lay, dec'd. Wit: Charles Draper, Ephraim Holleager. Within deed ackn. 5 May 1769.

31. Matthew Wilson from Boaz Manlove, Sheriff. 3 Aug 1769. Goods and chattels of John Clowes, Senr. and John Clowes, Junr.

were levied a sum of money which Joshua Fisher and son in the Court of Common Pleas recovered against them and several tracts were seized, among which were lots in the bounds of Lewes Town bounded on the northeast side of a lot belonging to Daniel Nunez, Esqr. and on the southwest side of a lot of Captain David Hall and on the southeast side of First Street (or Kollocks Street) and on the northwest side of the road that leads out of town by the meeting house. Lots were sold for £41 on 29 July 1769. Wit: Wm. Hazzard, Rhoads Shankland. Within deed ackn. 3 Aug 1769.

31. Burton Waples, blacksmith, Sussex Co., from Thomas Prettyman, Junr., Sussex Co., planter. 3 Aug 1769. Two tracts in Indian River Hundred one of which was granted by proprietary warrant to William Waples of Sussex Co. who devised same to his son William Waples who by deed of sale conveyed same to Thomas Prettyman, the elder and he by deed of gift conveyed to Thomas Prettyman the Younger, party to these presents. And the other of which two tracts was granted by warrant dated 27 May 1717 to Thomas Prettyman of said county and he dying intestate it became the property of his son Thomas Prettyman afsd. the Elder and by his deed of gift conveyed it to his son Thomas Prettyman the Younger, party to these presents. Beginning at a corner post being the head corner of a tract called the Cheet now in the possession of Burton Waples afsd. and from thence along the line of a tract called Batchelors Lott now in the possession of Dirickson Waples ... to a corner tree of William Waples ... dividing line between tract and land of the heirs of John Marriner, dec'd. 129 acres for £145. Wit: Wm. Peery, Hugh Stephenson. Within deed ackn. 3 Aug 1769.

32. Isaac Chace, Sussex Co., yeoman, from Wilson Lee, Sussex Co. 2 Aug 1769. Land in the forrest of Broadkill Hundred being part of a tract granted Richard Parrimer, dec'd. 80 acres for £30. Wit: Rhoads Shankland, Samuel Shankland. Within deed ackn. 3 Aug 1769.

33. Hugh Stephenson, Sussex Co., from Joseph Atkens and wife Mary, Sussex Co. 4 Aug 1769. Tract in Broadkill Hundred being part of a larger tract granted by a proprietary warrant to Benjamin Stockley who assigned it to heirs of Daniel Copes and afsd. Mary being one of the heirs of afsd. Daniel Copes received 1/5 part of afsd. tract. Beginning at the edge of Sockrocket Branch. 85 acres for £10. Wit: Wm. Peery, James Stephenson. Within deed ackn. 3 Aug 1769.

34. James Black, cordwinder, Sussex Co., from William Wheeler, Sussex Co., taylor. 3 Aug 1769. Land in Cedar Creek Neck and Hundred granted by warrant to Robert Hudson, 400 acres and he conveyed it to Henry Bowman and said Bowman conveyed 200 acres of afsd. tract to Joseph Booth, Esqr. and he conveyed same to Peter Goyle and he by his last will devised same to Peter and Mary, son and daughter of Ruth Williams and Peter dying in his nonage it fell to the said Ruth who married Joshua Bowler who conveyed it to Robert Cade and he dying intestate William Wheeler, one of the heirs of said Robert Cade petitioned the orphans court for a

division of the land and it was determined that the land would not lend itself to division and the land was allotted to said William Wheeler. For £164. Wit: Wm. Peery, George Black. Within deed ackn. 2 Aug 1769.

35. Bond. Wilson Lee, yeoman, Sussex Co., to Absolom Little, carpenter, Sussex Co., for £90, 11 March 1769. Wilson Lee is bound to Absalom Little for £45.

35. George Black, Junr. from George Clindaniel, Baker Johnson and wife Margret and Elizabeth Loughland of Sussex Co. 9 July 1769. Whereas there is a tract being part of Robert Hart's 900-acre tract in Cedar Creek Neck and Hundred being part of that part that was sold and conveyed by deed of indenture from Robert Hart to John Clandaniel as by deed dated 10 April 1715 for 200 acres and also part of a subdivision of 196 acres surveyed and divided of to John Clandaniel by order of an Orphans Court held 26 Nov 1747. Boundary runs to a line of the land surveyed for Abraham Wynkoop ... new division line between the said John Wheelers and the place of Thomas Hinds, late dec'd. Containing 96 acres. Wit: Isaac Watson, Dormon Lofland. Within deed ackn. 2 Aug 1769.

36. Nathan Campble, Sussex Co., from Jacob Hellings and wife Mary, Kent Co., Delaware. 2 Aug 1769. Land on south side of the Coolspring Branch in the forrest of the Broadkill Hundred. Runs to a line of Josias Martin's land. Contains 100 acres being part of a larger tract called the Coolspring formerly the property of James Campble dec'd. and Rebeckah Campble his wife and after the decease of the said James Camble the above said tract fell to his heirs except for a provision for 1/3 part to Rebeckah Campble during her lifetime. Wit: Thos. Gray, Robert Hood. Within deed ackn. 2 Aug 1769.

37. Walter Frankland and Samuel Franklin of the City of New York, merchants, from Abraham Mitchell of the city of Philadelphia, hatter, Thomas Lightfoot, William Lightfoot, late of Philadelphia, merchants, now living in Worcester Co., Maryland. 9 Nov 1768. Abraham Mitchell, Thos. Lightfoot and William Lightfoot have jointly or severally purchased several parcels of land and procured sundry warrants and located some parcels thereon in the counties of Worcester, Dorsett and Somerset in Maryland now likely to belong under the government of Newcastle, Kent and Sussex on Delaware and in the county of Sussex all of which tracts of land and warrants have been procured for the use and promotion of Pine Grove Furnace now erected on Deep Creek and whereas said Walter and Samuel Franklin are justly interested with the said Abraham Mitchel, Thomas Lightfoot and William Lightfoot in all the said lands, furnace, buildings and appurtenances and have paid for two equal fifth parts of all the purchase money and other expenses. For £5, two fifth parts in parcel of land in Deep Creek in Worcester Co. containing 390 acres called Partnership with furnace, sawmill, gristmill, dams, houses and buildings thereon and millpond near afsd. tract called Adams Folley containing 2 acres; also two

undivided equal fifths of another tract adjoining Partnership called Ireland of 500 acres which was bought by William Lightfoot, one of the conveyancers of James Hurst, also two equal undivided fifth parts of another tract in Broadkill forrest in Sussex Co., called Cooks Chance of about 250 acres which tract was bought by Thomas Lightfoot one of the conveyancers of Samuel Paynter, also two equal undivided fifth parts of another tract near the head of Cares Neck on Gravelly Branch in the forrest of Broadkill Hundred containing 859 acres which was bought by Thomas Lightfoot one of the conveyancers of William Darter and two undivided equal fifth parts of all the iron ore and mines found or to be found on and in a certain tract called Miles End containing about 300 acres and also on or in another tract of about 100 acres known as Pilsons Lott which last mentioned two tracts lay adjoining each other on Barren Creek in Somerset Co. in Maryland and are in possession of Benjamin and Joseph Vennebls with full and free privilege at any and all times to all iron ore; also equal fifths of tract on Lewis Branch in Dorset Co. adjoining lands of Matthew Smith and others containing 22 acres which tract was taken up by virtue of a warrant from the Maryland Office; also two fifth shares of several warrants yet to be located, one from Governor John Penn in favour of Abraham Mitchel and others dated 29 Aug 1764 for locating 2000 acres in or near Northwest Fork, one other warrant in favour of Abraham Mitchel and others for locating 200 acres near Deep Creek, one other warrant from Governor John Penn in favour of Abraham Mitchel and others for locating 5000 acres of land between Deep Creek and Broad Creek, Nanticoke River and Stoney Branch and 5 other warrants from the Maryland Land Office in favour of Abraham Mitchel for different quantities on of which the last described 22 acres is surveyed; also one other warrant from Maryland Office in favour of Thomas Lightfoot one of the conveyancers for 50 acres. Wit: James Allison, Richard Templin. Within deed ackn. 3 Aug 1769.

38. Robert Burton, Sussex Co. from George Hearne, Worcester Co. Maryland, planter and his wife Comfort. 3 Aug 1769. Tract in Angola Hundred being part of a tract formerly belonging to John Hill dec'd. who by his last will devised it to his son Absolom Hill and he conveyed it to George Parker of Somerset Co. in Maryland and he conveyed it to Comfort, wife of afsd George Hearne and widow of Joseph Houston in the time of her widowhood. For £11.5, 10 acres to be laid out of the 100 acres. Beginning at a corner oak being a line tree of John Stockley and John Hill and in the division line of said lands. Deed ackn. 3 Aug 1769.

39. Thos. Grove, Sussex Co., yeoman, from John Heavelo, Sussex Co., cooper. 4 Aug 1769. Whereas Thomas Grove died intestate seized of a tract on the south side of Prime Hook Creek and the west side of Little Creek leaving issue Thomas Grove, Samuel Grove and Susanna Grove who pursuant to law had division in the lands of their father and 280 acres part of the said tract divided and laid out for Samuel Grove, beginning at a corner maple standing at the run of the Beaver Dam ... post standing on the side of Little Creek ... And whereas said Samuel Grove died

intestate and afsd. Thomas Grove administered the estate of Samuel Grove. For £420. Wit: David Conwell, Henry Smith. Within deed ackn. 4 Aug 1769.

40. John Heavelo, Sussex Co., cooper, from Thomas Grove, Sussex Co., yeoman. 4 Aug 1769. [See above - same tract.] Ackn. 4 Aug 1769.

41. Perry and Leatherbery Barker from William Barker, Sussex Co., yeoman. For £50 paid by his brothers, Peery Barker and Leatherbury Barker of the said county rights which may fall to him by the death of either of his afsd. brothers and to that tract that Job Barker, father of the afsd. Perry, William and Leatherbery did devise to them which land is part of a tract that afsd. Job Barker purchased from Samuel Cary by deed of bargain and sale dated 14 Nov 1749 for 150 acres and as by another deed of bargain and sale from John Russel dated same day for 75 acres which land is situated in Indian River Hundred on the south side of Middle Creek proceeding out of Rehoboth Bay and called Tanners Hall. Wit: Philips Kollock, Daniel Nunez. Within deed 19 Aug 1769.

45. Peter Robinson, late of Worcester County but now of Sussex Co., miller, from Elias West and his wife Sarah admr. and widow of Joseph Warrington, Junr. 5 Sep 1769. Joseph Warrington by a bond of conveyance was bound to Peter Robinson regarding a tract in Drake Neck in Indian River Hundred of Sussex Co., 333 acres called Blacksmiths Hall which tract was devised by the last will of Thomas Warrington of Sussex Co. to his son, the afsd. Joseph Warrington, Junr. For £360. Wit: Thomas Robinson, Daniel Nunez.

46. Petition of Elias and Sarah West to convey above referenced land.

46. Edmon Dickson, Sussex Co., from Joseph Cord, Sussex Co., ship carpenter, and wife Jane. 6 Sep 1769. Whereas Joseph Cord, father of the afsd. Joseph by his last will devised to his son afsd. Joseph, a tract in fee tail in Broadkill Hundred. And Joseph, the son, suffered a common recovery of the land whereas Joseph Earle was demandant against sd. Joseph Cord. For £250 paid by Edmon Dickson. Land on the east side of Long Bridge Branch ... to a corner oak on the southwest side of the widow Stevens' plantation. 400 acres. Wit: David Hall, John Shankland. Within deed ackn. 6 Sep 1769.

47. Elizabeth Milbey from Peter Robinson, a mortgage. 6 Sep 1769. Peter Robinson of Sussex Co., miller, and Elizabeth Milbey, same county, a minor and daughter of Nathaniel Milby, dec'd. Tract in Drakes Neck in Indian River Hundred, 333 acres called Blacksmiths Hall, as will appear in a deed of bargain and sale from admr of Joseph Warrington, Junr., dec'd. to afsd Peter Robinson, dated 5th instant. For £50 to be paid by Peter Robinson before 30 Aug next. Wit: Boaz Manlove, Reece Woolf, Junr. Deed ackn. 6 Sep 1769.

14

48. Thos. Prittiman, Sussex Co., from Bettey Lingo admx of John Lingo, Sussex Co. who died intestate. 27 July 1769. For £101.10. Beginning at a corner of John Prettyman's land ... to a white oak standing in the line of Robert Burton's land, 321 acres as by survey made on 20 April 1736. Which land was conveyed by John Fasset to the heirs of afsd. John Lingo as by deed from said John Fassit. Wit: Mary Kollock, Daniel Nunez.

49. Joseph Russel, Sussex Co., yeoman, from Joseph Carpenter, Sussex Co., weaver. 7 May 1734. For £52 a tract on the south side of the Broad Kill and adjoining the land of said Joseph Russel's land, beginning at a corner post in the fork of Peters Gutt ... to the mouth of Fishers Gutt that runs into the Broad Kill which said marsh land was formerly granted to Jacob Warring as appearing in the warrant dated 20th of 12 month 1693 who died possessed of the same at whose decease the same marsh lands descended to his nephew the above Joseph Carpenter. 100 acres. Wit: Rd. Holt, Phil. Russel. Deed of sale ackn. May Court 1734.

50. John Hemmons from Constant Marriner, Sussex Co., yeoman. For £21.7.6, paid by John Hemmons, conveys a tract in Indian River Hundred and on the head or near the head of Abrahams Branch adjoining afsd. John Hemmons and being a part of the tract of afsd. Constant Marriner on the west side of the road from the Chappel to Warwick, 44 acres which belonged to Thomas Marriner of Sussex Co. and who willed it to afsd. Constant Marriner. Wit: Evan Morgan, Moses Marriner. Within deed of sale ackn. 8 Feb 1769.

50. Reece Woolf, Junr., Sussex Co., yeoman, from Patience Jacobs, widow and admx of Nathaniel Jacobs, yeoman who died intestate. 8 Nov 1769. Tract in Rehoboth Hundred being part of a larger tract or patent called Linning and Warring which lately belonging to Thomas Hall, senr., late of the county afsd., dec'd., yeoman. 127 acres. Whereas Nathaniel Jacobs on 4 April 1769 by an article of agreement with Reece Woolf, that for an amount stated Nathaniel Jacobs would convey to Reece Woolf the above 127 acres. Wit: Isaac Smith, Rhoads Shankland. Within deed ackn. 9 Nov 1769.

52. Reece Woolf, Junr. from Nathaniel Jacobs. Bond. Bound for £293. April 1769. Upon the payment of £146.11.7 with lawful interest the land which lately belonged to Thomas Hall of 127 acres. Wit: William Gill, John Rodney.

52. Petition of Patience Jacobs to convey [above described] tract.

52. John Little, Sussex Co., merchant, from John Holmes, Sussex Co. yeoman. 4 Aug 1769. Tract in Lewes and Rehoboth Hundred being part of a tract called Watsons Patent, on Long Love Branch. 150 acres for £120. Wit: Samuel Darby, Andrew Collings. Within deed ackn. 9 Nov 1769.

53. Benjamin Mifflin, Sussex Co., from David Forman, Sussex Co.,

yeoman. 17 Feb 1769. For £10, undivided moiety of a tract in Cedar Creek Hundred bounded by lands of William Carpenter, William Lofley and Tow(?) Bridge Branch containing in the moiety 106 acres, the whole of the tract 112 acres [sic]. Wit: Isaac Draper, Prisgrave Steal. Within deed ackn. November Term 1769.

54. Isaac Draper, yeoman, Sussex Co., from Benjamin Mifflin, Sussex Co., yeoman. 1 Nov 1769. Whereas John Clowes, John Jones and Benjamin Mifflin by sundry conveyances purchased a large tract in the forrest of Green Dranes and whereas said parties being joint tenants did make partition thereof and release to each other their several shares, the northeast part of which appointed to said Mifflin, bounded by the division of said John Clowes, the northward by lands of Andrew Collings, Junr., the late John Spencer, Esq., Foster Donavan and James Reed, eastward by lands formerly John Wright's and John Fowler's and southward by lands of the said Isaac Draper, Richard Reynolds and James Pettyjohn, formerly called Cord Tract. Benjamin Mifflin for one shilling conveys to his son in law, Isaac Draper. 100 acres. Wit: John Clowes, Prisgrave Steel. Within deed ackn. 8 Nov 1769.

54. John Carlile, Sussex Co., from Wm. Loffley, Sussex Co., yeoman. 2 Aug 1769. Tract in forrest of Cedar Creek Hundred surveyed by virtue of a warrant granted to afsd. William Lofley, dated 19 Nov 1756, laid out for 150 acres. Bounded to a line of land surveyed for John Loffley. For £50. Wit: Thomas Cary, Rhoads Shankland. Within deed ackn. 8 Nov 1769.

55. James Hall from Philip Huggens, Sussex Co. For £20 releases and quit claims to James Hall that part of a tract in Cedar Creek Hundred called Silver Plains, containing 149 acres, on the west side of Mire Branch which is a part of a larger tract surveyed by virtue of a proprietary warrant granted to John Coverdale, Junr., and assigned by said Coverdale to afsd. Philip Higgens containing in the survey 255 acres, made 20 Jan 1756. Wit: Thomas Lindall, Joseph Lindall. Within deed ackn. November Term 1769.

56. Joseph Lindel from Philip Huggens, Sussex Co. For £55, part of a tract in Great Neck in Cedar Creek Hundred called Silver Plain, 140 acres, on the east side of Mire Branch, being part of a tract granted to John Coverdale, Junr. and assigned by him to Philip Huggens, containing by survey 255 acres. Wit: Thomas Lindall, James Hall. Within deed ackn. November Term.

56. Abraham Harris, Sussex Co., carpenter, from Charles Clark, Worcester Co., Maryland, yeoman. 6 Nov 1769. Charles Clark had granted to him by proprietary warrant, 200 acres in Broadkill on the north side of Rennals(?) Branch, dated 9 June 1743. 185 acres surveyed on 11 Dec 1743. For £60. Wit: John Clowes, Agothey Christopher. Within deed ackn. 8 Nov 1769.

57. John Maull from Nehemiah Maull and Mary his wife and James Maull and Jane his wife, Sussex Co., pilots. For £60, release and quit claim to John Maull of Sussex Co., shipwright, tracts or lots of land which John Maull, date, dec'd., father to the afsd.

parties, died possessed of, on the bank of Lewes Creek, 5 acres. Beginning at corner post of the bank of Lewes Creek being a corner of land of Joseph Bailey which formerly belonged to Jonathan Bailey, dec'd. father to afsd. Joseph Bailey. Wit: Wm. Lewis, John Field. Note: One of the afsd. lots was sold and conveyed by Margery Miers and the other by James Claypoole to John Maull, pilot, who died intestate leaving issue, Nehemiah, John, James, Mary and William Maull who became seized of the land and the afsd. Nehemiah and James now being of full age to convey land. Within deed ackn. Dec 1769.

58. John Caid, Sussex Co., house carpenter, from Solomon Knock, Sussex Co., yeoman and Comfort his wife. May 1769. Tract on the south side of Prime Hook Creek being part of a larger tract known as Hasholds Fortune purchased by Andrew Fullerton, late of the county afsd. from George Hashold of New Marlborough, Hampshire Co., Massachusetts Bay in New England and Fullerton by his deed of sale dated 1 Aug 1757 conveyed the lands and tenements to Samuel Hopkins who on 2 Aug 1758 conveyed same to Solomon Knock one of the parties to these presents, who for £89.3.3, convey same to John Caid. Laid out for 89 acres and 26 perches. Wit: William Stephenson, Elisha Nocks. Within deed ackn. 4 May 1769.

59. Rees Meridith and John Mifflin, City of Philadelphia, merchants, from Robert Warren, Sussex Co., yeoman. 23 Nov 1769. Tract in Broadkill Forrest of Sussex Co. adjoining and formerly taken up by John Cord, Ephraim Darby, Samuel Pettyjohn and Thomas Dodd which was granted to said Robert Warren by virtue of a proprietary warrant dated 24 May 1749 and surveyed in the year 1756 at which time it was called Two Strings to a Bow, beginning at a corner oak being a corner of John Cord's land. 160 acres. For the sum previously paid by Samuel Pettyjohn plus the further sum of £6 now in hand paid by Rees Meridith and John Mifflin. Wit: Benjamin Mifflin, Isaac Draper. Within deed ackn. 8 Feb 1770.

60. Solomon Wright, Sussex Co., yeoman, to Benjamin Mifflin, Sussex Co., yeoman. 21 Nov 1769. Whereas the proprietary warrant dated 26 Feb 1739 did grant to John Wright of said county and father of the said Solomon a tract in the forrest of Sussex Co. called Bryer and Thistle adjoining the swamp and marsh called Green Dranes surveyed and laid out for 513, acres part whereof the said John Wright sold and conveyed to James Pettyjohn and John Wright by his last will dated 1 Aug 1752 devised to his two sons, Edward and the above mentioned Solomon all his remainder part of said tract. For £25. Wit: John Clowes, Boaz Manlove. Within deed ackn. 8 Feb 1770.

61. Burton Waples, senr., blacksmith of Sussex Co., from William Waples, Senr., Sussex Co., yeoman. 7 Feb 1770. Tract on the north side of Indian River about 2 miles from the town of Warwick being the northernmost end of a larger tract granted to William Waples by commissioner's warrant and surveyed and laid out to said William Waples, father to both parties. William Waples by his last will bequeathed said land to his son William Waples.

For £5.4. Land beginning at a corner oak being a corner tree of a tract formerly belonging to John Marriner now dec'd. standing in or near the head line of a tract taken up by Thomas Prettyman, the Elder, now dec'd. 13 acres. Wit: John Harmonson, Wm. Peery. Within deed ackn. 7 Feb 1770.

62. William Ware, Sussex Co., pilot, from Thomas Rowland, Sussex Co., pilot. 1 Jan 1770. For £30, tract or lot which was conveyed to afsd. Thomas Rowland by a deed from his father William Rowland, dec'd, beginning at a corner stone on the bank of Lewis Creek being a corner of a lot which afsd. William Rowland conveyed to Joseph Conwell or to some of his children. Wit: Luke Shield, Thos. Gray. Within deed ackn. 6 Feb 1770.

63. Elias Hugg, Sussex Co., merchant, from Thomas Gray, Sussex Co., Innholder. 9 Feb 1770. Lot in Lewes Town whereof afsd. Thomas Gray now dwells and whereas the lot was conveyed by a deed of sale from William Plumstead and Samuel Neve of the City of Philadelphia as executor of the last will of Richard Metcalf, late of Sussex Co. to afsd. Thomas Gray, beginning at the south corner of Market and Second St. and on the northwest by a lot lately possessed by William Arnal, on the northeast end by Front Street and on the southeast side by Market St. containing 60 feet front and 200 feet in length. For £155. Wit: Alexr. Shankland, Rhoads Shankland. Within deed ackn. 9 Feb 1770.

64. Simon and Samuel Darby, Sussex, farmers, from Elizabeth Darby admx. of John Darby of Sussex Co., dec'd. 8 Feb 1770. John Darby died intestate with insufficient personal estate to discharge his debts. Hence Elizabeth Darby, the admx., was allowed to sell a small parcel of land for £61, beginning at a corner post being a corner of the land of Jacob Kollock, Junr., ... to a corner post of the line of Jonathan Bailey, dec'd. ... containing 4 acres and 53 square perches. Wit: J. Anderson, Robert Burton, Junr. Within deed ackn. 8 Feb 1770.

64. Samuel Rowland, Sussex Co., pilot, from Catharine Russel admx. of Ephraim Russel of Sussex Co. who died intestate. 8 Feb 1770. The personal estate of Ephraim Russel was insufficient to discharge his debts. Hence Catharine Russel was allowed to sell 43 acres for £64.10. Wit: Danl. Nunez, Jno. Russell. Within deed ackn. 8 Feb 1770.

65. George Frame from Nathan Frame. Mortgage. 6 Feb 1770. Tract in Indian River Hundred whereof Robert Frame died intestate, possessed of. Nathan Frame being the eldest son of Robert Frame received 2 shares of the estate. The tract beginning at the north end of Doe Bridge at the head of Indian River ... to the chimney of the dwelling house ... to the millpond ... containing 183 acres, for £124.18. Wit: Charles Rawlins, Leath. Barker. 7 Feb 1770.

66. John Oakey from James Gorden, Sussex Co., yeoman. 6 Feb 1770. Tract in Indian River Hundred on Cow Bridge Branch being part of a larger tract containing 210 acres, surveyed and laid

out for Robert West in 1717. 110 acres for £30. Wit: David Shankland, Rhoads Shankland. Within deed ackn. 7 Feb 1770.

67. Moses Wilson, Sussex Co., yeoman, from Richard Bloxsom, Sussex Co., yeoman. 2 Aug 1769. Two tracts in Broadkill Hundred on the west side of Mill Branch which have descended down to afsd. Richard Bloxsom by a deed of sale from William Wyatt dated 3 May 1764. Beginning on the west of Mill ... to a corner of land of David Rankens ... 200 acres for £150. Wit: William Henry, Rhoads Shankland. Within deed ackn. 7 Feb 1770.

67. Levi Rigs from Peter Rigs, William Rigs, John Rigs, William Murphey and Ann his wife, William Simson and Elizabeth his wife, Thomas Poynter and Susanna his wife, Robert Simpson and Rachel his wife, all of the counties of Kent and Sussex, of Delaware. 30 Jan 1770. Tract in Cedar Creek Forrest granted to Solomon Truit by the Proprietary for 100 acres. Whereas Solomon Truit in consideration of another tract conveyed afsd. land to Peter Rigs and whereas Peter Rigs died intestate and the land descended to his several children as above described, Peter Rigs, William Rigs, John Rigs, Ann Rigs wife of William Murphey, Elizabeth Rigs wife of William Simpson, Susanna Rigs wife of Thomas Poynter and Rachel Rigs wife of Robert Simpson. 100 acres for £50. Wit: Levin Crapper, Richard Hays. Within deed ackn. 8 Feb 1770.

69. Wrixam Lewis, Sussex Co., shipwright, from Rees Woolf, Junr., Sussex Co., yeoman and wife Mary. 25 Nov 1769. Tract in Rehoboth Hundred about 3 miles from the town of Lewes being part of a larger tract called Warrens Choice which William Warren had granted to him by patent and by sundry devises and conveyances became the right of William Wesley who conveyed to above said Reece Woolf, Junr. And part thereof was conveyed to said Reece Woolf by Patience Jacobs admrs. of Nathaniel Jacobs, dec'd. who purchased it, with more, of Thomas Hall by way of public sale. Beginning at the end of a ditch cut by afsd. Wrixam Lewis and the afsd. Thomas Hall in the division line ... to a corner stone standing in a line between Stephen Green and said land ... about 2 perches from a marked white oak called Nancy. 30 acres for £40. Wit: Mary Kollock, Parker Alif(?). Within deed ackn. 7 Feb 1770.

70. Joseph Truitt, Junr., Sussex Co., yeoman, from Benjamin Truitt, Sussex Co., yeoman. 22 Feb 1770. Tract in Cedar Creek Hundred being part of a larger tract surveyed to Benjamin Truitt for 500 acres which small tract is laid out on the southwest side of afsd. larger tract beginning at a corner stake in the line of Annanias Hudson's land ... to a stake standing in the line of Francis Roberts, 135 acres. Wit: Jno. Rodney, John Wiltbank. Within deed ackn. 6 May 1770.

70. Jacob and Rachel Conwell, son and daughter of Joseph Conwell, pilot of Sussex Co., from John Conwell, Sussex Co., yeoman. Bill of sale. For 5 shillings. Negro girl called Pheabe. Wit: Elias Conwell, John Conwell. Recorded 2 April 1770.

71. John King. Patent. Edmund Andros, Esqr. senr. Tract near the whore Killin called Peach Blossom on Rehoboth Bay which by virtue of a warrant hath been laid out for John King beginning at Warrens Creek running east upon the bay to Kings Creek. 900 acres. 3 March 1676. John King assigns to Wm. Futcher 300 acres 8 June 1680. John Futcher assigns within mentioned patent to Richard Payntor, 12 April 1710. Wit: Philip Russel, Rodger Corbet.

72. Know that we, Jonas Morris of the City of Corke, merchant, and Mary Morris, wife of said Jonas Morris appoint Joseph Jacobs of the City of Philadelphia, merchant our attorney to convey all our estate in Pennsylvania or elsewhere in America. Wit: Wm. Ellis, George Ellis, City of Corke, Kingdom of Ireland. 24 July 1766.

72. Know that I, Ann Morris now of the City of Dublin, Ireland, spinster, appointed Joseph Jacobs of the City of Philadelphia, merchant, my attorney to convey all my estate in Pennsylvania or elsewhere in America, particularly the land called Morris Land and formerly called Ditchers Hill in Pennsylvania. Wit: Joseph Barcroft, Wm. Ellis, City of Cork. 24 July 1766.

73. Samuel Russel from Parker Robinson, Esqr., exr. of last will of Joseph Russel of Sussex Co., yeoman. 1 May 1770. Joseph Russel in his lifetime on 24 June 1766 under penalty of £190 agreed to convey to Samuel Russel a tract in Broadkill Hundred called the Head of the Bever Dam, binding north upon Samuel Rowland, dec'd., south upon land of Ephraim Russel and west upon land of Hill Staton, containing 80 acres except 1 3/4 acres which Joseph Russel sold to Ephraim Russel and the said Joseph Russel not having conveyed the land in his lifetime. Wit: John Wiltbank, Wm. Parker. Within deed ackn. 1 May 1770.

74. Samuel Russel from Joseph Russell. Bond. Whereas Joseph Russell is bound to Samuel Russel to convey land. [See above.] Wit: Jno. Clowes, Hannah Heavelo. Bond proved 1 May 1770.

74. Isaac Draper, cooper, from Thomas Pettyjohn, Sussex Co., yeoman. 5 Jan 1770. Whereas by virtue of sundry warrants said Thomas Pettyjohn became seized of a tract in Broadkill Forrest called Green Drains bounded by lands of Andrew Collings, Obediah Messick and Absolom Phips, containing 600 acres which said Thomas Pettyjohn by his deed dated 1 May 1765 conveyed to John Clowes, Benjamin Mifflen and John Jones, resurveying to himself 30 acres called Bushy Thicket beginning at a corner tree of a tract laid out for John Cord now in possession of Richard Reynolds ... to a line of land granted by Benjamin Miffln to said Isaac Draper. 30 acres for £5. Wit: Benja. Mifflin, Wilson Lee. Within deed ackn. 2 May 1770.

75. Thomas Carey, Sussex Co., yeoman, from Mary Wynkoop, John Vining and Phebe his wife and Benjamin Wynkoop, surviving exrs. of the last will of Abraham Wynkoop, Sussex Co. 15 April 1770. Whereas by virtue of a warrant of resurvey dated 10 Oct 1744

there was surveyed and laid out for Edward Evans and Rebecca his wife and Elizabeth Clark, daughters and heirs of Wm. Clark the Younger, late of said county, dec'd., a tract in Cedar Creek Hundred containing 1245 acres and Edward Evans and Rebecca his wife and Elizabeth Clark by their indenture dated 1 March 1745 conveyed to said Abraham Wynkoop the said tract and he in his will of 15 Nov 1753 directed that all land of Kent and Sussex Counties not mentioned in his will, should be sold and did constitute his wife Mary, his daughter the said Phebe Vining, his son Thomas Wynkoop and his son the said Benjamin Wynkoop (which Thomas Wynkoop is since dec'd.) exrs. Land beginning at a stake, corner of Benjamin Truitt's land ... to a white oak in the line of said Thomas Carey's land ... line of the manor of Worminghurst. 260 acres for £130. Wit: Hap Hazzard, Miers Fisher. Within deed ackn. 2 May 1770.

76. Nathaniel Williams, Worcester Co., Maryland, from William Steel, Sussex Co. 1 May 1770. Tract in Broadkill Hundred granted by a proprietaries warrant to Ephraim Darby for 212 acres who conveyed it be deed of sale to afsd. William Steel who conveys 113 acres for £50. Boundary runs to .... post by the road from Evans's Mill... Wit: Wm. Peery, James Steel. Within deed ackn. 1 May 1770.

77. John Owens, Sussex Co., farmer, from Abram Wynkoop's surviving exrs. (Mary Wynkoop, John Vining and Phebe his wife and Benjamin Wynkoop) 27 March 1770. By virtue of a warrant dated 25 Nov 1748 to lay off 200 acres to Richard Coverdale the land was surveyed 18 Dec 1749 in Cedar Creek Forrest adjoining Magdaline Manlove, Richard Coverdale, senr. and Arthur Fowler and called Honey Comb Tract. Beginning at a large white oak on a ridge being a boundary of the widow Manolve's land ... to an oak of Richard Coverdale, senr. ... to a corner oak of Samuel Royal's land which land was sold to Abram Wynkoop by said Richard Coverdale and after the demise of Abram Wynkoop was conveyed to Mary Wynkoop, John Vining and Phebe his wife and Benjamin Wynkoop, surviving exrs. Sale dated 5 May 1762. For £50 the land is conveyed to John Owens. Wit: Thomas Cary, Miers Fisher. Within deed ackn. 1 May 1770.

78. Ahab Clandaniel, Sussex Co., house carpenter, from David Warren, Sussex Co., Yeoman. 1 May 1770. Whereas Caleb Currier of Sussex Co., wheelright, obtained a warrant for 200 acres in the Broadkill forrest adjoining lands of David Smith and Lawrence Ryly dated 17 March 1757 and said Caleb Currier on 3 Jan 1759 assigned the warrant (except 30 acres on the north east corner which was sold to Edward Roberts) to David Warren for £25. Wit: John Clowes, John Ingram. Within deed ackn. 1 May 1770.

78. Burton Waples, Junr., Sussex Co., blacksmith, from Joshua Richards, Sussex Co., cooper. 2 May 1770. Tract in Indian River Hundred called Warwick which did formerly belong to William Burton of Worcester Co., Maryland, dec'd. who caused part of the tract to be laid out in lots for a town which he named Warwick under the yearly rents of 6 shillings and 8 pence to be paid on 1

Jan yearly. And William Burton by his last will desired that these rents be paid equally amongst his 6 children. Whereas Richard Burton one of the said children gave his obligation to Henry Draper conditioned for the making over and conveying to Henry Draper dated 8 Feb 1752, a lot of 10 acres being part of the land devised by said William Burton to his children but Richard Burton died before the title was made. His exrs. Elizabeth Burton and Job Ingram by indenture dated 5 Feb 1756 conveyed the said 10 acres to Henry Draper, land bounded on the southwest by the land of Elizabeth Burton now Elizabeth Prettyman, one of the legatees and devisees of said William Burton and on the northeast on the land formerly belonged to Catharine Morris, one of the legatees of William Burton but now belonging to Burton Waples, father to afsd. Burton Waples and on the south by the Indian River. For £64 paid by Burton Waples, Junr. Wit: Thomas Robinson, Peter West. Within deed ackn. 2 May 1770.

79. Thomas May, Sussex Co., Delaware, from Avery Draper, Junr., and James Thistlewood and Sarah his wife, all of the county of Kent, yeomen, Delaware. 2 Feb 1770. Whereas there is a tract, marsh and cripple containing 100 acres being part of a larger tract purchased by Jonathan May and Henry Draper, fathers to the afsd. Thomas May and Avery Draper, Junr. and Sarah Thistlewood of Thomas Davis, late of the county of Sussex called Marsh Patent as by a deed from Thomas Davis to the afsd. Jonathan May and Henry Draper and the afsd. Henry Draper having died intestate leaving 7 children the land was divided into 8 shares and the afsd. Avery Draper, Junr., James Thistlewood and Sarah his wife came lawfully seized of 2/8 of one part. For 25 pounds. Wit: Levin Crapper, Azariat Richardson. Within deed ackn. 2 May 1770.

80. George Rickards from Mary Poor and Richd. Shockley admrs of Nehemiah Poor who died intestate. 2 May 1770. Whereas Mary Poor and Richard Shockley sold the land hereafter mentioned being part of the tract that William Daniely devised by his last will to his daughter Kesiah the wife of William Bennit of Kent Co. and the same that William Bennit and Kesiah his wife by a deed of bargain and sale sold to the exrs. of Abraham Wynkoop and the exrs., to wit, Mary Wynkoop, John Vining and Phebe his wife and Benjamin Wynkoop died by deed of bargain and sale dated 5 May 1762 sell and convey same to afsd. Nehemiah Poor. For £80. Wit: Wm. Hazzard, Joshua Rickards. Within deed ackn. 2 May 1770.

81. Napthaly Carpenter, Sussex Co., yeoman, and James Carpenter, Sussex Co., taylor. Deed. 2 March 1770. Whereas Nephaly Carpenter, father to the afsd. Nepthaly and James was seized of two several tracts and marsh by virtue of the last will of Thomas Price which said Nepthaly Carpenter, the Elder, died intestate leaving 5 children, minors, three of whom being dec'd. in their minority, the tracts became the property of first mentioned Nepthaly and James Carpenter which land is located on the north side of Slaughter Creek in Slaughter Neck, beginning on the north side of Slaughter Creek being a corner of Thomas Hinds' land ... east side of Barns's Branch ... containing 416 acres and 64

perches. Beginning at a corner post standing on the beach being a corner of William Tills Marsh. John Clowes, Thos. Gray. Within deed ackn. 2 May 1770.

83. Henry Killen from James Hemmons. 3 May 1770. Between Danielly Loughland of Dobbs Co., North Carolina, yeoman, by his attorney James Hemmons and Henry Killen of Kent Co., Del., yeoman. Whereas Danielly Loughland by power of attorney dated 19 Feb 1770 authorized and impowered James Hemmons of Dobbs Co. to sell and convey two tracts in Sussex Co. Whereas by virtue of a warrant a tract was granted from the proprietaries dated 10 Dec 1740 to Dormon Loughland late of Sussex Co., dec'd., father of the afsd. Danielly Loughland for 200 acres in the forrest of Slaughter Neck in Cedar Creek Hundred and on the west side of Bridge Branch adjoining a tract formerly surveyed for Thomas Wilson (called Wilsons Folley) and the afsd. Dormon Loughland by his last will dated 25 Dec 1749 devised the said land to his son Danielly Loughland afsd. reserving 50 acres to his son Dormon Loughland. Beginning at a corner oak formerly surveyed to Thomas Wilson. 250 acres. Wit: Naphtaly Carpenter, William Shankland. Within deed ackn. 3 May 1770.

84. James Hemmons from Daniel Lofley. Power of Attorney. Danielly Lofley of Dobbs Co., North Carolina, appoints James Hemmons, planter, attorney to receive of Isaac Watson or any other person, rents and damages done to tract containing 250 acres joining Isaac Watson's land and 170 acres near Benjamin Riley's land and also the money that is in Dormon's Lofley's hand; also to convey said lands. 19 Feb 1770. 26 April 1770 appeared Benjamin Chadwick aged 25 years who deposeth that he saw Danilly Lofland sign the within power unto James Hemmons.

84. John Russel of Sussex Co., cordwayner, from Comfort Prettyman, Sussex Co., widow of William Prettyman, and daughter of Shepard Kollock, of same co., dec'd. 5 May 1770. Tract near Lewes Town containing 41 acres being part of a larger tract formerly belonging to above named Shepard Kollock called Middleborough originally granted to Alexander Molleston, dec'd. and by sundry conveyances by deeds and descents became the property of above named Shepard Kollock who by his last will devised same to his wife Mary Kollock during her widowhood and she dying intestate, administration of her estate was granted to her eldest son George Kollock whereupon a commission was appointed of David Hall, Gilbilsher Parker, Esqr., Stephen Green, John Wiltbank and Peter Parker to divide the land and who set forth in their return with a plat annexed thereto. For £99.10, 41 acres, land beginning at a corner post of David Hall, Esqr. ... to line of Jacob Kollock, Esqr. ... to line of divident or part of same tract allotted to Herculous Kollock for and a part of said afsd. Shepard Kollock died possessed of at the head of afsd. tract, 25 acres of which lies upon the northwest side of the road that leads from Lewes Town to Rehoboth Neck beginning at a corner of the land of David Hall, Esqr. to a division line with Herculous Kollock, the other 16 acres being woodland on the southeast side of the said Rehoboth Road. Wit: Simon Kollock,

Perry Prettyman. Within deed ackn. 8 May 1770.

85. Israel Brown, Motherkill Hundred, yeoman, from Sarah Brown of Motherkill Hundred, Kent Co., widow and admx. of John Brown late of said place. 3 May 1770. Whereas John Bowman, Sussex Co., dec'd. by sundry Mesne conveyances became possessed of part of a large tract formerly surveyed to Henry Bowman called Sawmill Range and situate in Cedar Creek Hundred on the south side of Mispillion Creek and said Bowman on 27 Jan 1736/7 by his deed conveyed to John Brown part of said premises to contain 100 acres beginning at the lower end of Ivey Island for which whole tract formerly belonging to Daniel Welch but now to Levin Crapper, Esqr. ... to Mispillion Creek for 100 acres (Liber G, folio 183). Whereas said John Bowman afterwards by one other deed dated 3 Feb 1741 conveyed to said John Brown one other part of the said premises containing 50 acres beginning on the south side of Mispillion Creek opposite a parcel of marsh on Kent Shore called Wild Oat Patch. And whereas John Brown being possessed of the said two parcels of land containing together 150 acres died intestate leaving issue 7 children, viz: Elizabeth, Mary, John, William, Jane, Israel (above named) and Rachel whereof Elizabeth and William are since dec'd. without issue and the said John Brown the Younger having entered into a bond with his brother the said Israel Brown dated 23 June 1768 under £60 conditioned for the conveyance by deed to him the said Israel Brown all the moiety or one-half of his share of the premises undivided, vizt. the said 150 acres, the said conveyance not being made to said Israel Brown by said John Brown in his lifetime, the widow and admx. of said John Brown, the afsd. Sarah Brown, conveys same to Israel Brown for 45 pounds. Wit: Wm. Chance, Junr., Nehemiah Davis, Junr. Within deed ackn. 4 May 1770.

87. Israel Brown from John Brown. Bond. John Brown, Kent Co., for £60 binds himself on 23 June 1768 to Israel Brown. That John Brown make over 1/2 of his right of the home place where Rachel Pinyard and Israel Brown and Levi Olaver now live to Israel Brown. Wit: Richard Pollet, Levi Olaver. Proved 4 May 1770.

87. Levi Olaver from John Brown. Bond. John Brown of Kent Co., is bound to Levi Olaver and Jean his wife for 60 pounds. 23 June 1768. That John Brown make over his right of the home tract where Rachel Pinyard, Israel Brown and Levi Olaver now live. Wit: Richard Pollet, Israel Brown. Proved 4 May 1770.

87. Petition of Sarah Brown, admx. of John Brown, late of Kent Co., dec'd., that whereas John Brown formerly of Cedar Creek Hundred in Sussex Co. was seized of 150 acres part of the Sawmill Range originally surveyed for Henry Bowman and being so seized died intestate leaving issue, 7 children of which the first above mentioned John Brown the late husband of the petitioner was oldest son and whereas John Brown, husband of the petitioner did on 23 June 1768 enter into a bond to convey his half of his father's estate to his brother Levi Oliver for a consideration. Petitioner prays to convey same to Levi Oliver.

87. Petition of Sarah Brown admx of John Brown sheweth that John Brown formerly of Cedar Creek Hundred died seized of 150 acres and part of the Sawmill Range originally surveyed for Henry Bowman and being so seized died intestate leaving issue, 7 children of which the first above mentioned John Brown, the late husband of the petitioner was the oldest son and whereas John Brown, husband of the petitioner, did on 23 June 1768 enter into a bond obliging himself to convey 1/2 of his share of the estate of his said father afsd., viz. the said 150 acres to his brother Israel Brown for a consideration. 3 May 1770.

88. Levi Olaver, Sussex Co., blacksmith, from Sarah Brown, relict and admx. of John Brown of Kent Co., dec'd. 3rd day of the 5th month 1770. Whereas John Bowman of Sussex Co., dec'd. did by deed dated 27 of 1st month 1736/7 also in and by one other deed dated 3rd day of the 2nd month 1741/2 to John Brown, Sussex Co., merchant, dec'd. father of the above John Brown of Kent Co., 2 tracts in Cedar Creek Hundred on the south side of Mispillion Creek, part of a large tract formerly granted to Henry Bowman known as Sawmill Range which two tracts contain in the whole 150 acres and whereas said John Brown of Kent Co., agreed to Levi Olaver for the sale of 1/2 of the dividend of the 150 acres for £35. John Brown entered into bond with Levi Olaver dated 23rd, 6th month 1768 conditioned for the conveying of the moiety of the divident and Sarah Brown doth release the land. Wit: Wm. Chance, Junr., Nehemiah Davis, Junr. Ackn. 4 May 1770.

89. Wm. Pointer, Sussex Co., yeoman, from John Depray, Sussex Co., yeoman. 8 May 1770. Whereas by an indenture dated 27 June 1769 Robert Morris of the City of Philadelphia, merchant, and Sarah Greenway of said city, spinster, exrs. of Robert Greenway, late of the city, dec'd., granted to said John Depray, inter alia, a tract in Sussex Co., being part of the proprietary manor of Worminghurst beginning at a corner oak in the line of a tract late of John Murphey, dec'd., and on the southeast side of Bowman's Branch ... to a corner tree of land late of Gabriel West, Senr. 266 1/4 acres and 36 perches called Neighbours Covet for £124.7.2. Wit: Wm. Chance, Junr., John Rickards son of John. Ackn. 8 May 1770.

90. John Depray from Robert Morris, City of Philadelphia, merchant and Sarah Greenway of said City, spinster, two of the exrs. of Robert Greenway, of said city, merchant, dec'd. 27 June 1769. Whereas by indenture dated 8 Dec 1750 Joseph Yeats of the said city, merchant, granted to said Robert Greenway, inter alia, a tract being part of proprietary manor of Warminghurst ... for £124.7.2, 248 1/2 acres, 6 perches. Wit: Elisha Morris, Littleton Townsend. ackn. 8 May 1770.

91. Caleb Cirwithin, Sussex Co., from John Cirwithin, Sussex Co. 2 May 1770. For £100, part of a tract of 600 acres known as Rich Neck in Primehook Neck in Cedar Creek Hundred originally granted to John and Samuel Watson by warrant from the court of Sussex dated 16th of 9th month 1683 and laid out on 14th of 12th month 1684 and confirmed to said John and Samuel Wattson by patent

dated 17th of third month called May 1688 under the hand of William Markham, Secretary, and John Goodson Commissioner appointed for the granting of lands and by a deed dated 5th of 4th month 1688 was conveyed by John and Samuel Watson to William Piles and acknowledged 5th, 6th, 7th and 8th days of the 4th month 1688; likewise two parcels of meadow or marsh both of which are part of a larger tract called Wattsons Marshes surveyed 14th day of the 12th month 1684 by virtue of a special warrant dated 5th of 5th month 1683 and confirmed to Luke [sic] by patent dated 5th of 1st month 1688 and by a deed from the said Luke Watson dated 5th of 4th month 1688, is conveyed to said William Piles and acknowledged 5, 6, 7, and 8th days of the 4th month by afsd. Luke Wattson to William Piles and by virtue of a conveyance from afsd. William Piles is confirmed part of the above said lands and marshes to Caleb Cirwithin the Elder by two deeds dated 10 Aug 1698 and on 1 Jan 1719 above said Caleb Cirwithin by his last will gave his above lands and marshes to his son Caleb Cirwithin and by virtue of the docking of the entail according to law and recorded 4 Nov 1768, John Cirwithin now has authority to grant the hereafter mentioned property that is one part of afsd lands and marshes on the north side of the Mill Pond about 11 perches west of the Mill Dam ... to a post on the edge of the Brook Branch supposed to be in Luke Wattson's patent line. 236 acres. The other part of marsh in Primehook Great Marshes adjoining the south side of Slaughter Creek and on the west by John Bellemy's 1000 acres being 1/2 part of 75 acres of marsh which above said Piles sold to Caleb Cirwithin; likewise, a grist mill and a saw mill on the head of Primehook Creek with two acres adjoining the south end of the mill dam in Broad Creek Hundred. Wit: Naphtaly Carpenter, James Carpenter. Within deed ackn. 3 May 1770.

93. William Steel, yeoman, from Boaz Manlove, Sheriff. 4 May 1770. To conserve the Peace at the Instance of John Clowes against James Richardson commending him by virtue of the writ of Venditioni exponas to expose to sale a tract in Broadkiln Forrest for the use of John Clowes, 260 acres. Wit: Wm. Chance, Junr., Mary England. 4 May 1770.

94. Joseph Carrel, Sussex Co., from Azariah Richardson and his wife Elizabeth, admrs. of Edward Carey of Sussex Co. 21 Feb 1770. Whereas Edward Carey was seized of a certain tract containing 150 acres and died intestate and left 4 small children and a personal estate not sufficient to pay his debts and maintain his children. 150 acres adjoining the lands of Nathaniel Poynter and the land surveyed for Rives Holt and the land surveyed for William Clark's heirs by Joshua Fisher their attorney. For £50. Wit: Levin Crapper, Wm. Hazzard. Within deed ackn. 4 May 1770.

95. John Little, Rehoboth Hundred, Sussex Co., from Benjamin Jacobs, Providence Township, Philadelphia Co., yeoman. 10 May 1770. Whereas on 26th of 3rd month 1685, surveyed and laid out for Stephen Whitman, a tract called Ditchers Hall on the north side of Braceys Branch, 600 acres, by virtue of a warrant dated 11th of 2nd month 1682 by the return of the survey under the hand

of Joshua Barkstead, surveyor will appear. Whereas said Stephen Whitman afterwards granted the tract to John How and Michael Sadler on 9, 10, 11 and 12th of 1st month 1686. After the death of Michael Sadler, John How on 5th of 4th month 1688 conveyed the tract to Jeremiah Scott of the town of Lewes as recorded in Book A, folio 128-130. And Jeremiah Scott in his last will dated at Marrow Bone Lane in the Liberty of Thomas Court dated Dublin January 17, 1705 devised to Thomas Pallen of Brabason Street, dyer, and William Kellet of Thomas Court, ale seller "whom I make joint exrs. of my last will" of which Thomas Pallen and William Kellet became vested with the title to said tract who by their lease and release dated last day of Feb and first of March 1708 conveyed said tract to Thomas Morris, of the City of Dublin, brewer, as recorded in Liber K No. 10, folio 234. And Thomas Morris on 19/20 March 1729 conveyed tract to John Mason of Tomalin, County of Kildare, farmer and John Baily of Mount Melick in Queens Co., farmer and to the survivors of them for the use and benefit of Thomas Morris grandchildren, the children of his then dec'd. son James Morris late of Moone, county of Kildare, namely Anne Morris, Samuel Morris and Mary Morris whereas authority was granted to John Mason and John Bailey to sell the land and by the said indenture recorded in Liber K No. 10, folio 235 and on 10 July 1749 John Mason and John Baily conveyed the land to the said grandchildren who were then of full age as recorded in Liber K No. 10, folio 237 and whereas the said Samuel Morris died and was interred in the church yard of the Parish of St. Mary Shandon on 6 Aug 1761 without issue, whereupon Anne and Mary Morris became vested with the land and Mary Morris afterwards married Jonas Morris and Anne Morris and Mary Morris and Jonas Morris granted power of attorney to on 30 Oct 1762 to Joseph Jacobs, merchant, of Philadelphia, to dispose of the land. The tract beginning near the improvement of Solomon Stokley ... corner of land originally surveyed for Luke Watson called Wattson's Choice ... along a line of land formerly surveyed for Richard Bundock called Arcadia ... to the main road from Indian River to Lewis Town commonly called the Indian River Road ... along the tract of William Foster to where the road crosses Dodds Branch ... to the water side of a mill pond ... to the mouth of Dodds Branch where it empties into Braceys Branch ... to the tract now in the possession of William Marriner ... 513 acres and 59 square perches. Wit: Boaz Manlove, Mark McCall. Within deed ackn. 7 Aug 1770.

98. William West, Sussex Co., pilot, from Samuel Paynter, Junr., Sussex Co., carpenter. 3 Aug 1770. Lot in town of Lewes in Mulberry Street bounded according to a deed of sale from William Cornwall and Rebeckah his wife, admrs of estate of Elias Fisher to John Paynter, Junr. dated 14 Dec 1727. For £17. Wit: Thos. Gray, Joseph Hosman. 3 Aug 1770.

98. John Maull, Sussex Co., shipwright, from David Rankens, Sussex Co., cordwainer and Mary Ranken his wife, Daniel Murphey of Sussex Co., pilot and Hannah his wife. 1 April 1770. Parcel of land on the bank of Lewes Creek being part of a larger tract which was formerly taken up by William Tom and by sundry

conveyances became the property of John Jacobs; reference being made to the deed which Henry Draper gave to said John Jacobs. And the afsd. John Jacobs dying intestate the right of said land descended to his two daughters, Mary and Hannah who married David Ranken and Daniel Murphy, party to these presents. Laid out for 5 acres for £60. Wit: Elias Hugg, Alexander Bruce. Within deed of sale ackn. 9 Aug 1770.

99. Peter Parker, Sussex Co., yeoman, from John Conwell, Sussex Co. yeoman. 4 Sep 1770. Whereas two tracts in the forks of Cedar Creek on the south side the widow Draper's mill pond which one of the small parcels of land was taken up by virtue of a warrant dated 29 Aug 1715 for David Smith, tayler, laid out for 200 acres, and said David Smith and wife conveyed by deed of sale to Robert Turk 1 Feb 1724 and Robert Turk being indebted to several creditors the land was sold by the sheriff at publick sale to John Conwell. And by virtue of a warrant for William Fisher, the land being on the south side of Cedar Creek and in the fork of said creek and joining to the above land. And William Fisher by his last will bequeaths afsd. 100 acres to John Conwell dated 10 May 1725 - in all 300 acres which John Conwell sold to John Walton by an article of agreement dated 2 March 1762 for which afsd. John Walton for a £180 assigns his right to Peter Parker. Wit: Anderson Parker, John Shankland. Within deed ackn. 4 Sep 1770.

101. I, Draper May of Sussex Co., yeoman, for 5 shillings and other considerations, paid by my brother Thos. May of said co. have released right to 4 parcels of land in Cedar Creek Neck and on Mispillion Creek one of which parcel was conveyed by deed of sale by Jonathan Shankland, High Sheriff to Jonathan May for 125 acres; the second parcel was conveyed by deed of sale from Thomas Davis to Jonathan May afsd. and Henry Draper for 199 3/4 acres; the third parcel by deed of sale from Thos. Clifton to James Harper for 50 acres; the fourth parcel of marsh lying within the bounds of a bank on Mispillion Creek and supposed to be within the bounds of Henry Pennington's patent and on the northwest or west side of a ditch cut between the afsd. Draper and Thos. May containing 12 acres and in the whole 386 3/4 acres. Wit: John Draper, William Shankland. Within deed of release ackn. 4 Sep 1770.

102. Thos. and Peter Robinson from William Burton. I, William Burton of Worcester Co., Maryland, for £65, paid by Thomas Robinson and Peter Robinson, both of the county of Sussex, merchants release claim to two part of a tract that Joshua Burton died intestate and possessed of in Indian River Hundred containing 217 acres, the original grant was made to William Kanning 11 April 1682 and surveyed 6 Sep 1682 for 300 acres and patent granted 26 March 1684 and William Kinning conveyed same part thereof to George Young by deed of sale dated 17 Sep 1685, recorded 1 Nov 1786 and at a court held June 1688 Cornelius Wiltbank and Jane his wife admr. of Isaac Bound obtained judgment against the afsd. George Young for a sum of money and afterwards assigned judgment to William Burton who caused the land to be

sold by the sheriff to said Burton on 17 Aug 1705 for 217 acres. William Burton by his last will devised as the residuary part of his real estate to said Joshua Burton his son having died intestate and left issue , vizt., William Burton, Jacob Burton, Ann the wife of John Wingate and Sarah Burton. Newcom White, John Eveans. Within deed of release ackn. 5 Sep 1770.

102. Nehemiah Davis, Junr., Sussex Co., taylor, from Thomas Groves, Sussex Co., yeoman. 8 Aug 1770. For £17, marsh on the south side of Prime Hook Creek ... laying before the south door of Henry Smith's house. 9 acres and 16 perches. Wit: John Wilson Dean, Isaac Smith. Within deed of sale ackn. 8 Aug 1770.

103. Nehemiah Davis, Junr., from Boaz Manlove, Sheriff. 8 Aug 1770. whereas there were several judgments recovered against John Cirwithin whereas the sheriff sold 28 acres of marsh on the north side of Cirwithin's Mill Creek alias Prime Hook Creek a little below said mill to Nehemiah Davis he being the highest bidder for £36. Wit: Jacob Hazzard, Dormon Lofland. Within deed ackn. 8 Aug 1770.

104. Nehemiah Davis, Junr., from Boas Manlove, Sheriff. 8 Aug 1770. Whereas there were several judgments recovered against John Cirwithin whereupon the sheriff sold 133 acres to Nehemiah Davis for £63, binding by the edge of the mill pond of Prime Hook Little Branch. Wit: Jacob Hazzard, Dormon Lofland. Within deed of sale ackn. 8 Aug 1770.

105. Andrew McDowel, Chester Co. from Joseph and Samuel Shankland, Sussex Co., iron masters. 1 Sep 1770. For £178.6, an undivided 1/6 part of 811 acres adjoining and including the head of Nanticoke River in Cedar Creek Hundred surveyed by virtue of a warrant granted to Joseph Shankland and the undivided 1/6 of a forge, gristmill and saw mill on said premises, as also 1/6 part of two other tracts, one called Loflands Fork Road adjoining the 811 acres which was surveyed for William Lofland by warrant and conveyed to Samuel Shankland containing 377 acres, the other part lying and including part of Gum Branch surveyed for Joseph Shankland, called Iron Valley, containing 200 acres. Wit: Boaz Manlove, Littleton Townsend. Within deed of sale ackn. 4 Sep 1770.

105. John Gault to John Evans. John Turvel Gault and Angelita his wife of Worcester Co., Maryland for £60, paid by their brother John Evens of Sussex Co., taylor, land which Thomas Eavens the Elder, father of afsd. Angelita, late of Sussex Co., died possessed of in Angola Neck which Thomas Evans purchased from John Potter in July 1762 and recorded in Liber I No. 9, folio 398. Wit: Thos. Robinson, William Burton. Within deed of release ackn. 14 Aug 1770.

106. John Vankerk, Sussex Co., from Thos. and Draper May, Sussex Co., yeomen. 7 Aug 1770. Tract granted by patent to Henry Pennington and by sundry means has descended to afsd. Thomas Draper. Beginning at a corner of Harts tract ... bounding

several water courses til it intersects with Mispillion Creek ... 120 acres. For £120. Wit: Thomas Homes, Ann May. Within deed of sale ackn. 8 Aug 1770.

107. Isaac Townsend, Sussex Co., from Charles Draper, Sussex Co., house carpenter. 8 July 1770. For £40.3.10, all the property that ever belonged to said Isaac Townsend being the same tract that afsd. Charles Draper purchased of said Isaac Townsend in 1769 being part of a tract that William Townsend willed to his son Costen Townsend, being on the east side of Cedar Creek joining Ebenezer Spencer's land on the west side and joining David Wattson's 2 acres on the east side containing 101 1/2 acres. Wit: Dormon Lofland, Isaac Wattson. Within deed of sale ackn. 8 Aug 1770.

107. William Johnson from Samuel Johnson. I Samuel Johnson of Sussex Co., yeoman, for £16, and love and affection, etc. release to William Johnson my right to land in Indian River Hundred granted to my father Samuel Johnson, dec'd. by warrant 3 July 1754 for 200 acres. Wit: Joseph Yoseph, Roads Shankland. Within deed of release ackn. 8 Aug 1770.

108. Jacob Kollock, Junr. to Fretwell Wright. A penal bill which bindeth Jacob Kollock, Collector of His Majesty's customs for the port of Lewes, to be paid to Fretwell Wright. 13 Aug 1770.

108. John Hall, Sussex Co., yeoman, from Joseph Hazzard, Sussex Co., mariner, for £85, tract at the head of Long Neck on the southeast side of Cow Bridge Branch on Sockrockat it being part of a larger tract formerly granted to Cord Hazzard called Sockarockah which warrant was dated 16 March 1738, beginning at a corner of land surveyed formerly for Thomas Walker, 150 acres. Wit: James Gordon, Marnix Virdin. Within deed of release ackn. 8 Aug 1770.

109. Robert Lacey, Worcester Co., Maryland, yeoman, from William Carey, Sussex Co., yeoman. 8 Aug 1770. Whereas Samuel Cary, Sussex Co., yeoman, dec'd., being at the time of his death seized of a tract at the head of Indian River and by his will dated 21 Jan 1754 bequeathed to his four sons, William, Joseph, Samuel and Elias, all the land whereon he did dwell and all adjoining thereto, containing 500 acres to be equally divided. For £31.5 William Carey's right to above property. Wit: James Gordon, Isaac Smith. Within deed of sale ackn. 8 Aug 1770.

109. Larrance Riley to Joseph Morris. 7 Aug 1770. Between John Crothers of Accomack Co., Virginia, yeoman, by attorney in fact, Larrance Riley, Senr. of Sussex Co., yeoman, and Joseph Morris of Somerset Co., Maryland, yeoman. John Crothers by his writing obligatory dated 3 Feb 1767 obligate himself to convey to Nehemiah Reed a tract of 150 acres in the penal sum of £100 and Nehemiah Reed on 16 Aug 1768 assign the writing obligatory to Dennis Morris who on 6 Aug 1770 assign said writing obligatory to afsd. Joseph Morris. Land begins on the south side of the edge

of the northwest fork of Pembertons Branch in the Broadkill
forrest being at the corner of Robert Cale's land ... to a line
of the land formerly laid out for Peter Lucas now in the
possession of Hannah Hall, containing 150 acres. Wit: Boaz
Manlove, Thomas Grove. Within deed of sale ackn. 9 Aug 1770.

111. Larrance Riley from John Cruthers. Power of Attorney to
convey above described land now in the possession of Nehemiah
Reed. Wit: John Ponder, Junr., Benjamin Riley. 4 April 1767.

111. Benjamin Carpenter, Sussex Co., cordwainer, from Ezekiel
West and wife Sarah, Sussex Co. For £9 that parcel that Robert
Hill of Sussex Co. died possessed of in Angola Hundred, about 100
acres which by the last will of John Hill dated 8 Jan 1725
devised to said Robert Hill. Wit: Hester Kollock, Daniel Nunez.
Within deed ackn. 7 Nov 1770.

112. Arthur Hazzard, Sussex Co., planter, from Benjamin
Carpenter, Sussex Co., cordwainer and Comfort his wife. 7 Nov
1770. Tract in Angola Hundred being part of a larger tract taken
up by Francis Meads and John Crawley called Soulsters Inheritance
as by deed William Smith, Rebeckah Smith to John Hill dated 4 May
1722 appears, and John by his last will devised same to his son
Robert Hill which Robert Hill died intestate and left issue, the
afsd. Comfort and Margret, his only heirs, which said tract
contains 73 acres. For £47.9 the moiety or half part. Wit:
Thomas Cary, Daniel Nunez. Within deed ackn. 7 Nov 1770.

113. Thos. May, Sussex Co., planter, from Boaz Manlove, High
Sheriff, Esqr. 7 Nov 1770. Tract on south side of Mispillion
Creek containing 100 acres being part of a larger tract that
Jonathan May and Henry Draper purchased Thomas Davis, Sussex Co.,
dec'd., known as Marsh Patent, and Henry Draper died intestate
and left issue, one called Isaac Draper whose property was
attached who possessed 1/7 part of said tract and in Aug Term
1770 the sheriff was ordered to sell the same which land was sold
to the highest bidder, Thomas May, for £10.10. Wit: Robert
Wright, J. Moore. Within deed ackn. 7 Nov 1770.

113. Alexander Laws, Worcester Co., Maryland, from John Laws,
Worcester Co., Maryland. 6 Nov 1770. For £50. Tract in Sussex
Co., called Addition to Fellowship surveyed 4 Feb 1755 for 170
acres lying between Johns Branch and Arthur Foster's plantation,
surveyed for Samuel Owens which he by deed of sale conveyed to
said John laws 4 Feb 1756. Wit: John Owens, William Owens.
Within deed ackn. 7 Nov 1770.

114. Alexander Laws, Worcester Co., from William Owens, Sussex
Co. 6 Nov 1770. For £75. Parcel of land called Williams
Security joining the southeast and northeast side of the lands
whereon the said Alexander now dwells. 159 acres. Wit: Edward
Carey, Henry Fisher. Within deed ackn. 7 Nov 1770.

115. Thomas Cary from Welches heirs. 20 Oct 1770. Between
Thomas Cary of Sussex Co., yeoman and Jacob Welch, John White and

Sarah White his wife and Ebenezer Welch of Sussex Co. Whereas John Welch of Dosset [Dorchester] Co., Maryland, dec'd., owned a parcel in Sussex Co. called John Welch's Bear Swell alias Welches Chance in Cedar Creek Hundred being the land whereon John Welch and Daniel Welch now live and whereas John Welch died intestate leaving no issue, the afsd. land descended to the sons and daughters of Daniel Welch brother to afsd. John welch being the only proper heirs, to wit, John Welch, Jacob Welch, Daniel Welch, Sarah Welch now Sarah White and Ebenezar Welch. For £9. Wit: Edward Cary, Thos. Cary Young. Within deed ackn. 7 Nov 1770.

116. William Shockley, Sussex Co., farmer, from Peter Parker, Sussex Co., yeoman. 6 Nov 1770. Parcel in Cedar Creek Hundred, part of which was granted to David Smith and surveyed 1 Aug 1716. For £100. Beginning on northwest side of the southwest branch of Cedar Creek. 250 acres. Wit: Boaz Manlove, Richard Shockley. Within deed ackn. 6 Nov 1770.

116. Jane Irons, Worcester Co., Maryland, from Majour Warren, Sussex Co. 11 May 1770. Tract in Broadkill Hundred of 300 acres being part of a larger tract of 700 acres granted to Josiah Roten which land layeth on the east side of a branch on the head of Bever Dam Branch proceeding out of the head of Indian River about 18 miles from town of Lewes between the forks of the roads that leadeth from Lewes to Somerset and Dorchester Counties called Forked Poplar and surveyed by virtue of a proprietary warrant, lying on the south and southwest side of the larger tract which land was conveyed to afsd. Majour Warrant from David Green and to David Green from afsd. Josiah Rotten. For £46.3. Wit: Joshua Morris, Simon Kollock. Within deed ackn. 7 Nov 1770.

117. John Draper, Sussex Co., Innholder, from Luke Watson, Sussex Co., yeoman. 15 Nov 1770. For £15. Grist mill land, late property of John Walton and also 2 acres laid off at the condemnation of the stream and 2 acres, 4 perches on the north side of the mill pond. Wit: Boaz Manlove, Richard Cade. Within deed ackn. Dec 1770.

118. Elisha Knock, Sussex Co., yeoman, from John Homes, Sussex Co., yeoman. 2 Aug 1769. 2 Aug 1769. For £200. Land granted by patent to afsd. John Homes on the south side of Mispillion Creek in Cedar Creek Neck, 128 acres. Wit: John Read, Rhoads Shankland. Within deed ackn. 8 Nov 1770.

119. John Reed, yeoman, from John Homes, Sussex Co., yeoman. 8 Aug 1770. Land in Cedar Creek Neck on the south side of Mispillion Creek being part of a larger tract granted by patent to afsd. John Homes 19 Jan 1759. 120 1/2 acres. Wit: Elisha Knock, Roads Shankland. Within deed ackn. 8 Nov 1770.

119. Richard Blocksom, Sussex Co., yeoman, from Solomon Knock, Sussex Co., yeoman. 8 Nov 1770. For £143.10, 143 acres, beginning at a corner post of Mills Field patent ... to a corner in Masons line ... to a corner of Stephenson's land bought of Isaac Wiltbank, being part of a tract containing 425 acres called

Luck by Chance lying in Cove Neck, granted by patent to Hermanous Wiltbank and by sundry conveyances or devises to Isaac Wiltbank and by said Wiltbank the 143 acres were conveyed to said Solomon Knock. Wit: Boaz Manlove, Thos. Grove. Within deed ackn. 13 Nov 1770.

120. Richardson Cade, Sussex Co., yeoman, from Wm. Willson and his wife Anna and Lodawick Warring of Sussex Co. 8 Dec 1770. Whereas Robert English, dec'd., Sussex Co., father to afsd. Anna, had granted to him by virtue of a proprietary warrant 250 acres in Broadkill forest which land said English did sell to Christopher Topham but made no deed of sale to him for the same and after the decease of Topham, Robert Gill, admr. of his estate sold said land to Neil McNeel which said McNeel by his last will bequeathed said land to his daughter Sarah which said Sarah with her husband Samuel Tam conveyed the land to the above named Lodowick Warring on 7 Feb 1755. The afsd. Anna Willson being the only daughter and legal representative of Robert English did claim the above said tract as her property whereupon the afsd. Lodowick Warring contracted with Wm. Moore her attorney for same and took a deed of sale from her the afsd. Anna signed by said William Moore dated 15 Oct 1759 for the whole tract excepting 50 acres reserved for said Anna which 50 acres lyeth on the east end of said land. Beginning at a corner oak standing in Rolphs line, containing 50 acres. For £10. Wit: Luke Walton, William Riley. Within deed ackn. 11 Dec 1770.

121. Joseph Warrington from James McIvain. I, James McIlvain of Sussex Co., yeoman, for £25 release and quit claim right to tract in the forrest of Indian River Hundred adjoining lands of Woodman Stockley, dec'd., containing 200 acres granted by Proprietors warrant to above named James McIlvain and to John Warrington, Sussex Co., dec'd., dated 20 June 1753. Wit: Daniel Nunez, Thomas Smith. Within deed ackn. 8 Nov 1770.

121. John Rodney, Sussex Co., from Elijah Skidmore and wife Mary, Sussex Co. 15 Dec 1770. Parcel on the south side of Broadkill Creek containing 180 acres being part of a larger tract granted by patent to Cornelius Wiltbank, dec'd., called Luck by Chance which said patentee conveyed 275 acres to James Fenwick, dec'd. who by his last will devised same and all his estate except his wife's thirds, to his 5 children, to be equally divided amongst them; the youngest dying first the land survived to the other four, Thomas, William, James and Mary. Thomas mortgaged his share (1/4) and then died without issue and his part was sold at public sale to discharge his mortgage and was purchased by afsd. William; afterwards the said James died without issue and William and Mary conveyed the 180 acres to Samuel Tam 1762. And Samuel Tam sold and conveyed the same to the above John Rodney. And whereas said Mary at the time of making the said conveyance to the afsd. Samuel Tam was under coverture having been married by the above named Elijah Skidmore several years before which said Elijah was absent in the province of North Carolina for upwards of 10 years before the making of the conveyance last. Nevertheless as he is now returned some

doubts have arose whether said Mary could legally convey her part of said land. Now for £80 pounds the land is released. Wit: J. Russel, Wm. Parker. Within deed of sale ackn. 15 Dec 1770.

122. Jane Mollinex, Sussex Co., widow of William Mollinex, from Bethual Watson, Sussex Co., farmer. 8 Nov 1770. Whereas Alexander Argu, Sussex Co., yeoman, now dec'd., on 26 Nov 1753 possessed of two parts of land, the one lying in the forrest of Cedar Creek Hundred between the head of Bowman's Branch, one of the branches of Mispillion Creek and on the side of a swamp called the Woolf Den called Jones Adventure containing 395 acres and the other part being in the forrest of Cedar Creek Hundred being formerly taken up and belonging to John Morris containing 99 3/4 acres did appoint Bethuel Watson his attorney to sell the land whereby Bethual Watson did on 11 Dec 1754 contract to convey the afsd. two tracts to Samuel Davis for £75 paid in part to Alexander Argu and the residue paid to Moses Argue his son and admr. Bethuel Watson was bound to Samuel Davis in a writing obligatory under the penalty of £500 on 19 May 1760 Samuel Davis assigned for £100 to William Mollinex afsd. now dec'd. Wit: David Hall, Samuel Davis. Within deed ackn. 8 Nov 1770. [The name is spelled Argu, Argue and Argoe.]

124. Power of Attorney to Bethuel Wattson from Alexander Argoe to sell above mentioned land. Wit: James Read, John Polk. Proved by oath John Polk, blacksmith, 7 Nov 1770.

124. Bond. Samuel Davis from Bethual Wattson. [See above deed.] Wit: James Read, John Read.

125. William Mollinex from Samuel Davis in assignment of bond [see above]. Wit: Pemberton Carlile (X), Warron Burroughs. 19 May 1760.

125. Abraham Potter from John Potter. Power of attorney. I John Potter of Rowans Co., North Carolina, planter, appoint my brother Abraham Potter of said county my attorney to recover, receive, etc. from all persons indebted to me in Sussex Co. and to make sales of all lands of mine in Sussex Co. Wit: Daniel Baley, John Harrison, David Stewart. ackn. 1 Aug 1770.

125. James Holland, Sussex Co., planter, from Simon and Samuel Darby, Sussex Co., planters. 5 Feb 1770. Whereas John Darby died intestate and Elizabeth Darby, admx. to his estate obtained an order of Orphans Court to sell his land and Simon and Samuel Darby were the highest bidders for £11.10 the parcel beginning at the corner of the land of Jacob Kollock, Junr. ... to a corner post standing in the line of Jonathan Bailey, dec'd. containing 453 acres and 53 square perches. Wit: J. Russel, William West. Within deed ackn. 5 Feb 1771.

126. Joseph Lane, Sussex Co., yeoman, from David Warring, Sussex Co., yeoman. 5 Feb 1771. Whereas John Webb had granted to him by virtue of a proprietors warrant dated 19 June 1747 a tract in Cedar Creek Forrest which he by deed of sale dated 2 May 1764

convey to afsd. David Warrington for 262 acres, part of the afsd. tract for £30. Now David Warrington for £30 conveys to Joseph Lane 100 acres being part of the above recited 262 acres. Wit: Elias Hugg, John Waples. Within deed ackn. 5 Feb 1771.

127. George Frame, Sussex Co., from Smith Frame, Worcester Co. Maryland. 6 Feb 1771. Whereas a tract in Broadkill Hundred whereof Robert Frame late of Sussex Co. died seized and Nathan Frame, eldest son of said Robert Frame had the land divided and 30 acres was allotted afsd. Smith Frame adjoining William Russel's land. For £6. Wit: Wm. Peery, James Black. Within deed ackn. 6 Feb 1771.

128. Barnet Vankerk, Sussex Co., yeoman, from John Coverdall son of Susanna, Sussex Co., yeoman. 6 Feb 1771. Parcel of land in forrest of Cedar Creek Hundred being part of a larger tract granted to afsd. John Coverdal in Great Neck being the east side of the larger tract; warrant granted to John coverdall 3 Oct 1745 on northwest side f a branch or Beverdam ... to a corner oak of land formerly Abraham Parsley ... containing 51 acres for £7. Wit: Thomas May, Saml. Shankland. Within deed ackn. 6 Feb 1771.

129. John Collins, Junr., Worcester Co., yeoman, from Mitchel Smith, Sussex Co., yeoman. 6 Feb 1771. Parcel of land in the forrest of Broadkill Hundred being part of a larger tract taken up by proprietaries warrant granted to Richard, Samuel and Daniel Hopkins and conveyed by deed of sale from them to afsd. Mitchel Smith by deed dated 3 Dec 1763 beginning at a corner of the land of Andrew Collings Junr., 50 acres for £25. Wit: Sam: Shankland, Rhoads Shankland. Within deed ackn. 6 Feb 1771.

129. Mathew Wilson, clerk for and in behalf of his daughter Polley Wilson, from David Gray, Sussex Co., mariner. Feb 1770. For 7 shillings, 6 pence and in consideration of the will and desire of his mother, dec'd., who desired her maiden land might be given to said Polley Wilson (her daughter Betsey having a small moiety) and inasmuch as said David Gray is by law (being the oldest and only surviving son) entitled to 2/3 of this land he to comply with the will of a parent doth sell to Mr. Wilson in trust of Polly Wilson a minor, tract in Lewes Hundred being part of a larger tract surveyed to Robert and John Shankland and by them divided 1 Jan 1731, vizt., the northwest side to John Shankland of 163 acres and southeast to Robert Shankland of 177 acres. This division was confirmed by warrant to both parties 1 April 1735. John Shankland at his death devised his part to be equally divided between his daughters Sarah and Hester, the former was afterwards sold to Mr. Nunez. The southwest part was Hester's part, beginning at a corner oak on a line of Roads Shankland's land near Cool Spring Road ... to Mr. Wiltbank's line ... containing 82 acres. Two parts of this land to which the said David Gray had a right he hath made over to Mr. Wilson. Wit: Jos. Shankland, Jno. Miller, Junr., George Knight. Within deed ackn. 6 Feb 1771. [A correction to the description of the land is added on 15 Feb 1782 and witnessed by Polly Marsh, Elizabeth Drain, Matthew Wilson, John Drain, Peter Marsh and

Rhods Shankland, Surveyor.]

130. Obediah Messick, Worcester Co., Maryland, from Joseph Lufton and wife Mary, Sussex Co. 7 Oct 1769. Parcel of land in Broadkill Forrest adjoining the land of said Obediah Messex, Andrew Collings and John Clowes, Junr., which said parcel was granted to the afsd. Mary when Mary West by virtue of a proprietary warrant. For £16 all the above recited land warrant and improvements except 100 acres on the north end of the same adjoining 40 acres on Gravelly Branch now in the possession of John Clowes, Junr. Wit: Rees Woolf, Jas. Warrington. Within deed ackn. 6 Feb 1771.

131. John Laws, Worcester Co., Maryland, from Samuel Owens, Worcester Co., Maryland. 6 Feb 1771. Whereas by proprietors warrant dated 29 June 1750 for James Owens to lay off 200 acres being all the vacant land between Arther Fowler, Jonathan Fowler, Joseph Morgins, William Laws, Thomas Statons, lying on both sides of Johns Branch in the forrest of Cedar Creek Hundred. For £100, Samuel Owens son of James Owens conveys 200 acres called Luck. Wit: Thomas May, Smith Fassit. Within deed ackn. 6 Feb 1771.

131. Alexander Laws, Worcester Co., Maryland, planter, from Levin Bounds, Sussex Co., planter. Feb 1771. Whereas by proprietors warrant dated 28 July 1748 for Arther Fowler, in the forrest of Cedar Creek Hundred, surveyed on 12 April 1748, 289 1/2 acres. For £30, 100 acres of the above described land which by deed to his son John Fowlers was conveyed, called Horse Pound Tract, the above 100 acres to be taken out of the northeast part of the larger tract. Wit: Samuel Owens, Junr., John Laws, Junr. Within deed ackn. 6 Feb 1771.

132. Isaac Wattson, admr. of Thomas Wattson, dec'd.. from Simeon Lewes and wife Elizabeth, yeoman. 27 July 1770. Whereas a tract in Cedar Creek Hundred being part of a larger tract granted to Henry Bowman for 1000 acres adjoining the bay side marshes containing 295 acres which land was sold by Henry Bowman to Mark Manlove and conveyed by John Bowman, representative of Henry Bowman, the patentee by his deed of bargain and sale dated 12 March 1752 and did convey to said Elizabeth Lewes and Purnal Wattson, Thos. Wattson and Isaac Watson the then representatives and heirs of Mark Manlove the above said purchaser. And Simeon Lewes and wife Elizabeth for £50 paid by Thomas Wattson, bricklayer in his lifetime. Beginning at a post in George Watson's line. 295 acres. Wit: Levin Crapper, Wm. Hazzard. Within deed of sale ackn. 6 Feb 1771.

133. Thomas Bounds from Levin Bounds. Feb 1770. Whereas a proprietors warrant dated 28 July 1748 for Arthur Fowlar for 289 1/2 acres in the forrest of Cedar Creek Hundred, surveyed on 12 April 1748. For £60 part of this tract, being 189 1/2 acres which was conveyed by Arthur Fowler to John Fowler and by John Fowler to Levin Bounds. Tract is called Horse Pound Tract. Wit: John Laws, Junr., Samuel Owens, Senr. Within deed ackn. 6 Feb

1771.

134. Smith Frame, Worcester Co., Maryland, from Joseph Warrington, Sussex Co.,. 28 Feb 1771. Tract in Indian River Hundred granted by Proprietary warrant to Samuel Johnson, late of Sussex Co., and the said Samuel Johnson by assignment on the back of said warrant made over his right to Robert Lacy who by his last will among other things devised to his son Parker Lacy who by deed of sale conveyed same to the above named Joseph Warrington. Beginning at a corner stone on the east side of the great road leading from the sawmill towards Philadelphia. 160 acres. Wit: Peter Parker, Peter F. Wright. Within deed ackn. 5 Feb 1771.

135. Benjamin Jacobs, Providence Township, Philadelphia Co., yeoman, from Jonas Morris, Anna Morris and Mary Morris, all of Ireland, by Joseph Jacobs of the City of Philadelphia, their attorney. 19 April 1769. Whereas by indenture on 15th of the 6th month 1688 between John How of Sussex Co. of the one part and Jeremiah Scott of the town of Lewes of the other part, the said John How conveyed to Jeremiah Scott that tract called Dichers Hill containing 600 acres which by divers conveyances and other assurances since become invested in the above named Jonas Morris, Anne Morris and Mary Morris. For 10 shillings. Wit: Isaac Jones, Jane Dennis. Recorded in City of Philadelphia 9 March 1770.

136. John Stockley from Olaver and Prettyman Stockley. I Olaver Stockley and Prettyman Stockley, for £32 have released and quit claimed rights to 330 acres in Angola, Sussex Co., being part of a larger tract formerly taken up by Francis Meads and John Crawly called Soulsters Inheritance. Wit: Wm. Peery, Elias West. Within deed ackn. 6 Feb 1771.

137. Wrixam Lewis, Sussex Co., Esqr., from Abraham Wiltbank, Sussex Co., pilot. 13 Feb 1771. Tract on bank of Lewes Creek bounded by land which afsd. Abraham Wiltbank purchased the estate of his brother, Jacob Wiltbank and on the land belonging to John Wiltbank, Esqr. and the same land that Abraham Wiltbank died seized of, containing 64 acres. For £217.10. Wit: Hannah Nunez, Daniel Nunez. Within deed of mortgage ackn. Feb 1771.

138. Rhoads Shankland, Sussex Co., yeoman, from Joseph and Samuel Shankland, Sussex Co., Gentlemen. 25 Jan 1771. For £1200. Tract on the southwest side of Pagan Creek called St. Martains granted by patent to Edward Southeron 15 Jan 1675 and conveyed by deed of sale from Mary Southern, widow and admx. of estate of Edward Southern, dec'd., dated 6th of 3rd month 1685 to Griffith Jones who assigned the land to Samuel Preston and said Samuel Preston conveyed same William Shankland grandfather of said Joseph and Samuel Shankland and the said William Shankland in his last will left the land to his son Joseph Shankland father of Joseph and Samuel Shankland and whereas Joseph Shankland the Elder was indebted to his son James Shankland and afsd. tract was seized and sold to afsd. Samuel Shankland as appears in deed of

sale from Daniel Nunez, Sheriff. Beginning on the north side of a small branch containing 410 acres. Wit: David Hall, James Thompson. Within deed of sale ackn. 8 Feb 1771.

139. John Collins, Junr., Worcester Co., from Obediah Messick, Worcester Co. 6 Feb 1771. Parcel of land at first granted to Mary West by Proprietors warrant and whereas Joseph Lofton married afsd. Mary West and whereas said Joseph Lofton and Mary by their deed of sale conveyed said land to afsd. Obediah Messick, said parcel being part of the above described tract, for £6. Wit: Reynalds(?) Williams, Rhoads Shankland. Within deed of sale ackn. 6 Feb 1771.

139. Purnal Watson and wife Mary, Sussex Co., from Isaac Wattson, admr. of Thomas Watson, Luke Watson and wife Mary, Draper May and wife Ann, all of Sussex Co. 30 July 1770. Tract in Cedar Creek Hundred being part of a larger tract granted to Henry Bowman for 1000 acres joining the bay side marshes containing 295 acres which land was sold by Henry Bowman to Mark Manlove who bequeathed same to his son Thomas Manlove and he dying without issue it fell to his two sisters, Mary and Elizabeth, and Elizabeth later married Thomas Watson and Mary married Nehemiah Davis and Thomas Watson purchased from Nehemiah Davis and Mary his wife their moiety or half part and Thomas Watson dying intestate the said land became the property of his son Thomas Wattson who died without issue leaving two brothers and two sisters, namely, Purnal, Isaac, Mary and Ann, parties to these presents. For £286.16.1 1/2. Beginning at a corner post on George Wattson's line. Wit: Levin Crapper, Thomas May. Within deed of sale ackn. 6 Feb 1771.

140. Robert Hood, Sussex Co., from William Peery, Sussex Co., and wife Mary. 8 Feb 1771. Parcel of land in Broadkill Hundred which James Hood died intestate seized of, the tract descended to Mary wife of afsd. William Peery, being one of the heirs. For £22. Wit: Elias King, William Stephens. Within deed of sale ackn. 8 Feb 1771.

140. Jonathan Rust, Sussex Co., yeoman, from Joseph Hazzard, Sussex Co., yeoman. 27 April 1770. For £16, tract in Indian River Hundred formerly taken up by warrant for Cord Hazzard and afterwards by his deed of gift conveyed to Joseph Hazzard. Beginning on the north side of Dutchman's Branch, 80 acres. Wit: Andrew McIlvain, Junr., Elias Hugg. ackn. 6 Feb 1771.

141. Henry Fisher of Lewes and Rehoboth Hundred, Innkeeper, from John Read, of Cedar Creek Hundred, husbandman. Lease for 5 shillings, parcel in Cedar Creek Hundred, containing 123 acres. Wit: Robert Done, Daniel Nunez. Within deed of sale ackn. 9 Feb 1771.

142. Henry Fisher from John Read. Common Recovery. Indenture Tripartite made 28 Dec 1770 between John Read of Cedar Creek Hundred, husbandman and Henry Fisher of Lewes and Rehoboth Hundred, Innkeeper, and Jacob Moore of Lewes and Rehoboth

Hundred. John Read for 5 shillings paid by Henry Fisher hath
released to Henry Fisher by virtue of a bargain and sale made by
John Read by indenture for one year, tract of land in Cedar Creek
Hundred, 123 acres and 95 square perches. Wit: Robert Done,
Daniel Nunez. Within deed ackn. 9 Feb 1771.

144. John Clowes, Sussex Co., from Ezekiel Jones(?), Worcester
Co., Maryland, yeoman. 13 Jan 1771. Tract in Broadkill Forrest
adjoining Jane West's marsh and on land now in the possession of
Foster Donavan and Andrew Heavelo which said tract was surveyed
to said Ezekiel Joynes(?) by virtue of a proprietors warrant
dated 1 Nov 1758. Beginning with a maple standing in the marshes
of the Bever Dam ... to lands formerly surveyed for Richard
Dobson now in the possession of Foster Donavan. 92 acres for
£25. Wit: John Ellegood, Thomas Ellegood. Within deed ackn. 8
May 1771.

145. Manlove Russel from Levi Russel. I Levi Russel, Sussex
Co., for 5 shillings paid by Manlove Russel of Sussex Co., ship
carpenter, one moiety of a larger tract conveyed by a deed of
sale from Joseph Feddeman to William Russel by deed dated 4 Nov
1760; land is on northwest side of Broadkill Creek, beginning at
a corner post standing at the northwest end of the Drawbridge
containing 140 acres. Wit: William Clark, Rhoads Shankland.
Within deed ackn. 8 May 1771.

145. Joseph Shankland, Sussex Co., ironmaster, from Boaz
Manlove, Sheriff. 7 May 1771. Whereas the property of Andrew
McDowell of Sussex Co. was ordered to be sold to levy the sum of
£420 which Joseph and Samuel Shankland have lately recovered
against him plus court costs and charges, the sheriff seized and
sold his 1/6 part of Unity Forge plus his right in said company
including land. For £120. which land consists of 1/6 of three
tracts in Cedar Creek the one whereon the forge stand of 811
acres called Shanklands Discovery, the other containing 377 acres
called Loftlands Fork Roads, the third containing 200 acres
called Iron Valley which lands were conveyed to Andrew McDowel by
Joseph and Samuel Shankland. Wit: J: Moore, Elias Conwell.
Within deed ackn. 8 May 1771.

146. George Walton, Sussex Co., from Spencer Chance, Sussex Co.
7 May 1771. Tract in Cedar Creek Hundred containing 74 acres and
139 perches being part of a larger tract which Abraham Wynkoop,
Esqr., dec'd., purchased of the heirs of Robert Hart called Harts
Choice and the said Abraham Wynkoop by his last will devised same
to his son Thomas Wynkoop, now dec'd., who by his last will
devised same to Benjamin Wynkoop who by his deed of sale dated 7
May 1760 conveyed the same to afsd. Spencer Chance, beginning at
a line on Robert Hart's land being a corner of William Pierce's
land. 74 acres and 139 perches. For £109.10. Wit: Wm. Hazzard,
James Rench. Within deed of sale ackn. 8 May 1771.

147. George Walton, Sussex Co., from Bethuel Wattson, Sussex
Co., yeoman. 7 May 1771. Parcel of marsh in Cedar Creek Neck on
the southwest side of Mispllion Creek adjoining land and marsh of

afsd. George Walton and Jonathan May containing 86 acres and 129 perches of marsh granted to afsd. Bethuel Wattson by warrant dated 4 June 1739. For 9 shillings paid by John Walton 12 Aug 1741 who then was a minor. Wit: Wm. Hazzard, Jas. Rench. Within deed of release ackn. 7 May 1771.

148. Thomas Robinson, Esqr., and Peter Robinson, Gentleman, both of Sussex Co., from John Evans, Worcester Co., Maryland. 6 March 1770. Tract in Angola Neck on the south side of Love Creek containing 474 acres and marsh, 400 acres whereof was conveyed by Elizabeth and Susannah Becket, extxs. of last will of William Becket, clerk, dec'd., to Coventon(?) Corbin, Gentleman in 1743 and by said Corbin conveyed to John Potter and by Potter conveyed by deed in 1762 to Thomas Eavans of Accomack Co., Virginia together with 74 acres and marsh included in a warrant of resurvey layed upon the premises by the afsd. John Potter and adjoining the other 400 acres. And whereas Thomas Eavens died intestate leaving a wife and several children whereof the afsd. John Eavans one of the parties to theses presents was the eldest whereupon the afsd. 474 acres became subject to a division. Wit: John Craige, Ezekiel West. Within deed ackn. 8 May 1771.

149. Samuel Rowland, Enoch Potter. Bond. I Enoch Potter of Duck Creek Hundred, Kent Co., Delaware, for £180, I bind myself this 20 March 1767. Grant right to tract containing 100 acres to Samuel Rowland. Wit: Peter Fretwell Wright, John Rowland. Within bond proved 9 May 1771.

149. Boaz Manlove Recognizance for the year 1770. At a Court of Quarter Sessions held 6 Nov 1770 whereas Isaac Smith and Nehemiah Davis, Junr., Gentlemen, of Sussex Co., and acknowledges owing the sovereign £700. Inrolled 28 Sept 1771.

150. John Clowes, Sussex Co., yeoman, from Boaz Manlove, Sheriff. 8 May 1771. The previous sheriff was order to seized the goods and chattles of Thomas Wilson of Sussex Co., in order to levy a certain amount recovered against him by John Clowes, Senr. and John Clowes, Junr. in a court of common pleas. The tract in Broadkill Hundred runs to a line of David Rorton's and contains 100 acres being part of a larger tract granted to Joseph Rorton by proprietary warrant and by his the said Josiah [sic] Rorton's deed of sale dated 7 Nov 1758 conveyed same to afsd. Thomas Wilson. Land sold for £35. Wit: Rhoads Shankland, John Wilson Dean. Within deed of sale ackn. 8 May 1771.

150. Joseph Earl, Kent County, Maryland, attorney at law, John Boyd of Baltimore Co., Maryland, physician, and William Buchanan of the same place, merchant, from Joseph Shankland and Samuel Shankland, iron masters, Sussex Co. 7 May 1771. For 5 shillings, two tracts, one called Shanklands Discovery of 811 acres on which is lately erected a double forge and other improvements, the other tract called Iron Valley containing 200 acres. Wit: Rhoads Shankland, Stringer Tilney, Andrew Paynter. Within ackn. 8 May 1771.

152. Levi Russel from Manlove Russel. Release. I, Manlove Russel of Sussex Co., ship carpenter, for 5 shillings, paid by Levi Russel of Sussex Co. release right to one moiety of a tract conveyed from Joseph Fiddeman to William Russel Nov 1760, lying in Broadkill Hundred on the northwest side of Broadkill Creek in small parcels the one containing 44 1/2 acres of wood land and the other containing 100 acres adjoining the creek bounds running to ... Green Branch ... to a corner post standing in a line of Wiltbank's land. Wit: Wm. Clark, Rhoads Shankland. 8 May 1771.

153. Foster Dulavan, Sussex Co., planter, from John Clowes, Sussex Co., marriner. 8 May 1771. Whereas John Clowes hath full title to tract in Broadkill forrest by virtue of sundry purchases made by him from William Daughters, Ezekiel Joyns, Thomas Wharton and a proprietary warrant. And whereas afsd. Foster Dulavan hath purchased of afsd. John Clowes two small parcels of said land out of the tracts purchased from William Daughters and Ezekial Joyne, witness that the parcel purchased by afsd. Foster Dulavan as afsd. out of Daughters Tract begins at a corner post of Andrew Collings, Junr's. land ... to a post on said Dulavan's Maryland line ... to a corner post in John Spencer's line ... containing 37 acres and 89 perches. And that part purchased by said Dulavan as afsd. out of Ezekiel Joynes his tract begins at a corner post of the afsd. Dulavan's Maryland land on the south side of the road afsd. ... containing 16 acres and 20 perches. For £40. Wit: Robert Lacey, George Walker. Within deed ackn. 8 May 1771.

154. Thomas Newcomb, Sussex Co., from Samuel Russel, Sussex Co., and wife Mary. 9 May 1771. Parcel in Broadkill Hundred for which a warrant was granted to William Trippett and Trippett assigned said warrant to John Hill and John Hill assigned said warrant to Charles Bright at whose request afsd. tract was surveyed and laid off for 300 acres and Charles Bright conveyed 90 acres, part of afsd. tract, to William Light and 210 acres, the remainder of the tract, to William Arey and said Arey by his deed of sale conveyed 120 acres of the land to afsd. William Light who was then seized of 210 acres and William Light dying intestate left heirs, one son and 3 daughters, to wit, John, Lacey, Mary and Elizabeth. Said Lucey [sic] married Benjamin Townsend and Mary conveyed their [sic] right to said John Light and Elizabeth conveyed to Mary Light and Elizabeth Newcomb whereby the said John Light became seized of 4 parts in five of the 210 acres and the said John dying intestate leaving issue, two daughters, to wit, Mary who married afsd. Samuel Russel and Elizabeth who married afsd. Thomas Newcomb. Samuel Russel and Thomas Newcomb having said land divided between them 105 acres thereof was allotted to said Samuel Russel in right of his wife Mary, beginning at a corner stake in the run of a branch called Getters Run alias Brights Beaver Dam containing 105 acres. For £35. Wit: John Shankland, Wm. Parker. Within deed ackn. 8 May 1771.

155. William Mitten, Sussex Co., yeoman, from Boaz Manlove, Sheriff. 9 May 1771. Tract in the fork of a Pemberton Branch being one of the branches proceeding out of the Broadkiln Creek,

beginning on the north side of the southernmost fork of said branch ... 210 acres. The same land being granted by warrant dated 13th of 11th month 1717 to Peter Lucas who by his last will bequeathed the same lands to his sister Sarah Lucas who conveyed same to William Stewart and conveyed by said William Stewart and his wife Mary to John Hall. The sheriff was ordered Aug Term 1770 to sell the land and the land was bought by William Mitten. Wit: Benja. Handy, Henry Fisher. Within deed 8 May ackn. 1771.

156. Jonathan Williams, Sussex Co., cordwinder, and Nathan Tharp, bricklayer and his wife Comfort, Sussex Co. 9 May 1771. Joseph Williams father of afsd. Jonathan Williams and Comfort Tharp was seized of and had title to a tract which Joseph Williams died intestate leaving four children, minors, two of whom being dec'd., the afsd. tract became the property of afsd. Jonathan Williams and Comfort Williams now wife of Nathan Tharp. Land is on south side of Cedar Creek in Slaughter Neck, beginning at a corner oak of Nicholas Turner's land ... to original line of John Dickeson's ... 149 acres adjoining the land of David Thornton which said western division contains 77 acres. wit: Joseph Turpin, Boaz Manlove. Within deed ackn. 9 May 1771.

157. Elijah Morgan, Sussex Co., yeoman, from Joseph Morgan, Sussex Co., yeoman. 8 May 1771. For £10, tract of 100 acres being in Cedar Creek forrest adjoining land of Manuel Manlove which said land was granted by the proprietors warrant to said Joseph Morgan 15 Aug 1748 and said Joseph Morgan assigned same to Magdalane Manlove and she for £10 paid by Elijah Morgan granted same to him. Wit: John Johnson, David Morgan. Within deed ackn. 8 May 1771.

158. Jacob Kollock, Sussex Co., Esqr., from Boaz Manlove, Sheriff. 25 May 1771. Goods and chattles of John Pettyjohn levied a certain sum of money which Jacob Kollock recovered against him. The sheriff seized 2 tracts supposed to contain 200 acres, the same whereon said John Pettyjohn lived. The land was sold to Jacob Kollock for £70. The land on 20th of 9th month 1716 granted to John Pettyjohn father of afsd. John Pettyjohn who assigned same to his son John and who on 6 Dec 1717 had surveyed the other tract by virtue of a warrant granted to Samuel Pettyjohn dated 30 Dec 1748 and the said Samuel Pettyjohn on 13 March 1753 assigned his right to afsd. John Pettyjohn. Wit: Henry Smith, J. Russel. Within deed ackn. 5 May 1771.

159. Peter Robinson. Recognizance. 10 Dec 1771. Peter Robinson, Esqr. high sheriff, Jacob Kollock and John Rodney and acknowledge themselves to owe our sovereign £700. The condition is that Peter Robinson shall faithfully fulfill his office.

159. Levin Crapper, Esqr. of Cedar Creek Hundred, from Catharine Holt and Penelope Holt Coward, admxs. of Rives Holt, Esqr., dec'd., both of town of Lewes. 8 Aug 1771. For £50. Tract on Mispillion Creek beginning at a corner sapling on the west northwest side of the head of Herring Branch, a corner of the land of Clark's heirs ... 383 acres. Land was surveyed to Ryves

Holt, Esqr. of Lewes formerly procured to be surveyed by Andrew McGill who sold his right in the same to Ryves Holt. Warrant was dated 12 Dec 1733. Wit: J. Moore, David Train. Within deed of sale ackn. 7 Aug 1771.

161. Levin Milby, Sussex Co., mariner, from Sarah Prittyman, widow of Isaac Prittyman, dec'd., Sussex Co. 7 Aug 1771. Tract in Indian River Hundred near the bottom of Long Neck, late the property of Thomas Leatherberry, dec'd., who died intestate leaving a widow and several children, whereof the said Sarah Prittyman was the eldest of the children. Elizabeth Leatherberry widow of William Leatherberry, dec'd., one of the heirs of afsd. Thomas Leatherberry petitioned the Orphans Court to divide the property which it was determined would not lend itself to division. Sarah Prittyman for £343 conveys same to Levin Milby, 246 acres [less the widow's thirds]. Wit: Boaz Manlove, David Train. Within deed ackn. 7 Aug 1771.

162. Thomas May, Sussex Co., yeoman, from John Crapper and wife Sarah, Sussex Co. 2 Aug 1771. Tract in Cedar Creek Hundred on Mispillion Creek, deed from Samuel Joyce to Jonathan May, dec'd. and to Sarah his wife who is not the wife of afsd. John Crapper. Beginning at the corner of Draper May ... to Harts line ... to a corner of Spencer Chance ... binding with the land of afsd. Thomas May ... to Joyce Gutt ... 200 acres for £210. Wit: David Train, Levin Crapper. Within deed ackn. 7 Aug 1771.

162. Arthur Hazzard, Sussex Co., planter, from Margret Hill, Sussex Co., spinster. 6 Aug 1771. Tract in Angola Hundred, part of a larger tract taken up by Francis Meades called Soulsters Inheritance as by deed of sale William Smith and Rebeckah Smith to John Hill dated 4 May 1722 and the said John Hill by his last will devised same to his son Robert Hill, which said Robert Hill died intestate leaving issue Comfort and afsd. Margret his only heirs which said tract contains 73 acres. For £47.9. Wit: Benja. Carpenter, Daniel Nunez. Within deed ackn. 9 Aug 1771.

163. Thomas Robinson, Junr., Sussex Co., from Boaz Manlove, Esqr. Sheriff. 7 Aug 1771. House and 2 lotts in town of Lewes adjoining northwest side of Mulberry Street and on the southwest side of the lot belonging William Arnal and the heirs of Samuel Arnal, dec'd. which lots Ada Boyd late Ada Robinson purchased at Philadelphia from Daniel Nunez, sheriff of Sussex Co. And at the suit of Robert Oakey against James Boyd of which said James Boyd married afsd. Ada who did attach all the said James Boyd's title and interest to the afsd. house and in May Term 1771. Judgement was obtained against said James Boyd agreeable to the act of assembly. Sale of house and lot and after duly advertising house and a lot and afterwards the lot was sold to said James Boyd Wright. For £10.1. Wit: John Hand, Daniel Nunez. Within deed ackn. 8 Aug 1771.

164. Robert Jones, yeoman, from Boaz Manlove, High Sheriff. Aug 1771. Sheriff ordered to levy the goods and chattles and lands now of said Sheriff, Beginning at a corner white oak being a

corner of 50 acres surveyed for 100 acres for Hudson then running down Kenney's Branch to the fork of said branch ... up the other branch called the Great Branch ... til it intersects the Maryland survey ... For £10.10. Wit: David Conwell, Hap Hazzard. Within deed ackn. 1 Aug 1771.

164. Joshua Bennit, Sussex Co., tayler, from Ebenezar Spencer, Sussex Co., planter. 30 July 1771. Parcel in Slaughter Neck adjoining the lands of John Young and William Wilson, beginning at a corner tree of Nehemiah Davis's land near a road that leads to Baker Johnson ... to a post of Henry Draper's land ... William Wilson's line ... resurveyed by Caleb Cirwithin containing 50 acres. For £100. Wit: David Watson, Littleton Townsend. Within deed ackn. 6 May 1771.

165. Ebenezar Spencer, Sussex Co., planter, from Isaac Townsend, Sussex Co., planter. 20 July 1771. For £200, tract in Slaughter Neck on the south side of Cedar Creek being part of a tract called Little Button and part of the same that belonged to Costin Townsend, dec'd., and adjoining the tract whereon said Ebenezar Spencer now liveth, beginning at a post one perch east or below David Wattson's Wharf by the edge of Cedar Creek ... to a post of David Watson's ... line of Thomas Lay, dec'd. ... corner of said Spencer's land that he first purchased of said Townsend ... 100 acres. Wit: Joshua Bennit, John Young. Within deed ackn. 6 Aug 1771.

166. John Rickards, Sussex Co., yeoman, from Alexander Laton, Sussex Co., planter. 7 Aug 1771. For £69. Parcel in forrest of Cedar Creek Hundred being part of a larger tract granted to John Webb by warrant dated 9 June 1747 which was conveyed by John Webb to above named Alexander Layton and recorded Liber I No. 9, folio 364. Beginning at a branch proceeding out of Cedar Creek ... to line that divides said land and land late of James Walker ... 123 acres. Wit: Moses Shankland, David Train. Within deed ackn. 7 Aug 1771.

167. John Clampit and Suffier his wife, from Robert Fleming and Margret his wife of Kent Co. in Mispillion Hundred 6 Aug 1771. For £50, parcel in Broadkill Hundred on the head of Coolspring Branch and being part of a larger tract called the Coolspring Tract being the property of the heirs of one Cample, dec'd. lying on the northeast side of the land of Hugh Virdin containing 100 acres. Wit: Levin Crapper, Richard Clampit. Within deed ackn. 7 Aug 1771.

168. Elijah Adams, Sussex Co., from Spencer Chance, Sussex Co. 6 Aug 1771. For £150, parcel in the forrest of Cedar Creek Hundred called Chances Folley granted by warrant dated 27 July 1752 to said Spencer Chance, beginning on the west side of Grubby Branch near a boundary of Charles Brown's land, containing 419 acres and 39 1/4 square perches. Wit: Wm. Hazzard, John Bell. Within deed of sale ackn. 7 Aug 1771.

168. Hugh Roberts, Philadelphia Co., Gentleman, from Rhoads

Shankland, Sussex Co., yeoman. 8 Feb 1771. Rhoads Shankland is bound to Hugh Roberts in the penal sum of £1000 to be void on the payment of £500 by 8 Feb next, with interest. To secure the loan Shankland releases to Hugh Robert parcel called Martins on the west side of the Kings Road that leads from Lewes Town to Philadelphia and on the southwest side of Pagan Creek at first granted by patent to Edward Southern and by sundry conveyances became the property of Rhoads Shankland, bounded on the southeast side by the lines of Isaac Wiltbank and John Woolf and the Kings Road and on the southwest side by John Prettyman's land, on the northwest side by the line of John Wiltbank's land and on the northeast by Pagan Creek, containing 400 acres, lying about 1 mile from Lewes Town. Wit: Jenney Hall, David Hall. Within deed ackn. 8 Aug 1771.

170. Thos. Fisher, Northampton Co., Virginia, farmer, from Joshua Spencer, Sussex Co., farmer. 9 Nov 1771. For £453, parcel called Hills Content, at Mispillion Creek, bounded by a ditch being a division line between said Joshua and Levi Spencer lately dec'd. and brother to said Joshua ... to a post in Spencer Chance's line ... corner of William Bagwell's land ... mouth of Spencer's Branch ... 259 acres and 53 perches. Wit: Isaac Watson, William Bagwell. Louisa Spencer, wife of Joshua Spencer confirms deed. Within deed ackn. 1771.

171. Benjamin Wynkoop, City of Philadelphia, merchant, from Samuel Walton, Sussex Co. yeoman, and George Walton of same place, yeoman and Mary his wife. 2 Nov 1771. For £79.15, tract beginning at a post on the edge of Mispillion Creek, a corner of the land of the heirs of John Brown, dec'd. ... the line of Benjamin Wynkoop's other land ... 58 acres and 21 perches. It is a part of a larger tract granted to Henry Bowman called The Saw Mill Range and which John Walton the father of the above named Samuel and George purchased of John Bowman and the said John Walton dying seized thereof by his last will dated 18 July 1731 devised same to his wife Naomy 1/3 part of his real estate during her life and devised remaining 2/3 to his sons Samuel and George and an infant then in the womb of its mother, which died in infancy. Wit: Wm. Hazzard, Dormon Lofland. Within deed ackn. 6 Nov 1771.

172. William Stevens, Sussex Co., planter, from Thomas Hardey, Sussex Co., cordwinder. 27 Sep 1771. Parcel in Indian River Hundred at the head of Swan Creek Branch being part of a larger tract granted by warrant to John Walker who devised in his last will said land to two of his daughters and John Parsons married one of the daughters and became invested in the right of the afsd. lands and said John Parsons conveyed said land to George Day of said county who devised in his last will afsd. lands to George Hill who conveyed lands to John Stevenson of said county and John Stevenson conveyed same to Thomas Marriner who conveyed same to afsd. Thomas Hardey. Lands bind on the lands of Barton Prettyman, Jessy Townsend, John Robinson, Ebenezar Cary and French Jack. 130 acres, for £66. Wit: Gillbn. Parker, Elias Hugg. Within deed ackn. 5 Nov 1771.

173. Benjamin Black, Sussex Co., from Jacob Stockley, blacksmith, Sussex Co. 26 Oct 1771. For £6, part of a tract in Indian River Hundred joining the side of Jacob Stockley's land late the property of Benjamin Stockley, dec'd. but in his last will bequeathed to his son Benjamin Stockley, containing 116 square perches. Wit: Wm. Prittyman, John Waller. Within deed ackn. 5 Nov 1771.

174. Jonathan Bryan, Sussex Co., bricklayer for £23.6.8 releases to Wrixam Lewis of Sussex Co., shipwright, parcel being part of a larger tract in Rehoboth Hundred called Warrens Choice which was conveyed by William Bryan and Ann Elizabeth his wife who owned the same by way of William Godwin, her father, to Cornelius Turner who conveyed 49 acres of afsd. tract which was in the southwest corner of afsd. tract to Lydia Bryan, Jonathan Bryan and Mary Bryan, it being 1/3 part of said tract, containing 49 acres. Wit: Joseph Hall, J. Moore. Within deed ackn. 3 Nov 1771.

174. John Hollaway, Worcester Co., yeoman, from John Adams, Sussex Co., pilot. 6 Nov 1771. For £300, parcel of 630 acres of land and marsh and part also of 991 acres, one moiety and half part that belonged to William Bagwell, dec'd., and part of a greater tract granted by patent out of the land office in New York to William Burton, Esqr. of Accomack Co., Virginia, called Long Neck which is situate in Long Neck between the Indian River and Rehoboth Bay joining the south side of Bagwells Creek and joining the south side of Robinsons Branch, one of the branches which proceeds from Bagwell Creek. Beginning at a corner post in the middle of Robinsons Branch being a corner between the widow Ann Burton and afsd. John Holloway, Senr., containing 150 acres of land and marsh. Boaz Manlove, Charles Draper. Within deed ackn. 6 Nov 1771.

176. John Russel of the town of Lewes, cordwainer, from John Clowes, Sussex Co., mariner, exr. of last will of John Clowes, Esqr. 10 Dec 1771. John Clowes in his lifetime bound himself to above named John Russel to convey a lot and whereas afsd. John Clowes died without complying. For £45, the lot is conveyed, beginning a corner stake of lots formerly belonging to Joseph Eldridge, dec'd. on King Street ... to lots formerly belonging Joseph Eldridge which he devised to two of his grandchildren, to wit, Thomas Eavans and Pheby Liping Cutt, containing 1200 square feet, being the same lots which John Clowes, dec'd., purchased of Joseph Eldridge, dec'd., by deed of sale dated 4 Feb 1728. Wit: Peter Robinson, Isaac Smith. Within deed ackn. 10 Dec 1771.

177. I, John Clowes, Esqr. am bound to John Russel, corwinder for £100, on 3 March 1769, obligated after the payment of £45, convey to John Russel a lot in Lewes Town, the same purchased by John Clowes of Joseph Eldridge. Wit: Thos. Gray, Perry Prittyman. Within deed ackn. 7 Nov 1771.

177. Petition of John Clowes to convey above mentioned land.

177. Joshua Rickards, Sussex Co., farmer, from Benjamin Stockley, Kent Co, Gentleman, Wm. Waples and Abigail his wife of Sussex Co. 7 Nov 1771. For £100, parcel in Indian River Hundred containing 330 acres, being all the land bequeathed by said Benjamin Stockley and his sister Abigail now the wife of William Waples as appears in the last will of Benjamin Stockley, Esqr., dec'd., part of which was conveyed to Benjamin Stockley, dec'd., by deed dated 8 Aug 1739 by Joseph Carter, the other part granted by warrant dated 24 Sep 1740. Wit: Richard Little, Lewis West, Jacob Stockley. Within deed ackn. 8 Nov 1771.

178. John Collings, Junr., Worcester Co., from Mitchel Smith, Sussex Co., yeoman. 6 Nov 1771. Parcel in the forrest of Broadkill Hundred being part of a larger tract conveyed by deed of sale to afsd. Mitchel Smith from Richard Samuels and Daniel Hopkins dated 3 Dec 1763, being the residue of said tract containing 50 acres. For £60. Wit: Luke Walton, Rhoads Shankland. Within deed ackn. 6 Nov 1771.

179. William Reynolds of Broadkill Hundred, yeoman, from Jacob and James Pettyjohn, both of Broadkill Hundred. 6 Nov 1771. For £60, 3 parts out of 4 of a tract in Broadkill Hundred on the west side of Long Bridge Branch called Stones Folley which land James Pettyjohn, dec'd., father of the above Jacob and James, died possessed of, divided of a larger tract belonging to John Cord in his lifetime and granted by John Cord to James Pettyjohn, dec'd. by deed dated 5 Aug 1742, laid out for 131 acres. Wit: John Collins son of Andrew, Rhoads Shankland. Within deed ackn. 6 Nov 1771.

180. Philip Cossey, Dorset [Dorchester] Co., Maryland, from Luke Walton, yeoman, Sussex Co. 6 Nov 1771. For £200.10, parcel in Cedar Creek Hundred, whereon said Luke Walton now dwells, 105 acres, being resurveyed 21 Dec 1719 for said Luke Walton, 2 acres adjoining John Draper's mill excepted for the use of said mill. Wit: John Draper, Rhoads Shankland. Within deed ackn. 6 Nov 1771.

181. Isabella Annett, Sussex Co., admx. of the estate of John Annett, dec'd., to John Clowes, Sussex Co., mariner. 9 Dec 1771. Parcel in south side of the Cyprus Branch, one of the branches of Primehook Creek called Strechers Hall containing 500 acres which was the property of Henry Strecher of Lewes Town, carpenter, who by deed of sale dated 5 March 1694 conveyed to James Stanford and James Thomas and said James Stanford's exr., Francis Chadds by his deed dated 4 May 1700 conveyed all the afsd. James Stanford's right to afsd. 500 acres to afsd. James Thomas who dying intestate the whole of the tract became the right of his brother Micah Thomas which said Micah Thomas also died intestate and the property became the property of his four daughters, Ann, Grace, Mary and Elizabeth, and said Mary with her husband William Barratt by their deed dated 5 Aug 1756 conveyed her 1/4 part to John Annet which said John Annet died intestate and so involved in debt that his personal estate was not sufficient to satisfy his creditors and his extx., Isabell Annet was allowed to sell

said land (for £39). Wit: Samuel Hand, Isaiah Johnson. Within deed ackn. 10 Dec 1771.

182. Essabella Annett, widow, from John Clowes, Sussex Co., mariner. 9 Dec 1771. Tract on the south side of Cyprus Branch called Strechers Hall [same as above] for £39. Wit: Samuel Hand, Isaiah Johnson. Within deed ackn. 10 Dec 1771.

183. Jacob Kollock, Esqr., Sussex Co., from William Steel, Sussex Co., laborer. Mortgage. 10 Dec 1771. Parcel in Broadkill Hundred being part of a tract that William Steel bought at sheriff's vendue of Boaz Manlove, Esqr., Sheriff., sold at the suit of John Clowes, as the property of James Buchanan, containing 150 acres, to be laid off on the north end of said tract and adjoining lands of Daniel Steel and Ezekiel Green being the improved part of said tract and now in possession of Prisgrove Steel son of William Steel. For £20. Wit: Thos. Robinson, John Wiltbank. Within deed ackn. 10 Dec 1771.

184. Daniel Nunez, Sussex Co., from Jacob Kollock, Sussex Co., exr. of Jacob Philips, dec'd. 28 Aug 1771. Jacob Philips authorized by his will dated 27 March 1760 his exr. afsd. to convey his real estate except for what was devised away in the will. For £148.10, tract called Two Little Necks, or Little Pasture Neck, in Lewes and Rehoboth Hundred adjoining the lands of Reece Woolf, Junr., William Gill and David Hall, Esqr. containing as by deed of release from william Till and Jacob Kollock, Esqrs., Trustees of General Loan Office dated 13 Nov 1744, 132 acres. Wit: Boaz Manlove, Peter Ft. Wright. Within deed ackn. 26 Dec 1771.

184. Philips Kollock, Esqr., from Jacob Kollock, Esqr., Sussex Co., exr. of Jacob Phillips. 28 Aug 1771. Tract in Broadkill Hundred being part of a tract granted to John Finch called Finch Hall by patent dated 15 Aug 1687, beginning at a hickory on the southeast side of the head of Round Pool Branch, 275 acres. Plat made 1 Aug 1748. Wit: Boaz Manlove, Peter Ft. Wright. Within deed ackn. 26 Dec 1771.

185. Jacob Kollock, Sussex Co., Esqr., from Philips Kollock, Sussex Co. 28 Aug 1771. Tract in Broadkill Hundred being part of a tract patented to John Finch, 275 acres. [See above entry.] Wit: Boaz Manlove, Peter Ft. Wright. Within deed ackn. 26 Dec 1771.

186. Alexander Draper, Cedar Creek Hundred, yeoman, from Boaz Manlove, Sheriff. 31 Aug 1771. Sheriff's sale of land of Henry Martin and Rebeckah his wife extx. of the last will of James Harper, Sussex Co., dec'd., to levy a certain sum of money recovered by John Coverdale, parcel being the same which afsd. James Harper purchased of afsd. John Coverdale. For £55. Wit: Benjamin Johnson, Burton Prittyman. Within deed ackn. 26 Dec 1771.

187. Richard Wells, Sussex Co., pilot, from Jacob Kollock, Exr.

of Jacob Philips, Esqr. 28 Aug 1771. For £80, lot in Lewes Town adjoining on the southeast side of the lot of Wrixam Lewis, Esqr. and on the northwest side of the lot of Elias Hugh, 200 feet by 60 feet, being the same that Jacob Phillips bought of William Arnal. Wit: Boaz Manlove, Peter Ft. Wright. Within deed ackn. 26 Dec 1771.

187. Jacob Kollock from Richard Wells, pilot. 29 Aug 1771. [Same lot as above described.] wit: Boaz Manlove, Peter Ft. Wright. Within deed ackn. 26 Dec 1771.

188. Benjamin Rickards from Benjamin Carpenter. Bond of conveyance. Benjamin Carpenter, Sussex Co., is bound to Benjamin Rickards of same county for the penal sum of £296, 13 May 1769. To convey tract on the west side of Cool Spring Creek, willed to Benjamin Carpenter by his father, Benjamin Carpenter, containing 300 acres of land and marsh, afsd. Benjamin Rickards now living on the premises, said Rickards taking on the encumbrances of a mortgage deed given John Fisher 5 instant. Wit: Andw. Camron, Rhoads Shankland.

189. John Ingram, Sussex Co., yeoman, from Thomas Ozbun, Sussex Co., ship carpenter. Mortgage. 20 March 1771. For £75, land adjoining east and north on the Broadkill Creek, west on land now in the possession of John Waller and south on lands of Samuel Hand and on the mouth of Round Pool Branch, containing 141 acres. To be paid on or before 20 March 1773. Wit: John Clowes, Samuel Hand. Within deed of mortgage ackn. 5 Feb 1772.

190. Luke Shield, Sussex Co., from Purnal Johnson and wife Sarah, Sussex Co. 7 Feb 1772. Part of a tract of land and marsh granted to Hermanus Frederick Wiltbank and conveyed by him to John Kirk, confirmed by a patent granted to him dated 19th of 3rd month 1686 and John Kirk son of afsd. John Kirk by assignment on the said patent dated 19 Nov 1691 assign same to William Piles who by his last will devised same to his three sons, William, Isaac and Joseph, the two first dying intestate and without issue, the lands descended to said Joseph who conveyed part of the same to William Burton who by his last will devised same to his grandson William Burton son of Richard Burton and the said William Burton, Junr., conveyed same on 7 Feb 1764 to afsd. Purnal Johnson. Beginning near bounder of Piles patent ... to corner hickory of Robert Shankland's land now the land of David Gray ... to a post which divides this land from John Piles' marsh now the lands of Benjamin Rickards ... 405 acres. Wit: J. Moore, Isaac Smith. Within deed of mortgage ackn. 7 Feb 1772.

191. William Burton, Sussex Co., Boatman, from John Adams of Indian River Hundred, pilot and wife Cornilea. 6 Feb 1772. For £84.10, tract in Indian River Hundred being part of a larger tract called Long Neck, granted to William Burton of the Colony of Virginia, Esqr. by patent dated 27 Sep 1677 by said William Burton conveyed to Thomas Bagwell by deed dated 29 Oct 1679 who by his last will dated 15 April 1690 devised same to his son William Bagwell, the grandfather of the said John Adams, in tail,

which descended which came to said John Adams after several
descents as heir in tail. Beginning at a corner post of other
land of said William Burton thence by land now in the possession
of the widow Ann Burton ... to a post corner of John Holloway's
land. 42 1/4 acres. Wit: Henry Fisher, John Woods. Within deed
ackn. 15 Feb 1772.

193. John Adams, Sussex Co., mariner, from John Holloway, Senr.,
Worcester Co., Maryland, yeoman. 6 Feb 1772. For £100, parcel
of 150 acres of land and marsh which afsd, Adams sold the same to
said Holloway per deed dated 7 Nov 1771, being part of a larger
tract of 630 acres, and part of 991 acres, the one moiety and
half part that belonged to William Bagwell, dec'd. and part of a
greater tract granted by patent out of the land office in New
York to William Burton, Esqr. of Accomack Co., Virginia, dec'd.,
called Long Neck, which afsd. John Holloway, Senr. conveys to
John Adams 50 acres out of his 150 as afsd. The land is between
the Indian River and Rehoboth Bay in Long Neck and joining the
afsd. Holloway's 100 acres on the east side and John Adams'
dwelling plantation on the west side and William Burton's 52
acres on the south and Bagwell Creek or pond on the north end.
Wit: John Shankland, Henry Fisher. Within deed ackn. 6 Feb 1772.

194. Caleb Cirwithin, Sussex Co., miller, from John Cirwithin,
Sussex Co., yeoman, sometimes carpenter. 25 Dec 1771. Parcel of
marsh in Prime Hook Neck surveyed 14th of 12 month 1684 by virtue
of warrant dated 5th of 5th month 1683 and confirmed to Luke
Wattson, Senr., containing 2000 acres of land and marsh whereas
Luke Wattson by his deed of sale conveyed to William Piles part
of the marsh who conveyed same to Caleb Cirwithin the Elder of
Sussex Co. by deed dated 10 Aug 1698 being 75 acres and the afsd.
Caleb Cirwithin in his last will bequeathed the said marsh to his
son Caleb Cirwithin and by an indenture 4 Nov 1768 John Cirwithin
the eldest son, recovered the above said 75 acres of marsh on 4
Nov 1768. Beginning at John Bellemy's lower corner tree ... to
Avery Draper's corner cedar post on the north side of a pond of
water in Tills line ... by the side of Slaughter Creek ... 44
acres of land and marsh. Wit: Joseph Collings, Stringer Tilney.
Within deed ackn. 29 Feb 1772.

195. Joseph Robinson, Sussex Co., yeoman, from Eli Cary, Sussex
Co., cordwinder. 5 Dec 1771. For £80, 250 acres, the same which
Samuel Cary father of the said Eli Cary devised to his four sons
then living, to be equally divided amongst them, and two of the
sons being since dead. The parcel is above Frame's sawmill near
the head of Indian River on the north side of the river. Wit:
Thos. Robinson, William Davis. Within deed of sale ackn. 5 Feb
1772.

196. George Hill, Sussex Co., from Peter Robinson, Sheriff. 1
Feb 1772. Land in Broadkill Hundred seized by the sheriff of
John Thomas, for £30.3 being part of a dividend laid off to Mary
Camble the youngest daughter of James Camble, dec'd., beginning
at a poplar in Mill Creek Branch alias Gittia Run below the

county road, 103 acres. Wit: Reynear Williams, Jno. Russell. Within deed of sale ackn. 5 Feb 1772.

197. John Truit, eldest son of Solomon Truitt, from Solomon Truitt, Sussex Co., yeoman. 18 Dec 1771. Surveyed and laid off for Solomon Truit on 5th of 7th month 1736 by virtue of a warrant dated 7th of 3rd month 1734, tract called Truitts Choice in Cedar Creek Hundred containing 443 acres and 143 perches including a survey made on the 4th of 3rd month 1723, being part of the proprietor's manor of Worminghurst. For good will and affection. Beginning at a post in a division line between said Solomon and his son Benjamin Truitt ... land in the possession of John Polk ... 204 acres. Land to be conveyed after the decease of said Solomon Truit and Mary his wife agreeable to the last will of said Solomon dated 12th of 10th month 1770. Wit: Wm. Hazzard, Thomas Cary. Within deed ackn. 5 Feb 1772.

198. John Plowman, Sussex Co., bricklayer, from George Black, Junr. and Sarah his wife, Sussex Co. 5 Nov 1771. Part of Robert Hart's 900 acre tract in Cedar Creek Neck and Hundred, being a part of that part that was conveyed from Robert Hart to John Clandaniel by deed dated 10 April 1715 for 200 acres and also part of a subdivision of 196 acres surveyed and divided of to(?) John Clandaniel by order of an Orphans Court held 26 Nov 1757. Boundary runs along the line of the land surveyed for Abraham Wynkoop,Esqr., dec'd. ... to a corner stone of John Whealer and the place of Thomas Hinds late dec'd. 96 acres as by a resurvey made 11 Feb 1766. Wit: Wm. Hazzard, James Black. Within deed ackn. 6 Feb 1772.

199. John Clowes, mariner, from Peter Robinson, Sheriff. 6 Feb 1771. Sheriff's sale of land of John Ennis to pay amount recovered by Jacob Kollock, Senr. and John Clowes, Junr., in Broadkill Hundred, beginning at the corner of land of Old James Pettyjohn's land to a line running between John Pettyjohn and Samuel Pettyjohn's land containing 100 acres, as also 200 acres contiguous and adjoining afsd. and to the afsd. John Ennis by virtue of a proprietor's warrant being all the land John Ennis held in Sussex Co., containing 300 acres. Jno. Russel, John Ingram. Within deed of sale ackn. 6 Feb 1772.

200. Moses Allin, Sussex Co., pilot, from John Lewis, Sussex Co., yeoman. 25 March 1772. Lot in town of Lewes bounded by 2nd Street, on the north by a lot of the heirs of James Simson, on the southeast side by a lot of Francis Cahoon, 60 feet by 200 feet, formerly the property of John Rhoads, Esqr. and by him conveyed to Rives Holt, Esqr. for the use of Comfort Jenkins, Innholder and the extx. of Rives Holt, Esqr. conveyed the said lot and all appurtenances thereunto the above mentioned John Lewis who bound himself to convey to Comfort Jenkins and whereas Comfort Jenkins by her last will bequeathed the lot to Mary Lewis, her niece who afterwards married Edward Craige who sold afsd. lot to afsd. Moses Allin. Wit: Wr. Lewis, William West. Within deed ackn. 28 March 1772.

201. George Walker, Sussex Co., from Peter Robinson, Sheriff. 29 Feb 1772. Sheriff's sale of land of William Prittyman for amount recovered by Peter Marsh against him. Land with a mill house, beginning at a post in Cool Spring Branch ... corner post of Warrington Woolf containing 4 acres and 44 perches and additional two acres condemned for the use of the said mill, for £26. Wit: Thos. Robinson, Wr. Lewis. Within deed ackn. 1772.

202. Jacob Walker, Sussex Co., from Elizabeth Stockley, Sussex Co., extx. of last will of William Stockley, Junr. who was exr. of the last will of Nathan Turner, dec'd. 29 Feb 1772. Parcel in Lewes and Rehoboth Hundred, beginning at a corner oak by a branch of the Cow Valley, 100 acres, as by a deed of bargain and sale from John Russel to Elizabeth Turner, Ephraim Turner, John Turner, Nathan Turner, William Turner and Mary Turner, dated 9 May 1755. Whereas Nathan Turner by his last will dated 29 Dec 1770 authorized afsd. William Stockley, Junr., his exr. to convey his land and he sold part of the land to Jacob Walker but has not conveyed the same in his lifetime which said part is part of the above described tract part of which Charity Turner purchased from the afsd. Ephraim and Elizabeth and devised same to her two sons the afsd. Nathan and William and the said Nathan afterwards purchased the said William's right in the whole tract which said Nathan's part is bounded by the land of John Wiltbank, Esqr. ... with a line parallel with the line of Coopers Hall to Jacob Kollock's mill pond near Wrixam White's containing 66 acres - for £62. Wit: Daniel Nunez, Peter Robinson. Within deed ackn. 29 Feb 1772.

203. Henry Fisher, Sussex Co., from Daniel Nunez, Sussex Co., and wife Hannah. 26 March 1772. House and lot in town of Lewes on the northwest side of Kollock's or First Street on the southeast side of the lot belonging to Elizabeth Paynter and fronting the Bank and Second Street, containing 200 feet by 60 feet which lot Jacob Philips purchased from Abraham Wiltbank and Naomy his wife and devised in his last will to afsd. Hannah. For £200. Wit: David Shankland, John Turner. Within deed ackn. 28 March 1772.

204. Daniel Nunez, Sussex Co., from Henry Fisher and wife Margret, Sussex Co. 31 March 1772. House and lot in town of Lewes ... [same as above entry which was conveyed to Henry Fisher]. £200. Wit: Wm. Davis, John ---. Within deed ackn. 25 April 1772.

205. William Burton, Broadkill Hundred, from Elizabeth Prettyman, John Stratton Burton, William Burton, joyner, William Bagwell and Ann his wife, all of Sussex Co., for £109.4, parcel of marsh of 91 acres that William Burton of Worcester Co., died possessed of and by his last will devised to his grandson Woolsey Burton who died intestate, situated in Broadkill Hundred and called Trumerters Island, resurveyed 1 Dec 1771, bounded by the marsh of Jacob Hazzard and James Fisher. Wit: Burton Waples, Lewes West. Within deed ackn. 25 April 1772.

206. Thos. Gray, cooper of the town of Lewes, from John Prettyman, Sussex Co., yeoman. 6 March 1770. For £115.12.6, a part of a tract formerly granted by a New York patent to Daniel Brown for 400 acres called Tower Hill dated 25 March 1676 and Daniel Brown assigned over the patent to Samuel Preston on 2 Nov 1693 who assigned the patent to James Peterkin on 7 Dec 1693 and Thomas Peterkin attorney of afsd. James Peterkin conveyed 200 acres (1/2 of the tract) to John Prittyman, Senr. on 8 Dec 1697 who conveyed 100 acres of the land to William Prittyman son of afsd. John Prittyman, Senr. on 8 May 1719 - being the northwest side of said tract of 400 acres, lying on the Bever Dam - and William Prittyman son of John Prittyman, Senr., conveyed the 100 acres to John Prittyman, minor, 23 Feb 1754, who bequeathed by his last will to William and John Prittyman, minor sons of the afsd. John Prittyman, the younger, father of the afsd. William and John Prittyman who obtained a warrant of resurvey 11 Dec 1754 and the resurvey dated 27 Feb 1756 for 175 1/2 acres and 12 square perches and after divided between said John Wiltbank and William and John Prittyman. William and John Prittyman agreed on 18 Jan 1766 to divide along the branch between them. The land lies in Rehoboth Hundred on the southeast side of the Bever Dam which cometh out of Cool Spring Creek alias Marshes Creek about 2 miles from town of Lewes, 100 acres and 100 square perches. Wit: Marnix Virden, David Shankland. Within deed ackn. 28 March 1772.

207. James Martin and Olaver Stockley of Sussex Co., yeomen, from Thos. Gray and Sophia his wife, Sussex Co. Mortgage. 28 March 1772. Parcel of 110 acres being of a tract formerly granted by a New York patent to Daniel Brown for 400 acres called Tower Hill in Rehoboth Hundred on the southeast side of the Beaver Dam which cometh out of Cool Spring where Thomas Gray now dwells and which Thomas Gray purchased from John Prittyman, deed dated 6 March 1767[sic]. For £124. Wit: William Peery, Jno. Russel. Within deed ackn. 28 March 1772.

209. Thomas May, Sussex Co., yeoman, from Cornelius Dewesse, Junr. and wife Elizabeth, Kent Co., yeoman. 10 Oct 1771. For tract of land and marsh purchased by Jonathan May and Henry Draper, father of afsd. Thomas May and Elizabeth Dewese, of Thomas Davis, late of Sussex Co. called Marsh Patent. Henry Draper having died intestate leaving seven children, the land was divided into 8 equal shares and afsd. Cornelius Dewese and Elizabeth his wife became seized of 1/8 of the parcel. For £14.8.9. Wit: Levin Crapper, Levin Collings. Within deed ackn. 29 Feb 1772.

209. William Fisher, Sussex Co., cordwinder, from John Turner, Sussex Co., taylor and Peter Adams and wife Mary. 3 Feb 1772. For £25, a parcel, part of a larger tract called Coopers Hall in the northernmost fork of Jacob Kollock's Mill Pond. Beginning at a post at the going over place, a corner of John Wiltbank's land ... containing 45 acres. The tract called Coopers Hall is fully recited in a deed of sale from John Russel dated 9 May 1755 to John Turner, Mary Turner, now the wife of Peter Adams and others. Peter Ft. Wright, Jacob White, Junr. Within deed ackn. 29 Feb

1772.

210. Thomas Prittyman, Sussex Co., yeoman, from Jacob Marriner, Sussex Co. 28 Feb 1772. For £60, a tract that John Marriner devised to his two sons, Joshua Marriner and Jacob Marriner, in Indian River Hundred containing 224 acres, originally granted to John Marriner, dec'd., by a warrant. Wit: Thos. Robinson, Henry Fisher. Within deed ackn. 28 March 1772.

211. Nathaniel Bowman Marriner from Elizabeth Lingo, surviving extx. of Richard Marriner. 8 March 1772. Tract on south side of Ivy Branch being part of a tract formerly belonging to Aminadat Hanzer, 100 acres, sold to satisfy debts for £51. Wit: Thos. Robinson, Constant Marriner. Within deed ackn. 28 March 1772.

212. Thomas Grice, Northampton Co., Virginia, planter, from Thomas Prittyman, Sussex Co., planter. 29 Feb 1772. Parcel in Indian River Hundred which by proprietors warrant dated 20 March 1735 for James Davidson of said co., dec'd., 300 acres - beginning at a corner of John Prittyman's land ... oak standing in the line of the tract (1100 acres) of Robert Burton, dec'd. - 321 acres as by the survey dated 20 April 1736 which land was conveyed to Nathaniel Bowman Marriner who conveyed same to John Fosset who conveyed same to Thomas Hardey all the land that lay on the northeast side of a road that leads from Robert Prittyman's to John Rigua and the now above granted land supposed to contain 230 acres as the remaining part left the said Hardy's part was laid off which said 230 acres was conveyed by said Fossit to the estate of John Lingo, dec'd., and Elizabeth (Betty) Lingo admx. of the estate obtained a court order to sell the land which she did sell to Thomas Prittyman. Wit: Boaz Manlove, J. Russel. Within deed ackn. 29 Feb 1772.

213. Peter Lindell, Sussex Co., yeoman, from John Lofland, Senr. of the forrest of Cedar Creek Hundred, yeoman. 29 Feb 1772. For £50, a parcel in the forrest of Cedar Creek Hundred first surveyed for afsd. John Lofland, Senr. 14 April 1748, called Knee Gum adjoining lands of said John Lofland and lands of Wm. Lofland - 115 acres. Wit: Peter Robinson, David Train. Within deed ackn. 1772. Within deed ackn. 29 Feb 1772.

214. David Shankland from Ephraim Turner, John Turner, John Ponder and Elizabeth his wife, Peter Adams and Mary his wife and Elizabeth Stockley extx. of William Stockley, Junr. who was extx. of Nathan Turner, dec'd. 28 March 1772. Parcel in Rehoboth Hundred being part of a larger tract that was granted to William Orr by a warrant dated 10th of 6th month 1715 and part of that part that Humphrey Turner bought from Daniel Fling bounded by a corner post in a line of the land of William Fisher ... to a line of the land of Jacob Kollock ... to said Kollock's mill pond ... 31 acres for £42.10. Wit: Henry Fisher, Daniel Nunez. Within deed ackn. 28 March 1772.

215. Benjamin Carpenter, cordwinder, Sussex Co., from Simon Kollock, Sussex Co., cooper. 30 Jan 1771. Lot or parcel of land

in or near the town of Lewes of 1 acre being part of that land
which formerly belonged to Shepard Kollock, dec'd. but is now in
possession of afsd. Simon Kollock son of afsd. Shepard Kollock.
Beginning on the southeast side of the Kings Road that leads to
the town of Lewes afsd. and at the north corner of the afsd.
Simon Kollock's land. Wit: ---, Gilbert Marriner. Within deed
ackn. Feb 1772.

216. The division of the land belonging to Nathaniel, Jas. and
Sarah Star. Whereas Nathaniel Star, James Star and Sarah Star,
widow and admx. of Jonathan Star, Sussex Co., dec'd., have
entered into bonds conditioned for the dividing a certain tract
in Cave Neck whereon Richard Star died possessed and willed to
his three sons afsd., and the afsd. Jonathan Star dying leaving
one child named Bethial Star who is now a minor, the afsd. Sarah
Star as admr. afsd. and guardian to her child with assistance of
Anderson Parker, Esqr. undertakes to stand to the division
submitted in the afsd. bonds. Survey finds the tract to contain
438 acres. Nathaniel shall have 146 acres bounded as appearing
on the plat as annexed except the marsh called the Point which
was devised to the afsd. Nathaniel Star as appears by the last
will of his father, Richard Star. Sarah Star widow of Jonathan
Star and his child Bethiah Star shall have 146 acres as shown in
the plat. James Star shall have 146 acres as shown on the plat.
2 March 1771. [See plat which is included.]

217. Benjamin Rickards, Sussex Co., yeoman, from Benjamin
Carpenter, Sussex Co., cordwinder. 6 May 1772. Tract in
Broadkill Hundred in Shetkill Neck that was granted to Hermanus
Frederick Wiltbank and conveyed by him to John Kirk and is
confirmed to John Kirk by a patent dated 19th of 3rd month 1686
and John Kirk son of afsd. John Kirk by assignment dated 19 Nov
1691 assigned patent to William Piles who by his last will
devised same to his son John Piles who by his last will devised
same to his son James Piles who conveyed same to Benjamin
Carpenter who by his last will devised same to his son Benjamin
Carpenter who is party to these presents. Boundary runs to
Coolspring Branch or Creek ... to a division line of Purnal
Johnson. 300 acres of land and marsh, for £250. Wit: Danl.
Nunez, Peter Ft. Wright. Within deed ackn. 6 May 1772.

218. Luke Shields, Sussex Co., from Benjamin Rickards and Esther
his wife of Sussex Co., yeoman. Mortgage. 7 May 1772. Part of
a tract of land and marsh granted to Hermanus Frederick Wiltbank
[see above entry] ... to his son Benjamin Carpenter who sold same
to Benjamin Rickards by a deed of bargain dated 6th instant.
Beginning at a oak standing near a landing on Coolspring Creek
... a oak near Peter Parker's Mill Pond ... to a dividing line
between said Benjamin Rickards and Purnal Johnson as also 45
acres of marsh adjoining at the bottom of the afsd. tract and
containing of land and marsh 300 acres. £70 to be paid by 6 Aug
next. Wit: Danl. Nunez, Peter Ft. Wright. Within deed of
mortgage ackn. 7 May 1772.

219. William Burton, Junr. of Indian River Hundred, yeoman, from

Wm. Burton his father, Long Neck in Indian River Hundred, planter. 8 May 1772. Tract of land and marsh in Long Neck in Indian River Hundred patented to Thomas and John Jones alls. Gollidge dated 26th of 1st month 1684 called The Brothers Portion containing 600 acres which patent was assigned by virtue of a letter of attorney from said Thomas Joans to John Parker and by the afsd. Joans to William Burton of Accomack, 5 Sep 1694, and William Burton by his last will dated 5 Jan 1695 devised same to his son Jacob Burton who devised same to his nephew the above named party to these presents in his last will dated 14 Nov 1716 - 223 acres. Wit: Simon Kollock, Philips Kollock. Within deed of sale ackn. 8 May 1772.

220. William Pointer from Levin Crapper, Esqr., Sussex Co. 7 May 1772. For £23, tract beginning at a corner of said tract standing in said Pointers Field ... to Landing Road containing 46 acres and 104 perches. Wit: Thos. Robinson, Parker Robinson. Within deed of sale ackn. 7 May 1772.

220. David Shankland, Sussex Co., carpenter, from Peter Adams and wife Mary of Sussex Co. 6 June 1772. For £10, a parcel of 7 acres being the northeast end of 37 acres conveyed by a deed of sale from Daniel Fling to Humphery Turner, dated 6 Feb 1744. Wit: Gilbs. Parker, Moses Allin. Within deed of sale ackn. 27 July 1772.

221. John Cample, Worcester Co., Maryland, from Charles Draper, Sussex Co. 5 May 1772. For the proportional part with the other land this day sold to the said John Campble of £900, parcel on the southeast side of Cedar Creek containing 27 acres being the same land that Charles Draper bought of Thomas Riley, dec'd. Wit: Thos. Robinson, Reynear Williams. Within deed ackn. 30 May 1772.

221. John Campble, Worcester Co., Maryland, from William Draper, Charles Draper, Alexander Draper and Joseph Draper, all of Cedar Creek Hundred. 13 May 1772. For £1950, tract in Cedar Creek Hundred, beginning at a red oak tree marked at the head of Emmots Branch containing 1100 acres, reserving an island within the above boundaries lying on Cedar Creek called Wynkoops Island and also the family burying ground. Wit: Robt. Greenall, J. Moore. Within deed of sale ackn. 30 May 1772.

223. John Draper, Sussex Co., yeoman, from Peter Parker, Sussex Co., yeoman. 27 June 1772. Tract in the forks of the branches of Cedar Creek which was surveyed to William Fisher by proprietors warrant dated 9th of 5th month 1700 and William Fisher in his last will dated 10 Dec 1725 bequeathed 100 acres to John Conwell who by his deed of sale dated 4 Sep 1770 conveyed to above said Peter Parker. For £25, 50 of described 100 acres, laid out on 11 Feb 1771. Wit: Peter Robinson, Jacob White, Junr. Within deed of sale ackn. 27 June 1772.

224. William Purnall, Worcester Co., Maryland, Gentleman, from John Black of Cedar Creek Hundred, yeoman, and his wife Naomi.

27 Nov 1772. By patent dated 3rd of 8th month 1692, granted to
Henry Bowman a tract on north side of Cedar Creek called Golds
Smiths Hall who died leaving it to John Bowman his eldest son who
on 3 May 1715 conveyed same to Thomas Goldsmith and William
Goldsmith the following parcel being part of the land recited in
the patent, that is to say, beginning at a glade of marsh which
runs up to Art Vankirk's land ... intersects with John Walton's
line ... to Thomas May's Gutt ... 130 acres, 80 acres to Thomas
Goldsmith and remainder to William Goldsmith. William Goldsmith
died leaving the 130 acres vested in said Thomas Goldsmith who by
his will dated 14 Dec 1741 devised same to his youngest sister
Jemima and Jemima later married Isaac Townsend and they by
indenture dated 3 May 1756 conveyed same to George Black father
of the above named John Black. Henry Fisher by deed dated 5 May
1743 [reciting that Henry Bowman, dec'd., sold to Thomas Manlove
since dec'd. a parcel of land near the mouth of Cedar Creek on
the north side thereof which deed of bargain was supposed to be
mislaid or lost and the said Thomas Manlove at the time of his
death did bequeath by his last will 100 acres, part of the said
land to his son Thomas Manlove who died leaving one only daughter
named Sarah who by her last will dated 27 Jan 1732 bequeathed 100
acres to said Henry Spencer and to make good the above mentioned
bill of sale and compleat the title to the said Henry Spencer,
John Bowman grandson and heir to said Henry Bowman did by his
deed dated 4 May 1743 conveyed the said 100 acres to the said
Henry Spencer] did convey to George Black the said 100 acres.
Beginning at a corner oak standing in the line of George Walton's
land ... running with a line of Goldsmith's land ... to a corner
of land lately in possession of Ann May dec'd. ... containing 100
acres. And whereas Art Verkirk of Sussex Co. by his indenture
dated 21 April 1730 [reciting that whereas there is a tract in
Sussex Co. formerly taken up by Josias Cowdrey containing 700
acres and said Josias Cowdrey dying without issue the same fell
to William Cowdrey, his eldest brother, and said William Cowdrey
sold to Art Verkirk 350 acres] conveyed to Richard Jacobs 200
acres part of the said land, beginning at a small distance from
Nicholas Branch ... to a corner oak on the south side of said
glade in John May's Pasture. And whereas Peter Hall, High
Sheriff, seized the tract last above recited to satisfy a debt
then due by above named Richard Jacobs did sell the tract to
Abraham Parsley, deed dated 4 Aug 1743 who conveyed one moiety or
half part of same 200 acres to said George Black [parcel
described], containing 110 acres, recorded in Liber H, page 44.
And whereas after the death of Abraham Parsley, James Havelo and
Frances his wife late Frances Parsley widow of said Abraham
Parsley, Anthony Parsley, Jonathan Jacobs and Sarah his wife late
Sarah Parsley, John Clandaniel and Prudence his wife late
Prudence Parsley, heirs and legal representatives of the said
Abraham Parsley dec'd., by their indenture dated 24 June 1746,
granted to Nottingham Jacobs the above recited tract of 200
acres, recorded in Book H No. 7, page 121(?). And whereas
Nottingham Jacobs on 25 April 1754 conveyed to said George Black
[after reciting the sale of a moiety of the said 200 acres to the
said George Black above recited and also the sale of the same to

the said Nottingham Jacobs, etc.] the other moiety or half part of the 200 acres, recorded in Book J, page 55. And whereas said George Black afterwards died leaving Ann his widow and issue 12 children and whereas at the Orphans Court in Feb 1772 George Black one of the sons of said George Black dec'd. preferred a petition stating that the above dec'd. George Black lately died intestate seized of a tract in Cedar Creek Hundred containing 600 acres, leaving 12 children of whom John Black was the eldest. [Allotment to the widow is described containing 80 1/4 acres. And remainder of land is described] This indenture is made for £749. Wit: Levin Crapper, William Bell. Within deed ackn. 28 Nov 1772.

230. George Black, Sussex Co., yeoman, from Azael Spencer, Kent Co. Delaware, yeoman. 29 July 1772. Tract in Cedar Creek Hundred being part of a tract purchased from the heirs of Robert Hart dec'd. by Abraham Wynkoop and by him devised to his son Benjamin Wynkoop and by his deed dated 2 Feb 1763 conveyed to Azael Spencer. 11 acres and 115 square perches for £25. Wit: William Hazzard, George Walton. Within deed of sale ackn. 13 July 1772.

231. George Black, Sussex Co., from Azael Spencer, Kent Co., Delaware, yeoman. 29 July 1772. Tract in Cedar Creek Neck formerly purchased by Henry Spencer from Robert Hart and sold by him to Mark Garden and by him possessed but never conveyed and Gabriel Gandron son to the afsd. Mark Gandron did for £13 assign his right to Joseph Spencer. And William Spencer son of afsd. Henry Spencer acknowledged and conveyed same to above named Joseph Spencer. And Donovan Spencer son to the said Joseph Spencer being seized thereof sold said dividend of land to Nathan Spencer who conveyed same to above named Azael Spencer by deed dated 6 Aug 1760. For £87, 40 acres. Wit: Wm. Hazzard, George Walton. Within deed of sale ackn. 13 July 1772.

232. Jno. Evans, Senr., on the seaside in Muddy Neck, Worcester Co., Maryland, yeoman, from John Hollaway, Senr., Worcester Co., Maryland, yeoman. 5 May 1772. For £200, a parcel being part of a larger parcel containing 150 acres of land and marsh which John Adams of Sussex Co., mariner, sold to the above named John Holloway, Senr. by deed 7 Nov 1771, and 50 acres sold to John Evans 8 Feb 1772 and the remainder in this sale being part of a larger tract of 630 acres of land and marsh and part of 991 acres the one moiety and half part that belonged to William Bagwell dec'd. and part of the great tract granted by patent to William Burton, Esqr. of Accomack Co., Virginia, dec'd. called Long Neck. Wit: Jno. Shankland, Sarah Shankland. Within deed of sale ackn. 5 May 1772.

233. David Thornton, Sussex Co., from Solomon Nock, Sussex Co. 4 May 1772. Parcel in Broadkill Hundred on the south side of Prime Hook Creek being part of a larger tract called Hasholds Fortune, purchased by Andrew Fullerton of Sussex Co. of George Hashold of Hampshire, Massachusetts Bay in New England who conveyed 200 acres thereof to Samuel Hopkins who conveyed the

same to within named Solomon Nock. For £60, 100 acres. Beginning at a corner maple standing on the south side of Hill Branch ... run of Sow Bridge Branch. Wit: John Clowes, Isaac Draper. Within deed of sale ackn. 6 May 1772.

David Thornton, Sussex Co., farmer, from Comfort Tharp, Sussex Co., widow of Nathan Tharp. 5 May 1772. Tract called Dickson Bevey, beginning at a corner dividing post of Jonathan Williams' land on the side of Cedar Creek, 44 acres for £44. Wit: Rhoads Shankland, James Carpenter. Within deed of sale ackn. 6 May 1772.

235. Jacob Stockley son of William Stockley, Junr., dec'd., Sussex Co., from Rhoads Shankland, Sussex Co. 6 May 1772. Parcel in Lewes and Rehoboth Hundred on Montius(?) Branch and another small branch, both proceeding out of Long Love Branch, being the tract which was by proprietary warrant granted to William White late of Sussex Co., surveyed 3 Jan 1718 containing 125 acres and whereas 1/2 deceased [descended?] to Ann Jeffers wife of William Jeffers and daughter of John Dickson dec'd and the said William Jeffers and Ann his wife by deed of bargain conveyed same half part to afsd. Rhoads Shankland. For £90. Within deed of sale ackn. 6 May 1772.

235. Isaac Draper, Sussex Co., cooper, from Lewis Davison of Bedford Co., Pennsylvania, yeoman. 30 Nov 1771. Parcel near the head of Broadkill Creek of 7 acres being part of a larger tract now in the possession of Boaz Manlove, on the south side thereof on which the house and orchard where said Lewis Davison formerly dwelt now stands and the larger tract now in the possession of Jacob Stafford and Rosanna his wife and whereas Rosanna Stafford after the decease of her husband Jacob Stafford by deed dated 9 Feb 1758 conveyed same to Lewis Davison. For £35. Wit: John Watson, John Clowes. Within deed of sale ackn. 6 May 1772.

236. Jonathan Williams, Sussex Co., shoemaker, from Comfort Tharp, widow of Nathan Tharp of Sussex Co. 5 May 1772. Tract called Dickson Bevey, beginning at a dividing post in Nicholas Turner's line ... 33 acres for £33. Wit: Rhoads Shankland, James Carpenter. Within deed of sale ackn. 6 May 1772.

237. Luke Townsend, Sussex Co., yeoman, from Robert Warring, Sussex Co., carpenter. 6 May 1772. Parcel in Cedar Creek forrest adjoining lands of Dormon Webb and the manor land containing 375 acres and conveyed to afsd. Robert Warring by deed of sale dated 16 June 1747 from William Loughland of Sussex Co. and Robert Warring gave to his son Wrixam Warring part of afsd tract but made no deed, which part was sold by Wrixam Warring to John Coverdal and laid off by said Robert Warring on the north northwest side of the whole tract and by sundry sales but no conveyances became the property of Luke Townsend and Levi Warring who divided the same by a line between them, beginning at a stake in Dormon Webbs line ... to division line laid off for John Coverdale ... on the southwest side of the dividing line. For £50. Wit: Reyner Williams, Wm. Davis. Within deed of sale ackn.

6 May 1772.

238. Levi Warring, Sussex Co., yeoman, from Robert Warring, Sussex Co., carpenter. 6 May 1772. Parcel in Cedar Creek Forrest adjoining land of Dormon Webb and the manor land containing 377 acres conveyed to the said Robert Warring by deed of sale dated 16 June 1747 [see above] - on the northeast side of the dividing line. Wit: John Clowes, John Wilson dean. Within deed of sale ackn. 6 May 1772.

239. Richard Durham, Sussex Co., carpenter, from Jonathan Dickoson, Sussex Co., yeoman. 6 May 1772. Parcel in Broadkill forrest adjoining afsd. Richard Durham's land containing 154 1/2 acres, about 60 acres of which is part of the same tract wherein Richard Durham now lives and the northeast end thereof was by deed of sale dated 4 Sep 1738 from Joseph Shankland conveyed to William Orr and the other part of said tract adjoining the said 60 acres towards the northwest containing about 90 acres is bounded on the southwest by Green Branch and on the northeast by Little Branch was surveyed by virtue of proprietors warrant to afsd. William Orr who by deed of sale dated 8 May 1751 conveyed afsd. 2 tracts to Jonathan Dickoson. For £77.10. Wit: John Clowes, Solomon Nock. Within deed of sale ackn. 6 May 1772.

240. John Clowes, Sussex Co., mariner, from Peter Robinson, Sheriff. 6 Feb 1772. To levy a certain sum of money recovered by John Clowes, Junr., against Thomas Walls, the sheriff seized and sold a tract of Thomas Walls. Beginning at a corner oak of Samuel Walls, land which Thomas Walls conveyed to afsd. Samuel by deed of sale dated 1 May 1764 - which land was granted to Thomas Walls by virtue of proprietors warrant. 160 acres for £33 to afsd. John Clowes on 5 Feb 1770. Wit: Robert Young, Isaac Draper. Within deed of sale ackn. 9 May 1772.

241. Petition by John Clowes to have above land conveyed to him.

241. Jonathan Dickoson, Sussex Co., yeoman, from Peter Robinson, Sheriff. 7 May 1772. Sheriff's sale of tract of Samuel Dickoson to levy sum of money recovered by Isaac Draper against him. Parcel in Broadkill forrest, beginning at a corner post on the northwest side of the Green Dranes, 106 acres, £50. Wit: Robert Young, Isaac Draper. Within deed of sale ackn. 7 May 1772.

242. Petition of Isaac Draper [to have above land conveyed to Jonathan Dickson, which land was bought by Draper and then sold to Jonathan Dickson]. 7 May 1772.

242. Hannah Fisher, Sussex Co., from George Kollock, admr. of Mary Kollock who died intestate and also all the estate with will annexed of Shepard Kollock unadministered by afsd. Mary Kollock the extx. of Shepard Kollock. 6 May 1772. For £160, land beginning a corner post about 3-4 perches from the pond ... to a corner post standing by the side of the county road from Lewes Town ... along the patent line to a corner post standing in the division line of the land of David Hall, 20 acres of land and

pond surveyed and divided from said tract on 16 Oct 1771. Wit: Hannah Nunez, Daniel Nunez. Within deed of sale ackn. 7 May 1772.

243. John Woods, Sussex Co., from Peter Robinson, Sheriff. 1 May 1772. Sheriff's sale of house and lot of Simon Edwards to levy sum of money which William Gill recovered against Simon Edwards. Said property was sold to William Gill for £15 who sold the same to John Woods for £12. Property is by the land of John Wiltbank, Esqr. and on the southwest side of the road leading down to the Canarikill Creek and on the northwest side of Ship Carpenters Street which same land was conveyed by Joshua Fisher, John Tilton and Comfort his wife, exrs. of Cornelius Wiltbank to afsd. Simon Edwards 23 May 1747, recorded in Book H, folio 169. Wit: William Gill, Samuel Edwards. Within deed of sale ackn. 6 May 1772.

244. Jennet Bailey wife of Nathaniel Bailey, Sarah Shankland wife of John Shankland and Mary Davison wife of James Davison, from her sister, Elizabeth Lewis wife of Noble Lewis, Sussex Co., spinster. Parcel of land being part of land John Miers sold to John Simonton the Younger by deed of sale dated 12 Dec 1748, containing 12 acres of land and branch and goes by the name of The Field, joining the southernmost street of Lewes Town on the north side of Simon Kollock, on the southwest end of Jennet Bailey's and Sarah Shankland's and Mary Davison's divident, on the southeast side thereof and the heirs of Thomas Cale's on the northeast end thereof, of which the afsd. John Simonton died before he came to full age, making no will and leaving no issue, only his four sisters, Jennet (Tennet?), Sarah, Mary and Elizabeth to whom the land descended. Wit: Alexr. Shankland, Peter White. Within deed of sale ackn. 6 May 1772.

245. Jennet Bailey wife of Nathaniel Bailey, Sarah Shankland wife of John Shankland and Mary Davison wife of James Davison, spinsters, to their sister, Elizabeth Lewis wife of Noble Lewis, Sussex Co. Rights to parcel of land of 12 acres that was left to them by their father, John Simonton, dec'd., by his will dated 29 May 1751 in which he bequeathed afsd 12 acres to his two youngest daughters, Comfort Simonton and Elizabeth Simonton. The said Comfort died before she came of age and left no issue and her share descended to the above said Jennet, Sarah and Mary. Land is in the town of Lewes on the northeast side of one of the branches of Pagan Creek, lying between Middle Street or Market Street and the southernmost street of Lewes Town and adjoining on the northeast end to a parcel of land claimed by the heirs of Jacob Kollock. Wit: Alexr. Shankland, Peter White. Within deed of sale ackn. 6 May 1772.

246. William Borroughs, Sussex Co., Gentleman, from William Willey, Noble Cordery and Nehemiah Smith, all of Sussex Co., Gentlemen. 5 May 1772. For £160, plantation in Cedar Creek Hundred containing 200 acres, the same that was warranted and surveyed to John Murphey and left by him to Nehemiah Tilney which by legal descents and conveyances became the property of afsd. William Willey, Noble Cordery and Nehemiah Smith. Wit: Levin

Crapper, Molton Crapper. Within deed of sale ackn. 7 May 1772.

247. Barnet Vankirk, Sussex Co., farmer, from Mary Wynkoop, New Castle Co, widow, Phebe Vining, Kent Co. widow and Benjamin Wynkoop of the City of Philadelphia, merchant - they being the surviving exrs. of last will of Abraham Wynkoop of Sussex Co., dec'd. 31 Aug 1771. For £30, tract in Cedar Creek Hundred, beginning at a corner oak, the last corner of John Loughland's land ... to the head of a small branch proceeding out of Gravelly Branch ... 137 acres, which tract was by virtue of a warrant dated 13 June 1744 granted to Abraham Parsley and called Golden Grove since sold by the heirs of said Parsley to William Shankland who conveyed the same to the above named Abraham Wynkoop, Esqr., dec'd. who by his bond obligatory dated 5 Jan 1753 sold same to afsd. Barnet Vankirk. Wit: J. Rodney, Joseph Oliver. Within deed of sale ackn. 6 May 1772.

248. Barnet Vankirk from Abraham Wynkoop. I Abraham Wynkoop, Sussex Co., merchant, [obliges himself to convey above land to Vankirk.] Wit: Robert Mears, John Bagwell. 5 Jan 1753. Proved 6 May 1772 by oath of Jacob Kollock, both evidences [Robert Mears and John Bagwell] being dead.

249. John Parker, sadler, Sussex Co., from Edward Eavans, City of Philadelphia, cordwainer and Rebecca his wife and Elizabeth Clark of the City of Philadelphia, spinster, the said Rebecka and Elizabeth being the daughters and only surviving issue of William Clark late of the City of Philadelphia, Gentleman, dec'd. by Rebecca his wife which said William Clark was the only son and heir of William Clark sometime of the City of Dublin, Ireland and late of Sussex Co., dec'd. by Honour his wife also dec'd. 27 Nov 1770. For £150, tract on the south side of Mispillion Creek, beginning at an oak on the edge of the bank of the Mispillion Creek near the store house of Levin Crapper being the corner of Israel Brown's land ... to the mill pond ... 300 acres ... part of a tract called Mill Range granted by patent to Henry Bowman who died seized thereof intestate whereupon administration of said Henry Bowman was committed to said William Clark the grandfather of Sussex Co., who obtained an order of Orphans Court to make the sale of the tract to sundry persons to the amount of £700 and which sawmill Range tract was in due form of law appraised by William Clark admr. at the full value of £200 which sum William Clark paid the settlement of his account whereas the said tract called the Saw Mill Range became vested in William Clark the elder and whereof William Clark died seized whereby the same tract devolved upon and descended to said Edward Evans and Rebecca his wife in right of her the said Rebecca and Elizabeth Clark as heirs. Wit: Purnal Johnson, Mark Killen. Within deed of sale ackn. 6 May 1772.

250. William Hazzard, Sussex Co., yeoman, from Mary Wynkoop, Sussex Co., widow, Phebe Vining of Dover, Kent Co., Delaware, widow and Benjamin Wynkoop of the City of Philadelphia, merchant, exrs. of last will of Abraham Wynkoop. 14 April 1772. For £220, tract in Cedar Creek Hundred, beginning at a post on the

southeast side of a branch of Mispillion Creek called Herring
Branch ... to a post standing in Thomas Cary's line ...
containing 220 acres being part of the overplus land contained in
the tracts called Pathalia and Cyprus Hall granted by virtue of
warrant dated 10 Oct 1744 and remaining in the survey for the
resurveying and laying out two tracts besides the said overplus
to Edward Evans and Rebeckah his wife and Elizabeth Clark, the
one in right of Daniel Leak called Pathalia and the other in
right of Thomas Bowstock called Cyprus Hall in Cedar Creek
Hundred in Sussex Co. which the said Edward Evans and Rebecca his
wife, and Elizabeth Clark by Joshua Fisher their attorney
recorded in Liber No. 7, folio 108, granted to Abraham Wynkoop
who died and in his last will dated 15 Nov 1753 devised to his
daughter divers legacies and devising several parts of his lands
to his two sons, Thomas and Benjamin Wynkoop and ordered all his
land not above disposed of which are lying and being in Kent and
Sussex Counties, Delaware to be sold. Wit: Ceasar Rodney, Miers
Fisher. Within deed of sale ackn. 1 Aug 1772.

253. Richardson Cade, of Broadkill Hundred, farmer, from Purnal
Johnson, Junr., Sussex Co. 29 Aug 1772. For £60. Tract being
part of a larger tract granted by Gilbert Marriner to Thomas
Davock who later died leaving in his will his sister Alice White
who died seized thereof and Mary Russell and Neomie Godwin
daughters of afsd. Thomas Davock became lawfully seized of the
same who afterwards by agreement had the same land divided
between them and the afsd., Mary then wife of Thomas Humphries
had her lot on the most westerly part up a Branch called
Pembertons Branch whereupon the said Mary Humphries after the
death of the afsd. Thomas Humphries by her last will bequeathed
Purnal Johnson her grandson all her right to the moiety laid off
to her, adjoining lands now in the possession of John Clowes, the
afsd. Richardson Cade and Thomas Reynolds, beginning at the
hickory standing in the line of the Dividend then a long a line
of old marked trees called Dyers line ... for 100 acres. Wit:
John Waller, Wm. Brittingham Ennis. Within deed of sale ackn. 29
Aug 1772.

254. James Black from John Black. 4 Aug 1772. Tract of land
and marsh in Cedar Creek Neck called Long Acre and purchased of
Abraham Wynkoop from the heirs of Robert Hart, the original
patentee and the said Abraham Wynkoop sold the same to George
Black, Sussex Co., who died intestate and without will leaving
several heirs one of which petitioned the Orphans Court for a
division of the said intestate's land and marsh in pursuance
whereof and John Black being the eldest son of said George Black,
dec'd., accepted the same according to Law, for the consideration
of £14, 30 acres. Wit: Wm. Hazzard, John Clowes. Within deed of
sale ackn. 4 Aug 1772.

254. George Black, Sussex Co., from John Black, yeoman. 4 Aug
1772. Tract of land and marsh in Cedar Creek Neck called Long
Acre which Abraham Wynkoop purchased of the heirs of Robert Hart,
the original patentee and Abraham Wynkoop sold said land and
marsh to George Black, dec'd., who died intestate and leaving

several heirs including John Black the eldest son who received an
allotment of land of which 30 acres he conveys to George Black
for £14. Wit: Wm. Hazzard, John Clowes. Within deed of sale
ackn. 4 Aug 1772.

255. David Thornton, yeoman, from Sarah Draper, exr. and
Alexander Draper, exr. of the last will of Nehemiah Draper,
Esqr., Sussex Co., dec'd. 31 May 1772. Nehemiah Draper was in
his lifetime bound to David Thornton to convey a tract for £350,
on the south side of Cedar Creek being part of two patents, the
one surveyed for William Page and granted to William Clark on 2nd
of the 6th month 1684 and the other tract granted to Robert
Twilley resurveyed for him 4th of 7th month 1686 called
Twillington and by sundry conveyances has descended down to said
Nehemiah Draper. But said Nehemiah Draper died before conveying
same. Boundary runs to a corner oak of the two acres belonging
to Drapers Mill. Containing 308 acres. Wit: Isaac Smith, John
Cirwithin. Within deed of sale ackn. 6 Aug 1772.

257. David Thornton from Nehemiah Draper. Bond. Nehemiah
Draper, Sussex Co., merchant, was bound to David Thornton of
Virginia, planter, on 9 Sep 1762, in the sum of £500 to convey
tract [see above]. Wit: Jonanath Milman, Ann Inglish (her mark).
Proved by oath of Jonathan Milman 6 Aug 1772.

257. George Walton, yeoman, from John Black, planter. 4 Aug
1772. Tract in Cedar Creek Neck called Long Acre which Abraham
Wynkoop purchased of the heirs of Robert Hart, the original
patentee and Abraham Wynkoop sold the same to George Black,
dec'd. who died intestate and John Black received an allotment
from the land of his father, afsd. George Black of which he now
conveys to George Walton 30 acres. Wit: Wm. Hazzard, John
Clowes. Within deed of sale ackn. 4 Aug 1772.

258. Joshua Spencer, Cedar Creek Hundred, farmer, from William
Bagwell of Cedar Creek Hundred, farmer and wife Mary. 6 Aug
1772. For £294.7.6 a parcel binding on the southwest side of
Mispillion Creek, beginning at a corner line of an old division
formerly run between Henry Spencer and Samuel Spencer, dec'd. ...
to the mouth of Spencers Branch ... to a corner of land belonging
to the heirs of Spencer Chance, dec'd. and the land lately sold
by said Joshua Spencer to Thomas Fisher ... running the division
lines between said Spencer and Bagwell's first line ...
containing 196 acres which said parcel is part of a larger tract
formerly devised by Henry Spencer to his son William who died
intestate leaving issue a son William and a daughter Elizabeth to
whom the land descended and Elizabeth later married John Bagwell
and they by indenture dated 10 July 1749 conveyed her allotted
part to said William Bagwell. Wit: Jacob Hazzard, Nichs.
Vandyke. Within deed of sale ackn. 6 Aug 1772.

259. Andrew Heavelo, Sussex Co., yeoman, from John Clowes,
Sussex Co. 5 Aug 1770. Parcel of 92 acres in the Broadkill
forrest on the head of Dobson's Marsh and surveyed by virtue of a
proprietors warrant dated 1 Nov 1758 for Ezekiel Joyns and called

Many Tryals which said Ezekiel Joyns by his deed of sale conveyed to afsd. John Clowes who conveyed same to Foster Donavan 16 acres thereof and conveys to said Andrew Heavelo the remaining 76 acres, bounded by a line of land formerly surveyed for Richard Dobson. Wit: Absolom Little, Thos. Gray. Within deed of sale ackn. 5 Aug 1772.

260. Edward Craige from Hamilton Craige, yeoman. For £5 paid by his son Edward Craige, Hamilton Craige releases two tracts conveyed by two deeds from John Harmonson to said Hamilton Craige, the one deed dated 3 Sep 1765 for 273 acres and the other deed of release dated 4 sep 1765. Wit: Thos. Robinson, Junr., Rhoads Shankland. Within deed of release ackn. 5 Aug 1772.

261. Alexander Reed, Sussex Co., yeoman, from William Stewart, Sussex Co., mariner. 1 Feb 1772. Parcel in the Indian River Hundred being taken up by Alexander Read late of the county afsd. father to the afsd. Alexr. Read which tract was conveyed by Allin Read as admr. to his father Alexander Reed by deed of sale dated May Term 1765 to William Stewart, being all that part of the afsd. tract lying on the west side of the county road from Lewes Town to the sawmill containing 100 acres, for £50. Wit: Thos. Whiteseth, Rhoads Shankland. Within deed of sale ackn. 5 Aug 1772.

261. Joseph Griffith, Junr. from Thomas Cary and Daniel Welch of Sussex Co. 7 Dec 1771. Tract in the forrest of Cedar Creek Hundred it being the tract formerly taken up by warrant granted to John Welch, dec'd. for 280 acres and surveyed 14 March 1769 - for £50. The moiety or half part of the 280 acres agreeable to a division line agreed to by the parties concerned, on the south side thereof it being that part thereon Daniel Welch now dwells. Wit: Wm. Hazzard, Benjamin Truit. Within deed of sale ackn. 5 Aug 1772.

262. Thos: Wilson, Cedar Creek Hundred, from John Reed, Sussex Co., yeoman. 3 Aug 1772. Tract on the south side of the main branch of Cedar Creek being a part of a tract formerly belonging to James Reed which was conveyed to said Reed by deed of sale from John Shankland, Sheriff, by deed dated 7 Feb 1737, on the north side of land belonging to Bethuel Watson. For £70, 123 1/2 acres. Wit: John Holms, Rhoads Shankland. Within deed of sale ackn. 3 Aug 1772.

263. Stephen Townsend, Sussex Co., yeoman, from Elias Townsend and Leah Townsend his wife. 29 Oct 1771. Part of a larger tract called Little Bolton that Stephen Townsend the Elder willed to his son William Townsend who died intestate leaving three daughters one named Leah being the eldest the now wife of afsd. Elias Townsend which parcel was surveyed 5 March 1771, beginning at the head of Emots Branch, laid out for 70 acres. For £35.10. Wit: Isaac Wattson, Thos. Watson. Within deed of sale ackn. 5 Aug 1772.

264. Thomas Staton from Anderson Parker, Esqr. attorney for

Sarah Star, admx. of Jonathan Star. 28 Aug 1772. Parcel in Broadkill Hundred being a tract whereof Richard Star, dec'd., seized of, who by his last will devised afsd. tract to his three sons, Nathaniel, Jonathan and James Star, said Jonathan dying said tract was divided. Sarah Star guardian of Bethiah Star, only daughter and heir of afsd. Jonathan Star and admx. as afsd. by Anderson Parker her attorney entered into bonds with afsd. Nathaniel Star and James Star to stand to and abide by the division which William Stevenson, Hugh King and Rhoads Shankland should make of afsd. tract who awarded to Sarah Star and Bethiah Star 146 acres, and 46 acres [described] was sold to pay the debts of Jonathan Star for £47.13. Wit: Benjamin Burton, Daniel Nunez. Within deed of sale ackn. 29 Aug 1772.

265. Solomon Parimore, Sussex Co., yeoman, from William Godwin, Sussex Co., yeoman. 29 Aug 1772. Whereas Thomas Tilton, Elizabeth Hill and Thomas Davock had granted to them and confirmed by sundry patents, several tracts on the north side of Long Bridge Branch and adjoining to the same 500 acres being the most southern part of the whole and bounded on the said branch, which by sundry conveyances became the property of Thomas Davock who by his last will dated 27 Jan 1718 among other things devised to his son Thomas Davock the above recited 500 acres and Thomas Davock the younger dying intestate and without issue the afsd. 500 acres became the property of his two sisters, Mary and Naomy who by mutual compact divided the said 500 acres by a line of marked trees [described]. Mary taking the upper part and most western part. And Naomi married Michael Godwin of Worcester Co. by whom she had several children and afsd. William Godwin being her eldest son, afsd. Naomi Godwin by her last will to her son William Godwin confirmed by the will of Michael Godwin dated Dec 1765 devised the moiety or half part of the 500 acres. For £300. Wit: John Waller, Wm. Brittingham Ennis. Within deed of sale ackn. 9 Aug 1772.

266. Ezekiel West, Sussex Co., yeoman, from Solomon Stockley, Sussex Co., cordwinder and Mary his wife. 4 Dec 1772. Part of a tract at the head of Laws Pond proceeding out of Bracey's Branch adjoining the west side of the line of said Law's land in Rehoboth Hundred and being part of a tract that was granted by warrant 13th of 1st month 1717 to Robert Davis for 200 acres and by virtue of afsd warrant was surveyed 12 April 1717 for 210 acres, called The Glades. For £73.6. Wit: Mary Kollock, Daniel Nunez. Within deed of sale ackn. 5 Aug 1772.

267. William Godwin, Sussex Co., yeoman, from William Robinson, Worcester Co. Maryland, yeoman. 1 Aug 1772. Parcel in Broadkill Forrest containing 200 acres on the south side of Kenny's Savanna near to Prettyman Day's first bounder, conveyed to afsd. William Robinson from Samuel Burton by his deed of sale dated 4 Sep 1758. For £27.10. Wit: John Clowes, John Reed, Junr. Within deed of sale ackn. 9 Aug 1772.

268. William Godwin, Sussex Co., yeoman, from Solomon Parrimore, Sussex Co., yeoman. 29 Aug 1772. Parcel in Broadkill forrest

about 15 miles southwesterly from the town of Lewes and adjoining lands now in the possession of Abraham Harris and Robert Talbert which tract was surveyed for Prittyman Day by virtue of a proprietor's warrant dated 9 June 1743 as 200 acres and Prittyman Day by his deed of sale dated 5 May 1752 conveyed same to John Gray who by his deed of sale dated Feb 1753 conveyed same to Nathan Brittingham who by his deed of sale dated 30 April 1759 conveyed same to afsd. Solomon Parrimore. Wit: John Waller, Wm. Brittingham. Within deed of sale ackn. 29 Aug 1772.

269. Philips Kollock, Sussex Co., from Gilbert Marriner and wife Elizabeth, Sussex Co. 28 Aug 1772. Part of a tract in Lewes and Rehoboth Hundred adjoining on the southwest side of the land of John Lewis, on the southeast side of the land of the estate of the late Jacob Kollock, Esqr., dec'd., and on the northeast end of the land that the afsd. Jacob Kollock in his lifetime bought from Herculous Kollock and on the northwest side of the Kings Road which said land is that part which was allotted and laid off to the afsd. Gilbert Marriner in the right of his wife, the afsd. Elizabeth as her part of the land that her father Shepard Kollock died seized of which said part is laid off for 40 acres as by the return of five appointed freeholders. For £180. Wit: Boaz Manlove, Daniel Nunez. Within deed of sale ackn. 29 Aug 1772.

270. Division of land of John Clowes, Esqr., late dec'd., amongst his children. John Clowes of Sussex Co., dec'd. by his will dated 8 April 1761 devised to his four sons and three daughters, William, John, David, Gurhardus, Catharine, Mary Junr. and Lydia Clowes all his land in said county to be equally divided. John Clowes, John Young and Catharine his wife, John Sheldon Dormon and Mary his wife, Jeremiah Conwell and Lydia his wife being at full age, heirs and legal representatives of the afsd. John Clowes dec'd, have caused a draught to be made as follows: Lot No. 1 of 1 acres except the ground on which the houses of Lot No. 2 stands, beginning at a stone and 8 feet below the Drawbridge; Lot No. 2 containing 1 1/2 acres [described] and 17 1/2 acres of Records' plantation called the Near Plantation [described]; Lot No. 3 of 50 1/3 acres of the Bridge Place called George Dodd's Plantation [described]; Lot No. 4 of the remainder of the afsd. Bridge Place being 51 1/3 acres; Lot No. 5 of 61 1/2 acres [described]; Lot No. 6 of 61 3/4 acres of Rickords or the Near Plantation [described]; Lot No. 7 containing the remainder of afsd. Ricords or Near Plantation. Wit: Wm. Burton, John Hazzard, Mary Millard. Signed by all parties 17 Dec 1772.

271. A Report of Peter Parker and Jonathan Stephenson. Whereas John Clowes, John Young and Catharine his wife, John Sheldon Dormon and Mary his wife, Jery Conwell and Lydia his wife this day entered into a writing obligatory agreeable to the last will of John Clowes, Esqr., dec'd., appointed the following subscribers to draw said lot for each of the heirs of John Clowes. [A plat is included which shows each lot.] Recorded 10 March 1773.

273. Rowland Bevans, Worcester Co., Maryland, from Levin Ennis, Sussex Co. 31 Oct 1772. Tract in Broadkill Hundred granted by a proprietor's warrant to Robert Warren of Sussex Co., who conveyed same to William Brittingham Ennis who conveyed same to above named Levin Ennis. For £50, 78 acres. Wit: William Peery, James Reynolds. Within deed of sale ackn. 1 Oct 1772.

273. Rowland Beavans, Worcester Co., Maryland, from John Pettyjohn, son of Hannah, Sussex Co. 31 Oct 1772. Parcel in Broadkill Hundred being part of a larger tract surveyed for Richard Pettyjohn or his widow Hannah, being 100 acres part of the afsd. larger tract containing 300 acres. For £65. Wit: James Reynolds, Rhoads Shankland. Within deed of sale ackn. 1 Oct 1772.

274. James Hall, Sussex Co., yeoman, from Daniel Nunez and Benjamin Burton, exrs. of last will of Hezekiah Cord, dec'd. 28 Aug 1772. Whereas Hezekiah Cord by his last will ordered that his land should be sold and the money applied to and amongst several of his relations, will dated 16 April 1767. For £45. Wit: John Rodney, James Fisher. Within deed of sale ackn. 26 Sep 1772.

274. James Reynolds, Sussex Co., from John Pettyjohn, Sussex Co. 31 Oct 1772. Tract in Broadkill Hundred being part of a larger tract granted by a proprietor's warrant to Richard Pettyjohn, dec'd. who by his last will devised the afsd. larger tract to his son the above named John Pettyjohn, party to these presents and he entered into a obligation to convey 100 acres of the above mentioned tract to Nehemiah Reed of Sussex Co. who assigned over the obligation to above named James Reynolds before the 100 acres was conveyed, beginning at a corner oak standing on the forks of the road from Lewes Town to Evans' Sawmill and Green Branch. For £75. Wit: Wm. Peery, William Shadly(?). Within deed of sale ackn. 31 Oct 1772.

275. James and Moses Tamplin [and others] from William Blizard. William Blizard, Sussex Co., yeoman, for £45 paid by Richard Tamplin, Sussex Co., since deceased, and now conveyed to sons and daughters of Richard Tamplin, dec'd, to wit: James Tamplin, Moses Tamplin, Thomas Tamplin, John Tamplin, Isaac Tamplin, Mary Tamplin and Richard Tamplin. Tract in Indian River Hundred, the same whereon Ezekiel Jackson formerly lived and formerly surveyed for Thomas Bryon called Devils Wood Yard, containing 115 acres. Wit: Levin Ennis, John Pettyjohn. Within deed of sale ackn. 31 Oct 1772.

276. Jno. Carlile, Junr., Sussex Co., from Wm. McCay and wife Patience, Sussex Co. 21 Sep 1772. Tract in Cedar Creek Neck on the north side of Bever Dam Branch which proceeds out of Cedar Creek being on the west side of Robert Heart's land and on the east side of the land of Thomas Hammons, Junr. and Robert Twelley containing 167 acres which tract was conveyed to John Manlove by Henry Molleston by deed of sale dated 4 Feb 1705/6. After death of said John Manlove afsd. tract became the property of Jonathan

Manlove who sold one-half part to William McCay party to these
presents dated 5 Feb 1760. For £150. Boundary runs to a
division line between afsd. William McCay and John McCay. Wit:
Levin Crapper, Wm. Hazzard. Within deed of sale ackn. 27 Sep
1772.

277. Margret Kollock extx. of Jacob Kollock, Esqr. Aaron Irons,
Worcester Co., Maryland, exr. of last will of Jane Irons of same
co., widow, dec'd. conveys two lots in the town of Lewes, the
first in breadth running along the bank of Lewes Creek up the
said creek 60 feet and in length southwestward to the extent of
the adjacent lots, the second on the street leading out of the
town by the house of David Hall for 90 feet and in length
southeastward to the land of the heirs of John Paynter being the
same lot which was give to the said Jane Irons by the last will
of her father Jacob Kollock the Elder dec'd. and the said Jane
Irons being so seized by her bond dated 15 May 1751, bound to
Jacob Kollock of the town of Lewes for £50. Whereas said Jacob
Kollock died having in his last will devised the use of the
premises mentioned above to his wife Margret during her lifetime
and after her death the said he devised same to his son Philips
Kollock and daughters, Hester and Mary wife of Nehemiah Field.
Whereas Hester Kollock hath married Jacob Moore of the town of
Lewes, attorney at law. Wit: Richard Bassett, Jno. Russell.
Within deed of sale ackn. 4 Nov 1772.

279. Petition of Aaron Irons. To the Court of Common Pleas Nov
1772. Aaron Irons, Worcester Co., Maryland. [To convey above
lots in accordance with the bond.]

281. Benjamin Truit, Senr., Sussex Co., to his son Benjamin
Truit. 1 Oct 1772. For £65, 101 acres begin part of a larger
tract in Cedar Creek Hundred of 200 acres granted to afsd.
Benjamin Truit, Senr. by warrant dated 9 June 1737 lying within
the bounds of the manor Worminghurst called Spittle Field. Wit:
Wm. Hazzard, Pemberton Carlile [his mark]. Within deed of sale
ackn. 4 Nov 1772.

281. Joseph Truit from John Hudson, Senr and Major Hudson of
Sussex Co. 2 Nov 1772. Tract in the forrest of Cedar Creek and
lying in the Proprietor's manor of Worminghurst adjoining the
land of William Hudson and Ananias Hudson, dec'd. and land of
Joshua Hudson and land of Henry Hudson which said tract was
surveyed and laid off 16 May 1765 for said John Hudson, 86 acres,
for £100. Wit: Benj. Truit, Wm. Hudson. Within deed of sale
ackn. 4 Nov 1772.

282. Manuel Manlove of Dorchester Co., Maryland and yeoman of
Sussex Co. [sic], from Richard Hays, Sussex Co., and son Richard
Hays. 3 Nov 1772. Parcel in the forrest of Cedar Creek Hundred
adjoining land of Manuel Manlove and land of the said Richard
Hayes, Senr. and land of Thomas Fisher of 63 acres and 17 perches
for £34. Joseph Truit, Unicy Hays. Within deed of sale ackn. 4
Nov 1772.

283. Charles Macklin, Sussex Co., yeoman, from Lowder Tatman, Sussex Co., yeoman. 3 Nov 1772. Parcel in the forrest of Cedar Creek Hundred in Stallion Head Neck on the west side of Gum Branch being on the north side of a larger tract containing 220 acres was conveyed by deed of sale from Isaac Ingram to William Tatman dated 5 May 1762 who conveyed same to afsd. Lower Tatman. For £85, 159 acres. Wit: Nehemiah Davis, Junr., Rhoads Shankland. Within deed of sale ackn. 4 Nov 1772.

284. William Blizard, Sussex Co., from Absolom Little, Bedford Co., Pennsylvania. 12 Sep 1772. Tract in Broadkill Hundred granted by proprietor's warrant to Charles Forgeson, dec'd. whereas the right of said warrant became the property of the four daughters of said Forgeson, to wit, Rosanna, Violinda, Mary and Sarah, who had the land surveyed for 212 acres and said Rosanna with her husband William Carhart conveyed her part to William Walls who married said Sarah and the said William Walls and wife Sarah and Hugh Stephenson and wife Mary (daughter of said Forgeson) conveyed their parts of said land to Absolom Little party to these presents. Beginning at an oak standing in the line of Griffin Jones' land ... to a division line between said land and Levin Clifton ... 159 acres for £35. Wit: Thomas Robinson, Peter Robinson. Within deed of sale ackn. 3 Nov 1772.

285. William Hudson, Sussex Co., from William Shockly, Sussex Co., yeoman. 4 Nov 1772. Tract in the proprietor's manor of Worminghurst and bounded by land of Francis Roberts and land in the possession of William Rickards now sold to John Hudson and joining other land of the said John Hudson and joining the plantation where William Hudson dwells and joining to the head of Roberts Mill Pond lying on Brierry Branch, 130 acres, £70. Wit: John Truitt, Daniel Nunez. Within deed of sale ackn. 4 Nov 1772.

285. Alexandr. McCay, Sussex Co., yeoman from Thos. May and wife Mary, Draper May and wife Ann, all of Sussex Co. 2 Nov 1772. Tract in Cedar Creek Neck on the south side of Mispillion Creek called Pennington surveyed for 400 acres of land and marsh 8 March 1685 at the request of Henry Pennington who conveyed the same to Thomas May who by deed of gift conveyed same to his son Thomas May who by his last will devised same to his son Jonathan May father of the first mentioned Thomas and Draper May, and Jonathan May dying intestate, the property descended to said Thomas and Draper May. For £100, 100 acres part of the afsd. 400 acres, joining at the head of a branch proceeding out of Mispillion Creek called Salterages Branch on the northeast side. Wit: Isaac Watson, William Mecay. Within deed of sale ackn. 4 Nov 1772.

286. Henry Hudson from John Hudson, Sussex Co., yeoman. 4 Nov 1772. Tract in the forrest of Cedar Creek Hundred, in the proprietor's manor Worminghurst adjoining land of Joshua Hudson and land now belonging to Joseph Truit binding on Bowman's Branch which said land was laid off 16 May 1664 at the request of John Hudson for his son Ananias Hudson, dec'd., who sold the same to his brother Henry for £50, laid off for 101 3/4 acres. Wit:

William Hudson, Boaz Borrough. Within deed of sale ackn. 4 Nov 1772.

287. Thos. Tilton, Kent Co., Delaware, from James Wallace, City of Philadelphia, merchant, and wife Elizabeth. 8 Dec 1772. For £5, plantation or tract in Slaughter Neck in Cedar Creek Hundred which once belonged to John Tilton, father of Thomas Tilton party to these presents and thereof he died, containing 300 acres. He died intestate, leaving seven children, Joseph, Thomas, James, Miah, Mary, Ann and Sarah to whom the premises descended and the afsd. Joseph later married Rachel Hilyard and by her had three daughters, Anne, Rachel and Sarah and soon after died intestate and after his death the three children died intestate and without issue, and Rachel afterwards married Richard Hoff and Rachel and Richard Hoff by their lease (6 Aug 1765) and release (7 Aug 1765) conveyed their interests to said James Wallace. Wit: Tho. McKean, Henry Malcolm. Within deed of sale ackn. 4 May 1773.

288. Received 9 Oct 1773 of Ezekiel West the sum of 40 shillings which was allowed me for damages by running road through my plantation by order of Court. Solomon Stockley.

289. An article between the heirs of Thomas Bagwell for the division of land. Ann Bagwell, John Bagwell, William and Thomas Bagwell minor by Ann Bagwell afsd. guardian the widow and sons of Thomas Bagwell, late of Sussex Co., dec'd., have mutually agreed and chosen John Wiltbank, Parker Robinson and Peter Robinson, Esqrs., any two of them that shall agree to make division and partition the land and tenements of which Thomas Bagwell was possessed, agreeable to the last will of said Thomas Bagwell dated 30 May 1772. Agreement made 31 Aug 1772. Wit: Benjn. Burton, Woolsey Burton.

289. Division of Thomas Bagwell's land and plat. The land divided as follows [see plat]: to Ann Bagwell, widow of Thomas Bagwell, 31 acres and 108 square perches of upland called No. 1 except one old frame of a house allotted to John Bagwell and 28 acres of marsh land called No. 2; secondly to John Bagwell 48 and 62 square perches of upland called No. 7 and 47 acres of marsh called No. 8, and old frame of a house standing on the widow's dividend, also a log shop standing in Thomas Bagwell's dividend and a barn and corn crib standing on William Bagwell's dividend; thirdly to William Bagwell 50 acres and 2 square perches of upland except barn and crib mentioned earlier called No. 5 and 40 acres of marsh land called No. 6; fourthly to Thomas Bagwell 54 acres and 154 square perches of upland excepting a log shop allotted to John Bagwell called No. 3 and 2 small parcels of marsh of 40 acres called No. 4 and No. 9. 24 April 1773. [Plat is included.]

291. Miers Fisher, City of Philadelphia, attorney at law from Mary Wynkoop, Phebe Vining and Benjamin Wynkoop, surviving exrs. of last will of Abraham Wynkoop, dec'd. 17 April 1773. Whereas Abraham Wynkoop was seized of a tract in Cedar Creek Hundred called Pathalia and Cyprus Hall and said Abraham Wynkoop in his

last will dated 15 Nov 1750 directed that his exrs. sell said the residue of the land not disposed of in the will in order to pay his debts and legacies. For £98, tract runs to a line of Benjamin Truit's land and thence by the land lately sold by said Mary Wynkoop, &c. to George Cowen, containing 98 acres and 100 perches. Wit: Tinch Tilghman, John Lyon. Within deed of sale ackn. 4 May 1773.

292. Samuel Campble, Worcester Co., Maryland, from William Shockley, Sussex Co., yeoman. 27 March 1773. Tract of 250 acres in Cedar Creek Hundred, part of which was granted to and surveyed for David Smith by proprietors warrant dated 29 Aug 1715 and by sundry conveyances became the property of Peter Parker who by deed of sale dated 6 Nov 1770 conveyed same to William Shockley. For £234.15, beginning on the northwest side of the southwest branch of Cedar Creek being the second corner of Smith's Survey ... near John Walton's fence. Wit: Charles Draper, Anderson Parker, Alexr. Draper. Within deed of sale ackn. 28 March 1773.

292. John Bell, Sussex Co., merchant, from John Heverlo, Sussex Co., cooper, and wife Hannah late Hannah Cord. for £100, tract in Broadkiln Hundred of which Joseph Cord, dec'd. by his last will dated 3 April 1738 devised to his son John Cord late husband of the above named Hannah Heaverlo; and also all her dower of a tract purchased of Elijah Killem by said John Cord. Wit: Boaz Manlove, Jno. Russel. Within deed of sale ackn. 6 Nov 1773.

293. John Bell, Sussex Co., merchant, from Henry Smith, Sussex Co., yeoman, and wife Mary late Mary Cord daughter and heir of John cord, dec'd. 6 Nov 1772. Two tracts in Broadkiln Hundred one of which was granted to William Clark and by him in his last will devised to his wife Honour Clark who on 4 June 1708 obtained a patent for land and by sundry deeds of conveyances the said tract became the property of Joseph Cord who by his will dated 3 May 1738 devised a part of the said tract to his son John Cord, beginning near the mouth of a small branch that makes out of Long Bridge Branch bounded by land the once belonged to Thomas Davock ... to a stake in John Hall's line ... corner of Joseph Cord's land ... swamp of Steven Revel's line ... to intersect with a line of two acres of land condemned for John Spencer, Esqr. dec'd to build a mill ... containing 588 1/2 acres resurveyed by Caleb Cirwithin at the instance of Henry Smith 23 Oct 1772. The other tract on northwest side of Long Bridge Branch called Kiliams Tract called Stone Folley, was originally granted to William Steward by warrant dated 15th of the 4th month 1718 and William Steward on 12 Dec 1738 assigned his right to said warrant to Jane Killamb and Elijah Killamb and Elijah Killamb sold his interest to said land to John Cord who died intestate leaving issue one daughter, said Mary Smith to whom the lands descended - beginning at a point about 20 perches above the old bridge being a corner of John Waller's land ... to a corner oak of William Reynolds opposite Solomon Dodd's house ... containing 140 3/4 acres, resurveyed 24 Oct 1772 by the instance of Henry Smith party to these presents. For £520. Wit: Boaz Manlove, Jno. Russel. 6 Nov 1772.

296. William Hudson, Sussex Co., farmer, from Benjamin Webb, Sussex Co. 4 Nov 1772. Parcel in the forrest of Cedar Creek Hundred being part of a larger tract surveyed for Jonas Webb by virtue of a warrant and said Jonas Webb by his last will gave the same to his son John Webb who died intestate whereby said land became the property of above named Benjamin Webb, 110 acres for £55. Wit: Jno. Truitt, Danl. Nunez. Within deed of sale ackn. 4 Nov 1772.

296. Ezekial Coston, from his father Benton Coston, Sussex Co., yeoman, for 5 shillings, a parcel in Broadkill Hundred being the northwest end of a larger tract granted to afsd. Benton Coston by proprietors warrant dated 29 March 1758, beginning at a corner of the land deeded by Benton Coston to his other son, Joshua Coston - 268 acres. Wit: John Waller, Rhoads Shankland. Within deed of sale ackn. 5 Nov 1772.

297. Benton Coston, Sussex Co., yeoman to his son Joshua Coston. For 5 shillings, eastern part of tract in Broadkill Hundred granted to Benton Coston by proprietors warrant dated 29 March 1758 - 2 acres. Wit: John Waller, Rhoads Shankland. Within deed of sale ackn. 5 Nov 1772.

298. Major Hudson, Sussex Co., planter, from Joseph Truit. Sussex Co., yeoman. 4 Nov 1772. Parcel in Cedar Creek Hundred in the forks of Long Branch laid off by Solomon Truit, dec'd., to his son Joseph Truit containing 122 acres being part of a larger tract running to a corner post of Benjamin Truitt's on the north side of Twilley's Road containing 132 acres which afsd. Solomon Truit bequeathed by his last will to afsd. Joseph Truit. For £100. Wit: Isaac Smith, John Bell. Within deed of sale ackn. 4 Nov 1772.

298. Stephen Mitchel of Somerset Co., Maryland, from Philip Cossey, yeoman, and wife Sary. 4 Nov 1772. Tract in Cedar Creek Hundred whereon the said Philip Cossey now dwells beginning at a tree in Cedar Creek Branch, 105 acres, resurveyed 21 Dec 1719. For £325. Wit: John Draper, Wm. Hazzard. Within deed of sale ackn. 4 Nov 1773.

299. Wm. McCay, Sussex Co., from Alexr. McCay, yeoman of Sussex Co. and Naomie his wife. 2 Nov 1772. Parcel in Cedar Creek Neck on the south side of Mispillion Creek called Pennington surveyed and laid out for 400 acres of land and marsh 8 March 1683 for Henry Pennington who conveyed it to Thomas May who by deed of gift conveyed same to his son Thomas May who by his last will devised same to his son Jonathan May who died intestate and the land devolved by right of inheritance to Thomas and Draper May they being the only surviving issue of Jonathan May, and Thomas and Draper May conveyed to Alexander McCay party to these presents 100 acres part of the afsd. 400 acres by deed. For £75, 50 acres of the afsd. 100 acres. Boundary runs to a post in a line of the whole and between the house where James Mitton now dwells and a house built by John MeCay. Wit: Wm. Hazzard, Isaac Wattson. Within deed of sale ackn. 4 Nov 1773.

300. Thomas Marvel, Worcester Co., yeoman, from James Reynolds, yeoman. Mortgage. 25 Nov 1772. For £25, tract that once belonged to John Pettyjohn and is the place where the said James Reynolds now lives lying in Broadkill Hundred. Wit: Robert Watson McCalley, Jno. Pettyjohn. Within deed of mortgage ackn. 29 May 1773.

301. Charles Draper, Slaughter Neck, husbandman, from George Reed of the town and county of New Castle, Delaware, Esqr. and wife Gertrude. 21 April 1773. For £632.8.2 Parcel in Prime Hook Neck. Beginning on Slaughter Creek being one of the corners of Mark Davis's land thence with a dividing line between said Draper and Davis ... to a post in the Hucklebury Swamp being a corner of the land of Nathaniel and Robert Young. 213 acres. And also that parcel of marsh in Prime Hook Neck beginning at a stake by Slaughter Creek ... to a line of Nathaniel and Robert Young ... 121 1/4 acres being part of that neck of land known as Prime Hook, to wit on 21 June 1671 granted by patent to Richard Perrot who by deed on 4 Jan 1672 conveyed same neck to Richard Perrott his son upon whose death the same descended to his son also named Richard Perrot who by deed dated 29 Oct 1718 conveyed same to Berkley Codd, Esqr. who having first granted divers tract on the south side of the said neck by his last will dated 29 Sep 23 devised the residue of the same neck to his wife Mary Codd who by her last will dated 26 Sep 1733 devised same residue to her great grandson Thomas Till who later in the month of Oct 1760 died intestate leaving Gertrude his wife and an only child named William who attained to the age of 5 years, 3 months and no more and on about 11 Dec 1762 died without having either brother or sister leaving the said Gertrude his mother his next of kin and to which the residue descended and Gertrude later married afsd. George Read. Wit: John Lyon, Theodore Morris. Within deed of sale ackn. 4 May 1773.

304. John Lofland, Senr., Sussex Co., from Wm. Winsley, Sussex Co., yeoman. 15 Sep 1772. Parcel in the head of Prime Hook Neck called Forrest on the north side of Lowbridge Branch one of the branches of Prime Hook Creek in Cedar Creek Hundred being part of a larger tract formerly granted by a Proprietors warrant to Thomas Lay dated 25 July 1741 called Primehook Ponds and said Thomas Lay conveyed same to above said Wm. Winsley by indenture dated 4 May 1748. For £55. Beginning at a corner post about 3 feet north of a tree in one of the lines of John Killingworth's land ... to a post in Absolum's Mosley's line ... to Joshua Turner's line ... 134 acres. Caleb Cirwithin, John Killingsworth. Within deed of sale ackn. 5 Nov 1773.

305. Nehemiah Field of the town of Lewes, pilot, from Cornelius Wiltbank, Broadkill Hundred, yeoman, and Rachel his wife. 4 Nov 1772. Whereas Cornelious Pluckoy alias Plooker(?) formerly of Sussex Co. was seized of two lots of ground in the town of Lewes, one of which is hereinafter particularly mentioned and described and so seized Cornelius Pluckoy and Judith his wife by their indenture dated 8 Dec 1693 conveyed said two lots to Cornelius Wiltbank grandfather of the above named Cornelius Wiltbank. And

whereas John Killingsworth late of said county was seized of a lot in the town of Lewes herein after also particularly mentioned and conveyed 1 Feb 1721 said lot to Cornelius Wiltbank as recorded in Book F No. 5, page 2-3. After the said Cornelius Wiltbank later died leaving issue, Isaac Wiltbank his only son whereas the premises vested in the said Isaac Wiltbank by descent and said Isaac Wiltbank died intestate leaving issue the above named Cornelius Wiltbank party to these presents and several other children. And whereas Joseph Millard who married Margret one of the daughters of the said Isaac Wiltbank dec'd. and the Orphans Court on petition a valuation was made on the land for £662 and Cornelius Wiltbank asked to pay the heirs their respective shares in order to take sole possession. For £47, contains in breadth northwesterly 60 feet and in length northeasterly 200 feet bounded on the northwest by the other lot above recited to be granted to said Cornelius Wiltbank by the said Cornelius Plookhey on the northeast by Lewes Town Creek on the southeast by a lot now the property of said Nehemiah Field and on the southwest by Front Street. The other lot contains in breadth on the said street 60 feet and in length to Lewes Creek 200 feet bounded on the northwest side thereof by said Nehemiah Field's lot on the northeast side by Lewes Creek and on the southeast by a lot late the property of John Miers but now of Nehemiah Davis, Junr. and on the southwest by said street. Wit: Jacob Kollock, J. Moore. Within deed of sale ackn. 4 Nov 1772.

307. William Davis, Sussex Co., yeoman, from Perry Prittyman, town of Lewes, blacksmith and admr. of Comfort Prittyman dec'd. who was a widow and admx. of William Prittyman dec'd. 27 Nov 1772. Parcel of marsh in the pasture of Wrixam White, Junr. near the wading place that leads to the Hawks Next containing 4 acres surveyed and laid off from a part of the same marsh which said William Prittyman in his lifetime sold to Jacob White. William Prittyman possessed of above described marsh died intestate and all his property was granted to Comfort Prittyman and she died intestate before she had past the accounts of her administration with the Orphans Court and commissary by means administration of the said Comfort Prittyman was granted to above Perry Prittyman who recorded the accounts of his administration 27 July 1772. For £5. Wit: Richard Little, Jno. Russell. Within deed of sale ackn. 8 Nov 1772.

308. Perry Prittyman, Sussex Co., blacksmith, from William Davis, town of Lewes, yeoman. 28 Nov 1772. Parcel of marsh containing 4 acres in Lewes and Rehoboth Hundred afsd. Perry Prittyman to said William Davis. [See above entry.] For £5. Wit: Richard Little, Jno. Russel. Within deed of sale ackn. 28 Nov 1772.

308. David Gray, Sussex Co., from William Burton, Broadkill, yeoman. 3 Feb 1773. For £74.13, 62 1/4 acres of marsh being the southeast end of 91 acres on the west side of Cool Spring Creek granted by a warrant to afsd. William Burton 12 Dec 1771 and resurveyed 8 Jan 1772 for 91 acres of marsh, 62 1/4 acres being bound as follows, at a corner post in Craig's line ... Wit: David

Hall, Joseph Hall. Within deed of sale ackn. 27 Feb 1773.

309. Henry Smith, yeoman, from John Clowes, exr. to last will of David Clowes, Sussex Co. 19 Feb 1773. Whereas David Clowes by virtue of the last will of John Clowes, Esqr. of said co. dec'd., was intituled to 1/7 of all lands of said John Clowes who was seized of as one heir to Gerhardus Clowes to 1/5 of said Gerhardus Clowes's lot and whereas said David Clowes ordered in his last will that if the remainder of his estate after giving sundry legacies was not sufficient to discharge his just debts then in that case his part of his father's estate should be disposed of to pay his debts and it was appealed to the Orphans court on 25 April last that his personal estate was not sufficient to pay his debts and therefore for £70, 1 1/2 acre was conveyed, beginning 10 feet below the Draw bridge together with the houses in which John Young now dwells, the logged kitchen, the small milk house and lowermost room of the store house and also was conveyed 1/5 part of 50 1/3 acres, being David Clowes part of Gerhardus Clowes lot of his dec'd. father's land which adjoins Hazzard's land. Wit: John Wilson Dean, William Burton, Within deed of sale ackn. 27 Feb 1773.

310. John Clowes, Sussex Co., mariner, from Henry Smith, Sussex Co., yeoman. 19 Feb 1773. For £70, 1 1/2 acres. [See above entry for same description.] Wit: John Wilson, William Burton. Within deed of sale ackn. 27 Feb 1773.

311. James Fisher, Sussex Co., yeoman, from William Burton, of Slutkill Neck, Sussex Co., yeoman. 4 Feb 1773. For £34.13, 28 acres and 130 perches of land and marsh being in Sluthkill Neck being a part of a larger tract formerly surveyed to Baptist Newcomb, beginning at a stake being the corner of the land late of William Craige, dec'd. now in the possession of Jacob Hazzard. Wit: Wm. Parker, Wm. Price. Within deed of sale ackn. 4 Feb 1773.

311. Samuel Rowland, Sussex Co., yeoman, from Thomas Rowland, Sussex Co., pilot. 2 Feb 1773. For £147.15, parcel of land and marsh binding on the northeast side of Pagan Creek and joining the afsd. Samuel Rowland's other lands on the southeast side and northwest side and afsd. Thomas Rowland's land on the northeast side and being part of a larger tract which formerly belonged to William Rowland of the same place, ship carpenter, dec'd. and being part of the land whereon the late dec'd. William Rowland did dwell and the said William Rowland for the love and affection which he bore his son Thomas Rowland and for the sum of 10 shillings he conveyed the above said parcel of land on 20 Jan 1763, beginning at a corner cedar post standing on the northeast side of Pagan Creek containing 49 1/4 acres. Wm. Lewis, Jno. Shankland. Within deed of sale ackn. 2 Feb 1773.

313. William Jones, Sussex Co., from John Stephenson, Sussex Co., yeoman. 24 April 1773. Parcel in Indian River Hundred being part of a larger tract granted to John Williams by the proprietor's warrant dated 20th of 6th month 1717. 112 acres,

the same surveyed 3 Aug 1724 as the property of William Waples who made over the same to John Stephenson on 2 Aug 1763. For £139. Wit: Alexr. Shankland, George Frame. Within deed of sale ackn. 24 April 1773.

314. Wm. Jones, Sussex Co., from Wm. Butcher, Sussex Co. 24 April 1773. Tract in Indian River Hundred being part of a larger tract taken up by the afsd. William Butcher, where John Stephenson's house now stands, containing 32 acres, for £11. Wit: Alexr. Shankland, George Frame. Within deed of sale ackn. 24 April 1773.

314. Nathaniel Bowman, mariner, from Thos. and Wm. Handzer, Sussex Co., mulattoes and yeoman. For £10.10, a parcel in Indian River Hundred of 350 acres it being the same where Nathaniel Bowman now lives, on the original grant that was made to Arrunadab Hanzer, mulatto, dec'd., reference being made to the patent granted being on the south side of Ivey Branch and bounded to the westward by the 1100 acre tract. 2 Feb 1773. Wit: Thos. Robinson, Newcomb White. Within deed of sale ackn. 3 Feb 1773.

315. William Parker, cooper, from Patience Jacobs, admx and widow of Nathaniel Jacobs who died intestate, of Sussex Co. 6 Aug 1772. Orphans Court granted Patience Jacobs authority to sell enough of dec'd. property to discharge his debts. William Parker for £111.10 is conveyed a parcel at the head of Monkeys Branch, the upper corner of the land sold by Nathaniel Jacobs in his lifetime to Reece Woolf, Junr. Wit: Phillips Kollock, Parker Robinson. Within deed of sale ackn. 3 Feb 1773.

316. George Read from Nathaniel and Robert Young, both of Prime Hook Neck, husbandmen. 8 April 1773. Nathaniel and Robert Young stand bound to George Read in the sum of £3200 conditioned for the payment of £400 on 25 March 1774 and annually up through 25 March 1782 and who confirm a parcel in Prime Hook Neck to George Read beginning at a corner stake on Slaughter Creek being the corner of Charles Draper's land ... stake by the side of the Huckleberry Swamp ... near Cattail Branch containing 842 acres. Wit: Mark Davis, Sarah Davis. Within deed of mortgage ackn. 4 May 1773.

318. George Read, of the town and county of New Castle, Delaware, from Mark Davis of Prime Hook Neck in Sussex Co., husbandman, and wife Sarah. 28 April 1773. Whereas Mark Davis stands bound to George Read for £1680 conditioned for the payment of the sum £400 on 25 March 1774 and £110 on 25 March 1775 and the annual sum thereafter of £110 through 25 March 1778 based on a debt of £840 have mortgaged their plantation and tract of land beginning at stake on Slaughter Branch about 75 perches above Bellamy's Corner ... to a division line run through Prime Hook Neck ... to a corner stake of Charles Draper's tract containing 461 1/4 acres; also the parcel of marsh in Prime Hook Neck beginning in Slaughter Creek ... to a corner stake of Nathaniel and Robert Young's tract ... containing 110 1/4 acres. Wit: Robert Young, Nathaniel Young. Within deed of mortgage ackn. 4

May 1773.

319. Samuel Rowland, Sussex Co., yeoman, from Mary Hammond of Duck Creek, Kent Co., Delaware, widow. 12 Oct 1772. For £90, parcel being part of a larger tract called Patent Burrow which Joseph Russel late of Chester Co. by Joshua Fisher his attorney conveyed to the said Mary Hammond by the name of Mary Potter, widow of Abraham Potter by indenture dated 13 March 1744 containing about 90 acres and about 10 acres adjoining thereto which she purchased of Jane Mark - being the same land which Enoch Potter son of the said Mary by his writing obligatory dated 20 March 1767 bound himself to convey to said Samuel Rowland. Wit: Rachel Pennington (her mark), Miers Fisher. Within deed of sale ackn. 4 May 1773.

320. Nathaniel and Robert Young of Prime Hook Neck, husbandmen, from George Read, town and county of New Castle, Delaware and his wife Gertrude. 21 April 1773. For £1848.15.10, plantation and tract in Prime Hook Neck, beginning a corner stake on Slaughter Creek being the corner of Charles Draper's land ... to a stake by the side of the Huckleberry Swamp ... containing 842 acres being part of Prime Hook Neck which on 21 June 1671 was granted by patent to Richard Perrot who by deed of 4 Jan 1672 conveyed same to Richard Perrot his son upon whose death the same descended to his son also named Richard Perrot who by deed dated 29 Oct 1718 conveyed same to Berkly Codd who having in his last will dated 29 Sep 1723 devised on the south side of same neck the residue of his property to his wife Mary Codd who by her will dated 26 Sep 1733 devised same residue to her great grandson Thomas Till who later in Oct 1760 died intestate leaving said Gertrude his widow and an only child named William who attained the age of 5 years and 3 months and no more and on or about 11 Dec 1762 died leaving the said Gertrude, his mother as next of kin as heir. Wit: John Lyon, Theodore Maurice. Within deed of sale ackn. 4 May 1773.

322. Thomas Purnal, Worcester Co., Maryland, Gent., from Benjamin Wynkoop, City of Philadelphia, merchant and Sarah his wife. 16 Dec 1772. Patent dated 26 Nov 1690 granted to Thomas May of Sussex Co. and Margret his wife called Spencer's Hall containing 500 acres. And whereas his wife Margret died leaving said Thomas May as surviving joint tenant who by his will devised the same to his son John May with the following words "I give unto my well beloved ... John May my Dwelling plantation and Land belonging to it and all other appurtenances ...," will dated 30 Jan 1725. And John May by his indenture dated 16 March 1737/8 conveyed same land to Abraham Wynkoop who devised same to his son Benjamin Wynkoop along with the land he purchased of the heirs of Robert Hart on the north side of Cedar Creek, the whole containing more than 1000 acres, and an island of marsh called the Island on the south side of Cedar Creek of 100 acres, this will dated 15 Nov 1753. This indenture: £861.18. Beginning at a post in a line of land late of Robert Hart now of William Bell ... land of Art Verkerk ... Blacks Bridge ... head of Mays Pond ... containing 507 acres and 149 perches. Wit: James Thompson, Nehemiah Field. Within deed of sale ackn. 5 May 1773.

324. Mark Davis of Prime Hook Neck, husbandmen, from George Read of town and county of New Castle, Delaware, and wife Gertrude. 21 April 1773. For £840, tract beginning at a corner stake on Slaughter Branch near Bellamy's corner ... containing 461 acres. and also that parcel of marsh in Prime Hook Neck beginning at a corner stake by Slaughter Creek ... to a corner of Nathaniel and Robert Young's tract ... to a corner of Charles Draper's marsh containing 110 1/4 acres. Being part of the neck of land known as Prime Hook granted by patent to Richard Perrott. [See above entry of Nathaniel and Robert Young for descent to Gertrude.] Wit: John Lyon, Theodore Maurice. Within deed of sale ackn. 4 May 1773.

327. Baptis Lay, Sussex Co., shipwright from Cornelius Wiltbank, Sussex Co. 5 May 1773. For £10, parcel on the southeast side of the Broadkill Creek adjoining Samuel Mountford's land and marsh which the said Mountford purchased of William Finwick, beginning at the north corner of William Fenwick's land and in the line of Samuel Mountford's land ... containing 18 acres of marsh. Wit: William Millard, Jno. Russel. Within deed of sale ackn. 5 May 1773.

328. William Draper, Sussex Co., from John Read, yeoman, and wife Martha, Sussex Co. 6 May 1773. For £264, parcel granted by patent to John Homes of Sussex Co. and by him conveyed by deed dated 8 Aug 1770 to John Read, on the south side of Mispillion Creek ... to a corner of James Black's land. 117 1/2 acres. Jno. Rodney, Jno. Russel. Within deed of sale ackn. 7 May 1773.

329. William Draper. Sussex Co., yeoman, from Elisha Knock, yeoman, and wife Margaret of Sussex Co. For £200, a part of a larger tract granted by patent to John Homes and by him conveyed by deed dated 2 Aug 1769, 128 1/2 acres to said Elisha Knock, bounded by Mispillion Creek ... to mouth of Walton's Gutt ... to George Black's line. Wit: J. Rodney, Jno. Russel. Within deed of sale ackn. 7 May 1773.

330. Laurance Riley, Sussex Co., yeoman, from Littleton Reed and wife Elizabeth of Accomack Co., Virginia. 29 Sep 1772. Parcel of 225 acres in the Broadkill forrest adjoining the lands of Edmund Read and William Tharp being the land whereon Benjamin Riley now dwells which land was the property of Smith Onley now dec'd which said Smith Onley died intestate and the tract became the property of his three children, John Only, Tabitha and Elizabeth one of the parties to these presents. Elizabeth and Littleton Reed having the right to 1/4 of the land, for £25.15. Wit: Wm. Conwell, David Train. Within deed of sale ackn. 5 May 1773.

331. Avery Draper, Caleb Cirwithin, Luke Watson, Jr., William Watson, Henry Smith and Luke Watson, Senr., all of Cedar Creek Hundred, owners of lands and marsh on the south side of Primehook Neck, of the one part and George Read of the town of Newcastle, owner of lands and marsh on the north side of Primehook Neck, of the other part. Their article of agreement. Whereas some doubts

have arisen between the respective owners afsd. as to the place where the line dividing the said lands and marsh through the Neck afsd. was originally run. Now for the quieting of those doubts and to the end that a dividing line may be fixed and known for the prevention of any controversies that might hereafter arise about the same these presents witness and it is hereby covenanted, declared and agreed by and between the said parties respectively for themselves that the said division line now is and forever after shall be continued deemed and taken to be as follows, to wit, beginning at a stake fixed on the marsh by the side of Slaughter Creek ... 13 Dec 1772. Wit: Mark McCall, Isaac Smith. Within agreement proved 4 May 1773.

331. Elizabeth McCay, admx. of John McCay dec'd. to Thomas Ozbun, ship carpenter of Sussex Co. 29 May 1773. For £146.2.3, parcel in Cedar Creek Neck on the north side of the Bever Dam Branch which proceeds out of Cedar Creek afsd. being on the west side of Robert Hart's land and on the east side of land that formerly belonged to Jonathan Hammond, Junr. and Robert Twilley containing 83 1/2 acres being part of a larger tract of 167 acres which land by sundry conveyances became the property of afsd. John McCay dec'd., beginning at a corner tree standing on the division line of afsd. John McCay and William McCay ... to a corner oak standing on Benjamin Wynkoop's line. Wit: Wm. Hazzard, Nehemiah Davis, Junr. Within deed of sale ackn. 29 May 1773.

332. Thos. Ozbun from Jno. McCay. A bond. John McCay, yeoman, of Sussex Co. is bound to Thomas Ozbun, ship carpenter of Sussex Co. for £292.5, 6 Oct 1770. That John McCay is to convey a tract of 83 1/2 acres it being one moiety or half part of 167 acres whereon said John McCay and William McCay now dwell on the north side of the Beverdam Branch which proceeds out of Cedar Creek on the west side of Robert Hart's land and on the east side of the land now belonging to one of the heirs of Thomas Hinds, dec'd. Wit: Wm. Hazzard, Azl. Spencer. Within bond ackn. 29 May 1773.

333. Petition of Elizabeth McCay, widow and admx of John McCay, Sussex Co., dec'd., who by a bond dated 6 Oct 1770 executed to Thos. Ozbun for the performance of a certain covenant ...[see above] she as admx wished to convey the land to said Thos. Ozbun. 29 May 1773.

333. Joseph Lindle, Sussex Co., yeoman, from John White, Sussex Co. 23 Feb 1773. For £30, parcel being part of the tract called Bashan on which the said John White now dwells in Great Neck and in the forrest of Cedar Creek Hundred of 100 acres, lying in the northeast part of the said tract Bashan being surveyed and laid out to him the said Joseph Lindel. Wit: Eli Parker, Joshua Dean. Within deed of sale ackn. 5 May 1773.

334. John Hickman, son of William of Sussex Co., from Thos. Smith, Sussex Co., yeoman. 29 May 1773. For £300, parcel in Slaughter Neck being part of a larger tract surveyed for John Nutter called Nutters Farms being the lower part of the said

tract containing 176 acres which was allotted to the said Thomas Smith as shown in the returns to the Orphans Court amongst the heirs of John Smith, bounded according to the survey and plat made 30 April 1767. Wit: Wm. Hazzard, Henry Smith. Within deed of sale ackn. 29 May 1773.

334. William Shockley, Sussex Co., yeoman, from Luke Carpenter, Sussex Co., planter. 26 June 1773. For £180, parcel granted by virtue of the proprietor's warrant dated 8 June 1737 requiring that 200 acres be laid out for Robert Lee in Cedar Creek Hundred at the head of Slaughter Neck and being on the northwest side of Primehook Creek Branch called Little Bridge Branch which land is called Grubby Plain being part of a larger tract, beginning at a corner post of the land of William Till ... 200 acres. And the said Robert Lee conveyed same on 4 May 1748 to James Carpenter who died intestate and the land devolved to his several children, the afsd. Luke Carpenter being the eldest male heir in place and having purchased his elder brother's right. Wit: Peter Robinson, Elias Townsend. Within deed of sale ackn. 26 June 1773.

335. Donovan Spencer, yeoman, Sussex Co., from Jos. Oliver, Junr., Sussex Co., son of Esther Oliver formerly Esther Spencer, dec'd. 26 Nov 1772. Two tracts in Cedar Creek Neck containing 140 acres, the one granted by patent dated 20 Sep 1667 to Richard Hill, the other purchased of Robert Hart and by sundry conveyances became the property of Joseph Spencer father of afsd. Donovan Spencer and the afsd. Esther, who died intestate and the land fell to his several surviving heirs and Esther being one of the said heirs did for the sum of £80 give said Donovan Spencer her bond to convey her right to the land and the said Esther Spencer later married Joseph Oliver and by him had one said son called Joseph, and she died without conveying said land according to contract. Wit: Wm. Hazzard, James Black. Within deed of sale ackn. 29 May 1773.

336. William Lofland, Sussex Co., yeoman, from Henry Killin, Kent Co., Delaware, yeoman. 3 May 1773. Parcel in the forrest of Slaughter Neck in Cedar Creek on the west side of the Lowbridge Branch adjoining a tract called Wilson's Folley which said tract was granted to Dormon Lofland by virtue of a proprietor's warrant dated 10 Dec 1740 who by his last will devised same, excepting 50 acres to his son Danilly Lofland which said Danilly Lofland by his attorney James Hemmons, his deed of sale dated 3 May 1770, conveyed all the afsd. tract except said 50 acres to afsd. Henry Killing for £50. Wit: Wm. Hazzard, Robert Cade. Within deed of sale ackn. 6 May 1773.

337. William Townsend, Sussex Co., yeoman, from Robert Waring, Sussex Co., yeoman. 5 May 1773. For £20, a parcel being part of a larger tract where said Robert Warring now dwells, beginning at a corner oak in Luke Townsend's field now dec'd. being a corner of said Warring's and said William Townsend's land ... 30 acres. Wit: John Clowes, Jacob Townsend. Within deed of sale ackn. 5 May 1773. 338. Isaac Townsend from Nathan Manlove, Kent Co. 21 June 1773. For £2 conveys the tract that Thomas Davis made over

to Mark Manlove, a grandfather to the above Nathan Manlove which
was taken up by John Otten who made it over to Henry Bowman who
willed it to his wife and child, containing 500 acres, beginning
at a corner maple in the line of Alexander Draper's land and at
the head of a small branch making out of the Beverdam of Cedar
Creek ... to the westward prong of the said branch where Purnel
Bennet's crossway crosses ... with side of the said branch within
the corner of the widow Lofland's field from thence along the
line of Pennington Patent till it intersects with the line of
William Wilson's Senr. then along the line of Thomas Davis' land
and from thence along the line of Charles Draper's Quarter and
from thence along Alexander Draper's patent line. Wit: Charles
Collings, William Draper. Within deed of sale ackn. 26 June
1773.

339. Dormon Lofland from Elizabeth Lofland, widow and extx. of
Gabriel Lofland. 4 May 1773. Parcel in Cedar Creek Forrest
adjoining the lands of Solomon Townsend and a survey made for
Charles Townsend which was granted by virtue of a proprietors
warrant dated 10 Nov 1740 to John Davis for 250 acres and by
sundry conveyances from the said Davis and his heirs the land
became the property of afsd. Gabriel Lofland who on 11 sep 1758
bound himself in the penal sum of £200 conditioned for the
conveyance of afsd. tract to Charles Williams who on 13 Dec 1759
assigned his right to the land to afsd. Dormon Lofland. Wit:
Henry Draper, Elias Townsend. Within deed of sale ackn. 5 May
1773.

339. Luke Clindaniel, Sussex Co., yeoman, from Jacob Townsend,
exr. of last will of Solomon Townsend, Senr. Sussex Co. 5 May
1773. Whereas Solomon Townsend on 7 July 1768 bound himself in
the penal sum of £48 to convey to afsd. Luke Clindaniel 100 acres
lying in Cedar Creek Hundred being part of a larger tract called
Bare Swamp and Solomon Townsend in his last will mentioned that
the land was sold to said Luke Clindaniel. The land begins at a
corner oak on Bennet's line. Wit: John Clowes, J. Russel.
Within deed of sale ackn. 5 May 1773.

340. Luke Clandaniel from Solomon Townsend. That we, Solomon
Townsend, Senr. and Solomon Townsend, Junr. are bound to Luke
Clandaniel, yeoman, to the sum of £48, to convey 100 acres [see
above] adjoining Stephen Bennet's survey and Thompson's Ridge.
Wit: George Morris, Eunice Morris, Wm. Townsend, Jacob Townsend.
Within bond was proved 5 May 1773.

341. Petition of Jacob Townsend exrs. of Solomon Townsend [to
convey above described land to Luke Clandaniel]. 5 May 1773.

341. John Wilson Dean, Sussex Co., farmer, from John Clowes,
Sussex Co., mariner. 5 May 1773. Parcel in Broadkill Hundred
beginning at a corner oak standing on the north side of a mill
pond being a corner of land called Talbert containing 111 acres,
the same being part of a tract called Carlisle's Mill Tract which
said 111 acres was by deed of gift from Charles Perry in his
lifetime granted to his daughter Margret Cale the wife of Thomas

Cale and they mortgaged said land to the trustees of the General
Loan Office of Sussex Co. and the land was sold to John Clowes by
the high sheriff and said John Clowes by his deed conveyed the
same to Richard Blackford who by deed of sale dated 13 May 1763
conveyed the same to Baptis Newcomb who by his deed of sale dated
2 Nov 1764 conveyed same to John Clowes party to these presents.
Wit: Jno. Russel, Thomas Grove. Within deed of sale ackn. 5 May
1773.

342. Micajah Truit, Sussex Co., yeoman, from Mary Annet, admx of
estate of Esabella Annet, Sussex Co. dec'd.   31 July 1773.
Whereas said Isabell Annet has title to a tract in the Broadkill
Hundred adjoining the lands of Isaac Jones, Robert Stephenson,
Samuel Hevelo, John Ponder and John Wilson Dean containing 220
acres part of which (about 94 acres) became the property of said
Isabella Annet by virtue of her father William Stephenson's last
will and the other part of about 126 acres being part of a larger
tract called Jersey Tract but originally called Strechers Hall by
sundry conveyances also became the property of said Isabella
Annet as followeth: Henry Strecher the original taker up by his
deed of sale dated 5 March 1694 conveyed the whole tract of 500
acres to James Stanford and James Thomas jointly - and Francis
Chads exr. of James Stanford conveyed 1/2 of the land to afsd.
James Thomas and said James Thomas dying intestate the land (500
acres) descended to his brother Micah Thomas who died intestate
and the land descended to his four daughters, Ann, Grace, Mary
and Elizabeth. Mary with her husband William Barrett by their
deed dated 5 Aug 1756 conveyed 1/4 part of land to John Annet who
died intestate and the land was sold to pay his debts to John
Clowes who conveyed same to Isabella Annet who died intestate and
Mary Annet admx. of Isabell Annet sold 116 acres of the land for
£59. Beginning at a stake on the south line of Strechers Hall
tract being a corner of Isaac Jones' land ... wit: Hap Hazzard,
Peter Robinson. Within deed of sale ackn. 31 July 1773.

343. William Johnson, Sussex Co., from Samuel Jump, Sussex Co.,
shop joiner. 15 May 1773. A warrant was granted to Philip
Wastcoat dated 23 Sep 1741 and said Wastcoat assigned said
warrant on 25 Jan 1743/4 to Thomas Bryan who the next day
surveyed a tracrt in Indian River forrest on the southwest side
of Harefield Branch on the county road on which the mill of the
late Andrus Simpler stands, on Gilbert Neck, being part of
Rosemerry Neck, on both sides of the county road but mostly on
the southwest side. 212 acres. Wit: Ann Shankland, Rhoads
Shankland. Within deed of sale ackn. 15 May 1773.

344. Noble Lewis from Nathaniel Bailey, Sussex Co., husbandman,
and Jean his wife; John Shankland of the town of Lewes, mariner,
and Sarah his wife; James Davison of the City of Philadelphia,
mariner (by virtue of a power of attorney from the said James
Davison to Mary Davison his wife dated 27 April 1773). Whereas
John Simonton late of Lewes Town, cordwainer, died seized of a
messuage and parcels of land in the town afsd. having made his
last will dated 29 May 1751 whereby he devised the house wherein
he then lived with a parcel of land adjoining called a garden to

his only son John Simonton who on or about 10 Aug 1761 died
intestate and without issue leaving four sisters, Jean, Sarah and
Mary, party to these presents and Elizabeth. And whereas
Elizabeth married Noble Lewis of the town of Lewes, cordwainer.
For £30. 27 May 1773. Wit: Wrx. Lewis, Henry Fisher. Within
deed of release ackn. 29 May 1773.

346. Philips Kollock, town of Lewes, merchant, from Noble Lewis,
town of Lewis, cordwainer and his wife Elizabeth. 29 May 1773.
For £140, a parcel adjoining the town of Lewes, beginning at a
post standing on the north side of Pagan Creek thence along
Middle Second or Market Street ... to a stake dividing this
property and that late of Cornelius Wiltbank ... containing 12
acres. Being the same that belonged to John Simonton and
descended to his four sisters and three of the sisters, Jean,
Sarah and Mary and their husbands released same on 27 May 1773 to
Noble Lewis. [See above entry.] Wit: Henry Fisher, J: Moore.
Within deed of sale ackn. 29 May 1773.

347. Moses Allin, town of Lewes, pilot, from Cornelius Wiltbank
of Broadkill Hundred, yeoman and wife Rachel. 4 Aug 1772.
Whereas Cornelius Pluckoo formerly of Sussex Co. was seized of
two lots in the town of Lewes and he and his wife Judith by their
indenture dated 8 Dec 1693 conveyed their two lots to Cornelius
Wiltbank, grandfather of the above named Cornelius Wiltbank and
said Cornelius Wiltbank died leaving issue, Isaac Wiltbank his
only son by reason whereof the premisses vested in the said Isaac
by descent and said Isaac died intestate leaving issue the above
named Cornelius Wiltbank party to these presents and several
other children and whereas Joseph Millard who married Margret one
of the daughters of the said Isaac Wiltbank at an Orphans Court 5
Aug last preferred a petition asking for a division of the land
and the court determined that the land would no bear division and
made a valuation and said Cornelius paid the other children the
amount valued. The lots beginning at a corner stone of a lot of
Nehemiah Field bought of the afsd. Cornelius Wiltbank being on
the northeast side of Front Street ... containing 1200 square
feet. Wit: Wrx. Lewis, Thos. Gray. Within deed of sale ackn. 4
Aug 1773.

348. John Cary, Sussex Co., from Brittingham Hill and wife Naomi
of Worcester Co, Maryland. 27 Feb 1773. Parcel whereof Michael
Godwin possessed which by his last will he devised to his
daughter, the afsd. Naomi Hill, beginning at a corner oak
standing on the east side of Long Bridge Branch near the wadding
place where the county road crosses said branch on the north side
of said road .. containing 100 acres. For £62.10. Wit: Thos.
Robinson, Burton Robinson. Within deed of sale ackn. 4 Aug 1773.

349. William Jones, Sussex Co., yeoman, from Burton Prittyman,
Sussex Co., yeoman. 24 Sep 1773. Tract in Indian River Hundred
granted by warrant dated 16 Sep 1748 to William Prittyman father
of Burton Prittyman which William Prittyman by his last will
devised to his son afsd. Burton Prittyman. For £27. Beginning
at a corner stake of Jones' land bought of John Stevenson ...

containing 54 acres. Wit: Thos. Robinson, Junr., Isaac Smith.
Within deed of sale ackn. 25 Sep 1773.

350. James Read, Broadkill Hundred, yeoman, from Elizabeth
Godwin of Worcester Co., Maryland. 28 Aug 1773. For £60. Parcel
in Broadkill Hundred adjoining lands in the possession of
Richardson Cade which said Cade purchased of Purnal Johnson,
Junr., part of a larger tract surveyed for Gilbert Marriner,
dec'd., by virtue of a proprietors warrant dated 21st of 12th
month 1714, surveyed 17th April 1716 for 200 acres. [Boundary
intersects Pembertons Branch.] Wit: George Frame, Wm. Holland.
Within deed of sale ackn. 8 Aug 1773.

351. Thos. Laverty, Sussex Co., yeoman, from Samuel Shankland,
iron master, Sussex Co. 5 Aug 1773. Parcel being a part of a
larger tract surveyed and laid out for William Lofland by virtue
of a proprietors warrant granted said Lofland and Thomas Hemond
which tract is called the Fork Roads and contains 106 acres. For
£100. Wit: Charles Polk, Junr., Rhodes Shankland. Within deed
of sale ackn. 5 Aug 1773.

351. Thos. Laverty, Sussex Co., from John White, Sussex Co. 3
Feb 1773. For £30, 100 acres being part of a larger tract called
Bashan surveyed for Warren Burroughs in the forrest of Cedar
Creek Hundred and Great Neck on the north side of the said tract.
Boundary intersects a line dividing part of the same tract to
George White and Joseph Lindle. Wit: Israel Coverdall, Charles
Polk, Junr. Within deed of sale ackn. 5 Aug 1773.

352. Richard Coverdall, Junr., Sussex Co., yeoman, from Sarah
Loughland, widow and admx to John Loughland of Sussex Co. 5 Aug
1773. Afsd. John Loughland died intestate leaving a tract of 300
acres in Cedar Creek Hundred adjoining lands now in the
possession of Absolom Warring, Solomon Townsend, Senr. and Junr.
and Wrixam Warring. The estate was administered at court 25
April last and found insufficient to pay dec'd. debts and
maintain his children until the eldest son should attain the age
of 21 or put them out apprentices and teach them to read and
write, whereupon the said Sarah Lougland admx. prayed said court
to order and allow her to sell part of said lands and the sale of
100 acres was authorized. Beginning at a corner post standing in
the line between Wrixam Warring and Solomon Townsend, Junr. ...
oak in the line of Absolom Warring ... to an oak in the line of
Solomon Townsend, Senr. ... containing 100 acres. Sold to
Solomon Townsend as the highest bidder for £24.10 who requested
that the deed be made to Richard Coverdale, Junr. Wit: John
Clowes, Boaz Manlove. Within deed of sale ackn. 5 Aug 1773.

353. Jehu Clifton, Sussex Co., from Major Poore, Sussex Co. 11
Dec 1772. Parcel in the forrest of Cedar Creek Hundred being
part of the maiden property of Mary Power widow of Nehemiah Power
and said Mary Power sold said land to her son Major Power.
Beginning at a stake on William Moor's line about 1/2 perch to
the east of an old corner oak of George Rickards' land ...
containing 100 acres. For £65. Reference to his dec'd mother

Mary Poore daughter of William Danielly. [The name is spelled both ways, as Poore and Power.] Wit: Joseph Truitt, John Truitt. Within deed of sale ackn. 5 Aug 1773.

354. Matthew Read, Sussex Co., from Benja. Miflin, City of Philadelphia, merchant. 6 May 1773. For £30, a tract which said Mifflin purchased of David Furman for 100 acres it being a moiety or half part of an undivided larger tract bounded by lands of the said Matthew Read, William Carpenter and by Sow Bridge Branch. Wit: Isaac Draper, David Firman (his mark). Within deed of sale ackn. 4 Aug 1773.

355. Thos. Tamplin, Sussex Co., from James Tamplin, Sussex Co. 3 Aug 1773. Tract in Indian River Hundred granted by proprietors warrant to Thomas Bryan, dec'd., who conveyed same to William Blizard who conveyed same to Ezekiel Jackson who by his writing obligatory obliged himself to convey it to Richard Tamplin but said Richard died before conveyance was made and said Ezekiel Jackson conveyed it to the heirs of said Richard Tamplin, the afsd. James Tamplin, eldest son of the said Richard Tamplin dec'd. A valuation was made on the land and accepted by Richard Tamplin. 119 acres. Wit: Samuel Dodd, Isaac Shelpman. Within deed of sale ackn. 4 Aug 1773.

356. Elias Townsend, Sussex Co., innholder, from Edward Strecher of the City of Philadelphia, house carpenter and wife Betty. 17 April 1773. Parcel of land and marsh in the bottom of Slaughter Neck being part of a tract and marsh formerly known as Bowmans Farms and the same fell to the above Betty Strecher by the death of her brother Isaac Davis, adjoining the lands of Nehemiah Davis, divided and laid out for said Betty Strecher on 18 March 1767 for 138 1/4 acres of land and marsh. Boundary runs by the side of a gut of the Loghouse Branch ... corner of a division line between Thomas and Nehemiah Davis [brothers] ... containing 138 1/4 acres. And there is a small parcel of land and marsh adjoining the above which also fell to the said Betty Strecher by the death of her brother Isaac Davis but is not part of the same patent as above but is part of the patent called Furlongs, laid off and divided to said Betty Strecher at the same time as above, 32 1/4 acres. For £250. Clear from any claim of John Snowden and his wife Sarah of the City of Philadelphia. Wit: Peter Robinson, William Davis. Within deed of sale ackn. 4 Aug 1773. [Another 28 acres is added to the above sale by annotation at the bottom.]

357. William Peery, Sussex Co., from Robert Fleming and wife Margret Fleming and Mary Hellings of Kent Co., Delaware; and Esther Campble admx of Nathan Campble of Sussex Co. 3 Aug 1773. Whereas there is a parcel of land in Broadkill Hundred called Coolspring Tract and whereas James Campble died being seized of the said land and leaving issue one son, the afsd. Nathan Campble and four daughters, Margret, Ann, Dorthea and Mary and the land was divided amongst them with 102 acres allotted to Dorthia Camble [described] and she died without issue with the land becoming the property of said Nathan Campble, Margret Fleming and

Mary Heklings, her brother and sisters. And whereas Nathan
Campble in his lifetime on 8 Aug 1771 together with Robert and
Margret Fleming and Mary Hellings, enter into a writing
obligatory in the penal sum of £100 conditioned for the
conveyance of his right to the afsd. William Perry and the Nathan
Campble dying before any conveyance was made. For £30. Wit:
James Vent, John Vent. Within deed of sale ackn. 4 Aug 1773.

359. Robert Fleming, Margaret Fleming and Mary Hellings of Kent
Co. Delaware and Nathan Campble of Sussex Co., are bound to
William Peery in the sum of £100 to convey a tract [see above
entry]. Within bond proved 4 Aug 1773.

359. Petition of Esther Campble admx of Nathan Campble, dec'd.
on 8 Aug 1771 entered into a obligation with Robert and Margret
Fleming and Mary Hellings, requests the court authority to sign
and acknowledge a deed of land to William Peery [see above
entries]. 4 Aug 1773.

360. Andrew Collings, Sussex Co., son of Andrew Collings of
Worcester Co., Maryland, dec'd., from John Clowes, Sussex Co.,
mariner. 4 Aug 1773. Whereas the said John Clowes in
partnership with Benjamin Miflin and John Jones, purchased in
Sussex Co. sundry tracts and parcels of land in the Broadkill
forrest and from a number of different people which were conveyed
to them in three equal parts to be divided and afterwards they
had their land surveyed by one general survey together with some
vacant land contiguous with the whole containing 4440 acres
called the Five Knatch'd Survey and dated May 1764 which said
survey was divided between them by a line, beginning at a post in
the horse savannah ... to Prittyman Day's line. Being the most
northern part of the said Clowe's part of the said Five Knatch'd
Survey which Andrew Collings devised by his last will to his son
Andrew Collings - for £100. Wit: Burton Waples, George Kollock.
Within deed of sale ackn. 4 Aug 1773.

361. Mitchel Jackson, Sussex Co., from Thos. and Peter Robinson,
Sussex Co., merchants. 4 Aug 1774 [1773?]. For £45, a parcel on
the north side of Indian River in Indian River Hundred at the
head of said river being part of a tract taken up by a
proprietor's warrant granted to William Carey who assigned same
to said Thomas and Peter Robinson, 100 acres. Wit: Luke Shield,
Parker Robinson. Within deed of sale ackn. 4 Aug 1773.

361. Eli Parker, Sussex Co., yeoman, from Mary Coverdale, extx.
of last will of John Coverdale, Sussex Co. 3 Aug 1773. At the
time of his death John Coverdale was held bound to John Johnson
to convey a tract of land, bound in the sum of £160 and whereas
John Johnson on 24 Feb 1761 assigned the obligation to James
Ingram who on 19 Oct 1762 assigned to William Paswaters who also
on 24 Dec 1763 assigned same to Levin Crapper who assigned same
to Eli Parker on 25 Feb 1765. For £60. The tract was in Cedar
Creek Hundred surveyed by virtue of a warrant dated 25 July 1758,
granted to John Coverdale as afsd. dec'd., 200 acres that lyeth
on the north side of a division line of the survey. Wit: Jno.

Russel, Woodman Stockley. Within deed of sale ackn. 4 Aug 1773.

362. Jno. Coverdale, Senr., to Jno. Johnson. A bond. 12 March 1739 [See above entry.] To convey tract in Cedar Creek Hundred of 200 acres adjoining land of Samuel Truit and Eli Parker and William Lofland. Wit: Richard Coverdall, Israel Coverdall. Within bond proved 4 May 1773.

363. Petition of Mary Coverdale [to convey above tract to Eli Parker].

364. Alexr. Draper, Junr. Sussex Co., merchant, from David Thornton, Sussex Co., yeoman. 4 Aug 1773. Parcel in Cedar Creek in Slaughter Neck formerly surveyed for John Nickson, for £16.5. Boundary runs to an original line of Robert Twilley's land ... containing 16 acres. Wit: Elia Mason, Isaac Watson. Within deed of sale ackn. 4 Aug 1773.

364. Thos. and Peter Robinson, Sussex Co., merchants, from Jacob Burton, Worcester Co., Maryland, house carpenter and joiner, for £32.10. A parcel of Joshua Burton who died intestate in Indian River Hundred, 270 acres, originally granted to William Kinning by the court of Sussex 11 April 1682 and surveyed for 300 acres and confirmed by patent granted 26 March 1684. William Kinning conveyed part of the land to George Young by deed of sale dated 17 Sep 1683. Cornelius Wiltbank and Jane his wife, admx of Isaac Bound, obtained a judgment against the estate of George Young and on 4 Sep 1704 assigned the said Judgment to William Burton who caused the land to be sold by the sheriff who sold the same to William Burton by deed dated 17 Aug 1705, from the sheriff, Luke Watson, as 217 acres. And also William Burton by another purchase from Kinning of a small dividend and William Burton by his last will devised at the residuary part of his real estate to afsd. Joshua Burton the said land and Joshua Burton having died intestate and left issue viz., William Burton, Jacob Burton, Ann the wife of John Winget and Sarah Burton. 3 Aug 1773. Wit: Jesse Townsend, John Brereton. Within deed of sale ackn. 4 Aug 1773.

365. Heirs and legal representatives of John Lofland, Junr., to wit, Weightman Loughland, Purnal Lofland, Isaac Lofland and Avis Lofland, minors, and Sarah Lofland, widow of said John Lofland, from Dorman Lofland, Sussex Co., yeoman. 4 Aug 1773. Whereas John Lofland on 9 Feb 1763 purchased of afsd. Dorman Lofland, 250 acres in the forrest of Cedar Creek Hundred for which he paid £100, and died before a conveyance was made. That parcel bounded by the lands of Solomon Townsend, dec'd. and a survey made for Charles Townsend now in the possession of Dennis Morris and lands now in the possession Wrixam Warring which said tract was formerly surveyed for John Davis and is now in the hands of the heirs of afsd. John Lofland, containing 250 acres. Wit: John Clowes, Rhoads Shankland. Within deed of sale ackn. 4 Aug 1773.

366. John Clowes, mariner, Sussex Co., from John Young and Catharine his wife; John Sheldon Dormon and Mary his wife; and

Lydia Conwell; of Sussex Co. 29 July 1773. Whereas John Clowes, Esqr. Sussex Co., dec'd., by his last will devised all his lands within the county afsd. to his seven children, William, John, David, Gerhardus, Catharine, Mary and Lydia, equally and whereas Gerhardus Clowes one of the afsd. seven children died without issue his rights became the property of his surviving brothers and sisters. Lot number 4 containing 51 2/3 acres became the property of afsd. Gerhardus Clowes [described], being part of Rickards Place commonly called the Near Plantation; lot number 6 became the right of Mary Dorman wife of John Sheldon Dormon; lot number 3 of 51 1/3 acres, part of the afsd. Bridge Plantation, became the property of afsd. Lydia Conwell now a widow [described]. Now said John Young and Catharine Young his wife for £12.10 assign their rights to lot number 4. Wit: Wm. Conwell, Boaz Manlove. Within deed of sale ackn. 4 Aug 1773.

368. George Cowan, Sussex Co., from Mary Wynkoop of New Castle Co., Delaware, widow; Phebe Vining of the town of Dover, Kent Co.; and Benjamin Wynkoop of the City of Philadelphia, merchant; the said Mary, Phebe and Benjamin being the surviving exrs. of the last will of Abraham Wynkoop. 6 July 1773. For £250, a tract in Cedar Creek Hundred beginning at a stake standing in the new manor line ... near the line of William Hazzard's land ... binding with Thomas Cary's land and land of Benjamin Truit ... 250 acres being the same, being part of the overplus land contained in the tracts called Pathalia and Cyprus Hall granted by virtue of a warrant dated 10 Oct 1744 ... besides the overplus to Edward Evans and Rebeckah his wife and Elizabeth Clark in right of Daniel Leah called Pathalia and the other in right of Thomas Bowstock called Cyprus Hall by indenture dated 1 March 1745 released to Abraham Wynkoop who by will dated 15 Nov 1753 bequeathed divers legacies to his daughters and devising several parts of his lands to his two sons, Thomas and Benjamin Wynkoop with all other lands in Kent and Sussex Counties to be sold. And Edward Evans and Rebecca his wife and Elizabeth Clark on 20 Jan 1765 confirmed to Joshua Fisher and Abraham Wynkoop and others by a letter of attorney to sell the land and accordingly the land was sold to George Cowan. Wit: James Thompson, John Woods. Within deed of sale ackn. 5 Aug 1773.

370. John Draper, Sussex Co., from Miers Fisher of the City of Philadelphia, attorney at law. 1 June 1773. For £140.11, a parcel in Cedar Creek Hundred being part of a larger tract called Pathalia and Cyprus Hall formerly belonging to Abraham Wynkoop, Esqr., dec'd. beginning at a post standing in the line of a tract called Farmers Delight ... to a post in the line of Benjamin Truit's land ... by the land lately sold by the exrs. of said Abraham Wynkoop to George Cowan [see above]. Containing 98 acres and 100 perches. Wit: James Thompson, Charles Logan. Within deed of sale ackn. 27 Nov 1773.

371. John Stockley, Sussex Co., carpenter, from Peter Robinson, Sussex Co., miller. 24 Sep 1773. For £187, 197 1/4 acres beginning at a corner stake in the line of Benjamin West's land ... being part of a larger tract called Blacksmiths Hall. Wit:

Hap Hazzard, Jacob Hazzard. Within deed of sale ackn. 13 Oct 1773.

372. Barnat Vankirk, Sussex Co., yeoman, from Joseph Lindal of Cedar Creek Hundred, yeoman. 2 Nov 1773. For £35, a parcel in Great Neck adjoining lands of George White and lands of Thomas Laugherty, part of a larger tract called Bashan first surveyed for Warren Burroughs and later deeded to John White. 100 acres. Wit: Nehemiah Davis, Junr., David Train. Within deed of sale ackn. 3 Nov 1773.

373. John Plowman, mason, Sussex Co., from Robert Hart, yeoman of Sussex Co. 27 Oct 1773. For £15, a parcel of marsh of 24 acres in the bottom of Cedar Creek Neck it being 1/2 of 48 acres which John Hart by his last will devised to his brother Robert Hart, party to these presents. Wit: Wm. Hazzard, Pemberton Carlile. Within deed of sale ackn. 13 Oct 1773.

373. Nathaniel Gorden, yeoman, from James Gorden, yeoman. For £200, real property devised to him, James Gorden, by the last will of his father Thomas Gorden, two patents, one called South Hampton and the other Martin's Vineyard in Lewes and Rehoboth Hundred; also 100 acres of marsh and broken land taken up by John Coe adjoining said patents. Wit: J. Rodney, Thomas Grove. Within deed of sale ackn. 7 Nov 1773.

374. Sarah Gray alias Hinds from Barbary Hinds. A deed of gift. Barbary Hinds of Sussex Co., to her daughter Sarah Gray commonly called Sarah Hinds daughter of Thomas Hinds, dec'd., two Negro boys, Essex and Isaac. 10 May 1771. Wit: Joseph Truit, Aram Williams (his mark).

375. Avery Draper, Sussex Co., yeoman, from Isaac Draper, Sussex Co., yeoman. 26 Feb 1774. Whereas Henry Draper, of afsd. county, grandfather to the afsd. Isaac Draper, by his last will devised to his two sons Henry Draper and Isaac Draper a parcel of 124 acres in Slaughter Neck being part of a larger tract called My Fortune which was by deed of sale dated 18 April 1730 from Alexander Draper conveyed to afsd. Henry Draper the Elder, beginning at a corner post in Loghouse Branch ... to Long Point Gut ... ; also 50 acres adjoining the 124 acres likewise conveyed to said Henry by the said Alexander by his deed dated 20 April 1730 that runs to the line that was Henry Draper's land ... corner hickory of Luke Davis; also 5 5/8 acres adjoining the above and conveyed to Henry Draper the Elder from Luke Davis by deed dated 18 April 1730. In all 4 tracts of 220 acres devised to Isaac Draper by his father, Henry Draper the Elder and Isaac Draper devised to his son, the afsd. Isaac Draper, party to these presents. Wit: John Clowes, James Read. Within deed of sale ackn. 26 Feb 1774.

376. Peter Robinson's Recognizance as sheriff for 1773. Bond confirmed 2 Feb 1774.

377. John Maull from Samuel Edwards, Sussex Co., pilot and Mary

his wife; and William Maull, shipwright, Sussex Co., for £60, tracts or lots which John Maull, dec'd. father of the afsd. parties died possessed of one of the said lots on the bank of Lewes Creek. Beginning at a corner of Luke Whield's ... to land of Samuel Rowland ... containing 5 acres. The other lot is on Lewes Creek beginning at a corner of land of Joseph Bailey which formerly belonged to Jonathan Bailey dec'd. father of said Joseph Bailey. Wit: Peter Marsh, Moses Allin. Within deed of release ackn. 1 Feb 1773.

378. Benjamin Burton, Esqr., from Peter Robinson, Sheriff. 7 Dec 1773. Sheriff's sale of property of James Perry, late of Sussex Co., miller, in order to pay £72.14 which Benjamin Burton recovered against him - sale of tract of 130 acres in Drakes Neck on the southwest side of the Middle Creek of Rehoboth Bay, beginning at a corner of the lands of Benjamin West ... to a corner stone of John Stockley's land bought of Peter Robinson, being part of a larger tract called Blacksmiths Hall. Wit: Levin Crapper, Isaac Smith. Within deed of sale ackn. 7 Dec 1773.

379. Nathaniel Gorden, Sussex Co., yeoman, from William Bignal, Sussex Co., yeoman and Rhoda his wife. 27 Nov 1773. For £125, a parcel of 100 acres being part of a larger tract called Martain's Vinyard which 100 acres was devised to Mary Bell by Thomas Gordon her father and said Mary by indenture dated 2 May 1732 conveyed the same to James Stevenson who conveyed the same to John Bignal dec'd. who by his last will devised the same to afsd. William Bignal. The parcel begins at a corner oak by the county road. Wit: Jno. Rodney, Thomas Grove. Within deed of sale ackn. 27 Nov 1773.

380. Richardson Cade, Sussex Co., yeoman, from Edmond Read, admr. of John Read, Junr., Sussex Co., yeoman. 2 Feb 1774. Parcel in Broadkill Hundred adjoining lands now in the possession of William Tharp, Benjamin Ryley, Littleton Lofland and John Clowes taken up and surveyed for John Read, Senr. and by him conveyed to his son John Read, Junr. who by a writing obligatory dated 2 March 1769 obliged himself to convey 100 acres of afsd. tract excepting a right for John Read, Senr., to live thereon during his natural life, to Edmond Read, which was not complied with in the lifetime of the said John Read, Junr. and the said Edmond Read for a consideration paid by Richardson Cade assigned to him the afsd. bond. The parcel begins at a corner post on the northwest side of Piney Run or Branch ... to a corner post of William Tharp's land ... to a corner of said Tharp's and Benjamin Rily's lands ... to a corner oak of said Riley's and Littleton Lofland's land. Wit: Samuel Hand, John Clowes. Within deed of sale ackn. 2 Feb 1774.

381. Edmund Read from John Read, Junr., yeoman, bond, for £50, on 2 March 1769, binds himself to convey 100 acres to Edmund Read, except for the use of John Read, Senr. during his lifetime. Assigned by Edmund Read to Richardson Cade, for £25, 1 Feb 1774. [See above entry.]

381. Petition of Edmund Read admr. of John Read, Junr. to convey land to Richardson Cade. [See above two entries.] 2 Feb 1774.

382. Samuel Lingo, Sussex Co., yeoman, from William Stuart, Sussex Co., yeoman. 7 Feb 1774. For £62, a parcel in Indian River Hundred on the east side of a country road that lead from St. George's Chappel to the sawmill adjoining on land formerly surveyed for William Dyer, John Prittyman and James Davidson; the afsd. tract surveyed by virtue of a warrant to Alexander Read dated 25 Nov 1747 and laid out of 265 acres called Partridge Tract, part of which said tract lying to the eastward of said county road, by an order of the Orphans Court 16 Feb 1763 granted to Allin Read admr of the said Abraham Read, to sell at publick sale a parcel containing 175 acres, which parcel was sold to William Stuart. Wit: Hap Hazzard, John Woods. Within deed of sale ackn. 2 Feb 1774.

385. Jacob Kollock, Sussex Co., merchant, is bound to Samuel Stephenson of Sussex Co., planter in the sum of £200, 2 Jan 1765. To convey a parcel in the Broadkill Hundred adjoining on the northwest side to the land of Thomas Ozbon and to the southwest side on the road leading from John Spencer's mill to Lewes Town and the southeast side adjoining on the land of Thomas Scidmore [Skidmore] and on the northeast side adjoining on the round Pool Branch and now in the possession of William Pride, the same being part of a larger tract whereon Matthew Ozbon Senr. formerly dwelled which said part was devised from said Mathew Ozbon to his son Matthew Ozbon the younger and was conveyed from said Mathew Ozbon the younger to afsd. Jacob Kollock and since the conveyance there has been a warrant of resurvey on the tract. Wit: Elias Hugg, Danl. Nunez, Junr. Within deed of sale ackn. 3 May 1774.

385. Edmund Read, Sussex Co., yeoman, from Richardson Cade, Sussex Co., yeoman. 2 Feb 1774. Parcel in Broadkill Hundred adjoining lands now in the possession of William Tharp, Benjamin Ryley, Littleton Loughland and John Clowes, taken up and surveyed for John Read, Senr. and by him conveyed to his son John Read, Junr. and by the admr. of the said John Read, Junr. 100 acres which was by a bond from said John Read to Richardson Cade confirmed to said Cade, except for the use of John Read, Senr. during his lifetime. Wit: Samuel Hand, Jno. Clowes. Within deed of sale ackn. 2 Feb 1774.

386. Jeremiah Joseph, Sussex Co., from James Tamplen, Sussex Co. 29 Jan 1774. Parcel in Indian River Hundred, on the northeast side of Sockarockets Branch containing 250 acres which land was granted by proprietor's warrant to Samuel Blundel and then became the property of James Blundel son of said Samuel Blundel and James Blundel assigned the warrant to Richard Tamplen who died intestate with the land falling to his son afsd. James Tamplen at valuation of the Orphans Court. For £78. Within deed of sale ackn. 29 Jan 1774.

387. Charles Waller, Sussex Co., yeoman, from David Stewart, Sussex Co., house carpenter and joiner, and wife Sophia. 27 Nov

1773. Whereas John Jones, father of Isaac Jones died intestate with his land descending to his several heirs and Ann Crow one of the heirs, by the consent of afsd. Isaac Jones in whom was vested the right of all the other heirs to a dividend of land. Beginning at a corner tree of land formerly belonging to Absolom Little and on the north side of Broadkill Creek ... to a corner post standing in the line of land in the possession of John Hevelo ... to a corner of Bryan Rowl's patent, containing 44 3/4 acres. Whereas said Ann Crow jointly with said Isaac Jones by their writing obligatory dated 7 March 1763 obliged themselves to convey said 44 3/4 acres to David Clowes and the land was conveyed by John Bound Jump and his wife Jemima admrs. of Ann Crow, and Isaac Jones, to David Clowes. And David Clowes by his last will devised same to his wife Sophia who later married David Stewart, part to these presents. For £66. Wit: Richardson Cade, John Hazzard. Within deed of sale ackn. 27 Nov 1773.

388. Thomas Burbyge, of Worcester Co., Maryland, from James Tamplin, Sussex Co. 29 Jan 1774. Tract in Indian River Hundred on the southwest side of Caw Bridge in Rosemerry Neck which said tract is part of the estate of Robert West who by his last will left the same to his son Solomon West who conveyed the same to George Chambers who conveyed the same to John Tamplin and after the death of John Tamplin it became the property of Richard Tamplin, father of afsd. James Tamplin. And one other tract in afsd. Neck beginning at a corner of the above recited tract - which said tract is part of a larger tract granted to Samuel Blundel and after his death becoming the property of his son James Blundel who assigned the warrant to said Richard Tamplin father of afsd. James Tamplin which two tracts contain 175 acres and afsd. Richard Tamplin dying intestate, afsd. James Tamplin petitioned the Orphans Court which made a valuation which said James Tamplin accepted. For £123. Wit: John Westly, Jeremiah Joseph (his mark). Within deed of sale ackn. 29 Jan 1774.

390. John Lacey, Sussex Co., yeoman, from Mary Smith, widow, Sussex Co. 17 Nov 1753. Whereas by virtue of a proprietor's warrant dated 11 Dec 1735 for Samuel Johnson Green, dec'd., 160 acres on Swan Creek including two small improvements adjoining to the west side of William Prittyman's land in Indian River Hundred called Newport. Samuel Johnson Green died leaving only child, a son who has died leaving afsd. Mary Smith, sister of Samuel Johnson Green and only heir. For £40. Wit: Thos. Bryan, Henry Brereton. Within deed of sale ackn. 1774.

391. Reece Woolf, Sussex Co., yeoman, from Wm. Parker, Sussex Co., cooper. 4 Feb 1774. Parcel in Lewes and Rehoboth Hundred, beginning at an oak standing on the south side of the head of Monkey's Branch, the upper corner of the land sold by Nathaniel Jacobs to afsd. Reece Woolf, ... to corner oak of Albert Jacobs' land ... containing and laid out as 111 acres and 119 perches 29 March 1773. For £174. Wit: Jno. Russel, David Train. Within deed of sale ackn. 4 Feb 1774.

391. John Lewis, Junr., from his father, John Lewis, Senr.,

Sussex Co., yeoman. For love and affection, a house and 4 acres and 39 square perches in Lewes Town, being the same house in which said John Lewis, Senr., dwells, as shown in a sheriff's deed dated 7 Nov 1753 to afsd. John Lewis. Wit: David Shankland, David Gray. Within deed of sale ackn. 4 Nov 1773.

391. Bond in which John Lewis Junr is bound to John Lewis Senr. for £100. 5 Nov 1773. To allow John Lewis, Senr. and his family to live on and occupy the land where the said John Lewis Senr. now dwells during his natural life which land was conveyed to John Lewis Junr by afsd. John Lewis, Senr. Wit: Philips Kollock, Comfort Kollock. Inrolled 15 Feb 1775.

392. James Gorden, Sussex Co., yeoman, from Robert Jones, Sussex Co., yeoman. 28 May 1774. For £65, a tract in Broadkill Hundred it being part of a larger tract which was conveyed to Thomas Staton, dec'd., by William Shankland then sheriff, dated 3 Feb 1746 which tract being part of a larger tract left by will to his son Thomas Staton who conveyed same to John Mustert by deed of sale dated 1 Sep 1761, said land surveyed and laid off 13 Jan 1761 as 100 acres. Beginning a corner oak near the Mill Creek. James Thompson, Richard Little. Within deed of sale ackn. 28 May 1774.

393. Jonathan Cohoon, Sussex Co., husbandman, from Edmund Dickoson, Sussex Co., house carpenter and joiner. 5 May 1774. For £110, 100 acres, being part of a tract of 400 acres in Broadkill Hundred on the east side of Long Bridge Branch formerly conveyed to said Edmund Dickoson by Joseph Cord. Wit: Parker Robinson, Jno. Russel. Mary Dickoson, wife of Edmund Dickoson, for 20 shillings, releases her claim. Within deed of sale ackn. 1774.

394. Constant Marriner, Sussex Co., from Nathaniel Bowman Marriner, Sussex Co., Gentleman. 6 Feb 1774. For £25. Parcel on the south side of Love's Branch in Indian River Hundred, taken up and surveyed for Aminadab Hanzer as sundry conveyances handed down to said Nathaniel Bowman Marriner, 228 acres. Wit: Thos. Robinson, Benjamin Truit, Junr. Within deed of sale ackn. 26 Feb 1774.

395. Solomon Baker, Sussex Co., yeoman, from Jonathan Hammons and wife Mary, admx of George Carpenter of Sussex Co. 28 Feb 1774. Tract in Piney Neck called Cabin Hill which was by virtue of a proprietor's warrant granted to William Carpenter who by his last will devised same to his son afsd. George Carpenter who by his bond dated 21 Feb 1772 obliged himself in the penal sum of £50 to convey said tract to Benjamin Johnson, who for £20 assigned same to Jacob Carpenter who for £20 assigned same bond to afsd. Solomon Baker. Wit: John Clowes, Joseph Darby. Within deed of sale ackn. 6 Feb 1774.

396. Bond from George Carpenter binding him to convey to Benjamin Johnson, carpenter, a piece of land his father willed to him in Piney Neck 1 Feb 1772. [See above.] Wit: Nehemiah

Messick, Levin Messick (his mark). Within bond was proved 26 Feb 1774.

396. Petition relative to the forgoing deed and bond.

397. John Ingram, Sussex Co., yeoman, from Robert Stephenson, Broadkill Hundred, blacksmith. 1774. For £465, a parcel of land and grist and fulling mill thereon, part of a larger tract which William Stephenson, father of afsd. Robert Stephenson died seized of, on the south side of Sow Bridge Branch being the same land which James Stephenson, dec'd., conveyed to said Robert Stephenson by his deed dated 1 March 1768, recorded in Liber K No. 10, folio 314, 160 acres. And also a parcel on the north side of afsd. Sow Bridge Branch part of a larger tract where Burton Robinson now dwells, containing 2 acres. Wit: John Heavelo, Nathan Spencer. Within deed of sale ackn. 26 Feb 1774.

398. Edmond Dickinson, Sussex Co., from Charles Harriss and wife Mary, Worcester Co., Maryland. 17 Feb 1774. Parcel in Broadkill Hundred on the east side of Long Bridge Branch, 200 acres being part of a larger tract which Joseph Cord devised to his son Joseph Cord who with Jane his wife by bond were bound to convey to Benjamin Atkinson said land and said Benjamin Atkinson assigned the bond to George Green who died intestate and the 200 acres became the property of several heirs of said Green, Mary Harris wife of Charles Harriss and daughter of the afsd. George Green being one of them. For £15, the convey their right to the 200 acres. Wit: Abraham Harris, Isaac Chaise (his mark). Within deed of sale ackn. 26 Feb 1774.

399. Andrew Simpler, Sussex Co., mill right, from John Hall, Sussex Co. 26 Feb 1774. For £140, parcel at the head of Long Neck at the southeast side of Cow Bridge Branch on Sockerockett which warrant dates 16 March 1738, part surveyed 5 Dec 1740, finished on 19 March 1766. Beginning at a corner of land surveyed formerly for Thomas Walker ... to the main run in the mill pond ... containing 150 acres. Wit: Andrew McIlvain, George Bonnem. Within deed of sale ackn. 26 Feb 1774.

400. Jacob Hazzard, Sussex Co., blacksmith, from James Fisher, Sussex Co., yeoman. 25 Feb 1774. For £18, a parcel of 16 acres and 21 perches being part of a tract formerly surveyed to Baptist Newcomb in Slutkill Neck, beginning at a corner of James Fisher's marsh ... to an oak on Trumpeter's Island ... clear from the claims of William Burton of Slutkill Neck. Wit: Philips Kollock, John Chance. Within deed of sale ackn. 26 Feb 1774.

401. William Millard, Sussex Co., shipwright, from John Young and wife Catharine of Sussex Co. 25 Feb 1774. Parcel of land and marsh in Broadkill Hundred on the east side of the mouth of a gut about 5 perches from Broadkill creek or mouth of the Mill creek ... which parcel is part of John Clowes' dec'd. and by virtue of his last will descended to afsd. Catharine Young, daughter of afsd. John Clowes. 9 1/2 acres for £4. Wit: John Ingram, Wm. Dellaney. Within deed of sale ackn. 26 Feb 1774.

402. Lewis West and Joshua Richards from William Fassit and wife Elizabeth and daughter and one of the heirs of John West, late of Sussex Co. For £60, their rights to two tracts which John West died, seized of, intestate, in Indian River Hundred, one deed from Elizabeth Lewis dated 4 Nov 1747 and a deed from Alburtus Jacobs and Sarah his wife dated 7 Nov 1753, for one tract containing 200 acres and the other deed from William West dated 2 Oct 1765 for 180 1/2 acres. Wit: Joseph West, Danl. Nunez. Within deed of sale ackn. 26 Feb 1774.

403. John Hall, Sussex Co., from John Stephenson and Adonijah Little, Sussex Co. 15 April 1773. Tract in Broadkill Hundred called Hare Fields Folley granted by proprietor's warrant to William Coulter who assigned same to James Stephenson who conveyed to afsd. John Stephenson, beginning at Harefield Branch ... to a line of land laid off to Thomas Oakey ... containing 150 acres. And one other tract in Broadkill Hundred adjoining on the east side of above recited tract granted to Hugh Stephenson by proprietor's warrant who assigned 1/2 of his right to the warrant to afsd. Adonijah Little ... 41 1/2 acres. For £75. Wit: Hugh Stephenson, George Benem. Within deed of sale ackn. 26 Feb 1774.

404. Purnal Johnson, Sussex Co., yeoman, from William Russell, town of Lewes, carpenter and Jane his wife. 8 Oct 1772. For £10, a parcel being part of a larger tract called Hashold's Fortune, beginning at a stake in Hills Branch ... to a line between this tract and Samuel Hopkins' land ... containing 200 acres of land and branch. Wit: William Henry, J. Moore. Within deed of sale ackn. 6 Feb 1774.

405. John Hemmons, Sussex Co., yeoman, from Constant Marriner, Sussex Co., yeoman. 2 May 1774. For £93, a parcel in Indian River Hundred being part of a larger tract which Thomas Marriner father of the afsd. Constant Marriner died seized of intestate, 92 acres. Wit: Manlove Morgan, Robert Marriner. Within deed of sale ackn. 4 May 1774.

406. Stockley Waples, Sussex Co., farmer, from Joshua Richards, Sussex Co., cooper. 4 May 1774. Tract called Cheet on the north side of Indian River in Indian River Hundred between Stevens Creek and Southrens Creek containing 775 acres granted by order of the court of Sussex and laid out 23rd of 2nd month 1684 confirmed by patent dated 3rd of 9th month 1684 to Thomas Welborne of Accomack Co., Virginia who by his letter of attorney dated 25 Jan 1685 by deed dated 8th of 12th month 1686 conveyed same to John Barker of Sussex Co. who by deed of sale dated 8th of 12th month 1686 conveyed same to William Burton of Accomack Co., Virginia, Gentleman, who by his last will devised to his son Joseph Burton of Sussex Co. and the tract descended to William Burton, Sussex Co., yeoman being the eldest son of afsd. Joseph Burton. William Burton by his deed of sale dated 3 Dec 1734 conveyed same to William Prittyman who obtained a warrant of resurvey dated 20 Jan 1735 and the tract was found to contain 1750 acres, then called Honesty and William Prittyman by his last will devised part of same to his son Isaac Prittyman

dated 20 Feb 1743. For £30 by his deed of sale dated 1766 conveyed to Joshua Richards. This conveyance of 30 acres is for £50. Beginning at an older corner oak in the division line of land sold from William Prittyman, dec'd. to Thomas Waples, dec'd. Wit: George Frame, Robert White, James Barr. Within deed of sale ackn. 4 May 1774.

408. Donovan Spencer, yeoman, Sussex Co., from John Black, planter of Kent Co., Delaware. 2 May 1774. Parcel of marsh called Long Acre which Abraham Wynkoop purchased of the heirs of Robert Hart, the original patentee, and the afsd. Abraham Wynkoop sold the same to George Black who died intestate having several heirs and after the valuation of the land and after deferring to the widow 1/3 part, it descended to John Black eldest son of George Black who for £21 makes this conveyance. Wit: Wm. Hazzard, George Walton. Within deed of sale ackn. 4 May 1774.

409. Dennis Morris, Sussex Co., yeoman, from Elias Townsend, Sussex Co., yeoman. 3 May 1774. Parcel of land and fresh marsh in Cedar Creek Hundred bounded by the lands of John Loughland, Senr., William Collings and a plantation that formerly belonged to Gabriel Loughland and being the same place where Charles Townsend, dec'd. formerly lived containing 350 acres. For £100, being 2/3 of the purchase money of the afsd. parcel and the other 1/3 part being paid to Ezekiel Collings and Hester his wife. Wit: John Wiltbank, Danl. Nunez. Within deed of sale ackn. 3 May 1774.

409. Moses Wilson, Sussex Co., yeoman, to John Little, Sussex Co., merchant. 11 April 1774. Tract in Broadkill Hundred now in the possession of William Peery on the northwest side of Mill Creek Branch and adjoining the lands of Whitely Hatfield of one side and David Ranken of the other, beginning at a corner post on the northwest side of a branch being a corner of the 50 acres belonging to William Coulter, 150 acres, for £51. Wit: Thomas Blaids Wildgoos, John Taylor. Within deed of sale ackn. 5 May 1774.

410. Samuel Stevenson, Broadkill Hundred, yeoman, from Margret Kollock, widow and extx. of the last will of Jacob Kollock, Esqr., late of the town of Lewes. 5 May 1774. Whereas Jacob Kollock was seized of a parcel of land in Broadkiln Hundred, beginning at the Deep Valley near the going over place at Round Pool Branch ... to the main county road ... 100 acres bounded on the northwest by lands now or late of Thomas Ozbon, on the southwest by the county road, on the southeast by lands now or late of Thomas Skidmore and on the northeast by the Round Pool Branch. Jacob Kollock later procured a warrant of resurvey and some vacant land added and on 2 Jan 1765 he signed a bond in which he was bound for £200 to above named Samuel Stevenson to convey a parcel in Broadkiln Hundred adjoining on the northwest side to the land of Thomas Ozbon and to the southwest side on the road leading from John Spencer's Mill to Lewes Town, the southeast side adjoining on the lands of Thomas Skidmore and on the northeast side adjoining on the Round Pool Branch and now in

the possession of William Pride, the same being part of a larger tract whereon Mathew Ozbon, Senr. formerly dwelled which said part was devised from the said Matthew Ozbon to his son Mathew Ozbon the younger who conveyed same to afsd. Jacob Kollock. Wit: George Read, J: Moore. Within deed of sale ackn. 5 May 1774.

412. Margret Kollock's petition to convey above mentioned land to Samuel Stevenson. [See above entry.]

413. Nathaniel Bradford, wheelwright, Comfort Wright widow of Edward Wright, Micajah Truit and his wife Sarah, all of Sussex Co., spinsters, from Samuel Heaverlo, Sussex Co., yeoman. 28 May 1774. Parcel being part of a larger tract on the south side of the Bever Dam Branch and on the north side of the Broadkill Creek about 2 miles north from the Draw Bridge in Broadkill Neck, containing 160 acres, and also 25 acres of marsh at the bottom of Walker's Neck being the north side of the Broadkill Creek being part of a larger tract of marsh of 250 acres which marsh was by patent dated 10 Sep 1702 granted to John Hill and it descended to John Walton dec'd. and by his exrs.' deed of sale dated 29 July 1763 to Samuel Heverlo, beginning at the south end of the 250 acres of marsh. Wit: Jno. Russel, Sarah Shankland. Within deed of sale ackn. 28 May 1774.

414. Jno. Rust, yeoman, from his father, Jonathan Rust, Sussex Co., yeoman. 3 May 1774. For £18, a parcel bounded by Rosemerry Branch, of 8 acres. Wit: Ann Shankland, Rhoads Shankland.

414. Edward Craig, Rehoboth Hundred, farmer, from Wm. Stockley of Rehoboth Hundred, farmer; Elizabeth Stockley, Rehoboth Hundred, widow; Jacob Stockley, same hundred, farmer and Esther his wife. 4 May 1774. Tract being part of a larger tract on Rehoboth Creek of 24 acres which William Stockley in his last will of 14 May 1771 devised to his son Jacob Stockley his plantation "whereon I now dwell also the plantation which I purchased of Rhoads Shankland ... belonging after his mother's marriage if she should again marry ..." he paying to his brother William Stockley when he arrives at the age of 25 the sum of £25. And if his son Jacob should die without issue that then the land should go to his son William. And the afsd, William soon after died thereof seized. This indenture if for £30 for all the premises except the mansion house wherein Elizabeth Stockley now dwells, all being part of a larger tract formerly the estate of John Crew, Mary Deprey and Jacob Kollock granted to them by warrant of resurvey dated 12 Jun 1707 and after the death of Mary Deprey her heir John Deprey conveyed same to Sanders Darby and the same was afterwards sold by public vendue to Elizabeth Darby and conveyed to her by the sheriff and Elizabeth Darby conveyed same to said William Stockley, Senr. being the same plantation formerly conveyed by Ephraim Darby to said William Stockley by deed 8 Sep 1753. Wit: Wrx. Lewis, Rhoads Shankland. Within deed of sale ackn. 4 May 1774.

416. Wm. Fisher, Sussex Co., cordwainer, from James Fisher, Peter Fretwell Wright and Hannah Darby lately Hannah Fisher,

98

surviving exrs. of John Fisher of Sussex Co., yeoman. 25 June 1774. Whereas John Fisher on 2 Jan 1763 by his writing obligatory was bound to said William Fisher in the sum of £240 pounds conditioned for the conveying of a parcel of land in Lewes and Rehoboth Hundred on the north side of Montius Branch being surveyed by commissioners warrant to William White who conveyed same to Francis Woolf who conveyed same to John Dixon the Elder dec'd. and after the death of John Dixon the elder the land descended to his children among whom was John Dixon the younger against whom John Little obtained a Judgment and caused the said John Dixon's share in the lands and also the land which descended to him by the death of his brother to be sold and afsd. John Fisher became the purchaser as by indenture dated 2 March 1762. This indenture is for £120. Wit: J. Rodney, Reece Woolf. Within deed of sale ackn. 25 June 1774.

417. John Fisher, Sussex Co., yeoman is bound to William Fisher, Sussex Co., cordwainer, in the sum of £240, 2 Jan 1769, to convey for £120 a parcel of land in Rehoboth Hundred on the north side of Montius Branch [See above deed.] Wit: John Gumly, Tabitha Brock. Within deed of sale ackn. 25 June 1774.

417. Petition of James Fisher, Peter Fretwell Wright, Hannah Darby, surviving exrs. of John Fisher, to convey above mentioned land to William Fisher. 25 June 1774.

418. Avery Draper's discharge as guardian to James Carpenter. This day I settled with James Carpenter, Junr. and paid him his part of his dec'd father and mother's moveable estate, when distributed 3 Sep 1765 is £181.17.2 1/4 with interest of £29.6.7 1/2 to 18 Nov 1768; and by the 1/2 part of his dec'd. sister and two brothers, vizt., Mary, Henry and Benjamin Carpenter, their moveable estate - £295.3.4. 1 April 1769.

418. Avery Draper's discharge as guardian to Naphtaly Carpenter. His part of his mother and father's moveable estate when distributed 3 Sep 1765 - £181.17.2 1/4 and 1/2 of his dec'd sister and two brothers, £245.3.4. 1 April 1769.

418. Joshua Hall, blacksmith, from Peter Robinson, sheriff. 2 Aug 1774. A lot on the southwest side of the town of Lewes, 130 feet front and 100 feet back being the same that Finwick Strecher, dec'd., by indenture dated 12 Sep 1743 conveyed to Elizabeth Godward who later married Robert Gill who is since dead and the said Elizabeth married James Brooks and they by deed of mortgage dated 18 Jan 1773 to the trustees of the General Loan Office for £12 and James Brooks failed to make payment and the sheriff sold the land to John Rodney for the use of said Joshua Hall for £18. Wit: Daniel Nunez, Jno. Rodney. Within deed of sale ackn. 4 Aug 1774.

419. John Wesley, Sussex Co., cordwainer; from Elizabeth Hosman of the town of Lewes, spinster; Stockley Hosman of the City of Philadelphia, house carpenter and Hannah his wife; Joseph Hosman of Sussex Co., sadler. 10 May 1774. Whereas Daniel Hosman was

seized of messuage and land in the town of Lewes of 11 1/2 acres and 20 perches and died intestate leaving a widow the afsd. Elizabeth Hosman and issue, two sons and two daughters, namely afsd. Stockley, Joseph, Jane and Comfort to whom the premises descended. And said Jane married William Russel who is since dead. For £150. Beginning at a corner of Mulberry Street ... to a stone on the north side of Market Street and on the southwest side of Finwick's Street ... behind the Second Street lot formerly belonging to Philip Russel, Senr., dec'd., called a 4-acre lot, containing in both lots 11 1/2 acres and 20 perches. Wit: David Hall, Peter White. Within deed of sale ackn. 5 Aug 1774.

421. John Wiltbank from Stockley Hosman. Power of attorney [to convey his part of above property.] 23 May 1774.

421. John Plowman, bricklayer, Sussex Co., from Wm. Pierce and Sarah his wife, yeoman. 29 July 1774. Tract in Cedar Creek Neck binding on Manlove's Branch and on the north side of Cedar Creek and the land formerly of Benjamin Wynkoop now of William Bell and binding on the land now the property of Thomas Ozbon containing 15 3/4 acres being part of a larger tract that Jonathan Manlove sold to John McCay and the said Jonathan Manlove by his deed of sale dated 6 Nov 1766 conveyed afsd. 15 3/4 acres to afsd. William Pierce. For £31. Wit: Levin Crapper, Benja. Truitt, Junr. Within deed of sale ackn. 3 Aug 1774.

422. William Conwell, Esqr., Sussex Co., from Thos. Grove, Sussex Co. 4 Aug 1774. Parcel of land on the south side of Prime Hook Creek and on the west side of Little Creek which proceeds out of Prime Hook Creek being three pieces cut off by straightening the afsd. Little Creek with a ditch, 14 acres as surveyed 20 June 1770. Wit: Wm. Davis, Jno. Russell. Within deed of sale ackn. 3 Aug 1774.

423. Jonathan Downam, Sussex Co., bricklayer, from Thos. Dodd, Sussex Co., yeoman. 20 Nov 1771. Afsd. Thomas Dodd and John Fowler had by proprietor's warrant dated 15 March 1754 laid out for them a tract in Broadkill forrest adjoining lands of John Right and Solomon Dodd and said Thomas Dodd and John Fowler by their deed of partition dated 1 Aug 1765 divided said tract between them [described boundaries] Thomas Dodd received the eastern part. For £15, 106 acres. Wit: Solomon Parrimore, William Reynolds. Within deed of sale ackn. 3 Aug 1774.

424. David Thornton of Cedar Creek Hundred, yeoman of the first part; Ann Williams, Sussex Co.,,, widow of Rynear Williams, physician of the second part; and the heirs and legal representatives of James Draper of the third part. Deed of partition. 3 Aug 1774. Whereas David Thornton was seized of a parcel in Cedar Creek Hundred bounded by a corner post on the north corner of St. Mathew's Church ... laid out for 122 acres and 23 perches being part of the land which David Thornton purchased of Nehemiah Draper in his lifetime and David Thornton was bound to Rynear Williams to convey afsd. land and Rynear

Williams died before a conveyance was made but in his will devised the land to his brother, James Draper, after the decease of his wife, will dated 1 April 1773. For £280 the land is conveyed in accordance with the will. Wit: Jacob Hazzard, William Burton. Within deed of sale ackn. 3 Aug 1774.

425. Jas. Fisher of Broadkill Hundred, yeoman, and Peter Ft. Wright from Thos. Fisher of Lewes and Rehoboth Hundred, yeoman. 5 Aug 1774. An agreement involving land in Broadkill Hundred on the northerly and westerly sides of a line beginning at the Broadkill Creek at the mouth of an old ditch and running up the ditch to the fork of Abraham's pond ... to Parker Robinson's line. Wit: David Hall, Junr., Dormon Lofland. Within deed of sale ackn. 5 Aug 1774.

427. William Thompson from James Newbold, yeoman, of Rehoboth Hundred, admr. of Thomas Layfield. Whereas Thomas Layfield by bond of 3 March 1774 was bound to William Thompson, yeoman, in the penal sum of £340 with a condition that Layfield would convey, for £170, a parcel of land in Lewes and Rehoboth Hundred being a part of the land of Hinman Rhoads, dec'd. and laid out for the heirs of Francis Newbold. And Thomas Layfield died before the conveyance of said tract. 85 acres. Wit: Gilb. Parker, David Hall. Within deed of sale ackn. 3 Aug 1774.

428. William Thompson from Thomas Layfield. Bond. 3 March 1774. [See above deed.]

428. James Newbold. Petition [to convey above mentioned land.]

429. William Thompson, Lewes and Rehoboth Hundred, from John Newbold of Worcester Co. Maryland, yeoman, and wife Rachel. 3 Aug 1774. For £30, parcel of land in Lewes and Rehoboth Hundred formerly granted and surveyed to John Newbold, dec'd., for 200 acres. Wit: Gilb. Parker, David Hall, Junr. Within deed of sale ackn. 3 Aug 1774.

430. Aaron Irons, Sussex Co., cooper, from Peter Robinson, yeoman, Sussex Co. 2 Nov 1774. Tract in Indian River Hundred of 130 acres being part of the tract that was devised by the last will of Thomas Warrington to his son Joseph Warrington, dec'd., who sold it to afsd. Peter Robinson and as no conveyance was made in the lifetime of Joseph Warrington the same was made by Sarah his widow and admx. who later married Elias West, the tract being called Blacksmiths Hall. For £192.10. Wit: William Perry, Henry Neill. Within deed of sale ackn. 2 Nov 1774.

431. Parker Robinson, Esqr. of Broadkill Hundred and James Fisher, Broadkill Hundred, from Thos. Fisher of Lewes and Rehoboth Hundred, yeoman, and wife Alice. 24 Sep 1774. Whereas John Fisher in his lifetime was seized of a certain messuage and plantation and in his last will dated 8 Feb 1770 instructed that the land be divided by a line [described] and he devised all the land and marsh above the line to his son Thomas Fisher and in the event of his death without issue then the same would go to his

son James Fisher. For £320.15, 150 acres. Wit: Samuel Rowland, David Hall, Junr. Within deed of sale ackn. 24 Sep 1774.

433. Isaac Smith, Sussex Co., yeoman, from Solomon Knock (Nox), yeoman, Sussex Co., and wife Comfort. 27 Aug 1774. Parcel in White Oak Neck of 100 acres being part of a larger tract of 400 acres called Swan Hill granted by patent to John Street who conveyed it to William Clark who conveyed same to Thomas Fisher who by his last will dated 17 Nov 1713 devised same to his son Joshua Fisher who by his deed dated 7 July 1744 conveyed same to Gershom Mott who by his deed dated 6 July 1750 conveyed 100 acres thereof to Solomon Nock, one of the parties to these presents. 100 acres for £190. Wit: Peter Ft. Wright, Hap Hazzard. Within deed of sale ackn. 27 Aug 1774.

434. John Plowman, bricklayer, Sussex Co., from John Whealer, Junr. of Sussex Co., James Caldwell, Junr. and Mary his wife. 3 Oct 1774. Parcel in Cedar Creek Neck, part of a larger tract called Harts Tract containing 101 acres, beginning at a corner post of John Clindaniel's land and William Bell's line ... George Walton's line ... to a corner post of John Plowman - which land was recovered at May Term 1758 at a suit brought by William Manlove, Kissiah Whealer and Margaret Chipman against Joseph Hickman, 75 acres of which was deeded to afsd. John Whealer and his brother Jonathan Whealer by said William Manlove, Paris Chipman and Margaret his wife, being the property of afsd. Kesiah Wheeler who died intestate being in possession of the afsd. 25 acres which at her death became the property of her several heirs, viz., William Manlove, Mary, John, Jonathan and Margaret, the said William having two shares. For £143.10 and the said James Caldwell and Mary his wife for £12.5 paid by John Plowman. Wit: Levin Crapper, George Black. Within deed of sale ackn. 2 Nov 1774.

435. Edmond Dickerson, Broadkill Hundred, yeoman, from Joseph Cord, Broadkill Hundred, yeoman. 3 Nov 1774. For £20, a parcel in the hundred afsd. being part of a larger tract which Joseph Cord conveyed a part of to the heirs of James Stevenson. 44 acres. Wit: Willm. Davis, David Train. Within deed of sale ackn. 3 Nov 1774.

436. Robert Burton, Angola Hundred, from Philips Kollock, town of Lewes, Esqr. and Comfort his wife. 6 Dec 1774. For £237.18, a parcel in Broadkill Hundred granted by patent dated 15 Aug 1687 to John Finch called Finch Hall, beginning at a corner post in the end line of the dividend being a corner of the land surveyed and laid off to Margaret Kollock as her dower. 183 acres, surveyed 23 Oct 1772. Wit: Danl. Nunez, William Brereton. Within deed of sale ackn. 6 Dec 1774.

437. John Miller from Isaac Killo. 1 Oct 1774. Tract in the head of Slaughter Neck in Cedar Creek Hundred, beginning at an oak in the line of Morgan Williams' land formerly being the line also of Twilley's ... containing 88 1/2 acres being part of a larger tract of 205 and 1/2 acres which by deed of sale with a

common warrant dated 4 Nov 1752 conveyed by Robert Miller to
William Bowness who in his last will dated 14 Jan 1762 devised
said land to his son William Bowness who conveyed by deed dated
18 July 1774 to Isaac Killo, party to these presents. For £110.
Wit: Jacob Hickman, Elisha Bratton. Within deed of sale ackn. 3
Nov 1774.

438. Isaac Killo, Sussex Co., farmer, from William Bonass
(Bowness) of Westchester Co., New York, surgeon. 18 July 1774.
Parcel in Cedar Creek Hundred, beginning in the line of Morgan
Williams' line, also of T. Willey's ... containing 205 1/2 acres
which was by deed with a common warrantee dated 4 Nov 1752
conveyed to William Bowness, father of afsd. William Bowness,
from Robert Miller and the said William Bowness, father of the
afsd. William Bowness, by his last will dated 14 Jan 1762 devised
said land to his heirs. For £170. Wit: Benjamin Johnson, Joseph
Darby. Within deed of sale ackn. 2 Nov 1774.

439. John Collings, son of Andrew, Sussex Co., from Thomas
Willing, Sussex Co. 2 Nov 1774. Tract in Broadkill Hundred
granted by proprietor's warrant being in Broadkill Hundred to
Benjamin Salmonds and surveyed for 66 acres, called Willings
Chance and Benjamin Salmons assigned his right to Thomas Donoaho
who assigned his right to above named Thomas Willing who by bond
obliged himself to convey the land to Jonathan Vaughan and
Company and Jonathan Vaughan in behalf of himself and company
assigned said bond to Andrew Collings who by his last will
devised same bond to his son afsd. John Collings. Bounded by a
corner dogwood of Richard Samuels' land. Wit: John Dean, Henry
Neille. Within deed of sale ackn. 2 Nov 1774.

440. Jacob Hickman, Sussex Co., yeoman, from Margaret White,
widow of James White, Sophia White, Elisha and Esabel Breton of
Sussex Co. For £105, a parcel being part of a tract which Joseph
Hickman, dec'd. bought of Henry Bowman, dec'd. called Hickman's
Fields in Slaughter Neck, beginning at a corner post of James
Kendrick, dec'd. ... to a post in Hays' line ... to a post in
John Miller's line likewise called Twilley's line ... to James
Kendrick's line formerly Hodges' line ... containing 80 acres.
Wit: Hugh Brattin, Laban Sturgis, John Miller. Within deed of
sale ackn. 2 Nov 1774.

441. Robert Stevenson, Sussex Co., from John Futcher, Sussex Co.
2 Nov 1774. Parcel in Indian River Hundred granted by
proprietor's warrant to Robert Richards and surveyed for John
Tuchbury admr. of said Richards for 400 acres who by deed
conveyed 250 acres of said tract to John Prittyman who by his
last will devised same to his son Thomas Prittyman who by his
last will devised same to above named John Futcher which said
tract is called Hooks Norton and whereas there is one other
parcel in Indian River Hundred adjoining the above mentioned
tract called Strife granted by proprietor's warrant to John
Prittyman and surveyed for 250 acres and John Prittyman by his
last will devised same to his son Thomas Prittyman who by his
last will devised same to afsd. John Futcher who conveyed 60

acres thereof to Robert Prittyman and 20 acres thereof to Micajah
Houston leaving a remainder of 420 acres which is hereby
conveyed. Wit: Wm. Peery, John Collings son of Andrew. Within
deed of sale ackn. 2 Nov 1774.

442. Wm. Tharp, Sussex Co., yeoman, from Laurence Ryley and John
Ryley Exrs. of Laurence Riley of Sussex Co. 6 Dec. 1774. Afsd.
Laurence Riley, dec'd., on 21 Sep 1772 by his bond obliged
himself to convey to afsd. William Tharp 55 3/8 acres, being part
of a tract whereon Benjamin Riley now dwells and also to defend
the land from Onley's heirs, beginning at a post on the south
side of a road that leads from said Laurence Riley's to John
Clowes. Wit: Paynter Stockley, Jno. Russel. Within deed of sale
ackn. 6 Dec 1774.

443. Laurence Riley is bound to Wm. Tharp for £83. A bond dated
21 Sep 1772. [To convey above mentioned parcel.]

443. Laurence and John Riley petition for the conveyance of
above parcel to Wm. Tharp. 3 May 1774.

443. William Hill, yeoman, Sussex Co., from Robert Hill, Junr.,
Sussex Co., yeoman. 2 Nov 1774. Parcel in Cedar Creek Neck
being part of the tract conveyed by deed from Samuel Spencer to
Ebenezer Spencer, recorded in Liber I No. 8, folio 220, binding
with Joseph Richards' line ... 50 acres according to the survey
dated 23 Aug 1759, for £50. Wit: John Dean, Hap Hazzard. Within
deed of sale ackn. 2 Nov 1774.

444. Wm. Hill, yeoman, Sussex Co., from Joseph Richards, yeoman,
Sussex Co. 2 Nov 1774. For £14, a parcel in Cedar Creek Neck on
the west side of Cedar Creek being a part of an ancient tract
that formerly belonged to John Richards, dec'd., being that part
that lies on the west side of Bever Dam and binding on the run of
said dam it being that part whereon William Richards formerly
dwelt, containing 30 acres. Wit: John W. Dean, Hap Hazzard.
Within deed of sale ackn. 2 Nov 1774.

444. John Little, Sussex Co., merchant, from Moses Wilson,
Sussex Co., yeoman. 12 Sep 1774. Two tracts in Broadkill
Hundred on the west side of Mill Branch and by sundry conveyances
descended to Moses Wilson, Senr., dec'd. father of afsd. Moses
Wilson, conveyed from Richard Bloxsom deed dated 2 Aug 1769 and
by Moses Wilson devised to his son afsd. Moses Wilson. Boundary
runs to a corner of David Rankin's land. 200 acres. Conveying
as was the earlier intention April last but because of a mistake
it was not. For 5 shillings. Wit: Joseph Hosman, John Tayler.
Within deed of sale ackn. 19 Sep 1774.

445. John Little, Sussex Co., merchant, from Elijah Atkens and
wife Hannah, both of Angola Hundred. 22 Aug 1774. Tract in
Angola and Indian River Hundred being part of a tract called
Arcadia granted by patent to Richard Bundick. Running to Long
Love Branch ... Whereas Hannah Atkens wife of the above said
Elijah Atkens became intituled by her former marriage to William

Hazzard now dec'd. to a third of the above said land. For £12.3.
Wit: John Tayler (his mark), Mycakiah Handcock. Within deed of
sale ackn. 19 Sep 1774.

446. Hannah Holland, widow of James Holland late of Sussex Co.,
yeoman, from Peter Robinson, sheriff. 27 Aug 1774. Whereas the
trustees of the General Loan Office recovered a Judgment against
John Lewis the elder, admr. of Thomas Stockley dec'd. for £50 and
the court ordered that the property of Thomas Stockley be sold.
For £40, a parcel in Lewes and Rehoboth Hundred in Warrens Neck
being part of tract formerly taken up by Otto Woolgast, dec'd.,
bounding on a branch which divides this land and that belonging
to Jonathan Henry dec'd., containing 160 acres. Wit: J. Russel,
Woodman Stokley. Within deed of sale ackn. 27 Aug 1774.

447. Anderson Parker, John Wiltbank, Esqr., Isaac Smith from
John Prittyman, Sussex Co., yeoman. 6 Dec 1774. For 30
shillings. Parcel beginning at a corner post in the southeast
prong of the Bever Dam branch about 1/2 perch above the going
over or fording place ... 145 perches of land and branch.
Property to be occupied as a school house and no other use. Wit:
Dd. Train, John W. Dean. Within deed of sale ackn. 6 Dec 1774.

448. Joseph Griffith from Manuel Manlove. Bond. Manuel Manlove
of Dorchester Co., Maryland, is bound to Joseph Griffith of
Worcester Co. in the penal sum of £300. 20 Oct 1772. Said
Manlove to convey 350 acres in Hindes Neck, 100 acres of which is
contained in a Maryland patent the other 250 acres containing in
a Pennsylvania warrant to afsd. Joseph Griffith. Wit: William
Marrick, Sarah Marrick (her mark). Within deed of sale ackn. 3
Nov 1774.

448. Joshua Burton from Levi Robins. Bond. Levi Robins, Sussex
Co., ship carpenter, is bound to Joshua Burton, Sussex Co., for
£200. 22 Sep 1768. To convey a parcel in Broadkill Hundred
adjoining north the land possessed by said Levi Robins, south by
land Elizabeth Rowland, easterly by land of David Gray and Parker
Robinson, containing 50 acres. --- Comly, Pherabah Keary (her
mark). Within deed of sale ackn. 6 Dec 1774. Proved by the
affirmation of Pherabah Bar, late Pherabah Keary.

449. David Hall, Esqr., town of Lewes, from Jacob Kollock, town
of Lewes. 6 June 1774. Jacob Kollock by his bond and warrant of
attorney is bound to David Hall for £480.8.4 conditioned for the
payment of £240.4.2 on 13 July next. Now Jacob Kollock for 5
shillings doth assign to David Hall two small parcels of land in
Lewes Creek whereon said Jacob Kollock now dwells, 34 acres and
the other parcel beginning at a corner post formerly belonging to
William Clark, dec'd. standing on the bank of Lewes Creek ... to
a corner post of the land formerly Phillip Russsel's ... to Pagan
Creek ... 37 acres being part of the tract called West India
Forty excepting a small part thereof being 9 to 10 acres formerly
conveyed by Peter Hall to Joshua Fisher. Wit: David Hall, Junr.,
Joseph Conwell. Within deed of mortgage ackn. 8 Feb 1775.

450. Wrixam Lewis, Sussex Co., shipwright, from Mary Bryan, Sussex Co., spinster. A release. For £23.6.8, a parcel being part of a tract called Warrens Choice, which was conveyed by William Bryan and Ann Elizabeth his wife who owned the same by the way of William Godwin, father of afsd. Ann Elizabeth, to Cornelius Turner who conveyed 49 acres of afsd. tract being laid off in the southwest corner of the afsd. tract to Lydia Bryan, Jonathan Bryan and Mary Bryan, party to these presents. Wit: Henry Niell, David Green. Within deed of sale ackn. 2 Nov 1774.

450. Thos. and Peter Robinson, merchants, from Elizabeth Clarkson, the only surviving exr. of William Becket and also the surviving and sole legatee of the real estate of the said William Becket. 10 Feb 1773. Parcel of woodland in Angola Neck and to the westward of Rehoboth Bay called Woodland Grove, granted by proprietor's warrant to William Becket dated 15 Oct 1740 and surveyed 15 March 1742, for 73 acres. Wit: Newcom White, James Francis Baylis. Within deed of sale ackn. 8 Feb 1775.

451. Levin Milby, Sussex Co., mariner, to Nathaniel Milby, Sussex Co., house joiner. 8 Feb 1775. Parcel in Drake's Neck on the north side of Herring Creek in Indian River Hundred called Golden Quarter late the property of Nathaniel Milby dec'd., father to afsd. parties who died intestate. £135. Runs eastward of the northeast end of Benjamin Burton's Mill Dam. 108 3/4 acres. wit: Samuel Darby, Burton Prittyman. Within deed of sale ackn. 8 Feb 1775.

452. John Harmonson and James Martin, Sussex Co., from George Walker, Sussex Co. 8 Feb 1775. Tract in Lewes and Rehoboth Hundred which was granted by patent to William Trotter 5th of 5th month 1684 who assigned his right to the tract to William Clark who assigned his right to same to Francis Cornwill who by his deed dated 13 Dec 1727 conveyed same to Thomas Walker and whereas there is one other tract in the hundred afsd. granted to Samuel Gray and David Gray heir of afsd. Samuel Gray conveyed 300 acres thereof to John Roads who conveyed 100 acres of same to Robert Lodge who conveyed the 100 acres to afsd. Francis Cornwill and Francis Cornwill conveyed same to Thomas Walker and after Thomas Walker's death said land was devised by the Orphans Court on 2 March 1742 by division of the land laid off 232 acres to afsd. George Walker on the west side of the whole tract binding on Coolspring Branch who sold a part of the said parcel to Jacob White. 110 acres, for £165. Wit: William Peery, George Kollock. Within deed of sale ackn. 8 Feb 1775.

453. John Potter, Sussex Co., planter, from Thomas Grove, Sussex Co., Gentleman. 8 Jan 1775. For £416.16.6, a parcel that Major William Dyor was possessed of by virtue of the last will of Nathaniel Walker containing 1000 acres called Walkers Choice and said Walker was possessed of the land by virtue of a warrant from the "Whorekill at Deal Court," and Major William Dyer by his last will devised to his son James Dyer 300 acres lying in the fork of the Broadkill part bordering on the Bever Dam and to the eastward of Prime Hook Creek with 100 acres of marsh. And James Dyer by

his deed of sale dated 18 Aug 1725 conveyed the same 400 acres to Thomas Groves who died intestate and as the land would not bear dividing Thomas Groves the eldest son accepted the land. Wit: Dirickson Waples, Stringer Tilney. Within deed of sale ackn. 8 Feb 1775.

454. John Ingram, Sussex Co., yeoman, from Robert Stevenson and wife Elinor, Sussex Co. 9 Feb 1775. Tract in Broadkill Hundred adjoining other lands of said John Ingram, called The Point, 100 acres, beginning at a corner cyprus tree standing in Sow Bridge Branch ... to the run of Hills Branch ... to Caleb Cirwithin's mill pond ... which by several conveyances became the right of afsd. Robert Stevenson. For £32. Wit: John Watson, Nehemiah Davis, Junr. Within deed of sale ackn. 8 Feb 1775.

456. Thomas Marvel, Worcester Co., Maryland, from James Reynolds, Sussex Co. 28 Jan 1775. Tract in Broadkill Hundred, being part of a tract granted by proprietor's warrant to Richard Pettyjohn of Sussex Co., who by his last will devised the afsd. larger tract to his son, John Pettyjohn who by bond was obliged to convey 100 acres of this land to Nehemiah Reed who assigned the bond to above named James Reynolds before the 100 acres was conveyed. Beginning at a corner oak standing in the fork of the roads from Lewes Town to Evans' saw mill and Green Branch, 100 acres for £100. Wit: Ann Shankland, Rhoads Shankland. Within deed of sale ackn. 28 Jan 1775.

456. Andrew Heaverlo, Sussex Co., from Joseph Parmer, Kent Co., yeoman. 7 Feb 1775. Two parcels of land and marsh conveyed by deed of sale from Daniel Dingee to afsd. Joseph Parmer, the one of 16 acres and the other parcel of marsh containing 25 acres in Broadkill Hundred, by which a moiety or 1/2 was conveyed, being part of Knight Howard, dated Feb 1768. For £18.15. Wit: William Millard, Rhoads Shankland. Within deed of sale ackn. 8 Feb 1775.

457. Stephen Townsend, Sussex Co., yeoman, from Alexander Draper and wife Rachel. 30 Jan 1775. Parcel being part of a tract called Little Buttin that Stephen Townsend the elder willed to his son William Townsend who died intestate leaving three daughters, one being Rachel the now wife of Alexander Draper. The land was surveyed 5 March 1771. Beginning at the head of Ennals Branch. 70 acres for £32.10. Wit: William Davis, Nehemiah Davis. Within deed of sale ackn. 8 Feb 1775.

458. Woodman Stockley, Sussex Co., yeoman, from Jehu and Robert West, Junr., Worcester Co. Maryland and sons of Thomas West, Senr. and Bridget his wife. 13 Jan 1775. For £120, paid by William Sharpe, Senr., dec'd., a parcel in Angola Neck on Bracey's Branch being the eastern most part of a larger tract in the right of Thomas Cary, dec'd., and by the last will of said Cary he devised the same to his wife Frances Cary during her lifetime and after her decease to the heirs of Thomas West, Senr. of Worcester Co., party to these presents beginning at a division line between Martha Cary and Frances Cary, widow of Thomas Cary, dec'd. ... to the head of Green Branch ... 147 acres. Wit: Thos.

Robinson, James Sharpe. Within deed of sale ackn. 8 Feb 1775.

459. James Sharpe, Sussex Co., yeoman, from Jehu and Robert West, Junr. Worcester Co., Maryland and sons of Thomas West, Senr. and Bridge his wife. 13 Jan 1775. For £120, paid by William Sharpe, Senr., dec'd., a parcel in Angola Neck on braceys Branch and to the northwest of the branch it being the westernmost part of a larger gract in the right of Thomas Cary dec'd and by his will he devised to his mother, Martha Cary for her lifetime and at her decease to the heirs of Thomas West and Bridget his wife. Wit: Thos. Robinson, Woodman Stockley. Within deed of sale ackn. 8 Feb 1775.

459. John Clowes, Sussex Co., yeoman, from Parez Chipman, Kent Co., yeoman. 26 Sep 1774. Whereas Elnathan Inkley, late of Sussex Co., died intestate, possessed of 250 acres, in Broadkill Hundred, on the head of Long Branch and said Inkly left issue three daughters, Anna, Mary and Sarah Inkley and 2/3 of said land is now in the possession of Monica Waller as heir to her father John Spencer, Esqr. and the heirs of Matthew Parrimer, dec'd., and whereas said Mary Inkley married afsd. Parez Chipman by whom she had issue, one daughter, and died intestate having not disposed of her equal 1/3 part of the afsd. land and whereas the daughter of afsd. Mary also died intestate and without issue never having disposed of her mother's equal third of the 233 acres falls to afsd. Parez Chipman. For £25. Wit: James Riggen, William Bowness. Within deed of sale ackn. 8 Feb 1775.

460. William Mathews, Northampton Co., Virginia, from Parker Robinson and wife Ruth, Sussex Co. 6 Dec 1774. A parcel in Broadkill Hundred called Abrahams Lot granted by patent dated 26th of 1st month 1686 to Abraham Potter for 300 acres and said Abraham Potter by his deed 1 March 1694 conveyed it to John Jones(?) who --- on April 1730(?) conveyed same to Christopher Topham who by his deed of sale dated 6 Aug 1734 conveyed same to Robert MacCarrel who by his will dated 2 April 1743 devised two shares of the tract to his son James McCarrel who by his deed dated 30 Aug 1748 conveyed same to Robert Craig. Charles Cade son of Robert Cade the elder conveyed his share of said tract being 100 acres by deed dated 10 Feb 1726 to Arthur Johnson and John Hambleton son and heir of Agness Johnson, widow and admx. of Arthur Johnson by virtue of an order from the Orphans Court conveyed the said 100 acres by deed dated 2 May 1739 to John Brice who by deed of mortgage pledged the 100 acres to the Trustees of the Loan Office of Sussex and not making sufficient payments the land was seized by the sheriff and sold to afsd. Robert Craig by deed 6 May 1752 and Robert Craig died intestate and left heirs, Hamilton Craig, John Craig, Mary White wife of Jacob White, the afsd. Ruth wife of Parker Robinson and Robert Craig, a minor son of Alexandr. Craig, dec'd., who by their deed dated 5 Aug 1763 conveyed their rights to said land to above mentioned Parker Robinson. Beginning at an oak standing by the edge of Coolspring Branch and on a corner tree of Samuel Rowland's land ... to a corner post of the line of George West's land ... 379 acres. Wit: Boaz Manlove, Ann Williams. Within

deed of sale ackn. 8 Feb 1775.

462. Jonathan Woolf, Lewes and Rehoboth Hundred, hatter, from David Hall, Esqr., town of Lewes. 24 Feb 1775. A parcel being part of a larger tract called St. Martins in Lewes and Rehoboth Hundred about 2 miles from Lewes Town in the fork of the Indian River and Kings Road, 4 1/4 acres, for £20. Wit: John Hemmons, Joseph Hall. Within deed of sale ackn. 25 Feb 1775.

463. Hap Hazzard, Sussex Co., yeoman, from Nathaniel Hickman, Sussex Co., yeoman, and wife Phebe late Phebe Robins, admx. of Levi Robins, shipwright who died intestate. 9 Feb 1775. Levi Robins died seized of a parcel being part of a larger tract in Broadkill Hundred called White Oak Neck containing 600 acres originally granted by patent to Henry Harmon, dec'd. known as Tayler's Hill. This parcel for 30 acres for £55. Wit: Jno. Russel, Isaac Smith. Within deed of sale ackn. 9 Feb 1775.

464. John Pool from Jacob Walls, Sussex Co., yeoman. 2 April 1773. For £12 and natural love and affection, a tract in Indian River Hundred granted to William Warrinton, Senr. by proprietor's warrant, 193 acres, being a part of the whole tract, conveyed by William Warrenton to George Olaver and from him the 193 acres to the said Jacob Walls, adjoining lands of Andrew Simpler and late of Tegle Walton and Levin Walls being part of the whole tract that adjoins the heirs of Edward Records. Wit: William Johnson, Andrew Simpler. Within deed of sale ackn. 1775.

465. Wm. Marriner, Sussex Co., from John Pool, Sussex Co. 25 March 1775. Tract of 93 acres in Indian River Hundred being a part of a tract called Death Bed for which a warrant was granted to William Warrington, Senr. and later conveyed to George Olaver who conveyed 193 acres to Jacob Walls and said Walls conveyed same to above said John Pool. And John Pool conveys said 93 acres to William Marriner, as surveyed 23 March 1775. Beginning at a corner post in a small glade being the bounds of land of Andrew Simpler. For £35. Wit: Andrew Simpler, William Johnson. Within deed of sale ackn. 25 March 1775.

465. George Rider, Sussex Co., farmer, from John Sherman (Shearman), yeoman. 25 Feb 1775. A parcel in Indian River Hundred on the north side of Cow Bridge Branch, 30 acres being part of a larger tract surveyed and laid out for Thomas Walker. For £12. Wit: Andrew McIlvain, Rhoads Shankland. Within deed of sale ackn. 28 Feb 1775.

466. Pemberton Carlile. Sussex Co., yeoman, from Nathan Hays, Sussex Co. 29 Oct 1774. For £30. A parcel in the forrest of Cedar Creek Hundred. 121 acres. Granted to said Nathaniel Hays by warrant dated 18 Dec 1758. Wit: Wm. Hazzard, Robert Cade. Within deed of sale ackn. 25 March 1775.

467. Moles Patterson, New Castle Co., from Benjamin Rickards. Sussex Co. 28 Jan 1775. Tract in Broadkill Hundred, late the property of Paull Simpler, part of which Paul Simpler bought of

John Coulter and part thereof he bought as the property of John
Hart and one other part he obtained by proprietor's warrant which
is bounded by lands of James Hall and Andrew Coulter on the north
by Clark Nottingham in the west and by Brights Bever Dam on the
south and by lands of Thomas Newcomb on the east and the said
Paull Simpler being indebted to several persons who obtained
Judgment against him and the land was seized and sold by the
sheriff, Roads Shankland, and sold for 500 acres to afsd.
Benjamin Rickards who now conveys same for £140.10. Wit: William
Peery, Peter Ft. Wright. Within deed of sale ackn. 8 Feb 1775.

467. John Rouse, Sussex Co., from William Peery, attorney to
Moles Patterson, New Castle Co. 25 Feb 1775. Parcel in
Broadkill Hundred late the property of Paul Simpler of Sussex
Co., whose land was sold by the sheriff [etc., see above] and
Moles Patterson sold 300 acres thereof to Hugh Hall which he has
now sold to afsd. John Rouse [described]. For £50 paid by Hugh
Hall. Wit: James Bar, Nehemiah Coffan. Within deed of sale
ackn. 25 Feb 1775.

467. William Peery granted power of attorney by Moles Patterson
of the Borough of Wilmington [to convey above mentioned tract].
25 Feb 1775.

468. Wrixam Lewis son of John Lewis and Fairn(?) his wife was
born 19 March 1757.
William Lewis son of John Lewis and Fairn(?) his wife, born 15
Feb 1760.

Deeds Liber M No. 12.

1. Sacker Wyatt, Sussex Co., from Smith Frame, Sussex Co. 20
Feb 1775. A parcel in Broadkill Hundred lately the property of
Robert Frame of Sussex Co., who died intestate whose eldest son
Nathan Frame petitioned to divide the land and a parcel of 30
acres was laid off to Smith Frame son of afsd. Robert Frame on
the east end of the said tract and adjoining lands of William
Russel, part of which Smith Frame sold to George Frame and the
remaining part to be conveyed by this deed, 17 1/4 acres. Wit:
William Peery, Samuel Paynter. Within deed of sale ackn. 25 Feb
1775.

2. William Wyatt, Sussex Co., from Elizabeth Burns, extx. of
William Lingo, Sussex Co. 11 Feb 1775. Whereas William Lingo
was seized of a tract in Broadkill Hundred being part of a larger
tract which Thomas Staton, dec'd., bought at sheriff's vendue,
and after the death of Thomas Staton the land became the property
of his two sons, Thomas Staton (rec'd the southern part) and Hill
Staton (rec'd. the northern part), and said Thomas the younger by
his deed conveyed his part to above mentioned William Lingo who
by his last will ordered that his exrs. sell 50 acres at the head
of the tract to pay his debts. Beginning at a post near the road
that leads from Coolspring to the Drawbridge over the Broadkill
Creek. 50 acres, for £58. Wit: Isaac Smith, Hap Hazzard.

Within deed of sale ackn. 25 Feb 1775.

3. Richard Jefferson from Henry Reynolds and wife Elinor, all of Sussex Co. 16 Oct 1773. Parcel in the forrest of Broadkill Hundred being part of a larger tract granted to Ezekiel Green by virtue of proprietor's warrant dated 29 March 1758 and being that part of afsd. tract devised to said Elinor Reynolds by her father said Ezekiel Green, on the west side of Kenney's Branch ... bounded by an oak of said Green's Maryland patent ... 100 acres, for £55. Wit: Rhoads Shankland, Samuel Shankland. Within deed of sale ackn. 9 Feb 1775.

4. James Reynolds, Sussex Co., planter, from James Pettyjohn, Sussex Co, yeoman. 25 Feb 1775. Parcel in Broadkill Hundred which has been conveyed by a deed of sale from Samuel Pettyjohn and his wife Ann, extx. of the last will of John Wright of Sussex Co., to afsd. James Pettyjohn. Beginning at a corner oak standing by Thomas Dod's fence ... 96 acres. Wit: Rowland Beavans, Rhoads Shankland. Within deed of sale ackn. 25 Feb 1775.

4. Levin Walls, Sussex Co., yeoman, from John Russel, town of Lewes, survivor [sic]. 25 March 1775. Parcel in the forrest of Indian River being part of a tract granted by proprietor's warrant to William Warrington, dec'd., called Death Bed Tract being the north side of said tract. Beginning at an oak standing in the middle of Dutchmans Branch in the line of land formerly surveyed for Cord Hazzard ... 193 acres. For £30. Wit: William Johnson, Andrew Simpler. Within deed of sale ackn. 25 March 1775.

5. William Lofland, Junr., Cedar Creek Hundred, yeoman, from Peter Lindal of Cedar Creek Hundred, yeoman. 8 Feb 1775. For £60, a parcel of land in the forrest of Cedar Creek Hundred called Kne Gum which was first surveyed for John Lofland 14 April 1748, adjoining the lands of said John Lofland and lands of William Lofland, Senr. 115 acres of land and swamp, which said parcel is the same which afsd. John Lofland by his deed dated 29 Feb 1772 conveyed to afsd. Peter Lindle. Wit: John Watson, David Train. Within deed of sale ackn. 8 Feb 1775.

6. John Cirwithin and others from Sarah Halbert. For love and affection toward John Cirwithin, Martha Cirwithin and Sarah Watson, my grandchildren, one Negro boy called Dick. [Other articles are also given.] 17 March 1775. Wit: Henry Smith, William Watson.

7. Thos. Marriner, Sussex Co., from Thos. Newcomb, Sussex Co., yeoman. 25 Feb 1775. For £25, a parcel in Indian River Hundred, taken up by a proprietor's warrant granted to Thomas Shearmon, dec'd., dated 26 June 1744 by the last will of said Thomas Shearman devised to his son George Sherman who by his deed dated 8 Feb 1764 he conveyed the same to the said Thomas Newcomb which said land is bound by the lands of John Lacy, George Rider and Andrew Simpler, called Woolf Den containing 160 acres. Wit:

Nehemiah Davis, Junr., Richard Little. Within deed of sale ackn.
25 Feb 1775.

8. Joseph Draper, Cedar Creek Hundred, yeoman, from John
Hickman, Cedar Creek Hundred, yeoman, and wife Mary. 7 Jan 1775.
Whereas David Smith of Sussex Co. Esqr. dec'd. was possessed of a
piece of land of 200 acres and by his last will devised to his
son John Smith, "... on the southeast side of the tract called
Lebanon containing ... 200 acres ... " dated 26 April 1753 and
John Smith died having made his last will devising to his son
John Smith, grandson of the above named David Smith, Esqr. said
tract of land inter alia, and some vacant land that he purchased
containing 350 acres, dated 5 Nov 1758 and said John Smith by his
last will devised to David Smith and Nutter Smith, two of his
sons, certain other tracts, and whereas said David Smith, Nutter
Smith and John Smith, all died intestate and without issue,
whereas the land descended to their surviving brothers and
sisters and their legal representatives to wit, Thomas Smith;
Comfort who married Dorman Loffland; Elizabeth; John Hickman
party to these presents and son of William Hickman and Sarah his
wife, which said Sarah was another sister of the said David,
Nutter and John Smith, dec'd.; Nehemiah Davis, Junr., Sarah and
Ann Davis, children of Mark Davis and Mary his wife which said
Mary was another sister to said David, Nutter and John Smith. A
dividend was assigned to John Hickman, minor, and son of William
Hickman and his wife Sarah, 200 acres on the county road in the
lines of the patent Lebanon. With 41 acres of land and marsh
including part of Black Walnut Island being part of the tract
what was willed by John Nutter dec'd., to David Smith, dec'd. and
the lower end of said tract next adjoining Hog Island being in
all 241 acres of land and marsh with about 79 acres of surplus
land in Lebanun Patent and 81 acres of surplus land in Pages
Patent in the bounds of 100 acres of being in allotted acres
which will make 360 acres and in all with the 40 acres in the
whole 401 acres, which surplus land of 160 acres that was
surveyed divided of by an agreement made in the lifetime of the
afsd. John and William Smith ... 360 acres ... according to the
survey of 26 -28 March 1767 ... For £130. Wit: Samuel Johnson,
Nehemiah Davis, Junr. Within deed of sale ackn. 7 Jan 1775.

10. Peter White, town of Lewes, house carpenter, from Hannah
Darby of Lewes and Rehoboth Hundred, spinster. 4 Feb 1775. For
£160, a parcel in Lewes and Rehoboth Hundred ... Boundary runs
along the land of David Hall, Esqr. ... 20 acres. Wit: Mary
Hall, David Hall, Junr. Within deed of sale ackn. 9 Feb 1775.

12. David Hazzard, Sussex Co., yeoman, from Dormon Lofland, High
Sheriff. 26 Dec 1774. Whereas John Rodney and David Hall,
Esqr., Trustees of the General Loan Office, recovered a Judgment
against John Russel surviving exr. of the last will of John
Russel the elder for £30 and it was ordered that the land of John
Russel in Indian River Hundred, dec'd., be seized by the sheriff,
and a parcel of 27 acres was sold, being part of a larger tract
whereof William Atkins the elder, died intestate, which was sold
and purchased for £17.5 by John Russel for the use of David

Hazzard, party to these presents. Beginning at a corner post in
the line of Cord Hazzard in a swamp thence along the line of
Robert Burton ... surveyed 28 March 1761 for 27 acres. Wit: Peter
Ft. Wright, David Train. Within deed of sale ackn. 31 Dec 1774.

13. John Rouse, Sussex Co., from Dorman Lofland, Sheriff. Feb
1775. Tract in Broadkill Hundred being a tract whereof Michael
Godwin, died, seized, who by his last will devised same to his
daughter Naomi who married Brittingham Hill and said Hill and
Naomi by their deed conveyed same to John Cary. Beginning at a
corner oak standing on the east side of Long Bridge branch near
the Wading Place where the County Road crosses the branch. 100
acres. And the said John Cary being indebted to Henry Harper of
the City of Philadelphia, merchant in the sum of £154 the said
Henry Harper obtained a Judgment against said John Cary (Aug Term
1774) and the sheriff sold the land to Unice Cary for £101 and
she later married John Rouse. Wit: Leatherberrry Barkert,
Emanuel Russel. Within deed of sale ackn. 8 Feb 1775.

14. Woodman Stockley, Sussex Co., yeoman, from William Sharp,
Junr, Worcester Co. Maryland, exr. of the last will of William
Sharp, Worcester Co. 8 Feb 1775. William Sharp, Senr. for £132,
paid by Woodman Stockley, which payment William Sharp, Junr. is
fully satisfied, tract in Indian River Hundred in Angola Neck and
on Braces Branch and on the south side of a branch that proceeds
out of Middle Creek it being the same that Thomas Cary devised to
his wife Frances during her life. Beginning at a marked hickory
which was the second bounder of a tract that Thomas Cary bought
of Thomas Warrington, dec'd. ... division line between Frances
Cary, widow, and said Thomas and Marthew Cary his mother
agreeable to the last will of said Thomas who left the afsd.
lands to his widow during her lifetime, and in will dated 28
April 1756 devised 2 shares of his lands to Thomas West, Junr.
son of Thomas West Senr. and Bridget his wife and the remainder
of his lands amongst the other heirs of Thomas West, Senr. The
afsd. parties, Thomas West, Junr; John West; Robert West; Thomas
West, Senr. and Bridget his wife; William Otwell and Naomie his
wife; George Thompson and his wife Bridget; Thomas Ingram and Ann
his wife; and Isaac Jones and Mary his wife; have conveyed to
William Sharp, dec'd., the 136 acres as by their deed dated 2 Feb
1768. And the afsd. William Sharp sold the above Woodman
Stockely and gave a bond. Wit: Andrew McIlvain, James Sharp.
Within deed of sale ackn. 8 Feb 1775.

15. Woodman Stockley from William Sharp. Bond. William Sharp
is bound to Woodman Stockley for £264 24 June 1774 to convey land
[see above entry]. Wit: Peter Robinson, William Sharp.

15. Joshua Burton, Sussex Co., taylor, from Nathaniel Hickman,
Sussex Co., yeoman, and wife Phebe, late Phebe Robins, admx. of
Levi Robins, shipwright who died intestate. 28 Jan 1775.
Whereas Levi Robins by his bond dated 22 Sep 1768 was bound to
Joshua Burton for the sum of £200, to convey a tract in Broadkill
Hundred adjoining north by lands of the same tract then possessed
by Levi Robins, south by lands of Elizabeth Roland, easterly by

lands of Parker Robinson, Esqr. and David Gray, containing 50 acres. And said Levi Robins having received £69.4.5 part of the consideration money, the residue being £16.5.7. The tract being in White Oak Neck being part of a larger tract of 600 acres originally granted by patent to Henry Harmon, called Taylers Hills. Beginning at a corner post on the road leading from Lewes Town to the Draw Bridge. Wit: Hap Hazzard, J. Russel. Within deed of sale ackn. 7 Feb 1775.

17. Richard Burton from Jacob Walker. Bond. Jacob Walker, Sussex Co., is bound to Richard Burton, Sussex Co., yeoman, for £16. 17 Dec 1743. To convey a parcel in Piles Neck containing 12 acres. Wit: Elizabeth Burton (her mark), Marget Talor (her mark). Know that I Robert Burton, son of the within named Richard Burton and by his last will heir to the within named 12 acres of marsh, have in consideration of £8.15 sold to Anderson Parker, 6 acres and 67 perches of the within named marsh. 12 Oct 1773. Wit: Joseph Grattin, James Fisher.

17. Nathaniel Bailey, Sussex Co., yeoman, from Stephen Green, Sussex Co., shipwright. Bond. For £12. 15 March 1768. To convey a parcel in Rehoboth [Hundred?], being part of a tract granted by patent to Jonathan Baily [Captain]. 6 acres. Wit: Ephraim Darby, Marth Green. Within deed of sale ackn. 7 Feb 1775.

18. Commissions to James Hamilton, Joseph Turner, William Logan, Richard Peters, Benjamin Chew, Thomas Cadwalader, Richard Penn, James Tilghman, Andrew Allin, Edward Shippen, Junr., Esquires, members of the Proprietary and Governor's Council. And to Benjamin Burton, Jacob Kollock, Wrixam Lewis, Gilbelcher Parker, Levin Crapper, Thomas Robinson, William Conwell, John Rodney, Anderson Parker, Parker Robinson, Boaz Manlove, John Wiltbank, Daniel Nunez, Nehemiah Davis, John Dagworthy, William Holland, William Alligoog, William Polk and Jonathan Bell, of Sussex Co., Justices of the Peace. 24 Oct 1774.

19. Commissions for Job Ingram, Joshua Hill, John Laws, Isaac Horsey, Jeremiah Cannon, Daniel Dinge and Luke Shield, Junr. of Sussex Co., Justices of the Peace. 2 Sep 1775.

19. Larance Riley, Sussex Co., farmer, from Jacob Morris, Sussex Co. yeoman. 3 May 1775. For £5, a parcel in the forrest of Broadkill Hundred being part of a tract surveyed to Christopher Topham, as also a parcel surveyed by proprietor's warrant to Jacob Morris. Boundary runs to a tract of 500 acres laid out of John Stevenson ... containing 20 acres. Wit: Littleton Townsend, Rhoads Shankland. 3 May 1775. Within deed of sale ackn. 3 May 1775.

20. Richard Hart, Sussex Co., yeoman, from John Clowes, Sussex Co., merchant. 3 May 1775. Parcel in the forrest of Broadkill Hundred being part of a larger tract surveyed for John Fowler and by him conveyed to John Ennis and John Clowes obtained a Judgment against afsd. John Ennis and the land was seized by the sheriff

and sold to John Clowes. 58 acres, for £21.15. Wit: Littleton
Townsend, Thos. Gray, Junr. Within deed of sale ackn. 3 May
1775.

21. George Rider, Sussex Co., farmer, from Robert Jones, Sussex
Co., yeoman. 25 Feb 1775. Tract granted by proprietor's warrant
to Thomas Hall dated 29 March 1758, in the fork of Kenney's
Branch and the Great Branch containing 200 acres, for £40. Wit:
Samuel Darby, Thomas Sirman. Within deed of sale ackn. 2 May
1775.

22. John Sharp, Sussex Co., yeoman, from Isaac Draper, Kent Co.,
cooper. 3 May 1775. Parcel in the forrest of Broadkill Hundred
conveyed by several deeds to afsd. Isaac Draper, the first tract
conveyed by James Pettyjohn, 222 acres, per deed dated 3 May
1768; the second tract conveyed by Benjamin Mifflin late of
Sussex Co. per his deed dated 1 Nov 1769, 100 acres; the third
parcel conveyed by Thomas Pettyjohn per deed dated 5 Jan 1770, 30
acres. The above mentioned parcels surveyed and brought into one
tract, bounded by a corner of a tract surveyed for John Cord and
a corner of Mifflin, Clowes and Jones. For £120. Wit: Henry
Draper, Rhoads Shankland. Within deed of sale ackn. 4 May 1775.

23. John Paynter, Sussex Co., house carpenter, from Nathaniel
Gorden, Sussex Co., yeoman. 3 May 1775. For £37.10, a parcel in
Rehoboth Neck being the southwest end of a larger tract called
Martains Vineyard, 30 acres. Wit: Leatherberry Barker, Rhoads
Shankland. Within deed of sale ackn. 3 May 1775.

23. John Draper, Sussex Co., miller, from Peter Parker, Sussex
Co., miller. 4 May 1775. For £60, 100 acres in the forks of
Cedar Creek granted by warrant to William Fisher and surveyed 4
May 1717 and by the last will of afsd. William Fisher devised to
John Conwell who conveyed same to Peter Parker, party to these
presents. Wit: Nehemiah Davis, Junr., Henry Smith. Within deed
of sale ackn. 27 May 1775.

24. William Hall, Sussex Co., yeoman, from Thomas Tamplin,
Sussex Co., yeoman. 10 April 1775. Tract in Indian River
Hundred granted by proprietor's warrant to Thomas Bryan late
dec'd. who by his deed conveyed same to William Blizard who
conveyed same to Ezekiel Jackson who by his bond obliged himself
to convey same to Richard Tamplin who died intestate before a
conveyance was made and the land was conveyed to James Tamplin,
eldest son of afsd. Richard Tamplin, who conveyed same to above
named Thomas Tamplin, party to these presents. 119 acres for
£30. Wit: Nehemiah Davis, Junr., Jno. Russell. Within deed of
sale ackn. 3 May 1775.

25. Benjamin Johnson and Branson Lofland, Sussex Co., from Thos.
Boyer, Kent Co., Maryland, yeoman. 27 May 1775. Tract on the
north side of Slaughter Creek adjoining lands of James Carpenter,
John Hickman, Mark Davis and marshes of Mr. Till, adjoining on or
near Haw Island which tract was formerly purchased of Christopher
Nutter by Alexander Draper who by his last will devised same to

his son Samuel Draper who by his last will devised same to his only child, a daughter who died in her minority and without issue and therefore his mother Elizabeth Boyer became intituled to the same and Elizabeth Boyer by her will devised same to afsd. Thomas Boyer, her son. For £100, 428 acres. One moiety or 1/2, to each. Wit: Peter Parker, Woodman Stockley. Within deed of sale ackn. 27 May 1775.

26. Lemuel Collison Paynter of Lewes and Rehoboth Hundred, yeoman, to George Frame, Indian River Hundred, yeoman,. 2 May 1775. For 5 shillings, a parcel in Lewes and Rehoboth Hundred, being part of a larger tract called Peach Blossom originally granted by patent dated 25 March 1676 to John King and which eventually became the property of Lemuel Collison Paynter. Beginning at a post by the side of Rehoboth Bay and from thence to and along Paynters Neck Road ... to Kollocks or Old Mill Road ... Valley of Warrings Branch ... 481 1/4 acres, for the rent of 5 shillings for the year. Wit: Boaz Manlove, Wrixam Lewis. Within deed ackn. 2 May 1775.

27. Isaac McDowell from Margret Kollock, town of Lewes, widow and extx. of Jacob Kollock. Two tracts in Indian River Hundred, one tract called Broad Water, 212 acres, being the same that was surveyed for John Day by proprietor's warrant dated 12 Feb 1735 and following the death of John Day descended to his son William Day and to satisfy the debts of William Day was sold by the sheriff (Rhoads Shankland) to Jacob Kollock by deed of 14 Feb 1767 (Book K, page 249). The other tract called Little Broadwater containing 70 acres being the same which was surveyed for John Warrington by proprietor's warrant of 29 Aug 1744 and sold as above mentioned to said Jacob Kollock as the estate of the above named William Day, for £136.17.5. Wit: John Hitchcock, J. Moore. Within deed of sale ackn. 27 May 1775.

28. Thos. Davis, Sussex Co., planter, is bound to Nehemiah Davis, Sussex Co., planter for £100, 28 Dec 1748, to make over a tract of marsh and some part of two islands, the number of acres not known yet, but is half of what marsh and land the above said Thos. Davis holds below Edward Furlong's line on the south side of the flat inlet when equally divided between Thomas Davis and Nehemiah Davis. Wit: John Hickman, Luke Heavelo. Within bond proved 27 May 1775.

28. Abraham Wynkoop, Sussex Co., Gent., is bound to Joshua Fisher, Sussex Co., Gentleman, for £300, 28 March 1746, to convey the moiety or half part of two tracts in Cedar Creek Hundred which tracts were conveyed to said Abraham Wynkoop by Edward Evans and Rebeckah his wife and Elizabeth Clark by deed dated 1 March 1745. Wit: Daniel Nunez, Anderson Parker, Robert Gill. On 4 Nov 1772 at a Court of Common Pleas came Daniel Nunez who examined the handwriting of Daniel Nunez and recognized it as that of Daniel Nunez [relationships not given] who was dead as well as the other two witnesses.

29. Thomas Martin, town of Lewes, labourer, from Peter Biggs,

City of Philadelphia, stone cutter, and wife Sarah. 4 March
1775. Three lots in the town of Lewes in Second Street, two of
which were originally granted by the Court of Sussex Co. 4th of
the 8th month 1687 to Alburtus Jacobs who on 7 Sep 1693 conveyed
said two lots with improvements to Charles Haynes, the other lot
adjoining the other two lots was also granted by the court afsd.
to Charles Haynes who by his deed dated 6 March 1693/4 conveyed
same to John Crouch who on 7 Dec 1694 reconveyed same to afsd.
Charles Haynes who by his deed dated 1 Dec 1696 conveyed same to
James Peterkin who by his deed of 9 Sep 1697 conveyed same to
James Simson who by his last will dated 27 Jan 1730 devised same
to his daughters Elizabeth and Margaret Simson and said Margaret
married James Holland by whom she had issue one daughter the name
Sarah the now wife of above named Peter Biggs and later died
being at the time of her death under coverture with the above
named Thomas Martin by means whereof the said Sarah became
intitualed to her mother's part or share of a house and afsd.
three lots, she being the only heir at law at time of her death.
Whereas the above named Elizabeth Simson and said Sarah became
tenants in common and by their agreement made 26 July 1774 caused
a division to be made of the said lots and Sarah's part is hereby
described, beginning at a corner in North Street ... to a corner
of Richard Wesley's lot ... containing one(?) thousand two
hundred square feet. For £70.11. Wit: Thos. Rowland, James
Justice, Wm. Ware. Within deed of sale ackn. 24 June 1775.

31. Brantson Lofland, Sussex Co., house carpenter, from John
Cirwithin, yeoman, or carpenter. 24 June 1775. For £90, part of
a tract of 600 acres originally surveyed by warrant granted to
John and Samuel Watson from the Court of Sussex dated 16th of 9th
month 1683 and confirmed by patent 17th of 3rd month 1688 and
called Rich Neck on the north side Prime Hook Neck in Cedar Creek
Hundred beginning at a corner gum by the edge of run of water of
the northernmost fork of Cyprus Branch ... John Cirwithin's land
... to a corner stone of Caleb Cirwithin and Nehemiah Davis's
land ... to a post at the head of Caleb Cirwithin's mill pond ...
100 acres. Wit: Nehemiah Davis, Junr., Henry Smith. Within deed
of sale ackn. 24 June 1775.

31. William Daniels, Junr., Sussex Co., from Dormon Webb, Sussex
Co., yeoman. 25 Aug 1775. Tract in the forrest of Cedar Creek
Hundred being part of a larger tract belonging to Dormon Webb,
and Thomas Posels, senr., bought the same of the said Dormon Webb
and paid him for the same which was £16 and he [Posels] died
before the land was conveyed and said Thomas Posels by his last
will devised said land to his grandson William Daniels, Junr.
Beginning at a corner stone of land belonging to John Postels and
of land of Dormon Webb. 20 acres. Wit: Thos. Pearson, John
Pearson. Within deed of sale ackn. 26 Aug 1775.

32. Micajah Houston, Sussex Co., tanner, from John Futcher,
Sussex Co., yeoman. 1771. For £16, a parcel in Indian River
Hundred about 10 miles south from the town of Lewes on Fishing
Branch, being part of a larger tract called Hook Norton.
Beginning at a corner ash of Abraham Branch at the Neck Road ...

21 1/2 acres. Wit: Rhoads Shankland, William Clark. Within deed of sale ackn. 2 Aug 1775.

33. Luke Watson, Sussex Co., yeoman, from Joseph Collings and Elizabeth his wife, John Killingsworth and Esther his wife of Sussex Co. 31 July 1775. Tract of land and marsh in Prime Hook Neck of 11 acres called Watson's Marsh all of which land formerly belonged to Captain Luke Watson who by his deed of gift dated 5 March 1696/7 conveyed to his son Samuel Watson 200 acres and by deed of gift dated 6 Feb 1704 conveyed the remainder to his son Luke Watson, Junr. who by deed of gift dated 4 Feb 1706 conveyed to his brother the afsd. Samuel Watson 100 acres and marsh and the said Samuel Watson by his last will devised his right to afsd. tract to his son Luke Wattson, father of the afsd. Elizabeth Collings and Esther Killingsworth and said Luke Wattson died intestate and the afsd. 300 acres became the right of his several children being nine in number. This conveyance for £50 of their rights to the property. Wit: Wm. Conwell, Caleb Cirwithin. Within deed of sale ackn. 2 Aug 1775.

34. George White, from his father John White, Sussex Co., Gentleman. 24 Feb 1773. 100 acres being part of a tract called Bashen, surveyed for Warren Burroughs in the forrest of Cedar Creek Hundred in Great Neck. Bounded by a corner stake of Thomas Laverty's and Joseph Lindel's lands, being part of the same tract ... 100 acres. Wit: Israel Coverdal, Charles Polk, Junr. Within deed of sale ackn. 3 Aug 1775.

35. Edmond Hurley, Dorchester Co., Maryland, from Thos. Bounds, Sussex Co. 3 Dec 1772. For £60, his right of a tract called Horse Pound in Cedar Creek Hundred first surveyed for Arther Fowler by virtue of a warrant in his name dated 28 July 1748, 289 1/2 acres, and Arther Fowler conveyed to Leaven Bounds, 189 1/2 acres of said land of the southwest part of the tract. Wit: George Polk, Charles Polk, Junr. Within deed of sale ackn. 18 Dec 1775.

36. Samuel Butler, Sussex Co., house carpenter, from Levi Bainum and Bartholomew Bainum, both of Sussex Co., yeomen. 7 Nov 1775. A parcel in forrest of Broadkill Hundred being part of a tract granted to John Virden and Joseph Brothern and from them conveyed to Robert Watson Macolly who conveyed his right to Elinor Bainum who by her last will dated 1 Sep 1771 devised same to her sons afsd., 90 acres, for £55. Wit: Wm. Millard, Rhoads Shankland. Within deed ackn. 8 Nov 1775.

36. Robert Watson McCalley, Sussex Co., yeoman, from Richard Reynolds, Senr, Sussex Co., yeoman. 8 Nov 1775. Tract called Good Will which was granted to afsd. Richard Reynolds by patent on 20 Dec 1741 under the Great Seal of Maryland, then called a part of Somerset Co., Maryland, on the south side of Green Branch and joining the western most end of Rackoon Savannah. Beginning at a drain of afsd. Savannah and it being the bounder of William Sheltman's land ... 100 acres. For £54.10. Wit: John Reynolds, Michel Scoot (his mark). Within deed of sale ackn. 8 Nov 1775.

37. Lawrence Rily, Kent Co. Delaware, house carpenter and joiner, from Edward Stapleford, Sussex Co., yeoman, and wife, Mary. 26 Aug 1775. Parcel in Broadkill Hundred in Kimballs Neck being the one moiety whereof William Robinson died and by his last will devised to two grandchildren, to wit, William Stewart and Mary Stewart which Mary Stewart married the afsd. Edward Stapleford. Beginning at a corner post of the lands of David Scuder dec'd. near Mill Creek ... to the line of the land of Jacob Walker ... to a post near the southeast end of William Stevenson's Mill Dam ... 116 3/4 acres, surveyed off and divided 29 July 1772. For £205.12.6. Wit: Wm. Hazard, Nehemiah Davis. Within deed of sale ackn. 8 Nov 1775.

38. John Woods, Sussex Co., mariner, from Dormon Lofland, Sheriff. 28 Oct 1773. A lot in the town of Lewes adjoining lands of said John Woods formerly Samuel Paynter's, dec'd., on the northwest, Second Street, on the northeast, South Street, 60 feet by 200 feet, and whereas Cornelius Kollock late dec'd. by his deed of mortgage dated 6 June 1749 to the trustees of the General Loan Office of Sussex Co. pledged the land for £35 and whereas he and his exrs. have failed to make payment, the land was sold by the sheriff. Wit: John W. Dean, Joshua Burton. Tract is supposed to be part of the original granted to Jacob Kollock the elder or by him purchased of the original patentee who by his last will devised same to his son the above Cornelius Kollock. Within deed of sale ackn. 7 Nov 1775.

39. Henry Smith and wife Priscilla Smith of Sussex Co., planter, to Peter Rust, Sussex Co., planter. 8 Nov 1770. For £152, part of a tract called Luck by Chance between the northeast and northwest forks of the Nanticoke River, 100 acres. Wit: Anderson Parker, John Woodgate. Within deed ackn. 8 Nov 1775.

40. Peter Ft. Wright, Sussex Co., tanner, from Dormon Lofland, sheriff. 10 Nov 1775. Whereas John Rodney and David Hall, Trustees of the General Loan Office recovered a Judgment against Joseph Bailey, admr. of Charles Perry for £60 and the sheriff seized a small lot in Lewes Town on the south side of a branch running into Pagan Creek containing 25 acres whereon the said Charles Perry formerly dwelled. Wit: J. Russel, Rece Woolf. Within deed ackn. 10 Nov 1775.

41. Mary Stockley, widow of John Stockley, Sussex Co., for love and affection toward her son Thomas Stockley, confirms to him a tract whereon she now lives, in Angola Neck of 330 acres, devised to her by the last will of her husband J. Stockley. Wit: William Peery, James Pollock. Within deed ackn. 14 Nov 1775.

41. Levin Dirrickson of Indian River, from Thomas Jones, swampman, for £20, a brown horse and saddle, cattle furniture and other articles. Wit: Jos. Dirrickson, Samuel Dirickson. Within deed of sale ackn. 18 May 1775.

42. Levin Dirrickson from Jno. Bratton, swampman, for £25, horse and saddle, furniture, and other articles. Wit: Nanny Miller,

Love Wingate. 18 May 1775.

42. Branston Lofland, George Rickets and Jehu Clifton, their article of agreement. 25 Jan 1775. Whereas William Donely of Sussex Co., died possessed of a parcel of land in the forrest of Cedar Creek Hundred, containing 689 acres which William Donely in his last will gave to be equally divided between his wife Mapp and his three daughters, Mary, Jemima and Casiah and in order to have a division made, Branston Lofland one of the heirs of the said Jemima Donely and assignee of the said Mapp Donely and George Rickets assignee of the said Casiah Donely and Jehue Clifton assignee of Mary Donely empowered a group of men to divide the land, and binding each other for the penal sum of £500. Wit: Bethuel Watson, John Draper, Jno. Cirwithin.

42. Bethuel Watson, John Draper, miller, and John Cirwithin, Gent., their award. [See above entry.] Whereas William Donely of Sussex Co., died possessed of 689 acres. First award to Branston Lofland and other heirs of Jemima whose maiden name was Donely. Beginning at a corner oak of Jerom Griffin's land ... to an oak by John Hudson's caper field ... to corner of afsd. Jehu Clifton's land ... to a stake in George Ricket's line ... 180 acres. Secondly awarded to Branston Lofland, assignee of Mapp Donely, widow of Mapp Donely ... by Benjamin Reyley's line ... 160 1/4 acres. Thirdly, the award to George Rickets assignee of Kezia Donely ... to Roberts Mill Pond ... 176 3/4 acres. Fourthly, award to Jehu Clifton, assignee of Mary Donely, dec'd., 106 1/4 acres. 17 April 1775. Wit: Bethuel Watson, Jno. Draper, Jno. Cirwithin.

44. Samuel Owens, Sussex Co., from John Rouse, Sussex Co., yeoman. 30 Dec 1775. Parcel in Broadkiln Hundred late the property of Paul Simpler which was sold by the sheriff to pay his debts, conveyed to Benjamin Rickards who conveyed same to Moles Patterson of New Castle Co. who sold 300 acres of the 500 acres to Hugh Hall and empowered William Peery to convey the 300 acres to Hugh Hall who ordered that the land be conveyed to afsd. John Rouse. For £40. Wit: Stephan Mitchel, James Barn. Within deed ackn. 30 Dec 1775.

45. Wrx. White from his mother Sarah Shankland, widow of William Shankland, Sussex Co. For £3, her right to a tract granted to her 26 Nov 1753 by proprietor's warrant for 150 acres adjoining her dwelling plantation in Rehoboth Hundred, surveyed and laid out 27 June 1772 for 89 acres. Wit: Robert White, Cornelius Waples, Betty Waples. Within deed ackn. 27 Jan 1776.

46. William Mathews, Broadkill Hundred, yeoman, from William Burton, Broadkill Hundred, yeoman and his wife Mary. 24 Feb 1776. Parcel in Broadkill Hundred on the south side of the Broadkiln Creek called Swan Hill granted by patent to John Street who conveyed same to William Clark who conveyed same to Thomas Fisher who by his last will devised same to his son Joshua Fisher who conveyed same to Gersham Mott who conveyed 100 acres thereof to Sollomon Nock and later said Gersham Mott conveyed the

remaining 330 acres of the tract to Absolom Little who by his
deed dated 2 Aug 1765 conveyed same to above named William
Burton. For £600. Beginning at a post in the line of the patent
on the south side of Woolf Pit Gutt. Wit: Anderson Parker, Isaac
Smith. Within deed ackn. 24 Feb 1776.

47. Sneed Johnson, Worcester Co., yeoman, to James Law, yeoman.
6 Feb 1776. Afsd. Sneed Johnson son of William Johnson, dec'd.,
for £100, 100 acres called Spring Garden in Deep Creek Hundred
being granted by Lord Baltimore to Jonathan Dolbe by patent 25
March 1757. Wit: Jno. Russel, Jacob Walker. Within deed ackn. 6
Feb 1776.

48. David Ranken, from John Clowes, Sussex Co., mariner. 7 Feb
1776. For £75, a parcel in Broadkill Hundred being part of James
Gray's patent called Milford, that part thereof on the east side
of Round Pole Branch, that part which was formerly the property
of Samuel Rowland and by the last will of Samuel Rowland it
became the property of his son Samuel Rowland, pilot, and part of
the land, 60 3/4 acres, became the property of afsd. John Clowes
by deed dated 6 Dec 1764 from the exrs. of said Samuel Rowland.
The other part of the land, 29 3/4 acres adjoining the above
mentioned land being part of two shares of Henry and Jonathan
Ozbon of the surplusage land surveyed for him and others on 9 Jan
1745/6 by virtue of a warrant of resurvey on James Gray's patent
for 1000 acres on land called Milford and by sundry conveyances
one moiety thereof became the property of Matthew Ozbon father of
afsd. Henry Ozbon and grandfather to afsd. Jonathan Ozbon and
Jonathan Ozbon on 10 March 1760 assigned his right to the afsd.
surplusage on the back of said warrant or resurvey to afsd. Henry
Ozbon, containing 82 acres and Henry Ozbon conveyed the land, 82
acres, to afsd. John Clowes by deed dated 8 May 1765, the two
parcels containing 95 1/4 acres. Beginning at a maple at the run
of Round Pole Branch being a corner also of a parcel sold bu
Samuel Rowland, pilot, to Baptis Lay ... to John Niel's land ...
in the line of land now in possession of John Burton. Wit: John
W. Dean, William Bowness. Within deed ackn. 7 Feb 1776.

49. William Bowness, Sussex Co., doctor, from Mary Annett,
Sussex Co. single woman. 7 Feb 1776. Parcel adjoining lands now
in possession of Robert Stephenson, Samuel Hevelo, John Ponder
and Micajah Truitt containing 100 acres being part of two tracts
late the property of Isabella Annitt, dec'd., of which 90 acres
became the right of said Isabella Annitt by virtue of a division
made by order of the Orphans Court of all the lands of William
Stephenson, her father, died seized of, 1 March 1762. The
remainder of said land became the right of said Isabella by
virtue of a purchase she made of the land formerly belonging to
Mary Barry adjoining the afsd. 90 acres and whereas the said
Isabella Annit died intestate leaving issue several children, the
afsd. Mary being one of them. For £200, 100 acres. Wit: John W.
Dean, Cornelius Waples. Within deed ackn. 7 Feb 1776.

50. Wm. Poynter, Junr., farmer, Sussex Co., from Jane Mullinex,
widow, and Richard Mullinex, Sussex Co., yeoman. 18 Dec 1775.

Alexander Argo, dec'd. by Bethuel Watson, his attorney, granted
to Jane Mullinex two tracts, one in the forrest of Cedar Creek
Hundred between the head of Bowman's Branch, one of the branches
of Mispillion Creek and the side of Woolf Denn Swamp, called
Jones's Adventure containing 395 acres, the other part in the
forrest of Cedar Creek Hundred formerly taken up and belonging to
John Morran containing 99 3/4 acres. For £133.5, 156 and 33
perches of the afsd. 395 acres, beginning at a corner oak of
William Parker and Alexander Argo's land ... to a blown down
corner black oak of Jane Warren's land ... to an oak of said
Warren's and William Mullinex's land ... surveyed 3 April 1775.
Wit: Wm. Hazzard, Rosley Poynter. Within deed ackn. 7 Feb 1776.

51. Robert Wood, Sussex Co., from William Frame, Sussex Co., and
wife Elizabeth. 8 Feb 1775. Parcel in Broadkill Hundred whereof
Robert Frame died intestate and his eldest son Nathan Frame
preferred a petition to the Orphans Court on 4 March 1766 to
divide the land and a division was allotted to afsd. William
Frame the youngest son of Robert Frame, his part, being part of a
larger tract granted to William Derval called Maiden Plantation
and handed down by conveyances from said William Derreval to the
said Robert Frame beginning at a corner post of the land allotted
to George Frame ... 248 acres, for £200. Wit: Job Ingram, Joseph
Piper. Within deed ackn. 7 Feb 1776.

53. Jonathan Hemmons, Sussex Co., planter, from his sister
Sealea [Celia] Hemmons, Sussex Co. 24 Feb 1776. For £15 to her
paid, a tract whereon her father's dwelling plantation was her
right being the third part of the whole tract supposed to
containing 200 acres first surveyed for Thomas Hemmons, Junr.,
who died intestate and a third part fell to said Sealia by
heirship in Great Neck on the west side of Merry Branch joining
on the east with John Lane's and James Hall's land and on the
northwest by Richard Coverdale and John Carlile's land. Wit:
Laurence Riley, Grace Riley. Within deed ackn. 24 Feb 1776.

53. William Ratliff, Sussex Co., farmer, from John Coverdale,
Sussex Co., yeoman. 24 Feb 1776. For £70, a parcel in the
forrest of Cedar Creek Hundred, being part of a tract surveyed
for John Coverdale by proprietor's warrant dated 3 Oct 1745,
beginning at a corner oak the bounder of John Lane's 100 acres
... in the line of Barret Kirk's land ... 250 acres. Wit:
Richard Green, Rhoads Shankland. Within deed ackn. 24 Feb 1776.

54. Francis Wright, Sussex Co., planter, from Robert Ross,
Sussex Co., planter. 23 Feb 1776. For £50, 52 3/4 acres called
Nutters Neglect, being the north end of said tract in Nutters
Neck on the west side of the main branch of the Nanticoke River
in that part formerly Dorchester Co., Maryland. Elijah Hatfield,
Mathew Ross (his mark). Within deed ackn. 23 Feb 1776.

54. Francis Wright, Sussex Co., from David Williams, Sussex Co.
23 Feb 1776. For £130, 76 1/4 acres of land called Rosses
Venture; also 8 1/4 acres called Bite the Biter, being the north
end of said tract in Nutters Neck on the west side of the main

branch of Nanticoke River that was formerly in Dorchester Co., first surveyed for James Ross and conveyed to said David Williams from said Ross. Wit: Robert Layton, Elijah Hatfield. Within deed ackn. 24 Feb 1776.

55. Levin Clifton, Sussex Co., bricklayer, from Francis Wright, Sussex Co., planter. 24 Feb 1776. Whereas Francis Wright became seized of a tract called Sapling Ridge formerly in Dorchester Co., Maryland but now Sussex Co., 40 acres of the tract was sold by Francis Wright to Levin Clifton, beginning at the first bounder of the afsd. tract on the north end of the afsd. tract near as the division was between Thomas Hickman and Mathew Dunkin and for £40. Wit: Robert Layton, David Williams. Within deed ackn. 21 Feb 1776.

56. Elijah Hatfield, carpenter and joiner, Sussex Co., from William Ross, Sussex Co., planter. 23 Feb 1776. For £55, 66 acres, being the south end of a tract called Rosses Venture, first surveyed for James Ross and he conveyed same to Robert Ross who conveyed same to afsd. William Ross, being part of Dorchester Co. in Nutters Neck and now Sussex Co., on the west side of the main branch of Nanticoke River and on the north side of Bridge Branch. Wit: Francis Wright, Thomas Dunkin. Within deed ackn. 5 March 1776.

57. Zephaniah Polk, Sussex Co., from Nathan Stafford attorney of Lydia Polk, Sussex Co. 25 Feb 1776. For £80, a tract called Wilsons Swamp Landing near the head of a drane called the Horse Pond Branch that issues out of the northwest fork of Nanticoke River near Wilsons Swamp, 87 acres. And another tract called Wales ... the northern side of Double Fork Branch that issues out of the East side of the Northwest Fork of Nanticoke River. 50 acres. Wit: John Wiltbank, Parker Robinson. Within deed ackn. 24 Feb 1776.

58. Nathan Stafford given Power of Attorney by Lydia Polk, Sussex Co. [See above entry.] 21 Feb 1776.

58. Nathan Stafford from Henry Stafford, Senr, Sussex Co. 24 Feb 1776. For £30, 50 acres of a tract called Staffords Lot to be laid off at the east end of said tract, the whole tract containing 150 acres and joins to a tract called Morrisses Venture. Wit: John Wiltbank, Parker Robinson. Within deed ackn. 24 Feb 1776.

59. Henry Stafford, Sussex Co., planter, appoints Zepheniah Polk as his attorney to convey to Nathan Stafford 50 acres of the tract Staffords Lot. 24 Feb 1776.

60. Henry Stafford, Junr, Sussex Co., from Henry Stafford, Senr., Sussex Co. 24 Feb 1776. For £80, parcel called Staffords Adventure, beginning at an oak standing by the side of a path that leads from said Staffords to Green Pond about 1/2 mile to the eastward of said Stafford's dwelling house. Wit: John Wiltbank, Parker Robinson. Within deed ackn. 24 Feb 1776.

60. Henry Stafford, Senr. planter, appoints Zephaniah Polk as his attorney to convey parcel of 53 acres of Staffords Adventure to Henry Stafford, Junr. Wit: Nathan Stafford (his mark), James Spence (his mark). Proved 24 Feb 1776.

61. William Rickards, Sussex Co., yeoman, from John Smith, Sussex Co., yeoman. 24 Feb 1776. Parcel in the forrest of Cedar Creek Hundred on the south side of the main branch of Cedar Creek containing 600 acres granted by patent to Luke Watson called Lebanon who conveyed same to Thomas Hardum, John Maughan and Richard Reynolds and by sundry conveyances and devises the land became the property of David Smith who his last will devised same to his two grandsons, John and David Smith, sons of William Smith, to be equally divided. For £100, 150 acres of his moiety. Beginning at a corner post of land of Mitchell Black's heirs on the hill near said Rickards' house ... surveyed 12 Aug 1774. Wit: Luke Townsend, Jacob Townsend. Within deed ackn. 24 Feb 1776.

62. Levin Connaway, Sussex Co., yeoman, from John Connaway, Sussex Co., planter. 10 Feb 1776. For £65, a parcel in Broad Creek Hundred, lately Worcester Co., granted by Lord Baltimore to Isaac Ingram by patent dated 16 Nov 1730 called Horse Head on the east side of Nanticoke River, a little to the southward of the head of Charles Tindal's Branch and about a mile to the westward of Philips Wingate's ... 100 acres. Wit: John Wiltbank, J. Russell. Within deed ackn. 10 Feb 1776.

63. Woodman Stockley, Sussex Co., planter, from John Abbot Warrington, Sussex Co., yeoman. 8 Feb 1776. A parcel in Indian River Hundred on the north side of Bracey's Branch being one of the branches of Rehoboth Bay, being part of a tract granted to Robert Bracey by patent called Webley, dated 29 Feb 1677 for 800 acres who conveyed same to William Clark who conveyed same to John Cary who conveyed same to Thomas Gray who mortgages same in the General Loan Office and sold by High Sheriff, Cornelius Wiltbank, to Robert Smith who conveyed same to Thomas Warrington who by his last will devised same to his son John Warrington who by his deed dated 4 May 1763 conveyed same to Jacob Warrington, father of the afsd. John Warrington, party to these presents which said Jacob Warrington died intestate leaving several children whereupon John Warrington petitioned the Orphans Court ordered a valuation which was accepted by afsd. John Abbot Warrington. Beginning at a corner of Woodman Stockey's land ... corner of James Sharp's land ... to the neck Road or Mill Road leading from St. George Chapel to Wiltbank's mill, dividing this land from lands of the late Cord Hazzard, dec'd. ... land dividing this land from lands of Arther Hazzard ... 198 acres, £288. Wit: David Train, Joseph Nock. Within deed ackn. 8 Feb 1776.

64. John Smith, yeoman, Sussex Co., from David Smith, ship carpenter, Sussex Co. 24 Feb 1776. Parcel in Cedar Creek Hundred on the south side of Cedar Creek Branch, 600 acres, granted by patent to Luke Watson and by sundry conveyances and

devises became the property of David Smith the elder now dec'd. and said David Smith the elder by his last will devised said tract to his two grandsons John and David Smith, sons of William Smith, to be equally divided between them. Beginning at an oak in Isaac Wattson's line ... land laid off for William Rickards ... line of land sold to Mitchel Black by afsd. John Smith ... Wit: Luke Townsend, Jacob Townsend. Within deed ackn. 24 Feb 1776.

64. David Smith, ship carpenter, Sussex Co., from John Smith, yeoman. 24 Feb 1776. Parcel in Cedar Creek Hundred on the south side of Cedar Creek Branch containing 600 acres granted by patent to Luke Watson and by sundry conveyances and devises became the property of David Smith the elder now dec'd. [See above entry.] Beginning at a oak in Isaac Watson's line ... land laid off for Wm. Ricords ... the line of land sold by John Smith afsd. to Mitchel Black ... Wit: Luke Townsend, Jacob Townsend. Within deed ackn. 24 Feb 1776.

65. George Adams, Sussex Co., from Job Smith, Sussex Co. 9 Feb 1776. Whereas David Smith of Worcester Co., Maryland, on 25 Aug 1745 resurveyed a tract called Smiths Delight Amended containing 100 acres and on 8 March 1757 conveyed the same to his son Job Smith then in Maryland and said Job Smith sold same to George Adams 5 Aug 1757 for £50, on the east side of Nanticoke River and north side of Deep Creek between Alexander Adams' and Caleb Bowman's land. Wit: David Train, Levin Connaway. Within deed ackn. 7 Feb 1776.

66. John Reed, planter, Indian River Hundred, from Joseph Warrington, farmer and wife Rachel, spinster, Sussex Co. 24 Feb 1776. Part of two tracts, one granted to John Parsons by proprietor's warrant 27th of 3rd month 1717, the other granted to Samuel Edwards 25 June 1740, with the parcel from the two tracts beginning at a corner post in a small field of Andrew McIlvain's land ... containing 250 acres, for £143.5. Wit: Rhoads Shankland, Smith Frame. Within deed ackn. 24 Feb 1776.

67. William Rickards, Sussex Co., Gentleman, from Charles Rickards and wife Charity, both of Sussex Co., yeoman. 28 March 1776. For £56, a tract called Rickards Delight in Somerset Co., now Sussex Co., 223 acres, being the same that Ann Rickards conveyed to Elizabeth and Charity Rickards by her deed dated 26 June 1764 called Rickards Delight in Tuskey(?) Branch to the westward of Broad Creek granted to said Ann Rickards for 561 acres. Wit: James Bayles, Thos. Robinson. Within deed of sale ackn. 9 April 1776.

68. James O'Neal, Sussex Co., planter, from his brother Thomas O'Neal, Sussex Co., planter. 9 April 1776. Whereas Thomas O'Neal's father, James O'Neal, had by his Lordship and Proprietor of Maryland a patent granted to him, which said Thomas was the oldest son of said James O'Neal that is living. For £100, a tract beginning on the east side of N. Savannah called Ackworths Savannah about 1/2 mile west of the main road that leads from

Broad Creek to Drapers Sawmill and about 3/4 mile northwest of the head of Miery Branch ... 100 acres. Wit: John Polk, Junr., John Ready. Within deed ackn. 9 April 1776.

69. Aron Ready, Sussex Co., planter, from John Ready, Sussex Co., planter. 9 April 1776. For £60, a tract called Byons Grave formerly in Worcester Co. now Sussex Co., between the branches of Wicomico River and the branches of Broad Creek, about 1 mile west of the Bald Cyprus Swamp above Edward Woollen's house ... 50 acres, granted to Joseph Parrimore by patent dated 15 June 1728. Wit: John Polk, Junr., William Bivins, Junr. Within deed of sale ackn. 9 April 1776.

69. William Bevins, Junr., planter, Sussex Co., from Wm. Bevins, Senr., Sussex Co., planter. 9 April 1776. For £50, a part of a tract called Callaways Neglect 1 mile east of Baldey Price's Branch issuing out of Broad Creek, 50 acres. Wit: Jno. Polk, Junr., Aaron Ready. Within deed ackn. 9 April 1776.

70. Joshua Coston from his father, Benton Coston, Sussex Co., yeoman, for 5 shillings, a parcel in Broadkill Hundred being the eastern most part of a tract granted to Benton Costen by proprietor's warrant on 29 March 1758. 20 March 1776. Wit: Rhoads Shankland, Thomas Gray, Junr. Within deed ackn. 9 April 1776.

71. James Jessop, Sussex Co., planter, from John Jessop and Eloner his wife, Sussex Co. 30 March 1776. Whereas John Jessop became possessed of a tract called Hog Range containing 313 acres by marrying Elinor Brown which land was devised to her by the last will of John Nutter, Dorchester Co. For £75, a parcel of 100 acres on the northwest end of afsd. tract. Wit: John Parker, Nehemiah Davis, Junr. Within deed ackn. 10 April 1776.

72. Philip Conway, Sussex Co., planter, from Jester Conningam, Sussex Co., planter. 22 Feb 1776. A parcel on the east side of Nanticoke River near the head of Deep Creek called Second Choice, being part of a tract granted to Arther Cunningam by patent of 80 acres for £30. Wit: John W. Dean, George Polk. Within deed ackn. 14 Feb 1776.

72. Samuel Cary, mariner, from Thomas and Peter Robinson of Angola and Indian River Hundred, merchants. 1776. Parcel in the hundred afsd. containing 119 acres being part of a tract granted by proprietor's warrant to William Cary (son of Thomas Cary, dec'd., and brother of afsd. Samuel Cary) who assigned the warrant to afsd. Thomas and Peter Robinson. Beginning at a corner of land formerly belonging to Robert Barton ... with Smith Frame's line ... to a corner post of John Collings ... for £107. Wit: John Wiltbank, Dav. Train. Within deed ackn. 9 April 1776.

73. John Potter, Junr., from his father, John Potter, Sussex Co. 8 Feb 1776. Tract where his son John lives containing 284 acres in Broadkill Hundred on the north side of the Beverdam Branch. Boundary runs to a dividing line of new marked trees of Thomas

Groves ... Also 6 Negroes, Moses, Sary, Jeanny, Robin, Leah, Sofier; 32 head of cattle; 11 head of hogs; 7 sheep; 30 geese and all household goods; all bonds due from son John Potter. For £552. Wit: Thos. Groves, Jno. Cady, Jno. Hazzard. Within deed ackn. 8 Feb 1776.

74. Wm. Mathews, Broadkill Hundred, yeoman, from Wm. Burton, Broadkill Hundred, yeoman, and his wife Mary. 24 Feb 1776. Parcel in Broadkill Hundred on the south side of Broadkill Creek called Swan Hill granted by patent to John Street who conveyed same to William Clark who conveyed same to Thomas Fisher who by his last will devised same to his son Joshua Fisher who conveyed same to Gersham Mott who conveyed 100 acres thereof to Solomon Nock and Gersham Mott conveyed the remaining part (330 acres) to Absolom Little who by his deed dated 2 Aug 1765 conveyed same to the afsd. William Burton. For £600. Beginning on the south side of Wolf Pit Gutt ... line of Joseph Cord's land ... corner of a patent called Maidenhead Thicket ... corner of 100 acres deeded by afsd. Gershom Mott to said Solomon Nock ... corner of the lands of the heirs of Levi Robins ... 330 acres. Wit: Anderson Parker, Isaac Smith. Within deed ackn. 24 Feb 1776.

76. William Burton, Broadkill Hundred, yeoman, from Wm. Mathews, Sussex Co., yeoman, and wife Ann. 24 Feb 1776. Parcel in Broadkill Hundred called Abrahams Lot granted by patent dated 26th of 1st month 1686 to Abraham Potter for 300 acres who by his deed dated 14th of 7th month 1686 conveyed same to Jacob Warren who by deed dated 1 March 1694 conveyed same to John Haynes who by deed conveyed same to Robert Cade whose sons Robert Cade and Thomas Cade by their deed dated 5 April 1730 conveyed their share, 2/3 of above tract, to Christopher Topham who by his deed dated 6 Aug 1734 conveyed same to Robert McCarrel who by his last will dated 2 April 1743 devised same to his son James McCarrel who by his deed dated 13 Aug 1748 conveyed same to Robert Craig. Charles Cade son of the afsd. Robert Cade the elder conveyed his right of said tract being 1/3 part by his deed dated 10 Feb 1726 to Arthur Johnson who admr. John Hammilton by virtue of an order of the Orphans Court conveyed same to John Brice by deed dated 2 May 1739 who mortgaged same in the General Loan Office which was late sold by Sheriff William Shankland to afsd. Robert Craige by sheriff's deed dated 6 May 1752 which tract was later valued by Orphans Court 1764 and accepted by Parker Robinson representative of the eldest heir of afsd. Robert Craig and Parker Robinson and Ruth his wife by their deed dated 6 Dec 1774 conveyed same to afsd. William Mathews. For £600. Beginning at an oak on the northwest side of the Cold Spring Branch being a corner of Samuel Rowlan's lands. 379 acres exclusive of 2 acres condemned for the use of a mill. Wit: Anderson Parker, Isaac Smith. Within deed ackn. 24 Feb 1776.

77. William Thompson, from James Newbold of Lewes and Rehoboth Hundred, yeoman, admr. of Thomas Layfield late of the said hundred. Whereas Thomas Layfield was seized of a parcel of land in Lewes and Rehoboth Hundred, 90 acres, and died intestate and James Newbold admr. of said Thomas Layfield sold the land by

order of the Orphans Court on 5 Dec 1774 for £173, beginning at a corner post standing on the division line of Henman Rhoads' land being a corner of William Thompson's allotment standing on the west side of the Neck road to the sea side ... line of George Young's patent ... head of Roads Pond ... Wit: Wm. Conwell, David Hall, Junr. Within deed ackn. 24 Feb 1776.

78. George Walker, Sussex Co., from Ebenezer Cary, Sussex Co. 2 Feb 1776. Tract in Indian River Hundred granted by proprietor's warrant dated 2 June 1757 to Thomas Cary, dec'd., who by his last will devised same to his son the afsd. Ebenezer Cary, beginning at the side of the Indian River ... post in John Burton's line ... 137 acres, for £150. Wit: Dormon Lofland, Arthur Hazzard. Within deed ackn. 24 Feb 1776.

79. John Lofland, Sussex Co., yeoman, from Wm. Winsley, Sussex Co., yeoman. 24 Feb 1776. parcel called Primehook Ponds granted to Thomas Lay by proprietor's warrant dated 25 July 1741 who by his deed dated 4 May 1748 conveyed same to afsd. William Winsley, along with a smaller tract adjoining which begins at a corner oak by the north side of Sow Bridge Branch ... of land laid out for Samuel Oliver ... containing 354 acres, surveyed 2 April 1742. About 100 acres of the above described land where Absolom Mousley now dwells the said Winsley has conveyed to him and 100 acres where the afsd. John Lofland now dwells the said Winsley conveyed on 5 Sep 1772 to John Lofland, Senr. father to the afsd. John. For £80, the residue of the above described 354 acres, i.e., 154 acres. To be held by William Winsley and his wife Tabitha during the natural lives and excepting 1/4 acre for a graveyard. Wit: John Clowes, Alexander Laton (his mark). Within deed ackn. 24 Feb 1776.

80. Caleb Balding, Sussex Co., planter, from Barkley Townsend, Sussex Co. planter. 9 April 1776. For £186, a tract being part of the tract called Indian Land on the south side of Broad Creek and adjoining Little Creek, 186 acres. Wit: John Polk, Junr, William Bivins, Junr. Within deed ackn. 9 April 1776.

81. Jester Cunningham, Sussex Co., planter, from John Conway, Sussex Co., planter. 23 Feb 1776. Parcel in the forrest of Broadkill Hundred being part of a tract granted to John Fleetwood by proprietor's warrant dated 2 July 1761. Nehemiah Fleetwood the son and heir of John Fleetwood sold to John Conway his right to afsd warrant as shown on back of warrant dated 21 March 1771, containing 70 acres, for £25. Wit: John Dan, George Polk. Within deed ackn. 24 Feb 1776.

82. John Polk, Junr., Sussex Co., planter, from Lowder Surman, Sussex Co., planter. 9 April 1776. For £90, a parcel called Readys Choice containing 50 acres, being a tract granted by Lord Baltimore to Isaac Ready by patent dated 20 Sep 1753 and sold to Lowder Surman, Worcester Co., now in Sussex Co., on the north side of the head of Asskutom Branch. Wit: John Ready, Aaron Ready. Within deed ackn. 9 April 1776.

83. Daniel Polk. Sussex Co., planter, from Charles Brown, the 3rd, planter, and wife Sarah. 24 Feb 1776. For £240, a tract called Tusse Wondoke near the head of Nanticoke River back in the woods from the water side. Wit: Willm. Davis, David Train. Within deed ackn. 24 Feb 1776.

84. Daniel Tree, Sussex Co., yeoman, from Ann Gawdy, Sussex Co., widow and extx. of last will of Moses Gawdy. 30 March 1776. Said Moses Gawdy by a bond dated 22 Aug 1772 obliged himself to Daniel Tree for £100, to convey parcel called Gawdys Delight, 75 acres, beginning north of the White Oak Swamp near a tract surveyed for John Williams. Wit: David Train, J. Russel. Within deed ackn. 30 March 1776.

85. Daniel Tree from Moses Gorday (Gordy). Bond. Moses Gordy, Senr. of Worcester Co., Maryland is bound to Daniel Tree of Worcester Co., Maryland for the sum of £100, 22 Aug 1772, obligated to convey [above 75 acres]. Wit: John Mitchell, Isaac Horsey. Proved 30 March 1776.

85. Naomi Green, widow, Richard Green, Stephen Green, John Green, Ambrose Green, Patty Green and Nelley Green, heirs of Stephen Green, dec'd., Sussex Co., ship carpenter, from John Lewis, Sussex Co., yeoman. 24 Feb 1776. Parcel of land and marsh on the southwest side of Lewes Creek and on the southeast side of Lewes Town being part of a tract called Middleborough being the east corner of afsd. tract, beginning at a post standing at the east corner of Cord's 20 acres ... corner post of Jacob White ... post standing near Pothooks Gutt ... containing 52 acres, for £70. Wit: Robert Shankland, Rhoads Shankland. Within deed ackn. 24 Feb 1776.

86. John Russel, Sussex Co., joiner, from Dormon Lofland, sheriff. 24 Feb 1776. Whereas John Rodney, Esqr., Trustee of the General Loan Office, obtained a Judgment against the above named John Russel, surviving exr of the last will of John Russel for £32 Nov Term 1775, a lot on the south side of Lewes Town, beginning at the eastern most corner of the land where Elizabeth Goddard's house formerly stood ... binding on the lands of the heirs of John Hill. For £25. Wit: John Rodney, W. Rodney. Within deed ackn. 24 Feb 1776.

87. Cornelius Bebens, Sussex Co., yeoman, from William Steel, Sussex Co. yeoman. 24 Feb 1776. For £50. Parcel, part of a tract surveyed for Joseph English in Broadkill Hundred, 100 acres. Wit: Anderson Parker, Rhoads Shankland. Within deed ackn. 24 Feb 1776.

88. Thos. Hickman, Sussex Co., from Francis Wright, Sussex Co. 24 Feb 1776. Francis Wright became possessed of a tract called Sapling Ridge formerly in Dorchester Co. but now Sussex Co., 80 acres of the afsd. tract Francis Wright hath sold to afsd. Thos. Hickman. Beginning at an oak at the northeast corner of Levin Clifton's deed, 40 acres of said tract, for £50. Wit: Robert Layton, David Williams. Within deed ackn. 24 Feb 1776.

89. George Relph, Sussex Co., yeoman, from William Relph, Sussex Co., planter. 30 March 1776. For £70, a parcel being part of a tract in Little Creek Hundred in Sussex Co., formerly Somerset Co., Maryland, called Good Luck at Last, originally granted by proprietor's warrant to William Relph, dec'd., 50 acres. Wit: J. Russel, Jean Russel. Within deed ackn. 30 March 1776.

90. Sacker Wyatt, Sussex Co., from Elizabeth, Mary and Ruth Russel, Sussex Co. 20 March 1776. Tract in Lewes and Rehoboth Hundred being part of a tract confirmed by patent to Roger Gum who conveyed it to John Fisher, and Thomas Fisher and John Fisher, sons and heirs of the first named John Fisher, conveyed same to Sarah Fisher who married William Spencer and they conveyed same to William Pettyjohn who conveyed 250 acres thereof to William Russel, father of the afsd. Elizabeth, Mary and Ruth Russel and William Russel conveyed 105 acres to Marnix Virden and and by his last will devised remaining part of 250 acres to his four daughters, Elizabeth, Mary, Ruth and Tabitha Russel which said remaining part is bounded as follows ... dividing line between this land and the land of John Hopkins, now surveyed for 203 1/4 acres. For £240. Wit: Emanuel Russel, Esther Russel. Within deed ackn. 27 April 1776.

90. Jathro Vaughan, from Levin Vaughan, Sussex Co., yeoman. For £10, a parcel being part of a tract in Nanticoke Hundred called Cox's Discovery which being part of a tract that William Vaughan of Somerset Co., father of the above named parties did by his last will dated 9 Nov 1742 devise to above named Jathro Vaughan in the following words, "I give unto Jathro Vaughan my well beloved son ... wife Mary Vaughan ... I give him the dwelling plantation whereon I dwell, 150 acres of land upon the south of the said plantation and to my son Ephraim Vaughan ... 100 acres out of the said tract upon the north side of the said manner plantation and a plantation I bought of Dudson Bacon and 50 acres joining to it ..." Wit: William Powell, J. Russell. Within deed ackn. 27 April 1776.

91. William Frame, Sussex Co., from Moles Patterson, borough of Wilmington, by Wm. Peery his attorney, Sussex Co. 22 April 1776. Parcel in Broadkill Hundred on Bever Dam Branch, 200 acres, part of a tract granted to John Coulter, late of the co. afsd. and the other of said two tracts was granted to Paul Simpler which said above recited part of said two tracts of land by sundry conveyances became the property of above named Moles Patterson who by bond obliged to conveyed the same to Robert Hood who assigned said bond to the afsd. William Frame. For £100. Wit: Samuel Owens, Junr., William Hall. Within deed ackn. 27 April 1776.

92. Mary Russel, Sussex Co., from Anderson Parker, Esqr., Sussex Co., admrs. of Thomas Staton 29 April 1776. Parcel in Broadkill Hundred part of which the afsd. Anderson Parker, attorney of Sarah Star, admx. of Jonathan Starr conveyed on 28 Aug 1772 to Thomas Staton. Land being sold to cover debts. 46 acres, for £98. Wit: Simon Kollock, David Train. Within deed ackn. 27

April 1776.

93. Arther Hazzard, Sussex Co., yeoman, from Margaret Stephenson, Sussex Co., admx. of Lemuel Collison Paynter, yeoman. 9 March 1776. Sale of land to cover debts. Parcel in Lewes and Rehoboth Hundred, part of a tract called Peach Blossom, originally granted by patent dated 25 March 1676 to John King and by several conveyances and descents it became the property of afsd. Lemuel Collison Paynter. 130 acres, for £295.15. Beginning at a corner post by the run of the branch of Warrens Creek about 10 perches below the house lately occupied by Elisha Nock ... road side dividing said land from lands of the heirs of Richard Paynter ... to the line obtained by and in possession of the heirs of Stephen Green ... Wit: Dav: Train, Isaac Bradley. Within deed ackn. 27 April 1776.

94. Margaret Stephenson, Sussex Co., spinster, from Arthur Hazzard, Sussex Co., yeoman. 16 March 1776. For £295.15, a parcel part of the tract in Lewes and Rehoboth Hundred called Peach Blossom originally granted by patent dated 25 March 1776 to John King. [See above.] Wit: Dav: Train, Isaac Bradley. Within deed ackn. 27 April 1776.

95. Robert Hill, Sussex Co., farmer, for love and affection, to his grandson Robert Covington of Sussex Co., a Negro girl Nance. 26 April 1776. Within deed of gift proved 27 April 1776.

95. Robert Hill, Senr. to his grandson, Robert Hill, Junr., for love and affection, a Negro girl Florah. 26 April 1776. Within deed of gift proved 27 April 1776.

96. Henry Draper, Sussex Co., from his father Avery Draper, Sussex Co., yeoman. 8 May 1776. For love and affection, a parcel whereon the said Henry draper now dwells being the same that Avery Draper purchased of Thomas Till, dec'd. by deed dated 6 Dec 1748, in Slaughter Neck. Beginning at a post in the line of the land laid out for Stephen Townsend. Wit: John Clowes, Thomas Grove. Within deed ackn. 8 May 1776.

97. William and James King from Hugh King. Parcel in Broadkill Hundred containing 200 acres being part of a tract which was granted to Garthwright Everson and called Orphans Choice, parcel being the southwest end of the afsd. larger tract by sundry conveyances became the property of Hugh King, dec'd. who by his last will devised said 200 acres to be equally divided between his sons James King father of William King, and James King, parties to these presents and Hugh King and they made division of the afsd. 200 acres. For 5 shillings. Wit: William Peery, Samuel Hudson. Within deed of release ackn. 8 May 1776.

98. Hugh King from William and James King. Tract in Broadkill Hundred containing 200 acres being part of a tract granted to Garthwright Everson and called Orphans Choice, being the south end of the afsd. larger tract. Wit: William Peery, Samuel Hudson. Within deed of release ackn. 8 May 1776.

98. James King from William King. Tract in Broadkill Hundred containing 200 acres which became the property of Hugh King who by his last will devised the said two 200 acres to be equally divided between his two sons, James King and Hugh King which said James King died intestate before any division was made, leaving issue two sons, William King (eldest son) and James King the parties to these presents which said Hugh King the younger, son of James King dec'd. made division of the said 200 acres among themselves agreeable to the will. Hugh to have the land on the northwest side of said dividing line and William and James to have 1/2 of 200 acres which now is surveyed to be 108 acres and William to have that part of 108 acres on the northeast side of the dividing line containing 72 acres being 2/3 thereof he being the eldest son and James King to have that part on the southwest side of the division line of 36 acres. Wit: William Peery, Samuel Hudson. Within deed of released ackn. 8 May 1776.

99. William King, Sussex Co., yeoman, from James King, Sussex Co., yeoman. For 5 shillings. Deed of release ackn. 8 May 1776. [Same tract as above.]

100. James Sharp from Woodman Stockley. 8 May 1776. For £60, parcel of land which John Abbot Warrington by his deed conveyed to Woodman Stockley in Indian River Hundred, surveyed 6 Jan 1775 for 139 acres. Wit: John Hazzard, Jno. Russel. Within deed ackn. 8 May 1776.

101. John Wootten, Worcester Co., Maryland, to Benjamin Wootten, Worcester Co., Maryland. 3 Nov 1763. For 5 shillings, a parcel called Inclosed(?) granted to Edward Wootten for 100 acres and conveyed by him to afsd. John Wootten and also a parcel called Hounds Hatch conveyed from William Bozman and Sarah his wife late of Somerset Co. to afsd. Edward Wootton for 500 acres, 300 thereof conveyed to said John Wooten, 150 acres of which said tract conveyed by said John Wooten to said Benjamin Wootten the said 150 acres to be laid off at the east end of the said tract. Wit: Wm. Allegood, George Layfield.

102. Isaac Bradley, Sussex Co., yeoman, from Tilghman Brown, Sussex Co., yeoman. 27 April 1776. For £140, tract called Proprietor's Dispute, in Northwest Fork Hundred, originally granted by the proprietary of Maryland to Charles Brown, dec'd, by patent dated 19 March 1754 for 158 acres and said Charles Brown by his will devised same to his son, afsd. Tilghman Brown, proved in Dorchester Co. Wit: John Russel, David Train. Within deed ackn. 27 April 1776.

104. James Steal (Steel) from William Steal (Steel). 27 April 1776. Parcel in Broadkill Hundred called Pasinous Ward granted to Ephraim Darby by proprietor's warrant dated 8 June 1737 who by his deed dated 3 Aug 1748 conveyed same to afsd. William Steal, 212 acres and the said William Steel by his deed of sale conveyed 113 acres thereof to Nathaniel Williams being the southwest and northwest part of the whole leaving at that time in his own right 99 acres on the southeast and northeast part. Now for £70 the 99

acres is conveyed. Wit: John Clowes, Samuel Hand. Within deed ackn. 27 April 1776.

105. Richard Firman, Sussex Co., yeoman, from John Clowes, Sussex Co., yeoman. 21 March 1776. Whereas John Clowes, Benjamin Miflin and John Jones by sundry purchases became possessed with 4000 acres of land in Broadkill Forrest and the most western part became the property of afsd. John Clowes. For £120, 171 acres of the western division of land. Beginning at Solomon Sammon's corner on Thomas Evans' line ... to a corner oak of John Day. Wit: William Peery, Samuel Hand. Within deed ackn. 27 April 1776.

106. Robert Layton, Sussex Co., planter, from David Williams, Sussex Co., planter. 24 Feb 1776. For £50, a tract called Young's Addition, containing 75 acres, which was granted to Nathan Young of Dorchester Co. on 29 Sep 1756. Beginning on the northwest side of the Bridge Branch that makes out of the head of the northeast fork of Nanticoke about 1/2 mile above the bridge. Wit: Francis Wright, Levin Clifton. Within deed ackn. 24 Feb 1776.

106. Obed Outten from Absolum Phipps. 30 March 1776. For £30, a tract called Good Neighborhood on the south side of Nanticoke River a little below Deep Creek. Beginning at a marked oak dividing it from the land of William Collings, 200 acres granted to Thomas Farnal 1 June 1687. Wit: Isaac Horsey, David Train. Within deed ackn. 10 March 1776.

107. John Collings, son of Darby, of Sussex Co., yeoman, from John Clowes, Sussex Co., mariner. 19 March 1776. A tract in the Broadkill Forrest, which by proprietor's warrant was surveyed on 19 Dec 1743 for Hugh Virdin who by deed dated 4 Feb 1761 conveyed same to William Boucher who by deed dated 7 Sep 17 62 conveyed same to John Clowes along with another tract and said John Collings having purchased a part thereof. Beginning at a corner oak on the northwest side of the road on the edge of Picture Hill ... land laid out for John Smith ... containing 193 1/2 acres except 82 acres conveyed by afsd. William Boucher to John Smith on the west side thereof. For £62. Wit: Henry Draper, David Ranken. Within deed ackn. 8 May 1776.

108. John Stuart, Sussex Co., yeoman, from John Clowes, Sussex Co., mariner. 24 Feb 1776. Parcel in Broadkill Hundred in the forrest being part of a tract conveyed to afsd. John Clowes by William Boucher. Beginning at a corner oak of John Day's land ... 100 acres. For £62.10. Wit: Henry Draper, David Ranken. Within deed ackn. 8 May 1776.

109. Joseph Knock, Sussex Co., yeoman, from Leatherbury Barker and wife Abigail, Sussex Co., yeoman. 9 April 1776. For £210, a tract on the south side of Middle Creek proceeding out of the western most side of Rehoboth Bay called Tanners Hall, granted to William Emmet by patent dated 1 Jan 1684, acknowledged on the back of the patent dated 6 July 1707 and said William Emmet

conveyed same to Francis Williams and by sundry conveyances the same land was handed down to John Russel who by his deed dated 14 Nov 1749 conveyed same to Job Barker who by his last will devised same to his two sons Peery Barker and Leatherbery Barker and they by deeds of release dated 26 Feb 1773 released to each other. 145 acres to Joseph Knock. Wit: James Bailis, Samuel Cary. Within deed ackn. 8 May 1776.

109. William Mumford (Moumford, Mountford), Sussex Co., from Joshua Robinson and wife Martha of Sussex Co. 8 May 1776. For £25, a tract in Prime(?) Neck near Indian River called Self Defense, taken up by a warrant of resurvey, the land being the same conveyed by James Rounds and Joshua Robinson to John Mountford on 7 Nov 1754 but because of a mistake in the deed a new deed is given to William Mountford heir of the afsd. John Mountford. Beginning at a marked pine standing near Paull Waple's fence to the southwestward of his house, 100 acres. Wit: Isaac Smith, Jacob Walker. Within deed ackn. 8 May 1776.

110. James Bar, Sussex Co., from David Rankin and wife Aby, Sussex Co. 8 Dec 1775. Two parcels in Broadkill Hundred, containing 160 acres, part of a larger tract called Timber Hill which was granted to John Vines and by sundry conveyances 160 acres became the property of Jonathan Scuder dec'd. father of the afsd. Aby Ranken. The other was part of a tract called Mill Plantation granted to William Clerk and by sundry conveyances the said 213 acres became the property of afsd. Jonathan Scuder and he died intestate leaving 5 children, David, Jonathan, Ruth, Aby and Hannah Scuder and said children made division of the two tracts among themselves. This portion beginning at a corner post by the edge of the run the Mill Creek Branch ... lands of William Peery ... lands of David McIlvain, dec'd., ... 70 acres for £100. Wit: Joseph Hall (his mark), Ann Fleming. Within deed ackn. 8 May 1776.

111. George Carter, Sussex Co., from James Johnson, Caroline Co., Maryland. 13 April 1776. For £50, a tract granted to Cornelius Johnson, grandfather of afsd. James Johnson who possessed the land by heirship. [Followed by a large blank portion.]

113. Lemuel Williams, cordwinder, from William Conwell, Esqr., Sussex Co. 2 May 1776. For £10, a parcel in Broadkill Neck and south side of Prime Hook Creek being part of a tract taken up by Nathaniel Walker and by sundry conveyances is now in the possession of said William Conwell. Wit: Thomas Grove, Caleb Cirwithin. Within deed ackn. 8 May 1776.

113. Francis Conwell, yeoman, from John Clowes, yeoman. 11 April 1776. Sundry parcels in the Broadkill Forrest by virtue of two deeds of sale, one from William Darters for part of the land granted to William Pettyjohn by proprietor's warrant and the other from Thomas Warton for all the land granted to him by proprietor's warrant dated 2 July 1757. Beginning at an oak of Andrew Collins part of the afsd. William Pettyjohn's survey ...

containing 100 acres, for £80. Within deed ackn. 8 May 1776.

114. Leatherbery Barker to his brother Perry Barker, Sussex Co., cordwinder. For £5, part of a tract that Job Barker, their father, by his last will devised to his three sons, Perry, William and Leatherbury in Indian River Hundred on the south side of Fishing Creek being the same that said Perry Barker and Leatherbery Barker now live on and called Tanners Hall. Wit: Jacob Stockley, Patience Stockley. 25 Feb 1773. Within deed of release ackn. 8 May 1776.

115. Perry Barker to Leatherbery Barker. For £5. Deed of release [to his part of the land - see above.]

116. Joseph Coulter from Robert and James Coulter. For 5 shillings and in obedience to a certain award under the hands and seal of William Tull, William Hand, John Neel and William Perry, arbitrators elected by afsd. Robert Coulter, James Coulter and Joseph Coulter to divide a tract in Broadkill Hundred whereof Charles Coulter, father of afsd. Robert, James and Joseph Coulter died, to be divided agreeable to last will of Charles Coulter. Wit: William Perry, Marnix Virden. Within deed ackn. 8 May 1776.

116. Robert Coulter from Joseph and James Coulter. For 5 shillings ... etc. [see above entry.]

117. James Coulter, Junr., from Robert and Joseph Coulter. For 5 shillings ... etc. [see above entries.]

118. Robert Coulter, Sussex Co., from James Coulter, Junr., Sussex Co. 22 March 1776. Tract in Broadkill Hundred, part of a tract whereof Charles Coulter, father of the afsd. James and Robert Coulter died and devised equally to his sons, Robert, Joseph and James. 100 acres, for £75. Wit: William Perry, Marnix Virden. Within deed ackn. 8 May 1776.

118. Molton Crapper, Sussex Co., yeoman, from John Parker, Sussex Co., sadler. 9 May 1776. For £150, a parcel on the south side of Mispillion Creek. Beginning at an oak on the edge of the bank of Mispillion Creek near the stone house late of Levin Crapper, Esqr., dec'd., being a corner of Israel Brown's land ... line of land called the Sawmill Range Tract ... which parcel is part of a tract formerly called The Saw Mill Range granted by patent to Henry Bowman who died seized thereof intestate and the admr. William Clark the elder died and the land devolved and descended to Edward Evans and Rebecca his wife in right of said Rebecca and Elizabeth Clark as heirs who by indenture dated 28 Nov 1770 conveyed same 300 acres to afsd. John Parker. Wit: Dav. Train, Benja. Truitt, Junr. Within deed ackn. 9 May 1776.

121. John Turpin, Sussex Co., from Hugh Eccleston and wife Elizabeth, and Joseph Ennals, Junr. and wife Mary, all of Dorchester Co. 6 Jan 1777. For £25, a tract on west side of the northeast branch of Nanticoke River called Sandy Neck, conveyed by John Trippe to John Twiford for 80 acres, part of the afsd.

tract, the residue containing 120 acres. Wit: Wm. Ennalls, Jos. Richardson. Within deed ackn. 22 Jan 1777.

122. George Howard Aydelott, Sussex Co., from his father John Aydelott, Sussex Co. 8 May 1776. For love and affection and 5 shillings. 400 acres being the residue of that part of a tract called Joynd Meadow which was conveyed by John Aydelott, Senr. and Mary his wife to afsd. John Aydelott by their deed dated 1 March 1742. Wit: Jona. Boyce, Joseph Aydelott. Within deed ackn. 8 May 1776.

122. John Fleetwood, Sussex Co., yeoman, from Nathaniel Bradford, Sussex Co., wheelwright. 25 May 1776. 25 acres of marsh laid off out of the 250 acres to above Nathaniel, Comfort and Sarah, as afsd. [sic] patent dated 10 Sep 1702 granted to John Hill and from him descended to John Walton, dec'd. and by his exrs. conveyed 29 July 1763 to Samuel Heaverlo which he by deed of sale 28 May 1774 conveyed to Nathaniel Bradford, in. Broadkill Hundred. Beginning at a corner stake in Samuel Heaverlo's line ... close by the road that goes down to Joseph Hazzard's from Samuel Heaverlo's land ... division line between Cornelius Wiltbank and afsd. Heaverlo ... 12 1/2 acres, divided off 30 Nov 1773. For £6.5. Wit: Dav. Train, Job Parrimer. Within deed ackn. 25 May 1776.

123. Ann Clay, New Castle Co., Delaware, widow, from Joshua Hill, Esqr., Baltimore Hundred. Deed of mortgage. 12 March 1777. Tract patented 9 April 1689 and granted to William Wittington then of Somerset Co., Maryland, on the south side of Indian (otherwise Baltimore) River in Somerset, later Worcester, now Sussex Co., called Springfield. Beginning at a stump by the side of Beaver Dam Branch and between a house where Rhodes Clark formerly lived and said Bever Dam ... 486 acres which by several conveyances is vested in afsd. Joshua Hill who stands bound to afsd. Ann Clay in the sum of £1600 for the payment of £800 by 12 March 1782. Wit: J. Rodney, J. Moore. Within deed ackn. 7 May 1777.

124. Abraham Adams, Sussex Co., from John Waller, Sussex Co., son and heir of George Waller late of Worcester Co., Maryland, planter. 25 May 1776. For £5, 11 at the head of a tract called Addition. Wit: Peter Robinson, George Black. Within deed ackn. 25 May 1776.

125. Abraham Adams, Sussex Co., planter, from William Reynolds, Sussex Co. planter. 25 May 1776. For £30, tract called Double Purchase in Grubby Neck on the north side of Authur's Branch issuing out of Deep Creek containing 13 acres. Wit: Peter Robinson, Nathaniel Milby. Within deed ackn. 25 May 1776.

125. Perry Prettyman, Sussex Co., blacksmith, from Jonathan Woolfe, Sussex Co., hatter, and wife Ruth. 25 May 1776. For £6.11.3, parcel in Lewes and Rehoboth Hundred in the forks of the Kings Roads leading from Lewes Town to the head of Indian River and from Lewes Town to Philadelphia. Beginning in the forks of

said road opposite John Wolf's door. 175 1/2 perches. Wit: J. Rodney, Penelope Rodney. Within deed ackn. 25 May 1776.

126. Abner Lamb from George Walker, Sussex Co., yeoman and Hester his wife. 27 July 1776. For £250, parcel beginning at the head of a small branch proceeding out of Cold Spring Branch on the southern side ... to a corner post of Reece Woolf ... branch dividing this land from the land lately sold by said George Walker to elders of the Presbyterian Church ... 119 acres. Wit: Phillips Kollock, Dav. Train. Within deed ackn. 27 July 1776.

127. George Handy, Somerset Co., merchant, from Joseph Parremore, Sussex Co., yeoman. 25 May 1776. For £45, a parcel in Broadkill Hundred, part of a tract called Good Luck at Last, originally granted by the proprietary of Maryland to William Relph by patent. Beginning at Percussion Branch ... 73 1/2 acres. Wit: Isaac Henry, W. Relph. Within deed ackn. 27 July 1776.

128. John McCullah, Sussex Co., from George Walker and wife Esther of Sussex Co. 24 March 1776. A parcel in Lewes and Rehoboth Hundred, 60 aces, of which 10 acres was part of a tract granted by patent to William Trotter called Batchelors Folly and by several conveyances became the property of afsd. George Walker, and the other 50 acres thereof a part of a tract granted by proprietor's warrant to William Shankland and by contract between said William Shankland and said George Walker it became the property of George Walker. Beginning on the east side of the Coolspring Branch ... 60 acres for £185. Wit: Wm. Peery, Hap Hazzard. Within deed ackn. 27 July 1776.

129. Nehemiah Stayton, Sussex Co., yeoman, from James Smith, Sussex Co., yeoman. 7 Aug 1776. For £9, a parcel of 9 acres and 12 perches, being part of a tract of 50 acres. Beginning at a stake on the fork of White Marsh and on the west side of the northeast branch of Nanticoke River ... to a point 29 perches from the beginning of a tract called Cliftons Lot. Wit: Thos. Gray, Junr., Morgan Williams. Within deed ackn. 7 Aug 1776.

130. Anderson Parker, Esqr., house carpenter from Perry Prettyman, blacksmith of the town of Lewes, and admr. of Comfort Prettyman who was the widow and admx. of William Prettyman. 31 Aug 1776. Parcel of marsh which said William Prettyman died seized of, being part of a tract in the ...? of Wrixam White, Junr., 4 1/4 acres, being part of a tract called Greenfield. ... For £15. Wit: Jehu Claypoole, James Cooper. Within deed ackn. 31 Aug 1776.

131. David Williams of Dorset Co., farmer, from Levin Crapper, Esqr., Sussex Co., merchant. Bond for conveyance of land. Levin Crapper is bound to David Williams for £1000 on 25 Jan 1768 to convey a parcel on the west side of Bowman's Branch which said Crapper bought of John Truitt and conveyed by Richard Hay, Senr. and one other tract whereon Nicholas Vughte, Junr. lately dwelt

adjoining the land, containing 509 acres. Wit: John Parker, David Train. Bond proved 9 Nov 1773.

131. Samuel Coulter, Sussex Co., farmer, from Joseph West, Sussex Co., yeoman. Bond for conveyance of land. Joseph West is bound for £200 on 8 Feb 1762. To convey a parcel in Slutkill Neck in the Broadkill Hundred containing 130 acres, part of a larger tract formerly belonging to Richard Dobson, dec'd., being the same land that was laid off pursuant to an Act of Assembly to Isable and Ann Dobson, two of the daughters of said Richard Dobson. Wit: Thos. Gray, Sophia Gray. Within deed ackn. 1776. The bond was assigned by Charles Coulter son of Samuel Coulter to Alexander Stockley of Sussex Co., carpenter for 19 shillings per acre, dated 24 Feb 1770. Later assigned by Naomi Stockley admx. of Alexander Stockley to Charles Coulter, 10 Jan 1771, who assigned the bond to Jesse Dean, yeoman, for 20 shillings per acre. Wit: James Gordan, Nathaniel Starr. On 9 May 1776 the bond and several assignments were proved.

132. William Morris, Sussex Co., yeoman, and Bevins Morris, Sussex Co., yeoman. Deed of partition. 27 May 1776. Whereas Bevins Morris father of the said William and Bevins Morris, by his last will devised to William and Bevins Morris all his lands to be equally divided and they have divided the land by mutual consent, in the Broadkill Forrest adjoining lands of Benjamin Mifflin, the heirs of Jacob Morris, Dennis Morris and Thomas Dutton, containing 300 acres. Beginning at a stake in Benjamin Mifflin's land being on the southwest part of the decedent's lands. William Morris to have the northwest portion, 110 acres. And Bevins Morris to have the southeast portion, 190 acres. Wit: Levin Connaway, John Dutton. Within deed of partition ackn. 6 Nov 1776.

133. William Cord, Sussex Co., from David Hazzard, Sussex Co. 5 Nov 1776. For £10, 12 acres of marsh being part of a tract called Middlesex and that part of said tract next and near the said Cord's land called Scearboroughs Neck, on the south side of Indian River. Wit: J. Russsel, Israel Holland. Within deed ackn. 5 Nov 1776.

134. David Hazzard, Sussex Co., from William Cord, Sussex Co. 5 Nov 1776. For £10, 8 acres being part of a tract called Scearboroughs Neck it being that part next to Moses Dazey's and at the west end of the said tract, on the south side of Indian River. Wit: J. Russel, Israel Holland. Within deed ackn. 6 Nov 1776.

134. Elihu Bridell, Worcester Co., Maryland, from David Hazzard, Sussex Co., cordwinder, and wife Sally. 7 Nov 1776. For £400, the tract whereon said David Hazzard now lives containing 250 acres being 1/2 or moiety of the tract called Middlesex as also 8 acres that the afsd. David Hazzard bought of William Cord as also 31 acres on the south side of the head of Barker's Branch. Wit: J. Russel, Israel Holland. Within deed ackn. 7 Nov 1776.

135. John Sharp, Sussex Co., farmer, from William Conwell, Esqr., Sussex Co. 7 Nov 1776. For £50, a tract that was taken up by John Kenman who conveyed same to William Darter who conveyed same to Christopher Topham who sold same to William Allin who conveyed same to afsd. William Conwell, 232 acres, surveyed 10 April 1722 at the request of William Darter. Wit: David Hall, Jacob Gum. Within deed ackn. 7 Nov 1776.

136. Burrel Jones from William Steel, Sussex Co., yeoman. 19 April 1776. For £80, a tract in Broadkill Hundred Forrest called Good Luck adjoining the lands of Cornelious Beavins it being a part of a tract the formerly belonged to James Ruksan(?) that Boaz Manlove sold at sheriff's sale containing 150 acres. Wit: James Steel, Nathan M---. Within deed ackn. 30 Nov 1776.

136. Able Nottingham from John Hall. 1 Sep 1776. Two parcels in Broadkill Forrest being part of two tracts, one taken by William Coulter, date of warrant 3 Sep 1740, the other taken up by warrant by Hugh Stephenson containing 130 acres. For £30, 70 acres of the afsd. tracts. Wit: William Perry, John Clampet. Within deed ackn. 30 Nov 1776.

137. Benjamin Steel from his brothers, Nathaniel and Daniel Steel, Sussex Co., yeomen. For 5 shillings. a parcel being part of a tract granted to Ezekiel Green who conveyed same to Daniel Steel, father to the afsd. Daniel, Benjamin and Nathaniel Steel, who by his last will devised same to Benjamin Steel, 83 acres lying to the northeast of said parcel. Wit: Cornelius Beavans, Rhoads Shankland. Within deed of release ackn. 25 Jan 1777.

138. Daniel Steel from Nathaniel and Benjamin Steel. Deed of release. For 5 shillings, ... devised to Daniel 83 acres being the home plantation. [See above entry.] ackn. 25 Jan 1777.

138. Nathaniel Steel from Daniel and Benjamin Steel. Deed of release. devised to Nathaniel 84 acres on the southwest end of said parcel. [See above entries.] ackn. 25 Jan 1777.

139. John Neal from his brother William Neal. For love and affection, 125 acres being part of a tract called Neals Folly containing 283 acres. Beginning about 30 perches to the eastward of Richard Clarkson's plantation. Wit: ----, Thos. Gray, Junr. Within deed ackn. 4 Feb 1777.

140. William Millard, Sussex Co., yeoman, from Thomas Gordon admr. of James Gordon, Sussex Co. 17 Feb 1776. For £111, tract in Broadkill Hundred being part of a tract conveyed to Thomas Staton, Senr., by William Shankland, then sheriff, by indenture, dated 3 Feb 1746, which said parcel being part of a larger tract left by will to his son Thomas Staton who conveyed same to John Mustard by deed dated 1 Sep 1761 who conveyed same to Robert Jones by deed dated 3 May 1769 who conveyed same to James Gordon by deed dated 28 May 1774, surveyed 30 Jan 1761 for 100 acres. Beginning at an oak near the Mill Creek. Wit: William Jefferys, Benjamin Ricords. Within deed ackn. 5 Feb 1777.

141. Starling Clarkson and Elizabeth Clarkson, Sussex Co., from Constantine Cannon and wife Starling, Sussex Co. 11 Jan 1777. For £10, by James Brown and White Brown, guardians to said orphans, parcel in the forrest of Mispillion Hundred. Beginning at a sapling at or near the road on the south side of a road that leads from Owingies(?) Bridge to Marshihope Bridge at or near the tract called Taylors Chance now in the possession Daniel Morriss, senr. Containing 130 acres. Wit: William Owens, Joseph Dawson. Within deed ackn. 5 Feb 1777.

141. James Gunby, Somerset Co., Maryland, yeoman, from James Salmon, Sussex Co., yeoman. 22 Feb 1777. For £300, a tract called Hickory Ridge in Broadkill Hundred in Deep Creek Forrest which was granted to Phillip Wingate by the Proprietary of Maryland by patent dated 29 Sep 1761 who by indenture dated 8 Nov 1770(?) conveyed same to afsd. James Salman. Beginning at an oak on the north side of a swamp about a mile from Windsor Branch and a short distance west of the plantation whereon Phillip Wingate formerly dwelt, 207 acres. Wit: D. Train, Willm. Davis. Within deed ackn. 22 Feb 1777.

142. Luke Thomas, yeoman, from William Godwin, Sussex Co., yeoman. 5 May 1773. For £12, a parcel in Broadkill Hundred, of a larger tract surveyed for Thos. English by proprietor's warrant called Hoggs Quarter. Beginning at a corner oak on the south side of Kenny's Savannah, 24 acres. Wit: Prisgrave Steel, Rhoads Shankland. Within deed ackn. 29 March 1777.

143. William Wilson from his brothers, John and Reuben Wilson, Sussex Co., yeoman. For 5 shillings, parcel being part of a tract granted to William Wilson, father to the above said John, Reuben and William Wilson who by his last will devised same to afsd. John, Reuben and William Wilson which said parcel being one moiety or half part and the southern most part thereof containing the manor plantation containing in the whole 330 aces. The moiety contains 165 acres. Wit: Robert Torbert, Rhoads Shankland. Within deed ackn. 29 March 1777.

144. Robert White, Kame Wilkins White and Isaac White, heirs of Isaac White and Jacob White, a minor son of Wrixam White, Sussex Co., from Perry Prettyman, Sussex Co., admr. of Comfort Prettyman who was admx. of William Prettyman. 7 May 1777. Whereas William Prettyman on 9 June 1768 by his bond obliged himself to Jacob White late of Sussex Co., dec'd. to convey 30 1/4 acres of marsh in Lewes and Rehoboth Hundred being part of one Cornwell's patent. Beginning at a post on the southeast side of Coldspring Creek and to the northeast side of Sheephole Gutt. For £75. Wit: Peter White, Rhoads Shankland. Within deed ackn. 7 May 1777.

144. Prisgrave Steel, Sussex Co., from Thomas Pettyjohn, Sussex Co. 29 March 1777. Tract in the Broadkill Forrest being part of a larger tract surveyed to said Thomas Pettyjohn by virtue of a warrant granted John Pettyjohn and assigned to the afsd. Thomas Pettyjohn 26 Feb 1761. Beginning at a marked oak of James

Pettyjohn's land ... Cyprus or Cambridge Branch ... 50 acres.
Wit: Samuel Shankland, Rhoads Shankland. Within deed ackn. 7 May
1777.

145. Thomas Croutch, cooper, from Cornelius Stockley. Bond for
conveyance of land. Cornelius Stockley is bound to Thomas
Croutch for £55 on 19 Oct 1763. To convey a tract in Slaughter
Neck Forrest in Cedar Creek Hundred containing 100 acres and
being part of a tract belonging to Robert Lee, Junr. lying
between Isaac Wattson's land and James Carpenter's land. Wit:
Isaac Wattson, Willm. Shankland. Within bond proved 9 March
1777.

146. Petition of Joseph Aydelott and wife Frances widow and
extx. of Cornelius Stockley. 31 March 1776. That Cornelius
Stockley on 19 Oct 1763 by his bond obliged himself to Thomas
Crouch [See above.] To convey land to Thomas Crouch.

146. William Shockley, Sussex Co., yeoman, from Joseph Aydelott
and wife Frances admx. of Corns. Stockley. [See above.] Wit:
John Chance, Isaac Wattson. Within deed ackn. 29 March 1777.

147. Zadock Lindal, Sussex Co., from John White, Sussex Co. 3
March 1773. For £50, part of a tract in the forrest of Cedar
Creek Hundred in Great Neck which tract is called Basham, first
surveyed for Warren Burroughs and deeded to afsd. John White who
has already deeded 300 acres on the north and east part of said
tract, and now to Zadock Lindal he conveys the remaining right of
the tract it being 200 acres. Beginning at a bounder of William
Mullinex's ... to a bounder of Ephraim Polk's land ... line
dividing part of said tract to Thomas Laverty to a post near the
edge of the Long Savannah ... with a line dividing part of said
tract to George White ... 200 acres. Wit: George White, Charles
Polk, Junr. Within deed ackn. 29 March 1777.

147. Bowden Hammond, Sussex Co., mariner, from Robert McCrea,
Worcester Co., Maryland, planter. 29 March 1777. For £798,
parcels, formerly in Worcester Co. but now Sussex Co., on the
south side of Indian River, called McCreas Lot, granted said
McCrea for 266 acres by patent and another tract called Richards
Struggle granted to Richard Tull for 50 acres. Wit: David Hall,
John Adams. Within deed ackn. 29 March 1777.

149. Charles Polk, Junr., Sussex Co., yeoman, from Isaac
Layfield, son of George Layfield of Worcester Co., Maryland,
yeoman. 19 March 1777. Tract called Fruitful Plain, 540 acres
on the main branch of Nanticoke River in Great Neck formerly
Smiths Neck adjoining lands of Francis Newbold, Unity Forge
Tract, originally granted by Proprietary of Maryland to George
Layfield by patent dated 15 July 1695, then a part of Somerset
Co., later Worcester Co., now Sussex Co. George Layfield died
without issue and the land descended to his brother's son Thomas
Layfield who died and by his last will devised same to his son
Thomas Layfield who resurveyed the same and died leaving issue
one son, Thomas Layfield to whom the land descended who died

intestate and without issue and the said lands descended to afsd. Isaac Layfield who is eldest son of George Layfield who was brother to Thomas Layfield, the son and devisee of the first above named Thomas Layfield the brother's sons of the original planter. For £150. Wit: Samuel Laverty, John Polk. Within deed ackn. 7 May 1777.

150. Jacob Coverdal, Sussex Co., from William Willey, Sussex Co., planter. 18 June 1774. For £20, a tract in Great Neck of 300 acres, binding on the north side by a survey made by Warren Burroughs and on the south by a survey made by John Loftland being a place first settled and improved by Andrew Dagg containing 300 acres, being taken up by virtue of a located warrant in the name of William Willey and formerly sold to Andrew Dagg. Wit: Israel Coverdall, Richd. Coverdall. Within deed ackn. 7 May 1777.

150. Ezekiel Brown, Sussex Co., yeoman, from John Clowes, Sussex Co. 4 May 1777. 50 acres at the head of Nanticoke River called Wigton which John Clowes on 29 May 1769 leased to James Willson for a term of years and afterwards in the same year sold the same under the encumbrances of said lease to John Sylavan and gave bond for conveyance thereof and said James Willson on 1 June 1769 assigned the lease to Messrs. Allexander Morton and John Fisher jointly. After the death of said Morton in 1776 the said Fisher being in debt to John Willett became insolvent and gave up his property to the creditors and Willett applied to said Clowes for a deed of conveyance for the said 50 acres [This land has too complicated a history to detail here. See actual deed.] £21.15. Wit: Jon. Anderson, Jos. Darby. Within deed ackn. 7 May 1777.

151. John Potter, from David Stuart and wife Sofiah, Sussex Co. Bond for conveyance of land. David and Sofiah Stuart are bound to John Potter for £560. To convey a parcel in Broadkill Hundred, 145 acres, whereon David Stuart now lives. 28 Nov 1775. Wit: Jehu Claypoole, Jno. Cade. Proved 31 Aug 1776.

152. Petition of Sophia Stuart, admx. of David Stewart, for leave of Court to convey land to John Potter. 11 June 1777. [See above bond.]

152. John Potter from Sophia Stuart. admx. of David Stuart. 11 June 1777. Parcel of land and marsh in Broadkill Hundred containing 145 acres being part of tract belonging to Thomas Grove conveyed from Thomas Grove, Samuel Grove and Susanna Grove to David Stuart. Beginning at a corner post standing on the south side of Primehook Creek. For £280. Wit: Thomas Grove, William Burton. Within deed ackn. 12 June 1777.

153. Jonathan Morgan, merchant, Sussex Co., from James Adams, Senr., Sussex Co., yeoman. 13 April 1766. Whereas by an indenture by Levi Gale, Esqr. to Henry Ennels, Deputy Surveyor of Dorchester Co., dated 10 April 1740, to survey a tract for Thomas Adams son of Roger Adams pursuant to order surveyed a parcel of land called Pore Luck then in Dorchester Co. now Sussex Co.

Beginning at an oak standing on the east side of the northwest
fork of Nanticoke River and about 3 perches north from the road
that crosses the upper bridge called Marshahope Bridge and about
1/4 mile from the said bridge, 58 acres, in Northwest Fork
Hundred, for £30. Wit: Constantine Cannon, Nathan Stafford (his
mark). Within deed ackn. 12 June 1777.

154. William Ross, Sussex Co., planter, from John Dawson, Sussex
Co., planter, and wife Leah. 2 June 1777. For £50, part of a
tract called Safford Venter in Northwest Fork Hundred, 51 1/4
acres. Wit: James Cooper and Jonathan Morgan. Within deed ackn.
12 June 1777.

154. Samuel Fountain and Major his wife of Caroline Co. of the
first part and Constantine Cannon of Sussex Co. of the second
part and from Roger Adams and Elinor his wife of Sussex Co. of
the 3rd part. 4 Feb 1777. Whereas in pursuance and by virtue of
a warrant dated 1740 called an Addition to Linkorn containing 41
acres, also two other warrants dated 1740 called Addition to
Backloss containing 77 acres and 1751 called Batchelors Quarter
containing 23 acres, also another warrant dated 1719 called
Linkorn containing 50 acres, also another warrant dated 1740
called Cliftons Delight containing 29 acres, also another patent
dated 1696 called Backeloss of 50 acres the whole of said tracts
containing 270 acres, late the property of Roger Adams, dec'd.
Roger Adams died leaving sundry issues among whom was Roger Adams
and Elinor his wife, Samuel Fountain and Major his wife and they
have deeded this land to Constantine Cannon. Roger Adams and
Elinor his wife and Samuel Fountain and Major his wife for £200
paid by Constantine Cannon to whom the land is conveyed. Wit:
Jonathan Morgan, Levin Cannon. Within deed ackn. 12 June 1777.

155. Peter Rea, Sussex Co., from William Ellegood, Sussex Co.
Bond for conveyance of land. William Ellegood is bound to Peter
Rea for £1000. 18 July 1777. To convey, after the sum of £158
is paid a part of a tract called Martins Hundred in Northwest
Fork Hundred on Herring Branch or Herring Run, boundary running
on a line of the land that was sold by said William Ellegood to
Isaac Williams now in the possession of Samuel Williams ... to a
line of Joshua Williams' land ... line of William Jewett's land.
Wit: Nathan Adams, Wm. Stayton. 173 acres.

156. Constant Mariner, Sussex Co., from Nathaniel Bowman
Mariner, Sussex Co. 5 Aug 1777. Tract in Indian River Hundred
being part of a larger tract formerly belonging to Aminadab
Hanser and was in the possession of Richard Mariner who by his
last will left his wife Elizabeth extx. and she by deed dated 28
March 1772 conveyed same to Nathaniel Bowman Mariner, being on
the south side of Joy Branch. 120 acres, for £85. Wit: Nehemiah
Davis, Junr., George Benson. Within deed ackn. 6 Aug 1777.

156. Daniel Polk, Sussex Co., planter, from James Jessup, Sussex
Co., planter. Sep 1776. For £41.16.3, part of a tract called
Hogg Range, 55 3/4 acres. Wit: John Laws, Thomas Laverty.
Within deed ackn. 7 Aug 1777.

157. Wateman Goslen, Sussex Co., from George Gullet and wife Mary, planter. 26 April 1776. For £75, a parcel on the east side of the Northwest Fork River of Nanticoke, part of the tract called Puzzle. Beginning about 50 perches to the south of William Richards plantation at the beginning tree of a tract called the Pessimon [Persimmon?] Bottom. 120 acres. Wit: James Cooper, John Laws. Within deed ackn. 7 Aug 1777.

158. Whitelay (Wheatley) Hatfield, yeoman, from Jacob Kollock, Senr., Esqr. Bond for conveyance of land. Jacob Kollock is bound to said Hatfield for £120. 1 March 1767. To convey at the receipt of £60, 106 acres which Jacob Kollock purchased of Gabriel Powell and Mary his wife on the southwest side of Mill Branch adjoining lands of Richard Blocksam and the heirs of William Dulavan. Wit: Mary Kollock, Danl. Nunez. Within deed ackn. 9 Sep 1777.

159. Margaret Kollock's petition to convey land to Whiteley Hatfield. [See above entry.] Granted 9 Sep 1777.

160. Whitelay Hatfield from Margaret Kollock, extx. of Jacob Kollock. [See above entries.] Beginning at an oak on or near Gitters Branch, on the northwest side and to the south of Kings Road that leads from Lewes Town ... division line between Charles Coulter and Timothy Dunnavan dec'd., laid out for 100 acres, being the same that was seized and sold by the sheriff to John Dunnavan in satisfaction of a debt, recovered by said Jacob Kollock. The afsd. Timothy Dunnavan was the highest bidder [sic] and John Dunnavan [sic] conveyed same to Mary Dunnavan on 7 Sep 1756 who later married Gabriel Powell and they conveyed same to Jacob Kollock, Esqr. on 16 Aug 1765. Wit: Hester Moore, D. Train. Within deed ackn. 9 Sep 1777.

161. William Wyatt, Sussex Co., yeoman, from Henry Lingo, Westmoreland Co., PA, yeoman. 19 Dec 1776. Whereas William Lingo, father of afsd. Henry Lingo was seized of two parcels joining each other in Broadkill Hundred and in his last will (his wife Elizabeth Lingo his extx.) directed that his extx. sell and convey 50 acres to pay his debts and devised the residue of said two parcels to his son afsd. Henry Lingo, reserving the use of the land to his wife Elizabeth during her lifetime. The parcels being the same that William Lingo purchased of Thomas Staton and Mary his wife by their deed dated 4 May 1768. Beginning at a corner post on the southeast side of Bever Dam Branch ... road that leads to widow Rowlan's ... division between said land and David Scudder ... 120 acres; and the other parcel beginning ... to corner post in the division line of the afsd. Staton and Scudder ... division line of Robert Jones and said land ... 15 3/4 acres. And is part of the land devised by Thomas Staton the elder to his son Thomas Staton, afsd. Except for 50 acres sold by Elizabeth Burns late Elizabeth Lingo. This conveyance for £70. Wit: William Conwell, Nehemiah Stockly, Joseph Pyles. Within deed ackn. 25 Jan 1777.

162. Power of attorney. Henry Lingo appoints William Wyatt his

attorney. Wit: William Conwell, Nehemiah Stockly. 30 Jan 1777.

163. John and William Wyatt, Junr., from William Wyatt, Senr. Bond for conveyance of land. William Wyatt of Worcester Co., Maryland, planter, is bound to John Wyatt and William Wyatt, both of afsd. county, in the penal sum of £400. 9 Dec 1774. To convey tract called Desire, 200 acres, that is, 100 acres to afsd. John Wyatt to be laid off convenient to the plantation or building whereon the said William Wyatt Senr. now lives and 100 acres to said William Wyatt, Junr., to the northwest end of the said tract. Wit: John Cod, Reuben Linch. [See John Coe's deposition recorded in Liber N, folio 339.]

163. Charles Draper from Alexander Draper. Bond for conveyance of land. Alexander Draper, Sussex Co., Sussex Co., is bound to Charles Draper of Sussex Co., yeoman, in the penal sum of £1000. 2 March 1773. To convey land called Drapers Quarter containing 276 3/4 acres of land and marsh excepting 27 acres in Neh. Davis pasture. Wit: Thos. Gray, junr., Nehemiah Davis, Junr. Proved 4 Aug 1779. [Added later]

163. May Term 1777. Petition of Nathaniel Young of Cedar Creek Hundred and Esther his wife (late Esther Draper) extx. of last will of Alexander Draper to convey to Charles Draper [see above bond].

164. Charles Draper from Nathaniel Young, Cedar Creek Hundred, yeoman, and wife Esther, extx. of Alexander Draper. Whereas Nehemiah Draper, father of the above named Alexander Draper, Esqr. was seized of 3 parcels in Slaughter Neck, one called Susans Palace being part of a larger tract called Bowmans Farm, another called Davis's Farm contiguous to afsd. tract, the other called My Fortune being part of a larger tract originally granted by patent to Edward Furlong adjoining to the last mentioned tract, died leaving a will in which he devised the same (inter alia) to his son Nehemiah who died without issue whereby the land became distributable and a valuation was made at 28 shillings per acre. And Alexander Draper became seized of the land and became bound to Charles Draper [see above entries]. Containing 276 3/4 acres. Wit: Joseph Draper, Benjamin Truitt, Brantson Lofland. Within deed ackn. 12 June 1777. Payment of £500 made in the lifetime of Alexander Draper. [Plat is included.]

166. John Tennent, Sussex Co., merchant, from Ezekiel Brown, Sussex Co., planter. 4 Nov 1777. For £150, tract called Bunkers Hill in Northwest Fork Hundred surveyed for said Ezekiel Brown by virtue of a warrant granted 23 Feb 1776, certificate dated 12 May 1776. 150 acres. Wit: Clement Bayly, Edmond Beachamp. Within deed ackn. 5 Nov 1777.

167. William Douglass, of Caroline Co., Maryland, iron master, from Isaac Brown, Sussex Co., planter, and wife Ann. Mortgage deed. 14 Aug 1777. Whereas said Isaac Brown and Levin Brown son of said Isaac and Ann Brown by one bond obliged themselves to William Douglass in the penal sum of £1000 conditioned for the

payment of £500 on 12 Aug 1780. To convey parcel called Poplar Ridge granted from Lord Baltimore on 12 Dec 1739 containing 50 acres with 208 acres and allowance of 6 per cent added thereto by virtue of a warrant of resurvey granted to said Isaac Brown by proprietaries of Pennsylvania and surveyed 9 Dec 1776 reducing the whole into one tract of 258 1/2 acres, still retaining the name Poplar Ridge. Also one Negro man named Benn, aged 24 years; Negro girl Patience aged about 16 years; and Negro girl named Seale aged 6 years. Wit: Thomas Laws, Joseph Dawson. Within deed ackn. 5 Nov 1777.

169. Levi Safford, Sussex Co., yeoman, from Nathan Safford, Sussex Co., yeoman and his wife Sarah. 30 Oct 1777. Parcel in Northwest [Fork] Hundred containing 150 acres called Safford Lot granted by patent to Henry Safford, first in Dorchester Co., Maryland now Sussex Co., for £70. Wit: Isaac Bradly, Henry Safford. Within deed ackn. 5 Nov 1777.

170. John Sheldon Dormon, Sussex Co., yeoman, from John Clowes, Sussex Co., yeoman. 1 March 1776. Whereas John Clowes, Esqr., father to the afsd. John Clowes, by his last will devised his lands to his seven children, equally to be divided by lots fairly drawn, will dated 17 Dec 1772 - by which allotment lot number 4 became the right and property of Lydia Conwell and Lot number 3 became the right of the heirs of Gerhardus Clowes, dec'd., and Lot number 2 the right of the heirs of David Clowes, dec'd., and Lot number 1 the right of afsd. John Clowes. See Liber L Number 11, folio 270. And the lot of David Clowes was sold to pay his debts and was purchased by Henry Smith, the highest bidder, and Henry Smith by deed of sale dated 19 Feb 1773 conveyed same to afsd. John Clowes. And Lydia Conwell by her deed dated 10 July 1773 together with John Young, Catharine Young, John Sheldon Dormon and Mary Dormon, conveyed her right to afsd. Lot number 4 and all their several rights to the afsd. Lot number 3 as heirs to afsd. Gerhardus Clowes, to afsd. John Clowes, party to these presents. For £360. Sale of lot numbers, 1, 2, 3 and 4, in Broadkill Hundred, Lots 1 and 2, beginning at the edge of the Broadkill Creek by the foot of the Draw Bridge, 8 feet below said bridge, 2 1/2 acres and Lots 3 and 4 lying a little to the eastward of the other two lots beginning at the mouth of a ditch emptying into said creek being a line of Hazzard's land containing 100 1/2 acres, reserving the right to use the draw bridge and crossway over the said Broadkill Creek to the heirs of John Clowes. Wit: Thomas Grove, Caleb Cirwithin. Within deed ackn. 5 Nov 1777.

171. Catharine Young, wife of John Young, from John Clowes, Sussex Co., mariner. 14 Feb 1776. Whereas John Clowes, Esqr., dec'd., father to the afsd. John Clowes and Catharine Young, by his last will devised all his lands to his seven children [see above entry] equally to be divided by lots fairly drawn, will dated 17 Dec 1772 - by allotment Lot number 6 containing 61 3/4 acres became the right of Mary Dormon wife of John Sheldon Dormon and Lot number 7 adjoining lot 6 containing and equal number of acres became the right of afsd. Catharine Young [see Liber L

number 11, folio 270 for the division]. And Mary Dormon with her husband John Sheldon Dormon by their deed dated 29 July 1773 conveyed lot number 6 to first mentioned John Clowes. For £80, Lot 6, beginning at the edge of the Mill Creek, 12 perches to the northwest of Hugh King's corner tree. Wit: J. Russel, Sacker Wyatt. Within deed ackn. 5 Nov 1777.

172. Nathaniel Waples, Sussex Co., sadler, from William Waples, Sussex Co., yeoman. 4 Feb 1778. Parcel being part of a tract granted by proprietor's warrant to Peter and Paul Waples on 1 March 1739 and the said Peter Waples died intestate and said land fell amongst his several heirs; the said William Waples being one of the said heirs, accepted the lands at valuation of 3 men appointed by the Orphans Court. Beginning at a hickory standing in the head line of a tract called Warwick formerly surveyed to Wm. Kenning ... 109 acres for £109. Wit: Rhoads Shankland, Draper May. Within deed ackn. 4 Feb 1778.

172. Parker Robinson, Esqr. from James Fisher, Sussex Co., yeoman, and wife Alice. Whereas Thomas Fisher of Sussex Co., yeoman, and his wife Alice by their deed dated 24 Sep 1774 conveyed to Parker Robinson, Esqr. and James Fisher above named, a parcel in Broadkill Hundred. Beginning on the Old Ditch on the northwest side thereof ... near the head of Peters Gutt ... corner post of Samuel Russel's land ... Broadkiln Creek ... 150 acres of land and marsh. And Parker Robinson and James Fisher have made division of the said land as following, beginning at a corner post. James Fisher and Alice his wife for 5 shillings. Wit: Ruth Rodney, Hannah Rodney. Within deed of release ackn. 4 Feb 1778.

174. James Fisher from Parker Robinson, Esqr. [Deed of release - establishing the division of land between Parker Robinson and James Fisher - see above entry] Beginning at the corner of Parker Robinson's land near the place mentioned in the last will of John Fisher, corner of the division between James and Thomas Fisher ... to a gutt leading out of Crab Ponds ... division line of 100 acres called the Old Point to Peters Gutt ... For 5 shillings. Wit: Ruth Rodney, Hannah Rodney. Within deed ackn. 4 Feb 1778.

175. Thomas Robinson, Junr., Sussex Co., yeoman, from Thomas Stockley, Westmoreland Co., yeoman. 5 Feb 1778. Parcel in Angola Hundred, 600 acres called Exchange, originally granted by patent to Francis Maggs and John Crolly and whereas William Bradford later became seized of the said land and whereby he transferred his rights to James Walker who by his indorsement on said patent transferred his right to William Simmons and John Hill who by their article of agreement made division of said lands whereby said Simmons became seized of one moiety who by his last will devised same to Jane Rost who married Samuel Rowland and they by their deed of gift transferred their right to Joshua Stockley who by his deed of sale conveyed same to Oliver Stockley who by his last will devised same to his four sons, John, Alexander, Oliver and Prettyman Stockley which Alexander, Oliver

and Prettyman Stockley by their several deeds of release
transferred their rights to said John Stockley who by his last
will devised same to his wife Mary Stockley who by her deed of
release transferred all her right to her son the afsd. Thomas
Stockley. Beginning at a poplar standing in the division line of
the land of John Hill ... 200 acres. Surveyed 3 Jan 1778. For
£309. Wit: Peter Ft. Wright, J. Russel. Within deed ackn. 4 Feb
1778.

176. Isaac Bradley, Northwest Fork Hundred, Sussex Co., yeoman,
from Charles Brown, Northwest Fork Hundred, Sussex Co., yeoman,
and wife Sarah; and John Brown, Northwest Fork Hundred, Sussex
Co., yeoman, and wife Rebecca. 2 Aug 1777. Parcel on the west
side of Nanticoke River in Northwest Fork Hundred called Rich
Bottom. Beginning at two red oaks being the first bounders of a
tract called Fax Hall. 200 acres, which was granted by patent by
proprietary of Maryland to Charles Brown the elder, dec'd.,
father of the afsd. Charles, and John Brown who by his last will
devised the same to his son Tilghman Brown who became seized of
same but died intestate and without issue and the land descended
to Charles and John Brown and Curtis Brown and Elenor Jessop,
late Elinor Brown wife of John Jessup as heirs and legal
representatives of said Tilghman Brown. And whereas afsd. Curtis
Brown, John Jessup and Elinor his wife by their deed dated 1 Aug
1777 confirmed to Charles and John Brown their rights to said
land. Wit: Daniel Polk, James Richards. Within deed ackn. 4 Feb
1778.

177. Charles and John Brown from Curtis Brown son of Charles
Brown the elder dec'd., and John Jessup and Elenor Jessup convey
their rights to tract called Rich Bottom for £30 paid by their
brothers Charles and John Brown. [See above entry.] Wit: Daniel
Polk, James Rickards. Within deed ackn. 4 Feb 1778.

179. Daniel Polk, Sussex Co., planter, from Curtis Brown, Sussex
Co., planter. 4 Feb 1778. For £130, tract called Browns's
Security in Northwest Fork Hundred. Beginning at a marked white
oak being the bounder of a tract called Turssewondock ... 171
acres. Wit: John Woodgate, Thomas Hickman. Within deed ackn. 4
Feb 1778.

179. David Thornton, Sussex Co., from John Rodney, Trustee of
the Land Office. 4 Feb 1778. Whereas Robert Stephenson late of
Sussex Co., dec'd., by a deed of mortgage dated 2 Aug 1759
mortgaged to Jacob Kollock and Ryves Hall, Esqrs. late trustees
of said Loan Office in condition of £60, whereof he did
acknowledge a tract in Broadkill Hundred being 2 shares in the
estate of his late father William Stephenson dec'd., computed to
be about 200 acres as by an allotment and division remaining on
record in the Orphans Court. And Robert Stephenson made but one
yearly payment to wit on 6 Aug 1760. For £500. Wit: John
Willson, Thomas Robinson, Junr. Within deed ackn. 4 Feb 1778.

180. Levin Hickman, Sussex Co., from Robert Nutter, Sussex Co.,
and his wife Sarah. 2 Feb 1778. Tract in Northwest Fork Hundred

called Nutters Lot which was granted by patent by the proprietary of Maryland to Christopher Nutter then of Dorchester Co. in 1760 who by his last will devised 200 acres of same land to afsd. Robert Nutter on the west side of the tract and made no mention of the remainder of the tract except that part that lay within his dwelling plantation and that part that was formerly called Part of Dublin ... for £86.11.7 46 1/4 acres in one parcel and 37 acres in the other parcel. Wit: Thomas Hickman, William Bagwell. Within deed ackn. 4 Feb 1778.

182. Levin Hickman, Sussex Co., from Joshua Hickman, Sussex Co., yeoman. 3 Feb 1778. Whereas said Levin Hickman is possessed of two tracts, one called Poplar Hill and the other called Poplar Hill Addition, both of which lie in Northwest Fork Hundred. Poplar Hill was granted by patent to William Layton of Dorchester Co., Maryland, who by his deed conveyed same to James Hickman. Poplar Hill Addition was granted by patent to James Hickman of whom the said Joshua Hickman is eldest son, and afsd. James Hickman after giving a bond to convey said two tract to Levin Hickman and before making conveyance, died. For £40, the one tract of Poplar Hill, 50 acres and the other tract of Poplar Hill Addition, 30 acres. Wit: Thomas Laws, Thomas Hickman. Within deed ackn. 4 Feb 1778.

183. Aaron Dodd, Sussex Co., yeoman, from Joseph Warrington, Sussex Co., yeoman. 3 Feb 1778. Parcel on Indian River Hundred, part of a tract granted to said Warrington by proprietor's warrant 30 April 1761. 146 acres. [Consideration not given.] Wit: William Wyatt, Draper May, Rhoads Shankland. Within deed ackn. 4 Feb 1778.

183. Cloe Bar, wife of James Bar and late widow of Jonathan Scudder late of Sussex Co., and Rachel Scudder, minor daughter of afsd. Jonathan Scudder from John Day and wife Hannah. 4 Feb 1778. Two tracts in Broadkill Hundred, one containing 100 acres and part of a tract called Timber Hill which was granted by patent to John Vines and by sundry conveyances became the property of Jonathan Scudder, dec'd., father of afsd. Hannah Day; the other tract containing 213 acres, part of a larger tract called Mill Plantation granted to William Clark and by sundry conveyances became the property of afsd. Jonathan Scudder. And afsd. Jonathan Scudder died intestate leaving issue, two sons and three daughters, the afsd. Hannah Day being one of the daughters who became entituled to one sixth part of the two tracts. For £32. Wit: James Coulter, Mary Peery. Within deed ackn. 4 Feb 1778.

184. John Jessep, Sussex Co., planter, from Charles Brown and Sarah his wife, Curtis Brown and John Brown and Rebecca his wife, all of Sussex Co. 2 Aug 1777. For £200. Tract called Ridge Point as by patent or mostly known by Bowndes Place, in Northwest Fork Hundred. 90 acres. Also part of a tract called Partnership containing 30 acres now in possession of Joseph Rickards. Wit: Daniel Polk, James Richards. Within deed ackn. 4 Feb 1778.

185. Curtis Brown, Sussex Co., planter, from John Jessep and Elinor his wife; Charles Brown and Sarah his wife; and John Brown, all of Sussex Co. 2 Aug 1778. For £150. Tract called Gladstower in Northwest Fork Hundred - 100 acres. Also tract called Clarance near the afsd. parcel - 94 acres. Wit: Daniel Polk, James Richards. Within deed ackn. 4 Feb 1778.

186. John Rust, Westmoreland Co., Virginia, from Joseph Dawson and wife Elizabeth, Sussex Co. 8 Nov 1777. For £177, 150 acres being part of a tract called Second Addition to Cannaan for which afsd. Joseph Dawson obtained a patent dated 21 June 1776. Wit: Constantine Jacobs, Henry Smith. Within deed ackn. 4 Feb 1778.

187. George Waters, Dorchester Co., Maryland, from Joseph and his son Charles Brown, both of Sussex Co. 10 Jan 1778. For £27, a tract called Wales. Beginning at a marked oak and cedar posts standing on the east side of said Waters plantation, they being the original bounders of the afsd. Wales and the Beginning of a tract called Double Purchase, containing 100 acres. Wit: Joseph Dawson, James Brown, Junr. Within deed ackn. 4 Feb 1778.

188. William Walls, son of Wm., dec'd., Sussex Co., from Thomas Walls, Sussex Co., yeoman,. For 5 shillings. A parcel in Broadkill forrest granted by proprietor's warrant 4 Oct 1738 to Jacob Kollock and assigned to said Walls 17 Oct 1738 being the southeast portion or moiety of the tract containing 240 acres ... division lines made by Thomas Walls and his brother William Walls, late of the same co. and containing in the whole 480 acres. Wit: John Craige, Rhoads Shankland. Within deed ackn. 4 Feb 1778.

189. Robert Mariner, Sussex Co., planter from Bowman Mariner, Sussex Co., farmer. 1777. Parcel in Indian River Hundred on the south side of Joy Branch formerly belonging to James Love, joining an 1100-acre tract, containing 100 acres, for £150. Wit: Constant Mariner, Thos. Gray, Junr. Within deed ackn. 4 Feb 1778.

189. Edmond Potter, Accomack Co., Virginia, from John Holmes, Sussex Co. Bond for conveyance of land. John Holmes is bound to Edmond Potter for £1500. 29 Dec 1774. To convey a parcel of land whereon he now lives binding on Musmillion Creek containing 224 acres. John Potter, William Draper. Within bond proved 4 Feb 1778.

190. Jonathan Bryan's certificate of marriage. To whom it may concern: We Jonathan Bryant and Margaret Stephenson did cause our intentions of marriage signed by one of the Justices for Sussex Co., dated 24 Dec last to be set up at said Justices door and a true copy thereof at the door of the courthouse in Lewes Town and have this 11th day of Feb ensuing, 1778, in the presence of witnesses, solemnized our said intention of marriage. Wit: Thomas Martin (his mark), William Jeffery, Thomas Andrews, Wm. Brittingham Ennis, Ann Parker, Mary Russul, Sarah Stockley (her mark), Ann Parker, Junr., Betty Parker, Mary Thompson, Shepard

Foster.

190. William Black, Sussex Co., cordwinder, from John Black, Augusty [Augusta] Co., Virginia. Bond for conveyance of land. John Black is bound to William Black for £8. 18 Oct 1768. To convey a parcel of land in Broadkill Hundred, being a part of a tract formerly belonging to Samuel Black, dec'd., and formerly called the Black Swamp. Wit: William Dellaney, James Martin. Proved 4 Feb 1778.

190. Elizabeth Carrel from her mother Margaret Carrel, widow, Sussex Co. Deed of Gift. For love and affection. Bed and furniture, colt bought of Molton Crapper, 1 ewe and lamb, 3 silver tea spoons at age 16. 20 March 1778. Wit: Thomas Evans, John Plowman.

191. Sarah Carrel from her mother Margret Carrel, widow, Sussex Co. Deed of Gift. For love and affection, bed and furniture, a heifer, pair of silver shoe buckles, 3 silver tea spoons and a pair of silver locket sleave buttons at age 16. 20 March 1778. Wit: Thomas Evans, John Plowman.

191. Peleg Walter, Sussex Co., from Joshua Hill, Sussex Co. Bond for conveyance of land. Joshua Hill is bound to Peleg Walter for £1000. 9 Jan 1776. To convey a parcel of land that John Robinson conveyed to Joshua Hill where the said Walter know dwells. Rec'd. of Peleg Walter £330 for the land and plantation - 29 March 1777 - /s/ Joshua Hill.

191. Isaac Shaver, Sussex Co., yeoman, from Levin Crapper, Sussex Co., merchant. Bond for conveyance of land. Levin Crapper is bound to Isaac Shaver for £300. 26 Jan 1771. To convey 231 acres adjoining the land whereon William Chance lately dwelled after the full purchase money is paid. Wit: David Train, Molton Crapper. Proved 6 May 1778.

192. Isaac Holland, Sussex Co., from John Walker, Sussex Co., yeoman. 5 May 1778. For £400, a parcel in Lewes and Rehoboth Hundred. Beginning at a corner poplar by the side of a large swamp being the corner of the land afsd. Isaac Holland now lives on ... corner of the lands the said Isaac Holland bought of the heirs of James Ricketts ... corner of the heirs of Westly ... land of William Holland ... 120 acres. Wit: Robt. Jones, William Holland. Within deed ackn. 6 May 1778.

192. William Polk, Sussex Co., planter, from Joseph and William Kinney, formerly of Sussex Co., planters. 26 Feb 1778. For £100, a tract called Kinney's Chance, beginning at a marked oak standing about 150 yards from Little Creek, 50 acres. Also tract called Good Neighbourhood, beginning about 50 yards from the third bounder of tract called the Desert, 50 acres. Also tract called Desert which fell to said Joseph and William Kinney by the will of their father William Kinney to be laid off by William Polk by the lines and limits described in the will of their father. Wit: Levin Polk, Robert Crouch. Within deed ackn. 6 May

1778.

193. William Fisher, Sussex Co., cordwinder, from William Holland, Sussex Co., yeoman. 31 Feb 1778. For £97.10, a parcel in Rehoboth Hundred about 4 miles from the town of Lewes on the northwest side of the road leading to Kollock's mill being part of 89 acres confirmed to said William Holland by a deed of sale from William Gill of said county dated 5 May 1767. Beginning at the first bounder of a tract laid out to William White ... line of the said Fisher and Jacob Stockley's land ... corner oak of land now in possession of David Shankland. Wit: Jams. Pettyjohn (his mark), Rhoads Shankland. 6 May 1778.

194. Nehemiah Coffin. Sussex Co., from Hugh Stephenson, Sussex Co. 6 May 1778. For £70, a parcel in Indian River Hundred, part of a tract granted to Benjamin Stockley and confirmed by said Stockley to the heirs of Daniel Coops and by Joseph Atkins and wife who married one of the daughters of said Coops, confirmed to Hugh Stephenson afsd. Beginning at an oak standing by Sockrocket Branch ... 85 acres. Within deed ackn. 6 May 1778.

195. Nehemiah Reed, Sussex Co., yeoman, from Edward Stephenson, Broadkill Hundred, yeoman, and wife, Margaret. 7 May 1778. Parcel in the forrest of Broadkill Hundred, 300 acres, called Collins Folly, originally surveyed to Joshua Collins on 2 Dec 1752 by virtue of proprietor's warrant dated 9 June 1743 and Joshua Collins by indenture dated Feb 1753 conveyed same to Isaac Brittingham of Worcester Co., Maryland who on 1 April 1760 conveyed same to Edward Stephenson. Boundary runs to a corner oak of land formerly surveyed for Abraham Parsley at the head of Pembertons Branch ... adjoining lands of Thomas Dutton (said to be the above mentioned land laid off or surveyed for the afsd. Abraham Parsley), Benjamin Mifflin, James Reed, dec'd., Zerubbabel Davis and Samuel Turner. For £130. Wit: D. Train, Mary Train. Within deed ackn. 7 May 1778.

196. John Sheldon Dormon, Sussex Co., yeoman, from Peter Dickerson and wife Catharine, Sussex Co. 20 June 1777. Whereas John Clowes, Esqr. (grandfather to afsd. Catharine Dickerson), dec'd., by his last will devised all his land to his seven children, William, John, David, Catharine, Mary, Lydia and Gerhardus, share and share alike by lots to be fairly drawn. William Clowes, father to the afsd. Catharine Dickerson, predeceased his father, and his share became the right of his four children, Catharine, Mary, Lydia and John. Whereas John, Catharine, Mary, Lydia, four of the seven children of John Clowes, along with John Young husband of afsd. Catharine [daughter of John Clowes], John Sheldon Dormon husband of afsd. Mary [daughter of John Clowes], and Jeremiah Conwell husband of afsd. Lydia [daughter of John Clowes] on 17 Dec 1772 entered into an agreement to divide the land which was done. For £85. 61 1/2 acres, 34 acres being part of the Bridge Plantation. Wit: John Neill, George Frame. Within deed ackn. 6 May 1778.

198. William Wilson, Sussex Co., from Salathiel Griffith of

Somerset Co., Maryland. 8 Dec 1777. For £24. Tract called
Dublin being within the lines clear of Owens' Fancy. Beginning
at a marked oak standing in Grubby Neck and near the bottom of
the neck and on Grubby Neck Branch, containing 41 acres, 56
perches. Wit: David Nutter, Francis Wright. Within deed ackn. 6
May 1778.

198. William Owens, planter, Sussex Co., from William Gaskins,
bricklayer, Sussex Co. 19 Feb 1778. A parcel conveyed by deed
of sale from David Owens to William Gaskins dated 14 Feb 1775
recorded in Worcester Co., 27 acres, Liber I, folio 570, dated 10
March 1775. For £60.10. Beginning on the east side of Zacharias
Swamp and on the east side of Northeast Branch of Nanticoke River
... Wit: David Owens, Ann Owens, Curtis Otwell. Within deed
ackn. 6 May 1778.

199. Peter Rea, Sussex Co., from William Ellegood, Esqr., Sussex
Co. 5 Feb 1778. William Ellegood by virtue of a deed of
conveyance from John Hooper then of Dorchester Co., became seized
of a part of a tract then in Dorchester Co. called Martins
Hundred in Northwest Fork Hundred and now in Sussex Co., who
later by deed of release confirmed to Isaac Williams 300 acres of
the northeastern most corner of the land and by another deed
released and confirmed to William Jewet 400 acres adjoining and
later by another deed released and confirmed to Thomas Williams
another parcel thereof adjoining a division line that was made
between John and Thomas Hooper with unconveyed 173 acres and 88
perches. For the remainder of the land, having received £15.10
from said Rea and Rea's bond and William Stayton's jointly for
the remainder with an additional payment made by Rea of £35
leaving a balance of £123. Wit: Henry Hooper, Elisha Ellett.
Within deed ackn. 6 May 1778.

201. The Rev. Sydenham Thorne, Sussex Co., and Betty his wife
(late Betty Crapper), surviving extx. of Levin Crapper, Esqr.
petition for leave of court to convey lands to the widow and
heirs of Isaac Shaver. 9 Jun 1778. Whereas Levin Crapper was
seized of a tract in Cedar Creek Hundred and by his bond dated 26
Jane 1771 was obliged to Isaac Shaver, yeoman, for £300, to
release their interest to 231 acres agreeable to a survey made by
Isaac Smith being part of a larger tract granted to Ryves Holt,
Esqr. for 383 acres, adjoining the lands whereon William Chance
lately dwelt. The bond was proved 6 May 1778 and recorded Liber
M No. 12, Folio 191. And Levin Crapper died before conveying the
land having first made his last will and appointed his wife
(petitioner) together with his son Molton Crapper (whom she hath
survived) as exrs. But Isaac Shaver hath died intestate leaving
Ann his widow and issue two sons, Levin and John Shaver, the
consideration already paid.

201. Ann Shaver and sons from Sydenham Thorne and wife Betty.
[See above entry.] The land beginning at a corner of Shadrick
Sturgis's land on the southeast side of the Landing Road ...
valley between said Shavers and William Chance's ... Wit: J.
Hall, J. Russel. Within deed ackn. 9 June 1778.

203. Luke Wattson, the younger from Thomas Jones, Sussex Co., yeoman, and wife Naomi (late Naomie Records), widow of John Records of Sussex Co., yeoman. Whereas John Records was seized of messuage and parcel of land containing 100 acres in Prime Hook Neck being the same which said John Records purchased of George Read, Esqr. and he by his last will devised same to his son Peter Records subject to his widow's thirds, she the afsd. Naomi. For £50. Wit: Luke Wattson, Sheriff, Isaac Wattson, son T. Within deed ackn. 9 June 1778.

204. William Robins, Sussex Co., carpenter, from John Clowes, Sussex Co., mariner. 15 March 1778. Tract in Broadkill forrest adjoining lands surveyed for John Johnston, Thomas McLane and Elinor Dobson, granted to John Needham by proprietor's warrant dated 4 Sep 1759 for 150 acres and said John Needham on 3 June 1761 assigned same to Woolman Dulavan who on 11 March 1762 assigned same to Elijah Collings who by his deed of sale dated 8 Aug 1765 conveyed same to afsd. John Clowes. Beginning at a corner of Thomas McLane's land ... to Johnston's now James Heaveloe's land ... 150 acres. For £60. Wit: Jos. Hall, Jno. Drain. Within deed ackn. 9 June 1778.

205. George Black admr. of John Holmes, petition for leave of court to convey lands to Edmond Potter. 7 May 1778. Whereas John Holmes by a bond dated 29 Dec 1774 was bound to Edmond Potter of Accomack Co., Virginia, for £1500, to convey a parcel where he then lived binding on Musmillion Creek containing 224 acres.

205. Edmond Potter from George Black, admr. [See above entry.] 7 May 1778. For £750. 224 acres. Parcel being part of a larger tract granted by patent to afsd. John Holmes in Cedar Creek Hundred. Beginning at the mouth of a Ditch parting the land from land of William Draper's part of the same tract and on the south side of Mispillion Creek. Wit: Jacob Hazzard, J. Russel. Within deed ackn. 10 June 1778.

207. Elihu Hazzard from Benjamin Scholfield, Sussex Co., farmer. Bill of sale for a Negro boy named Zacker. For £80. 13 June 1778. Wit: Jon. Nottingham, Lambeth Caulk.

207. Robert Hood from Mary Hood, Sussex Co., widow of James Hood, yeoman, Magdalin McKnett of Kent Co., Delaware, widow, Elizabeth Black of Sussex Co., widow, William Peery, Sussex Co., Gentleman and his wife Mary (late Mary Hood) which said Magdalin, Elizabeth and Mary were daughters of said James Hood. Whereas James Hood was possessed of a parcel in Broadkill Hundred containing 250 acres, part of a larger tract 907 acres called Maiden Plantation and by deed of indenture dated 14 Oct 1738 was conveyed from Thomas Harrisson to said James Hood (Liber G No. 6, folio 277). For £185. Wit: Robert Shankland, Robert Stevenson. Within deed ackn. 10 June 1778.

208. Anderson Parker, from Thomas Robinson, Esqr., Sussex Co. Bond for conveyance of land. Thomas Robinson is bound to

Anderson Parker for £190. 7 Aug 1775. David Johnson and Joseph
Johnson sons of David Johnson and Hannah his wife, and half
brothers to Robert Craig, dec'd. who was son of Alexander Craig
dec'd. and the present Hannah Johnson his wife, shall when they
arrive to full age, convey a parcel in Rehoboth Hundred east of
Peter Parker's mill pond it being the same that Alexander Craig
bought of William Davis, gaoler, containing 70 acres. Wit:
Leatherbery Barker, Levin Milbey.

209. Sacker Wyatt, Sussex Co., yeoman, from Tabitha Russel,
Sussex Co., spinster. 5 Aug 1778. A parcel in Lewes and
Rehoboth Hundred being a part of a larger tract originally
granted by patent to Roger Gum who by deed conveyed same to John
Fisher who died intestate leaving issue two sons, Thomas and John
Fisher to whom the land descended who by their deed conveyed same
to Sarah Fisher who later married William Spencer and they
conveyed same to William Pettyjohn who conveyed 255 acres to
William Russel, father of the afsd. Tabitha Russel and William
Russel conveyed 105 acres to Marnix Virden and later by his last
will dated 19 April 1770 devised the remaining part of 255 acres
to his four daughters, Elizabeth, Mary, Ruth and Tabitha. And
whereas said Elizabeth, Mary and Ruth Russel by their deed dated
20 March 1776 conveyed their right to afsd. Sacker Wyatt, which
remaining part is bounded by a division line between this land
and the lands of John Hopkins ... dividing line between this and
the land conveyed to Marnix Virden ... 203 1/4 acres. For £80.
Wit: William Bradley, J. Russel. Within deed ackn. 5 Aug 1778.

210. David Shankland, Sussex Co., house carpenter, from William
Fisher, Sussex Co., cordwinder. 4 Aug 1778. For £48. A parcel
in Rehoboth Hundred about 4 miles southwest from the town of
Lewes, being the one moiety of 16 1/2 acres conveyed by William
Holland to said William Fisher dated 31 Feb 1778. Wit: Gillb.
Parker, Rhoads Shankland. Within deed ackn. 5 Aug 1778.

211. John Rodney, Esqr., Sussex Co., from John Neill, Sussex
Co., yeoman, and wife Bathiah. 20 Nov 1777. For £150. A tract
in Broadkill Hundred containing 100 acres being part of a larger
tract called Springford Patent, granted to George Martin who
conveyed same to Joshua Fisher who conveyed same to Robert Neill
who by his last will devised same to John Neill who sold the
above mentioned 100 acres being part of the said patent, to James
Black but never properly conveyed the same and the said James
Black sold the same to John Rodney and requested that John Neill
and Bethiah his wife convey the same to John Rodney. Land
adjoins the lands of James Doughoty and the lands which John
Rodney purchased of Samuel Tam being the northeast corner of said
patent containing 100 acres. Wit: James Black, Margret Neill.
Within deed ackn. 6 Aug 1778.

211. Joseph Waples, Sussex Co., from William Waples, Sussex Co.
7 April 1778. Tract laid out to Thomas Prettyman on 27 Feb 1714,
53 acres, for £100. Wit: Rhoads Shankland, Perry Prettyman.
Within deed ackn. 6 Aug 1778.

215. Smothers Wattson (Watson). Sussex Co., from his mother Mary
Wattson (Watson), Sussex Co. Deed of gift. All her goods and
chattels. 10 Aug 1778. /s/ Mary Watson (her mark). Wit: Paul
Waples, Thomas Hudson (his mark). Was delivered by Mary Watson
to Smothers Watson, two feather beds and furniture.

215. Joshua Williams, planter, from Spencer Williams, planter.
Bond. Spencer Williams is bound to Joshua Williams for the penal
sum of £500. 1 May 1775. That Spencer Williams agrees and
stands to a division of land made between him and Joshua
Williams, made and concluded by William Stayton a surveyor, the
land being part of a tract called Martins Hundred. Wit: Isaac
Williams, Nancey Handsworth.

216. Rachel Pridow and Lova Mitchell Smith of Sussex Co., from
Constantine Cannon, Sussex Co. Bond. Constantine Cannon is
bound to Rachel Pridow and Lova Mitchell Smith in the penal sum
of £500. 10 Jan 1778. To cause the conveyance of the tract
called Nutters Adventure, by its owners when they become of age.
25 acres and 50 perches. Wit: Wm. Stayton, William Owens.

216. Albertus Jacobs, Senr. is bound to Hannah Jacobs, John
Jacobs, John Mollison and Albertus Jacobs, Junr. of Sussex Co.
and George Morgan of Kent Co., Delaware, Gent. Bond. In the sum
of £100. The condition is such that whereas John Kipshaven of
Sussex Co., by his last will dated 14 Jan 1700 ordered that his
two grandsons, John Jacobs since dec'd., and above said Albertus
Jacobs Senr. by Martha his daughter should enjoy one moiety of
his lands and personal estate and his above said daughter the
other moiety during her natural life and after her decease to
descend to his two grandsons above said to be equally divided.
Now upon the death of the testator's daughter the above said
Albertus Jacobs, Senr. has agreed with Hannah Jacobs, John
Jacobs, George Morgan, Jno. Mollison and Albertus Jacobs, Junr.
heirs to John Jacobs above, dec'd. to divide a certain tract
containing two little necks called Kick In and Kick Out, being
the property of above said testate and is bound to stand by the
division. 20 April 1746. Wit: Willm. Shankland, Thomas Gordon,
William Gill. Within bond was proved 5 Nov 1778.

217. Between Albertus Jacobs and the heirs of John Jacobs.
Award. We, William Shankland, Thomas Gordon and William Gill of
Sussex Co., Gent., Greetings. Whereas there is a dispute arisen
lately between Albertus Jacobs, Senr. of Sussex Co., Gent. and
Hannah Jacobs, John Jacobs, John Molleston, Albertus Jacobs,
Junr., and George Morgan concerning the division of a tract
devised to the two grandsons of John Kipshaven, to wit, John
Jacobs since dec'd. and afsd. Albertus Jacobs Senr. and whereas
all concerned agreed and became bound to each other to abide by
the decision of the arbitrators, William Shankland, Thomas Gordon
and William Gill who were to submit their decision by 20 April
1746. The division line was made beginning at a corner post
standing on a point of land on the bank of Kickinn ... That afsd.
Albertus Jacobs, Senr. may carry away a kitchen lately built by
said Albertus adjoining the house he now lives in. That afsd.

Albertus Jacobs senr. execute a deed of release of all the lands on the southeast side of the said several lines mentioned. 28 March 1746.

218. Joseph Dirickson, Sussex Co., late Worcester Co., from Benjamin Mifflin, late of Philadelphia, merchant, now a resident in Delaware, yeoman. 14 Aug 1777. Whereas Selby Hickman of said county, yeoman, by a deed of conveyance dated 22 July 1769 (Worcester Co., Liber H, folio 63-65) conveyed to said Mifflin a saw mill pond, timber, swamp, upland and cartway between his two tracts, one called Long Lot and the other Long Acre. For £80. Wit: Jos. Harney, Caleb Evans. Within deed ackn. 7 Sep 1778.

218. Robert Tolbert, Sussex Co., yeoman, from John Clowes, Sussex Co., mariner. 25 March 1776. Two tracts in Broadkill forrest which were conveyed to John Clowes by William Boucher by deed dated 7 Sep 1762. One tract was surveyed for said William Boucher by virtue of proprietor's warrant dated 9 June 1743, 250 acres - 100 acres of which lying on the west side of a line of marked trees from a corner oak being a corner of John Day's land, that John Clowes conveyed to John Stuart. For £112.10. Wit: Samuel Hand, James Heaverlo. Within deed ackn. 7 Sep 1778.

220. David Richards from Robert Nutter, Sussex Co., and wife Sarah. 31 July 1777. A tract in Northwest Fork Hundred called Nutters Lot containing as per patent 592 acres which was granted by the proprietary of Maryland to Christopher Nutter of Dorchester Co. of whom Robert Nutter is heir at law or first son and the said Christopher Nutter by his last will made no mention of the afsd. tract by which Robert Nutter became seized of. For £170. ... intersects a line of the land called Dublin ... Wit: Danll. Polk, Isaac Bradly. Within deed ackn. 10 Sep 1778.

221. Rhoads Shankland, Sussex Co., surveyor, from Elizabeth Martin, widow of Josiah Martin, Sussex Co. 30 Oct 1778. Parcel in Angola Neck on the west side of Rehoboth Bay late the property of Moses Shankland, dec'd. Beginning at a post by Comfort Henning's fence ... 135 acres. For £20. Wit: Thos. Turner (his mark), Jams. Conwell (his mark). Within deed ackn. 4 Nov 1778.

222. Henry King, Sussex Co., planter, from Ann Knott and John Linch, both of Sussex Co. 2 Nov 1778. For £14. Part of a tract called Courtesy in Northwest Fork Hundred containing 30 acres, formerly belonging to John Wine, dec'd. - 45 acres [in all?]. Wit: Shiles Moor, Nellay Grumbles. Within deed ackn. 4 Nov 1778.

222. Thomas Lafferty, Delaware, from Samuel Shankland, Delaware. 6 Aug 1778. For £80. Residue of a tract called Loflands Fork Roads containing 277 acres and 31 perches. Wit: Joseph Waples, Rhoads Shankland. Within deed ackn. 5 Nov 1778.

223. Prettyman Stockley, Sussex Co., yeoman, from James Thompson, Sussex Co., farmer. 5 Nov 1778. Parcel being part of a larger island in Lewes Creek known as Shanklands Island which said parcel is bounded beginning at a post of Saml. Paynter's

part ... to the creek at the Cape Channell ... 6 acres, for £36.
Wit: William Burton, Rhoads Shankland. Within deed ackn. 5 Nov
1778.

224. William Polk, Esqr. from William Moor, Sussex Co., yeoman.
Parcel in Cedar Creek Hundred, 400 acres called Widow's
Contrivance binding on the main branch of Cedar Creek called the
Church Branch in the fork thereof and a small branch making into
the same called Burrobung Branch, originally granted to Elizabeth
Poor, mother of the afsd. William Moor, who died intestate. For
£30. Wit: James Walker, J. Russel. Within deed ackn. 5 Nov
1778.

224. Caldwell King, Sussex Co., yeoman, from George Messeck,
Sussex Co. 5 Nov 1778. Tract in Broad Creek Hundred called Hogg
Quarter granted by patent from the Proprietary of Maryland to
Andrew Collings 19 May 1748. Beginning at a marked oak on the
north side of Gum Branch that runs into Pocomoke River and near
Grays Shingle Road, 25 acres, for £50. Wit: William Bevins,
Junr., William Driskell. Within deed ackn. 5 Nov 1778.

225. Peter Fretwell Wright, Lewes Town, tanner, from Thomas
Moor, Burden Town, Burlington Co., tanner. 5 Nov 1778.
Messuage, tanyard, orchard and parcel of land in Lewes and
Rehoboth Hundred which Joseph and Mary Eldridge by their last
wills devised to their two grandsons, the afsd. Thomas Moore and
Obediah Eldridge as tenants in common. And whereas Thomas by
Jacob Moore, Esqr., his attorney, and the said Obediah by Jabez
Fisher, Gent., his guardian, caused an amicable action of
partition to be entered in a Court of Common Pleas, May Term,
year afsd, which was done. 7 acres, for £340. Wit: Rhoads
Shankland, Perry Prettyman. Within deed ackn. 8 Dec 1778.

226. Article of Agreement between the heirs of John Houston,
dec'd. on division of his lands. Be it remembered that we John
Polk and Mary his wife formerly the widow of John Houston and
Leonard Houston, John Houston, James Houston, minor sons of the
said John Houston by Robert Houston their guardian have mutually
chosen John Mitchel, Chas. Moore, Levin Vaughan, Isaac Cooper and
Barkley Townsend, to divide and lay off to said Mary her thirds
and dower of the lands which John Houston in his last will dated
29 June 1775 devised to his three sons, above named, subject to
the thirds or dower of his then wife, the above named Mary. Each
binds himself in the penal sum of £500 to hold to the partition
of land on or before 1 Feb following. 27 Jan 1779. Wit: Cha.
Moore, Isaac Cooper.

227. Award on Division of John Houston's lands. We, John
Mitchell, Charles Moor, Isaac Cooper, Levin Vaughan, Berkley
Townsend, all of Sussex Co., send Greetings. Whereas John
Houston of Sussex Co., dec'd., was seized of land in Broad and
Little Creek Hundreds and in his last will devised to his three
sons, Leonard, John and James Houston, certain parcels of land
subject to thirds or dower of his then wife, Mary Houston. And
whereas by a certain writing obligatory dated 27 Jan 1779 between

John Polk and Mary his wife who was widow of the said John
Houston and Leonard Houston, John Houston and James Houston,
minor sons of the said John Houston, dec'd. by Robert Houston
their guardian. John Mitchell, Charles Moor, Isaac Cooper, Levin
Vaughan and Barkley Townsend were chosen arbitrators in the
partitioning of said Mary's thirds or dower and in the lands
afsd. containing 753 acres; her share containing 186 acres. Also
1/3 of a saw mill standing on saw mill lot and utensils, liberty
of the roads to and from the mill and granting the same liberty
to the orphans when of full age and 1/3 of the dwelling house
[and other].

228. Kezia Hubbert and Jeremiah Cannon to Peter Hubbert and
others. Deed of gift. 15 Feb 1779. We the subscribers [Kezia
Hubbert and Jeremiah Cannon] freely give to the under named nine
children of Peter Hubbert, dec'd., of Sussex Co., the following
goods and chattels, at or before our deaths at our election. To
Peter Hubbert, bed and furniture, square mahogany table. To
Thomas Hubbert, horse, cedar desk, half dozen quilt walnut framed
pictures. To Catharine Hubbert, a Negro named Mess(?), set of
silver table spoons and her father's picture. To Anastasia
Hubbert, a Negro boy named Charles, one dozen silver tea spoons
and a small quilt framed looking glass. To Michael Hubbert, a
horse and saddle, cow and calf. To Joseph Hubbert, cow and calf
and bed and furniture. To Jeremiah Hubbert, bed and furniture,
small mahogany desk, sow and pig. To Edward Hubbert, a mahogany
oval table, six plates, two dishes and one iron pot. To Sarah
Hubbert, a Negro girl named Patty, 1 silver cream pot, 1 silver
pepper castor, a chest of drawers. Wit: Matthew Cannon, Levin
Dirickson.

228. Thomas Wilson, Sussex Co., from Isaac Killo and wife Sarah,
admrs of Jacob Hodson, Sussex Co. 2 Feb 1779. For £110.10, a
parcel in Slaughter Neck on the south side of Cedar Creek
adjoining the lands of Aaron Oliver on the west and the land of
James Beavan on the east side and ends near about the Neck Road
that leads from Thomas Evans' Tavern to the Bayside and joins the
lands of John Young being part of the same tract that formerly
belonged to Robert Hodson, dec'd., containing 50 acres. Wit:
William Shockley, Collings Truitt. Within deed ackn. 3 Feb 1779.
[Plat is included.]

232. Release of Dower. Sydenham Thorne and wife from Daniel
Rodgers guardian of Zadock. I Daniel Rogers guardian of the
estate of Zadock Crapper, a minor orphan son Molton Crapper,
dec'd., who was a devisee and heir at law under the last will of
Levin Crapper, Esqr. hereby transfer to Sydenham Thorne and Betty
his wife late Betty Crapper widow of Zaddock Crapper the dower or
thirds of the said Betty Crapper to the land delineated on the
map annexed. That it to say, 1/3 of all rents and advantages
arising from a grist mill within the bounds of the said plot or
map to the said Sydenham and Betty during the term of her natural
life. And all the land included within the yellow lines. Within
deed of release ackn. 9 Dec 1778.

233. John Linch, Sussex Co., yeoman, from Andrew Collings, Sussex Co., yeoman. 10 June 1777. Whereas Andrew Collings hath good right to 400 acres in Broadkill forrest by virtue of proprietor's warrant called Partnership, for £30, 105 acres. Beginning at a bounder of a tract called Brandywine belonging to John Collings. Wit: John Clowes, Levi Russel. Within deed ackn. 3 Feb 1778.

233. Rhoads Shankland, Sussex Co., surveyor, from Joseph Dodd, tanner, and wife Sarah, Sussex Co. Deed of sale. 3 Feb 1779. For £5, a parcel being part of a larger tract granted to Jacob Shaltman, father to afsd. Sarah now the wife of said Joseph Dodd and by sundry means and deaths the said land has become the maiden land of the said Sarah being the same land whereon said Jacob Shaltman lived and died, it being her part and share of the land now divided, containing 60 acres. Wit: Sumerset Dickerson, John Chance. Within deed ackn. 3 Feb 1779.

234. Joseph Dodd, from Rhoads Shankland. 3 Feb 1779. For £5. [same land as above entry.] Wit: John Chance, Sumerset Dickerson. Within deed ackn. 3 Feb 1779.

235. Nancy Stuart from Catty Stewart, a Negro girl. Know that William Stuart late of Sussex Co., dec'd., by his last will after sundry legacies, desire that all the remainder of his estate should be mine after which in said will he also desired that his Negro girl named Poll should be his daughter Nancey Stuart's property which two desires are so entangled as that in time may cause dispute between my heirs and the said Nancey Stuart or heirs. And to comply with the desire of the testator my dec'd husband and for the love and regard for my daughter Nancey Stuart, I [relinquish claim to said Negro]. 17 March 1777. Wit: Robt. Jones, John Walker. Within deed of release ackn. 3 Feb 1779.

235. John Fleming, Sussex Co., taylor, from Joseph Hall, Sussex Co., yeoman. Deed of sale. 3 Feb 1779. For £62.10, a parcel being part of a larger tract taken up by Joseph Warrington by virtue of the proprietor's warrant granted in 1762. Beginning at a corner gum being also a corner of Moses Dodd's land, containing 100 acres. Wit: Francis Johnston, Rhoads Shankland. Within deed ackn. 3 Feb 1779.

236. William Millard, Sussex Co., shipwright, from William Bowness, Sussex Co., doctor. Deed of sale. 3 Feb 1779. A parcel adjoining land which belong to Robert Stephenson and Micajah Truitt and lands now in possession of John Ponder and Samuel Heaverlo containing 100 acres being part of two tracts late the property of Isabella Annett now dec'd. of which said land, about 90 acres became the right of said Isabella Annett by virtue of a division made by order of Orphans Court of all the lands of William Stephenson her father who died seized of said land as shown in the records of the Orphans Court dated 1 March 1752. The remainder of the land became the right of said Isabella by virtue of a purchase she made of the lands formerly belonging to Mary Barry adjoining the afsd. 90 acres and whereas the said Isabella Annett died intestate leaving issue several children, Mary Annett being one of

them and she sold the land to William Bowness party to these presents on 7 Feb 1776. 100 acres, £500. Beginning at a corner of Micajah Truitt's land and running thence partly with the line of John Ponder's land ... to a corner post of Robert Stephenson's line. Wit: John Heavelo, Samuel Dodd. Within deed ackn. 3 Feb 1779.

237. George and Nelson Waller, Sussex Co., yeomen, from Nathl. B. Mariner and son Robert Mariner of Sussex Co. yeomen. 3 Feb 1779. For £50, a tract on the south side of Ivey Branch in Indian River Hundred formerly granted by the Commissioners warrant to Thomas Blizard and from him assigned to John Hastings and by him conveyed by deed of sale to Peter Deal. Boundary runs with the line of John Stockley's land ... intersecting Burton's mill pond ... 170 acres. Wit: Constant Mariner, Rhoads Shankland. Within deed ackn. 4 Feb 1779.

238. Prettyman Stockley, Sussex Co., weaver, from George and Nelson Waller, sons and heirs of George Waller, dec'd of Sussex Co., yeomen. Deed of sale. 3 Feb 1779. For £400, a tract in Indian River Hundred on the south side of Ivey Branch formerly granted by the Commissioners warrant to Thos. Blizard and from him assigned to John Hastings and by him conveyed by deed of sale to Peter Deal. 170 acres. [See above entry.] Wit: Constant Mariner, Rhods Shankland. Within deed ackn. 3 Feb 1779.

239. John Evans from Uriah Hazzard, Sussex Co. Deed of sale. 4 Feb 1779. Whereas the Lord Proprietary of Maryland granted on 28 Jan 1688 to Mathew Scarborough the tract called North Pethernton on the Sea board side of afsd. co. Beginning at the southeast corner of a salt pond. 500 acres. William Scarborough by his deed on 28 Oct 1702 granted all afsd. land to Rodger Thomas, who by his last will dated 20 June 1703 devised same to John Stockley and William Hall and by sundry agreements and mutations part of the afsd. tract called North Peathurnton became the property of above afsd. Uriah Hazard. For £11.5.6. Bounds on a tract called Atkins Lot ... 11 acres. Wit: William Evans, Jonathan Wharton. Within deed ackn. 4 Feb 1779.

239. John Evans, Cedar Neck, husbandman of Sussex Co., from Ezekiel Hopkins, Sussex Co., cooper, and wife Sarah. 23 Sep 1778. For £625, a tract called Hopkins Discovery, on the south side of Indian River near the head of Blackwater Creek that issues out of the said Indian River. And witnesses that Josiah Hopkins and John Hopkins obtained a right in the same tract of 360 acres. John Hopkins father of afsd. Ezekiel Hopkins was seized part of the above tract Hopkins Discovery as per the patent and died intestate and his son Ezekiel afsd. his eldest son according to Maryland became his heir at law and has now sold all his right to the tract that is not already sold of or taken away by elder survey which is estimated to be 170 acres. Wit: John Evans, Senr., Jonathan Wharton. Within deed ackn. 4 Feb 1779.

240. William Wroe, Sussex Co., from John Mitchell, merchant, Sussex Co. 2 Feb 1779. For £200, tract called Manlove's Grove in

Broadkill Hundred on the north side of Broad Creek containing 500 acres according to the patent. Wit: Cha. Moor, John Nottingham. Within deed ackn. 4 Feb 1779.

241. Thomas Lewis, Dorchester Co., Maryland, planter, from Thomas White and wife Margett, Somerset Co., Maryland, planter. Deed of sale. 4 Dec 1771. For £70. Messuage or tenement called Whites Industry in Dorchester Co. Beginning at a marked oak standing near the head of Clay Swamp ... containing 100 acres. Wit: Dan Sulivan, James Muir.

242. James Gray, now of Sussex Co., from William Coffin son of John Coffin of Worcester Co., dec'd. Deed of sale. 28 Nov 1778. Whereas said John Coffin in his lifetime for £240 agreed to convey 45 acres, said William Coffin in consideration of his father's obligation conveys a parcel on Assawamon Creek at the head of Assawamon Bay. Beginning at a marked oak on a small drean that runs into Indian Assawamon Creek on the south side of the said creek it being the first bounder of a tract called Scotchish Plott which was formerly in possession of Hugh Tingle. Wit: Dennis Comfort Walker, Adah Boyd (her mark), Wm. Riley Evans. Within deed ackn. 3 Feb 1779.

243. Francis Cornwell, Sussex Co., yeoman, from Margaret Kollock, town of Lewes, widow and extx. of Jacob Kollock of Sussex Co., Esqr. 20 Feb 1779. Whereas Jacob Kollock was seized of a tract in the forrest of Broadkill Hundred and by his will empowered his extx. the above named Margaret Kollock to sell as conveniently might be. 210 acres, for £205. Wit: J. Russel, Samuel Hand. Within deed ackn. 9 March 1779.

244. Daniel Murphy, town of Lewes, from Moses Allen of Indian River Hundred, pilot, and wife Elizabeth. 2 May 1778. For £160, that messuage and lot of land in the town of Lewes bounded on the front by Second Street and on the northwest by a lot of the heirs of James Simpson, dec'd., and on the southeast by a lot now belonging to Francis Calhoon, 60 feet by 200 feet. Wit: Isaac Smith, Robert Massey. Within deed ackn. 9 March 1779.

245. Joseph Hall, Senr., Sussex Co., from Joseph Warrington, Sussex Co., and wife Rachel. 24 Feb 1776. Tract in Indian River Hundred adjoining lands of Moses Dodd, Aaron Dodd, Jonathan Rust and William Black. 251 acres for £58. Wit: George Frame, Rhoads Shankland. Within deed ackn. 4 Feb 1779.

246. William Molliston's receipt to Alburtus Jacobs. 5 Aug 1766. Receipt of Albert Jacobs the sum of £120 in full for my mother's estate and 3 stears sold and likewise for my dividend of Mrs. Jacobs estate and any part of land sold him.

246. Benjamin Sylvester receipt to Albertus Jacobs. Received 7 Nov 1770 of Albertus Jacobs by his bond of this date the sum of £16.10 for the full sum due to my wife for her share of what was due to her from her grandmother's estate and also in full for her part of her grandfather's land that lay on Rehoboth Hundred, viz.,

that of place called Kickin and the land adjoining on Coolspring Branch which descends to her by the death of mother Martha Morgan and the afsd. grandfather and grandmother which the said Albertus Jacobs was admr. to. Wit: Danl. Nunez.

246. Jacobs Morgan receipt to Albertus Jacobs. Rec'd. 8 Nov 1770 of Albertus Jacobs by his bond of this date, one bond to myself for £16.10 payable 1 Nov next and another to my brother Robert Morgan who I am appointed guardian for, for the sum of £16.10 payable 1 Nov next in full for my share and the said Robert's share of our grandmother's estate and also in full for one share of our grandfather's land that lay in Rehoboth Hundred called Kickin and the land adjoining on Coolspring Branch which descended to us by the death of our mother Martha Morgan and the afsd. grandfather and grandmother which the said Albertus Jacobs is admr. to. Wit: Danl. Nunez.

246. John Clowes, Sussex Co., mariner, from Adam Short, Sussex Co. yeoman. Deed of sale. 21 March 1776. Whereas Adam Short has surveyed by virtue of proprietor's warrant on 12 June 1761 a small tract in the Broadkiln forrest called Shorts Luck. 52 1/4 acres. For £22. Wit: Samuel Hand, John Baker.

247. John Draper, house carpenter, Sussex Co., from Benj. Johnson and Brantson Lofland, Sussex Co., yeomen. 5 May 1779. Parcel on the north side of Slaughter Creek. Boundary runs to a corner post of Jno. Hickman's land ... dividing post of Richard Shockley's land ... line of marsh belonging to the heirs of Thomas Hinds ... 113 1/2 acres of land and marsh. Also a parcel of marsh of 92 1/2 acres. Which said land and marsh was formerly purchased of Christopher Nutter by Alexander Draper who by his last will devised same to his son Samuel Draper who by his last will devised same to his only child a daughter who died in her minority and without issue and therefore her mother Elizabeth Boyer became intituled to the same and she by her last will devised same to Thomas Boyer her son who by his deed of sale dated 27 May 1775 conveyed same to Benjamin Johnson and Brantson Lofland. For £200. Wit: J. Russel, Paris Chipman. Within deed ackn. 5 May 1779.

248. Jessee Gray, Worcester Co., from John Collings, Worcester Co., Maryland. 27 March 1779. For £200, tract called Forten originally in Worcester Co., Maryland, now in Sussex Co., 100 acres, agreeable to the grant. Wit: J. Dennis, Caleb Wyatt, Joseph Gray. Within deed ackn. 5 May 1779.

248. Jessee Gray, Worcester Co., Maryland, from Miles Hudson, Sussex Co. 21 April 1779. For £100, a tract called Chance whereon the saw mill dam now stands with a long square so as to contain the banks on both sides of the said mill and dam which is at the head of Saint Martins River, containing 5 acres. Wit: Caleb Wyatt, Joseph Gray. Within deed ackn. 5 May 1779.

249. Brantston Lofland, Sussex Co., from Richard Shockley, Sussex Co. 5 May 1779. For £200, a parcel in Slaughter Neck on the north side of Slaughter Creek, this tract bought by Thomas Copes of Mary

Bowman, widow and extx. of John Bowman, 200 acres, surveyed 22 May 1759. Wit: J. Russel, John Draper. Within deed ackn. 5 May 1779.

250. Jacob Kindred, Sussex Co., planter, from Thomas Lewis, Caroline Co., planter, and wife Mary. 11 Feb 1779. For £200, tract called Whites Industry in Northwest Fork Hundred. Beginning at an oak standing near the head of the Clay Swamp and close on the south side of a small swamp ... 100 acres ... also a tract called First Choice in the hundred afsd. ... 91 1/2 acres. Wit: James Brown, Junr., Paris Chipman. Within deed ackn. 11 Feb 1779.

251. William Brittingham Ennes, Sussex Co., yeoman, from John Clowes, Sussex Co., mariner. 12 April 1779. Whereas John Clowes on 30 May 1771 purchased of Rhoads Shankland, High Sheriff, lands and tenements, the property of John Ennis, 80 acres. For £9, adjoining the lands of said Wm. B. Ennis, 80 acres, Wit: Jno. Wiltbank, Wm. Polk. Within deed ackn. 5 May 1779.

252. Thomas Wilson, yeoman, Sussex Co., from John Clowes, Sussex Co., mariner. 23 April 1779. Parcel in Broadkill forrest being part of a larger tract called Forked Poplar granted to Josiah Roton who by his deed of sale dated 7 Nov 1758 conveyed same to Thomas Willson. Boundary runs to a line of the lands of David Roton. 100 acres, and the said Thomas Willson being in debt the land was sold to John Clowes at public vendue by the High Sheriff and Boaz Manlove, Esqr. the then high sheriff conveyed same dated 8 May 1761 to said John Clowes. For £59. Wit: Jno. Wiltbank, Wm. Polk. Within deed ackn. 5 May 1779.

253. Thomas Crouch, Sussex Co., yeoman, from Brantson Loftland, Sussex Co., carpenter. 23 May 1777. For £150, part of a larger tract formerly surveyed by virtue of a warrant granted to William Danely in the forrest of Cedar Hundred. Beginning at a corner oak of John Bennet's land ... by Benja. Riley's line ... 160 acres. Wit: J. Russel, John Draper. Within deed ackn. 5 May 1779.

254. Richard Shockley, yeoman, Sussex Co., from Benja. Johnson and Brantson Loftland, Sussex Co., yeomen. 5 May 1779. Parcel on the north side of Slaughter Creek. Beginning at a corner post of John Draper's marsh in the line of the marsh belonging to the heirs of Thos. Hinds ... corner of John Hickman's land then by Mark Davis's line ... 229 acres, which was purchased of Christopher Nutter by Alexander Draper who by his last will devised same to his son Samuel Draper who by his last will devised same to his only child a daughter who died in her minority and without issue and her mother Elizabeth Boyer became intituled to the same and by her last will devised the same to her son Thomas Boyer who by his deed of sale dated 27 May 1775 conveyed same to afsd. Benjamin Johnson and Brantson Loftland. For £200. Wit: Paris Chipman, Jno. Russel. Within deed ackn. 5 May 1779.

255. Peleg Walter from Joshua Hill, Esq. Bond for conveyance of land. Joshua Hill is bound to Peleg Walter for £100. 9 Jan 1776. Wit: Sidah Hall, Comfort Walker. Proved 5 May 1779.

255. William Cahoon, Sussex Co., from John Fowler, Sussex Co., yeoman. 6 May 1779. For £304, a parcel in Broadkill forrest, part of a tract granted to said Fowler by proprietor's warrant dated 15 March 1754. Boundary runs to land of John Sharp ... line of a former survey made for William Daughter now in the possession of afsd. John Sharp ... land between John Fowler and his son William Fowler ... 95 acres. Wit: Phillips Kollock, Rhoads Shankland. Within deed ackn. 8 June 1779.

256. James Brown, Junr., Sussex Co., planter, from Mary Clarkson, widow of Richard Clarkson, of Sussex Co. planter. Bond. Mary Clarkson is bound to James Brown for £3000. 31 March 1779. To convey her thirds of widows dower of the plantation where said Richard Clarkson her late husband formerly lived, during her lifetime. Wit: John Tennent, Christopher Williams.

256. Richard Tull to Thomas and John Ange for performance of an award. Bond. Richard Tull of Sussex Co., is bound to Thomas Ange and John Ange of Sussex Co., in the sum of £15. 2 July 1779. To perform the award and judgment of John Flowers of Sussex Co. and Ezekiel Reed and Spencer Waters of Dorchester Co. arbitrators. Wit: Jesse Tull, John Turpin.

257. Award. 6 Aug 1779. As there is a sawmill and grist mill in partnership between Richard Tull and Thomas Ange and John Ange and there has been some dispute about making use of them when it was not their proper time to make use of them we the said arbitrators do order that neither of the parties shall offer to meddle or molest or concern with the said mills or utensils when it is not his proper time to make use of them, at the expiration of each man's time of working of the said mills he shall leave the stock yard and ways clear to roll on stocks to the said sawmill without any hindrance to any of the other parties. And the said Richard Tull shall pay and deliver to Thomas Ange when required the full quantities of 37 feet of good merchantable pine plank and deliver up 1/4 part of the timber cart that the said Tull bought of Samuel Shelton Slaughs and pay to John Ange when required the full quantity of 1189 feet of good inch pine plank and deliver 1/4 part of the timber care that he bought of Samuel Shelton Slaughs. And that Richard Tull lay off and convey 80 acres and 26 square perches of land agreeable to the plat laid off by Joseph Turpin being part of a tract called Tulls Addition. [For more details actual records.] Wit: John Flower, Ezekiel Reed.

258. Job Paremore, yeoman, from Mary Paremor, Sussex Co., widow and admx. of Mathew Paremore, yeoman. 29 June 1779. Whereas Mary Paremore after having fully administered the personal estate of the said Mathew Paremore preferred a petition to the Orphans Court 28 May 1774 praying for the sale of a tract in Broadkiln Hundred, 107 acres which land was sold to Job Paremore for £55.2. Wit: J. Russel, Jacob Stockley. Within deed ackn. 4 Aug 1779.

259. Mary Paremore from Job Paremore. 30 June 1779. For £55.2. Tract in Broadkiln Hundred containing 107 acres, bounded by the lands of William Godwin, westerly by the lands of Purnal Johnson,

and southeast by the land of Ann Cord and is part of a tract originally granted by a proprietor's warrant dated 15 of the 1st month 1714 to Walter Reed being the same parcel of land which Matthew Paremore died intestate seized and by said Mary Paremore as his administrator conveyed to Job Paremore. Wit: J. Russel, Jacob Stockley. Within deed ackn. 4 Aug 1779.

259. James Pettyjohn from Henry Smith. Bond for conveyance of land. Henry Smith of Sussex Co., yeoman, is bound to James Pettyjohn for £300. 8 March 1764. Tract in the forrest of Broadkiln Hundred, 300 acres, surveyed by virtue of proprietor's warrant, granted to John Cord late of Sussex Co., dec'd., binding east on the land of afsd. James Pettyjohn and southwest and north on land of Thomas Pettyjohn which said tract descended by the decease of said John Cord who died intestate to Mary the wife of above bounden Henry Smith and only surviving daughter of afsd. John Cord she being a minor. Wit: John Clowes, Lydia Clowes. Within deed ackn. 4 Aug 1779.

260. Ezekiel Williams, Sussex Co., planter, from Leah Wildredge, Sussex Co., widow. Deed. 5 Aug 1779. Tract on the head of the sound and on the south side of Indian Creek. Boundary runs to division between William Jurdon Hall and afsd. Leah Wildredge ... being part of a tract lately belonging to William Woodcraft dec'd. and now in the possession of Leah Wildredge. For £705. Wit: Wm. Jordan Hall, William Butcher. Within deed ackn. 4 Aug 1779.

261. Thomas Taylor, Sussex Co., planter, from Leah Wildredge, Sussex Co., widow. Deed. 5 Aug 1779. A parcel being part of a larger tract on the head of the sound and on the south side of Indian Creek. Beginning at a marked oak being the first boundary of Jordan Hall and Ezekiel Williams, part of the same tract and near the watering hole, 35 acres, lately the property of William Woodcraft, dec'd., now in the possession of afsd. Leah Wildredge, for £352. Wit: Wm. Jordan Hall, William Butcher. Within deed ackn. 4 Aug 1779.

262. William Jordan Hall, Sussex Co., from Leah Wildredge, heir at law to William Woodcraft of Sussex Co. Deed. 5 Aug 1779. Two tracts called Cow Quarter and Dumfries. Beginning at a marked oak at a place called Water Hole, 35 1/4 acres, for £500. Wit: William Butcher, Ezekiel Williams. Within deed ackn. 4 Aug 1779.

262. Uriah Hazzard, yeoman, from Phillips Kollock of the town of Lewes, yeoman, and wife Penelope. Deed. 24 March 1770. For £600. Beginning at a post on the north side of Pagan Creek or Branch, then along a street known by the name of Middle, Second or Market Street ... land late the property of Cornelious Wiltbank ... 12 acres - being the same that formerly belonged to John Simonton of the town of Lewes who died seized thereof intestate, the land descending to four sisters, Jane wife of Nathaniel Baily, Sarah wife of John Shankland, Mary wife of James Davison, and Elizabeth wife of Noble Lewis. The sisters, Jane, Sarah and Mary by their deed of release dated 27 May 1773 released and confirmed the land to Noble Lewis and Elizabeth his wife who on 29 May 1773 conveyed

same to Phillips Kollock. Wit: J. Rodney, D. Train. Within deed ackn. 25 March 1779.

263. Elenor Hitchcock, Sussex Co., widow, from Uriah Hazzard, Sussex Co., yeoman, and wife Sarah. Deed of mortgage. For £200, a parcel adjoining the town of Lewes. Beginning at a post on the north side of Pagan Creek or Branch, thence along at street called Middle, Second or Market Street ... being the same that formerly belonged to John Simonton ... 12 acres. [See above entry.] also bed and furniture, a horse, a gelding and cattle. Wit: J. Rodney, D. Train. Within deed ackn. 4 Aug 1779.

265. John Norman from James Cavender, Sussex Co., planter. 2 Aug 1779. Deed. For £55, tract called Smiths Folly, 108 acres. granted by Maryland proprietor's warrant dated 10 Sep 1740. Beginning at the southernmost side of Grubby Neck Branch that issues out of the northeast fork and on the west side thereof near a water hole ... Wit: Daniel Polk, John Jessep. Within deed ackn. 4 Aug 1779.

265. John Collings, Sussex Co., yeoman, from Collings Truitt, Sussex Co., yeoman. Deed. 29 April 1779. Whereas Andrew Collings by his last will devised to his grandson afsd. Collings Truitt, four parcels of land, one that he the said Andrew Collings purchased of Samuel Atkinson, 200 acres, called Allins Design as described in the patent granted to Robert Allin on 10 April 1747; another that he purchased of Thomas Evans and his wife Elizabeth Evans of 48 acres, called Bettys Purchase as described on the patent to Elizabeth Smith dated 5 Dec 1749; another of 10 acres adjoining the afsd. 48 acres which he the said Andrew Collings purchased of John Clowes; another tract adjoining the Green Drains granted to afsd. Andrew Collings by proprietor's warrant dated 8 June 1757 called Bundelin Folly, 80 acres. Total 338 acres, for £1000. Wit: Luke Wattson, Mary Wattson. Within deed ackn. 4 Aug 1779.

266. Bethuel Wattson, Sussex Co., from Benjamin Webb, Sussex Co. Deed. 4 Aug 1779. For £160. Parcel on Cedar Creek of 200 acres, devised to Elizabeth Burton by the last will of Henry Pennington, and conveyed by her attorney, Samuel Cary, to Edward Callaway who sold same to Benjamin Webb. Said premises bound on a Buroghbung Branch. Wit: John W. Dean, Dormon Lofland. Within deed ackn. 4 Aug 1779.

267. Elijah Fassett, Sussex Co., from Thomas Hall Parker, Accomack Co., Virginia. Deed. 4 Aug 1779. For £90, two tracts, one called Dumfries, the other Brotherhood, patented by proprietor's warrant of Maryland, on the seabord joining on Assawammon Bay, 85 acres. Wit: Charles Draper, John Purkins. Within deed ackn. 4 Aug 1779.

268. John Hudson, Sussex Co., yeoman, from William Rickards, Sussex Co., yeoman. 4 Aug 1779. Tract in forrest of Cedar Creek in the manor of Worminghust bounded by lands of John Postel, William Danels, Junr., Hezekiah Truitt, William Hudson, Benjamin Hudson and afsd. John Hudson, being the dwelling planation where

William Rickards once lived. For £200. Jno. Rodney, Phillips Kollock. Within deed ackn. 4 Aug 1779.

268. John Cade, Sussex Co., house carpenter, from Thomas Grove, Sussex Co., house carpenter. Deed. 4 Aug 1779. Parcel on the south side of Prime Hook Creek, being a part of a larger tract called Haphoots Fortune. For £20. Beginning at a corner stone of the lands of Jacob Gum, Thomas Grove and John Cade. Wit: Saml. Laverty, Adam Black. Within deed ackn. 4 Aug 1779.

269. Joshua Lofland from Charles Draper. Deed. 6 Aug 1779. For £200. A parcel in Slaughter Neck adjoining the lands of Purnall Bennett on the north and the land of John Young on the south being the same whereon the said Joshua Lofland now lives. 116 1/4 acres. Wit: John W. Dean, Jacob Hazzard. Within deed ackn. 4 Aug 1779.

270. Benjamin Hudson, John Hudson, William Shockley, husbandmen, from Elisha Bratton (Braughton) and Isbal his wife and Asa Hall and Sophia his wife, of Kent Co., Delaware. Deed. 4 Aug 1779. For £186, a parcel beginning at a corner post of land formerly belonging to David Smith ... to a corner of marsh formerly belonging to Thomas Price ... to a corner of Thomas Price and marsh formerly belonging to William Till ... to a corner of William Hickman ... 62 acres of marsh. Being part of a larger tract of marsh in Slaughter Neck taken up by Thomas Grove by virtue of a warrant from Proprietor of Pennsylvania, signed to him 19 July 1736 for 150 acres of vacant marsh and by deed dated 5 Aug 1741 conveyed the afsd. 62 acres to James White who by his last will dated 16 Sep 1763 devised same to his two daughters, Isbel and Sophia. Elisha Braughton and Isbel his wife and Asey Hall and Sophia his wife make over their right of half part of the above 62 acres to Benjamin Hudson and 1/4 part to John Hudson and 1/4 to William Shockley. Wit: Silvester Dibety, J. Russel. Within deed ackn. 4 Aug 1779.

271. Hugh Stephenson, Sussex Co., from Charles Coulter, Sussex Co. Deed. 26 April 1779. Tract in Broadkiln Hundred and the northwest side of Mill Creek Branch, granted by patent dated 2nd of the 2nd month 1786 to John Richardson for 500 acres and said patent as assigned to Charles Coulter and Samuel Coulter (father of afsd. Charles Coulter) by John Fisher by virtue of which assignment the said Samuel Coulter became seized of 175 acres on the south side of afsd. tract and said Samuel Coulter by his bond dated 15 Feb 1743/4 obliged himself to convey 175 acres to Richard Tamplin for 35 pounds and Richard Tamplin died intestate before a conveyance was made and James Tamplin, eldest son and admr. of the estate of Richard Tamplin assigned over the said bond to Sacar Wyatt who assigned same to afsd. Hugh Stephenson and afsd. Samuel Coulter died intestate and the right of said 175 acres devolved to afsd. Charles Coulter son of afsd. Samuel Coulter. Boundary runs to a line of John Neill's land ... corner post in the line of Edward Stephenson's land ... for £35. Wit: Joseph Hazzard, John Harmonson. Within deed ackn. 4 Aug 1779.

272. John Russell, Caroline Co., Maryland, farmer, from Hon. Edward Lloyd, Annapolis, Maryland, and Elizabeth his wife. Deed.

6 March 1779. For £352.15, that part of a tract called Loyds Forrest. Beginning at a marked post standing in the province line where the northern most line of Jarvey Safford's part of said land crosses the same ... 166 acres. Wit: Thos. White, Arthr. Bryan. Within deed ackn. 4 Aug 1779.

273. Henry Safford, Sussex Co., farmer, from Hon. Edward Lloyd, Annapolis, Maryland. Deed. 6 March 1779. Tract called Morrisses Venture, 50 acres, and 25 acres, part of tract called Daniels Venture in Northwest Fork Hundred and on the south side of Double Fork Branch. Wit: Thos. White, Arthur Bryan. Within deed ackn. 4 Aug 1779.

273. John Cample, Sandy Branch, Sussex Co., from James Murray, Sussex Co., yeoman. Deed. 2 Aug 1779. That said James Murrow [sic] for £30, tract called Addition, 20 acres. Wit: Adam Black, Edward Jones. Within deed ackn. 4 Aug 1779.

274. John Tingle, house carpenter, Sussex Co., from John Purkins, Gentleman, Maryland. Deed. 4 Aug 1779. For £207.10, a tract called Friendship. Beginning at the original bounder standing at or near to the head of a creek that Turkey Branch empties into and on the north side thereof and it being a corner tree of a tract of land formerly surveyed for Nathaniel Rackliff and now in the possession of Capt. Joseph Miller ... line to divide between the said Tingle and George Dirrickson ... 82 acres. The above said tract was granted to Joshua Hill on 10 May 1770 (in Maryland) and in May 1774 said Joshua Hill conveyed same to afsd. John Purkins. Wit: Charles Draper, John W. Dean. Within deed ackn. 4 Aug 1779.

275. Hezekiah Smith, Sussex Co., ship carpenter, from Thomas Bradley, Sussex Co., joiner. Deed. 30 July 1779. For £50, a tract called White Level in Northwest Fork Hundred, 50 acres. Wit: Daniel Polk, Elijah Wyatt. Within deed ackn. 4 Aug 1779.

275. Manuel Dodd from Moses Dodd and his sister Meriam which he has purchased her right, Agness Dodd, Ruth Dodd (alias Conway) and Aaron Dodd, Wm. Phinix and his wife Darcus, all of Sussex Co. Deed. For £5. A tract laid out for Joseph Dodd, father of the above, called Woodland Range, the same land whereon Manuel and Aaron Dodd now dwell. Wit: Thomas Walker, Rhoads Shankland. Within deed ackn. 4 Aug 1779.

276. Moses Dodd from Manuel Dodd and Tabitha Dodd, Agnes Dodd, Ruth Dodd (alias Conway), Aaron Dodd, William Phenix and his wife Darcus, all of Sussex Co. Deed. For £5. A tract surveyed and laid out for Joseph Dodd, father of the above, 1 Jan 1717 lying near the head of Coldspring branch on the north side of Dereval's land being one moiety of the afsd. tract containing in the whole 210 acres being all their right of the said moiety, 105 acres. Wit: Thomas Walker, Rhoads Shankland. Within deed ackn. 4 Aug 1779.

277. Aaron Dodd, from his brother Manuel [Manlove] Dodd, Sussex Co., yeoman. Deed. Tract called Woodland Range formerly surveyed

and laid out for Joseph Dodd the elder father of the above, being one moiety of said tract according to the division now made by said Manuel and Aaron Dodd. 110 acres. Signed: Manuel Dodd (his mark) Wit: Thomas Waker, Rhoads Shankland. Within deed ackn. 4 Aug 1779.

277. Peter White, Sussex Co., house carpenter and joiner, from Edward Craige and wife Sarah late Sarah Shankland, admx. of Jno. Shankland. Deed. 1 March 1779. Two lots which John Shankland was seized of in Lewes Town on the southwest side of the Meeting House Lot. Beginning at a corner post of the Meeting House lot standing in the line of Hall's land. For £60. Wit: Thomas Walker, John Orr. Within deed ackn. 4 Aug 1779.

278. Edward Craige, Sussex Co., yeoman, from Peter White, town of Lewes, house carpenter and joiner and wife Elizabeth. Deed. 2 March 1779. Two lots in Lewes Town. [Same lots as above entry.] Wit: Wit: William Hall, Adam Hall. Within deed ackn. 4 Aug 1779.

279. John Laws, Esqr., Sussex Co., from James Owens, Sussex Co., planter. Deed. 4 Aug 1779. Parcel in Johns Neck of 194 acres called Gorhans Addition which was granted by patent to Robert and Samuel Owens 18 Sep 1727 and Robert Owens by his deed released to afsd. Samuel Owens all his right to the tract and Samuel Owens by his last will devised same to his son James Owens who by his last will devised same to two of his sons, the afsd. James Owens, party to these presents, and William Owens and that the same should be divided between them by a drain that runs through the land called the Long Swamp Drain, the northern part to James and the other part to son William. For £500, 94 acres. Wit: Jacob Hazzard, Daniel Rogers. Within deed ackn. 4 Aug 1779.

280. John Winwright, Sussex Co., yeoman, from William Tully, yeoman, Sussex Co. Deed. 21 Sep 1778. For £100, a parcel of a tract called Tullys Addition originally granted by the proprietor of Maryland by patent 14 Sep 1774 to afsd. William Tully, including that part of afsd. tract called Tullys Addition that lies in the east side of the line that divides the state of Maryland and Delaware, 104 acres. Wit: Joseph Venables, Wm. Turpin, Isaac Henry. Within deed ackn. 4 Aug 1779.

281. William Turpin, Somerset Co., Maryland, from William Tully, Sussex Co., yeoman. Deed. 28 Sep 1778. For £260, a parcel being part of a larger tract called Orphans Lot on the north side of Blackwater Branch. Beginning at the divisional line between Joseph Hardy and the said William Tully, 1777 3/4 acres. Wit: Isaac Henry, Wm. Winder, Joseph Venables. Within deed ackn. 4 Aug 1779.

282. Richard Blocksom, son of William Blocksom, Sussex Co., yeoman, from Thomas Whorton, Sussex Co., yeoman. Deed. 4 Aug 1779. For £75, a parcel in the forrest of Cedar Creek Hundred near Marks Savanah being part of the tract whereon Thos. Whorton now dwells. Beginning at a corner post in the line of Whorton's lands ... to a corner oak of land surveyed to Jarom Griffith ... to the line of Thos. Crouch's land ... 50 acres. Wit: Benjamin Webb (his mark), Rhoads Shankland. Within deed ackn. 4 Aug 1779.

283. John Purkins, Worcester Co., Maryland, from Levin Dirrickson, Sussex Co., empowered to make sale of confiscated goods and chattels. Deed. 4 Aug 1779. For £54.15, a resurvey granted to Joshua Hill on a tract called Friendships Addition on 2 March 1776, the part taken in for said Hill is on the east side of Turkey Branch Road. 9 acres and 12 perches of Friendships Addition which is patent land and also 9 acres of Sandy Ridge in a small tract by itself both of same date, 9 July 1760. 169 1/2 acres. Wit: John W. Dean, Charles Draper. Within deed ackn. 4 Aug 1779.

284. George Dirrickson, Sussex Co., yeoman, from John Purkins, Maryland, Gentleman. Deed. 4 Aug 1779. For £507.10, a tract called Friendship. Beginning at a corner post about 1/2 mile from a creek that Turkey Branch empties in and on the north side thereof nearly adjoining to a tract called Buckridge now belonging to Capt. Joseph Miller and another tract formerly surveyed for Charles Rackliff and now in the possession of Joseph Miller ... towards a road that leads from Cedar Neck to Peleg Walter's ... 82 acres. This tract was granted to Joshua Hill on 10 May 1770 and it appears that on --- May 1774 the said Joshua Hill conveyed the above to John Purkins (recorded in Worcester Co.) Wit: John W. Dean, Charles Draper. Within deed ackn. 4 Aug 1779.

284. Joshua Hall, Broad Creek Hundred, blacksmith, from William Hall, town of Lewes, blacksmith. Deed. For £72.10, 200 acres, which Thomas Copes and Elizabeth his wife by their deed of sale dated 11 May 1763 conveyed to Joshua Hall and William Hall as tenants in common (recorded in Worcester Co., Liber E, folio 510, 511). 23 Aug 1777. Wit: J. Russel, Jean Russel. Within deed ackn. 4 Aug 1779.

285. William Fisher, Sussex Co., from Robert Fleming and his wife Margaret, John Clampet and his wife Sophia, all of Sussex Co. Deed. 9 Feb 1778. A parcel in Broadkiln Hundred called Coolspring which was granted by patent dated 2nd of 2nd month 1686 to William Clark and by sundry conveyances became the property of James Campbell who was father of afsd. Margaret Fleming; and James Campbell died intestate and the afsd. tract was divided amongst the several heirs, and 102 acres was laid off to afsd. Margaret Fleming as her full share. Beginning at a post in a line dividing the Coolspring Tract from land belonging to the heirs of David McIlvain dec'd. and being a corner of William Perry's lands ... to a corner oak of James Martin's land ... which was conveyed by Robert Fleming and his wife Margaret to afsd. John Clampet and his wife Sophia but an error was made in the deed and they join now in this deed so as to correct the error and make the deed good to William Fisher. For £230 to said John Clampet. Wit: Isaac Smith, Mary Smith. Within deed ackn. 4 Aug 1779.

286. Arthur Fowler to Jessee Fowler, Sussex Co. Bond. Arthur Fowler is bound to Jessee Fowler for £800. To convey by John Laws, Esqr. and Wm. Stayton, the rights of Arthur Fowler to the following tracts, Staytons Adventure, Fowlers Fancy, Fowlers Chance and Fowlers Adventure, lands that formerly belonged to Arthur Fowler, dec'd., which were by his last will left to Arthur and Jesse to be

equally divided between them. Wit: John Laws, Alexander Laws, Wm. Stayton.

287. Award and platt on division of Arthur Fowler's lands. Whereas there is a reference to us John Laws and William Stayton by bond dated 14 March 1777 between Arthur Fowler and Jessee Fowler of Sussex Co., to divide their shares of lands of Arthur Fowler dec'd. equally between them, do in pursuance of the said bond, award the division as follows, vizt., to begin at marked gum standing in Johns Branch also standing 41 perches on the 26th line of a tract of said lands called Fowlers Fancey ... [Plat is included.] 21 March 1777. Signed: John Laws and William Stayton.

287. Article of agreement between Charles Brown and wife and Abraham Cannon on division of lands. We, Charles Brown, son of Charles, of Sussex Co., yeoman, and Sarah his wife, late Sarah Cannon, widow of Thomas Cannon late of Sussex Co., and Abraham Cannon, a minor son of said Thomas Cannon, by James Brown, Junr., his guardian, have mutually agreed and chosen Daniel Polk and Robert Clarkson to divide and lay off to the above said Charles Brown and Sarah his wife, her thirds or dower in a certain plantation containing 100 acres called Poplar Hill in Northwest Fork Hundred which Thomas Cannon by his last will dated Jan 1773 devised to his son, afsd. Abraham Cannon subject to the thirds of his then wife the above named Sarah Brown. Wit: Wm. Polk, Isaac Bradly. Signed 9 Sep 1779.

288. Award on Division of Thomas Cannon's lands. Daniel Polk and Robert Clarkson send Greetings. Whereas Thomas Cannon of Northwest Fork Hundred by his last will dated Jan 1773 devised to his son Abraham Cannon a plantation or tract containing 100 pounds called Poplar Hill in the hundred afsd. subject to dower of his then wife Sarah Cannon and whereas by bond dated 9 Sep 1779 mutually made between Charles Brown son of Charles and Sarah his wife late Sarah Cannon widow of said Thomas Cannon and Abraham Cannon a minor son of said Thomas Cannon by James Brown, Junr., his guardian. We the said Daniel Polk and Robert Clarkson were chosen arbitrators to divide and lay off Sarah's thirds, 33 1/2 acres. Beginning at the first beginning of the afsd. tract called Poplar Hill ... 27 Sep 1779.

288. John Neill, planter of Broadkiln Hundred, from David Rankin, Mount Pleasant Township, Westmoreland Co., PA. Power of attorney. 9 Dec 1778.

289. Moses Mariner, Sussex Co., yeoman, from Luke Wattson, Sheriff. Deed. 4 Nov 1779. Whereas Thomas Whitesides late of Indian River Hundred was seized of a parcel in Indian River Hundred containing 270 acres, the same which Bowmans Marriner and Jacob Marriner conveyed to Thomas Whitesides and Arthur Whitesides and the said Arthur Whitesides by deed of release, conveyed same to said Thomas Whitesides who by indenture of mortgage dated 24 May 1776 mortgaged the same to John Rodney, Esqr. of Sussex Co., Trustee of the General Loan Office for £72 in bills of credit. And whereas Thomas Whitesides and Margaret Whitesides admx. of said

Thomas Whitesides while she was sole and the afsd. Moses Marriner who lately married with the said Margaret made default in the payment of the third quota of the said mortgage money - whereupon the land was sold to the highest bidder by the sheriff for £156. Wit: Nehemiah Davis, Junr., D. Train. Within deed ackn. 4 Nov 1779.

291. Robert Houston, Junr., Sussex Co., farmer, from Robert Houston, Senr., Sussex Co., farmer. Deed. 2 Nov 1779. A parcel on the northwest side of Indian Town Branch issuing into the Indian River, surveyed and taken up by Tekel Walton by patent who by his deed conveyed to afsd. Houston, Senr. Beginning at a marked oak on the northwest side of Indian Town Branch afsd. ... 100 acres. For £100. Wit: Jacob Burton, Lidy Winsor. Within deed ackn. 4 Nov 1779.

291. Anthony Heavelo, Junr., Sussex Co., from his father and mother, Anthony Heavelo, Senr., yeoman, and Margaret his wife. Deed of gift. 6 Sep 1779. Parcel in Broadkiln Hundred, 500 acres, where Anthony Heavelo Senr. now lives, part of a larger tract granted to said Anthony Heavelo, Senr. For love and affection, 200 acres, part of the tract whereon Anthony Heavelo, Senr., now lives, to be laid off of the south side thereof being that part whereon said Anthony Heavelo Junr. now lives. Wit: D. Train, Isaac Smith. Within deed ackn. 3 Nov 1779.

293. Jonathan Heavelo, yeoman, from his father Anthony Heavelo, Broadkiln Hundred, yeoman, and wife Margaret. Deed. 30 Aug 1779. A parcel in Broadkiln Hundred on the north side of Broadkill Creek whereon Jonathan Heavelo now lives containing 266 acres, 126 whereof Anthony Heavelo purchased of William Heavelo, 100 acres more thereof from Andrew Heavelo dec'd. and James Heavelo both of the county afsd. dec'd., 40 acres the residue thereof he purchased of Elias Samples and Sarah Samples his wife, late Sarah Heavelo daughter of Andrew Heavelo late of the county dec'd. by whom the land descended to the said Sarah. The 266 acres, above described, are part of a larger tract of 500 acres originally granted to Anthony Heavelo the grandfather. The afsd. Anthony and Margaret Heavelo for love and affection, and £5 convey same to Jonathan Heavelo. Wit: D. Train, Isaac Smith. Within deed of gift ackn. 3 Nov 1779.

294. Nathaniel Milbey, Sussex Co., house carpenter, from Joseph West, Sussex Co., yeoman. Deed. 3 Nov 1779. A parcel, part of a larger tract in Drakes Neck which formerly belonged to the heirs of John West. Beginning at the corner of the 200 acres and said to be in the land of Milbey's land ... from the northeast end of Benjamin Burton's Old Mill Dam ... 10 acres. For £240. Wit: Rowland Beavans, Rhoads Shankland. Within deed ackn. 3 Nov 1779.

295. John Cornwell, Sussex Co., from Nehemiah Coffin, Sussex Co., yeoman. Deed. 3 Nov 1779. For £750, a parcel in Indian River Hundred, part of a tract granted to Benjamin Stockley and confirmed by him to Danl. Coopes, and by Joseph Atkins and wife who married one of the daughters of said Coopes confirmed to Hugh Stephenson

who confirmed same to afsd. Nehemiah Coffin. Beginning at an oak standing by Sockrockett Branch ... 85 acres. Wit: William Hall, Rhoads Shankland. Within deed ackn. 3 Nov 1779.

295. Thomas Willen, yeoman, from George and Nelson Waller, sons to George Waller, dec'd. and heirs of John Waller, dec'd., their brother, Sussex Co., yeoman. 3 Nov 1779. Whereas the afsd. George Waller dec'd. on 10 July 1767 by his writing obligatory in the penal sum of £200 obliged to convey 70 acres being part of a tract called Waller's Choice and 89 acres being part of a tract called Addition which said two tracts were granted to George Waller dec'd. by patent from the Proprietor of Maryland, i.e., Waller's Choice on 30 March 1742, 30 acres of which said Waller by his deed conveyed to Thomas Evans, and Addition patented 9 Aug 1742, 11 acres of which he conveyed to William Runnels which patent contained 100 acres - which there remained unconveyed with said Waller, 159 acres adjoining each other on the south side of the head of Nanticoke River. George Waller died intestate within the jurisdiction of Maryland and title of the land became vested in his eldest son, afsd. John Waller who died intestate with the land now established as being in Sussex Co., and John Waller leaving no issue nor brothers or sisters except for the said George and Nelson Waller, the land became vested in afsd. George and Nellson as heirs to their said brother. For £100. Wit: Benjamin Dirrickson, Rhoads Shankland. Within deed ackn. 3 Nov 1779.

297. Avory Stephens, Cedar Creek Hundred, yeoman, from Bethuel Wattson, Cedar Creek Hundred, yeoman. Deed. 4 Nov 1779. For £120, a parcel in Cedar Creek Hundred called Watsons Island containing 200 acres. Wit: D. Train, Robert Shankland. Within deed ackn. 4 Nov 1779.

297. Richard Jefferson, Sussex Co., yeoman, from Benjamin Dirrickson, Sussex Co., millright. Deed. 3 Nov 1779. For £200, a tract called Hudsons Addition. Beginning at a marked oak, a bounder of a tract formerly surveyed to Thomas Walker on the east side of a branch issuing out of Indian River called Kinney Branch and in Old Bridge Neck about 1/2 mile from the mouth of said branch ... 50 acres. Wit: Robert Shankland, Rhoads Shankland. Within deed ackn. 3 Nov 1779.

298. Solomon Grace, Sussex Co., farmer, from John Fisher, Kent Co., Delaware, farmer. Deed. For £48, a parcel called Fishers Swamp in Northwest Fork Hundred, 40 acres. Wit: Robert Broadie, Thomas Higgnott (his mark). Within deed ackn. 3 Nov 1779.

298. Peter Millman, Sussex Co., yeoman, from Mary Millman, Sussex Co., widow. Deed. 31 Dec 1778. A parcel in the forrest of Cedar Creek on the north side of the northern most main branch of Cedar Creek in the manor of Worminghust which land was the property of Samuel Truitt of Sussex Co., dec'd., who by his last will left the same at the disposal and sale of his wife Mary who later married Jonathan Millman and Jonathan and Mary Millman sold the same to Peter Millman. 110 acres, for £50. Wit: John Rickards, Michael Milman. Within deed ackn. 4 Nov 1779.

299. Robinson Savage, Accomack Co., Virginia, from Edward Stephenson, Sussex Co., and wife Margaret. Deed. 27 Aug 1779. A tract in Broadkill Hundred, containing 236 acres, part of which land is part of a tract granted by proprietor's warrant to Andrew Fullerton on 23 Jan 1745 and part of said 236 acres is included in the bounds of a patent granted to John Richardson which said two parcels Andrew Fullerton by deed of sale dated 1 May 1760 conveyed to afsd. Edward Stephenson. Beginning at a post in the line that divides the land from the lands of Hugh Stephenson ... to a stone in the line of Moses Dodd's land. For £944. Wit: James Thompson, James Martin. Within deed ackn. 3 Nov 1779.

300. Peter, Jemmy and Nancey Wootton from James Fusham, Sussex Co., yeoman. Deed of gift. James Fusham for love and affection for his sons and daughter in law, Peter, Jemmy and Nancy, children of Benjamin Wootton, dec'd., by his wife Maron, gives to the said children, all personal and real estate - on condition of their behaving as dutiful children and "staying with me until they become of lawful age or married." Signed: Jas. Fusham and Maron Fusham (her mark). [Adding at end a Negro wench named Hannah.] Deed was made void by James Fusham by his oath that repeated breaches of said conditions had been made by his wife. 31 Dec 1779.

301. Joshua Hill from Robert Dennis, Sussex Co. Bond for conveyance of land. Robert Dennis is bound to Joshua Hill for £1000. 19 Nov 1773. To convey all that part of a tract called Friends Discovery, 266 acres, which lies to the southward and westward of Joshua Robinson's house and the land he is now in possession of and adjoining to Assawamon Creek. Wit: J. Dennis. Riley Evans.

302. Joshua Hill from Robert Dennis. Bond for conveyance of land. Robert Dennis is bound to Joshua Hill for £500. 19 Nov 1773. To convey 5 1/2 acres of land and marsh laying between where Jones Rickards now lives and Millers, by 1780 or sooner, part of a tract called Friends Discovery. Wit: J. Dennis, Riley Evans.

302. Nathaniel Waples, Esqr., Sussex Co., from Robert Lacey, shopjoiner(?) and wife Mary, Sussex Co. Deed. 18 Jan 1780. Robert Lacey, father of the afsd. Robert Lacey, late of Sussex Co., dec'd., being seized of a parcel on the east side of the Cow Bridge Branch at the head of Indian River and whereas the afsd. Robert Lacey the Elder by his last will dated 13 March 1753 devised to his son Robert Lacey, joyner, all the lands on the west side of Old Indian Road til intersecting Samuel Cary's land, it being a part of a tract called Mount Joy and another tract surveyed for afsd. Robert Lacey the Elder including all the land between the afsd. Indian Road, the afsd. Samuel Cary's land, the Cow Bridge Branch and a tract surveyed for John Cary called Strife containing 100 acres, for £4300. Wit: Joseph Waples, William Waples. Within deed ackn. 9 Feb 1780.

303. Luke Burton, Sussex Co., from his father Robert Burton, Senr. of Angola and Indian River Hundred, yeoman. Deed. 7 April 1779. For love and affection and 20 shillings. A parcel in the bottom of

Angola Neck whereon Robert Burton now dwells, all the lands and
marsh from the bottom of the neck to Long Point Gut and from thence
across the neck where the Old Gate formerly stood near where the
Old School House stood ... to Rehoboth Bay, (being the same tract
which was originally granted by patent to William Kanning and
devised to said Robert Burton by his father who then possessed the
same and the devise thereof to the said Robert Burton was
afterwards confirmed to him by the will of his grandfather). Wit:
Woodman Stockley, John Abbot Warrington, Joseph Houston. Within
deed ackn. 9 Feb 1780.

304. Robert Burton, Junr., from his father, yeoman, Robert Burton,
Senr., of Angola and Indian River Hundred, the Elder. Deed. 7
April 1779. For love and affection and 20 shillings. Tract
adjoining the south side of Bracys Branch. Beginning at a corner
oak near William Little's line thence along the division line
between this and lands formerly in possession of William Brereton
... to a post near the dwelling house of the late Benjamin Stockley
dec'd. 200 acres, being the same which Daniel Hossman and
Elizabeth his wife by their deed dated 4 Feb 1768 conveyed to afsd.
Robert Burton, the Elder. Wit: Woodman Stockley, John Abbott
Warrington, Joseph Houston. Within deed ackn. 9 Feb 1780.

305. John Burton, yeoman, from his father Robert Burton, the Elder
of Angola and Indian River Hundred. Deed. 7 April 1779. For love
and affection and 20 shillings. After the death of said Robert
Burton, a parcel in Broadkiln Hundred being part of a larger tract
originally granted by patent to John Finch and called Finch Hall.
Beginning at a corner post in the end line of the dividend being a
corner of the land surveyed for Margaret Kollock for her dower of
and in the said dividend ... 180 acres. Wit: Woodman Stockley,
John Abbott Warrington, Joseph Houston. Within deed ackn. 9 Feb
1780.

307. William Burton from Robert Burton, the Elder of Angola and
Indian River Hundred. Deed. 7 April 1779. For love and affection
and 20 shillings, a parcel in Angola Neck which Robert Burton
bought of Thomas, Peter, Joseph, Burton and John Robinson whereon
Luke Buron now dwells, that is all the said tract of land and marsh
above Long Point Gut from the mouth thereof up the said gut or
ditch to Wolf Pit Pond thence up the middle of the slash of the
pond ... 66 acres. Wit: Woodman Stockly, John Abbot Warrington,
Joseph Houston. Within deed ackn. 9 Feb 1780.

308. John Laws, Esqr., Sussex Co., from Robert Houston, Sussex
Co., acting exr. and John Polk and Mary his wife, extx. of the last
will of John Houston, dec'd. Deed. 5 Feb 1780. Whereas John
Windsor of Somerset Co. being seized of a tract called Coxes
Performance of 1000 acres by virtue of a proprietor's grant of
Maryland, by his will devised 150 acres, part of afsd. tract, to
his grandson John Windsor, late of Worcester Co., Maryland in fee
tail who died so seized of the same 150 acres leaving issue only
one daughter named Mary Windsor to whom the same descended in fee
tail as afsd. who became possessed thereof and later by her deed
with covenant of common recovery conveyed same to afsd. John

Houston who thereupon sued forth and obtained one perfect recovery and became seized in fee simple and died without devising the same and the Orphans Court ordered the land sold to pay his debts and John Laws was the highest bidder on 150 acres of £250. Wit: Jonathan Bell, William Boyce, Levin Vaughan. Within deed ackn. 9 Feb 1780.

309. Robert Houston, Esqr., Sussex Co., from John Laws, Esqr., Sussex Co. Deed. 9 Feb 1780. John Laws stands possessed of 150 acres being part of a tract called Coxes Performance in Broad Creek Hundred by virtue of a deed of bargain and sale made by Robert Houston. [See above entry.] Wit: Alexr. Laws, Wm. Polk. Within deed ackn. 9 Feb 1780.

310. George Messick, Sussex Co., yeoman, from Job Ingram, Sussex Co., yeoman. Deed. 11 Feb 1780. A parcel in Broadkiln Forrest granted by proprietor's warrant to Thomas Parker who by deed of sale dated 1 Feb 1737 conveyed same to Jacob Ingram who by his last will devised same to afsd. Job Ingram for 150 acres. Beginning at a corner marked oak standing on the south side of a branch providing out of Nanticoke River called Gravelly Branch ... for £100. Wit: Isaac Smith, J. Russel. Within deed ackn. 9 Feb 1780.

311. William and Solomon Deputy from Nunez Deputy and Silvester Deputy, Sussex Co. yeoman, Richard Hudson son of John Hudson, yeoman, and Betsy his wife late Betsy Deputy, Benjamin Hudson of Sussex Co., yeoman, son of William Hudson and Polly his wife late Polly Deputy. Deed of release. For £5 they assigned their right to a parcel in the forrest of Cedar Creek Hundred which was allotted to them as their respective shares of the lands of their father Solomon Deputy, that is all that was allotted by the Freeholders, 130 acres and to Solomon Deputy all that 120 acres allotted to him. Wit: John Laws, Anne Laws. Within deed ackn. 9 Feb 1780.

312. Josiah Polk, Esqr. from David Forman. Power of Attorney granted to Josiah Polk by David Forman to deliver to William Horsey, Isaac Horsey and William Polk, one indenture "which I have already sealed dated 25 Nov 1779, purporting a lease of all lands which were the estate of Joseph Forman late of Sussex Co.," dec'd., lying on the south side of Broad Creek for 10 years from 1 Dec next. Wit: Cha. Moor. Within Power of Attorney proved 9 Feb 1780.

312. William Horsey of Somerset Co., Maryland, and Isaac Horsey and William Polk, of Sussex Co., from David Forman of Kent Co., Maryland, admr. of Joseph Forman of Sussex Co. Deed of lease. 25 Nov 1779. For a yearly rent of the taxes due, the estate of Joseph Forman of Sussex Co., dec'd., at the time of his death on the south side of Broad Creek, reserving to David Forman, timber, woods, etc. and they shall rebuild two saw mills, one on Little Creek and the other on Turkey Branch. Wit: Ben Chambers, Cha. Moor, Gustavus Scott. Within deed ackn. 9 Feb 1780.

313. George Messick, Sussex Co., yeoman, from Isaac Ingram, exr. of last will of Isaac Ingram, late of Sussex Co. yeoman. Deed. 11

177

Feb 1780. Whereas Isaac Ingram in his lifetime being possessed of a parcel in Broadkiln Forrest which was granted to Abraham Ingram by patent for 50 acres called Barbadus dated 4 July 1741 who by his last will devised the same to afsd. Isaac Ingram dec'd. Beginning at a marked oak 4 perches from the north side of Maple Branch, a fork of Gravelly Branch proceeding out of Nanticoke River ... And whereas said Isaac Ingram dec'd. by a writing obligatory dated 30 March 1748 obliged himself to convey to George Messick the above mentioned land. Wit: Isaac Smith, J. Russel. Within deed ackn. 9 Feb 1780.

314. James Fassett, Worcester Co., Maryland, mariner, from Levin Dirrickson, Sussex Co., Esqr. Deed. 9 Feb 1780. Sale of confiscated land. For £301, a tract resurveyed and granted to Joshua Hill late of Sussex Co., which said tract now called Conclusion to Friends Desire, containing 542 acres bounded according to the return of resurvey granted to said Hill 2 March 1776, 298 acres, part of the above said 542 acres being patented formerly to John Lane of Maryland and since became the property of afsd. Joshua Hill. Wit: Charles Polk, Junr., Rhoads Shankland. Within deed ackn. 9 Feb 1780.

315. John Spence, Sussex Co., from Marmaduke Story, Kent Co., Delaware, and Ann his wife, Joseph Story, Sussex Co. and Lucreasey his wife, and Elizabeth Fitsjarrel of Sussex Co. Deed. 31 Jan 1780. For £1000, a parcel and plantation whereon John Spence now dwells in the Northwest Fork Hundred near Marshehope Bridge, being also part of a larger tract formerly surveyed for Marmaduke Story, dec'd., 6 Feb 1753 by virtue of proprietor's warrant dated 13 Nov 1750. Beginning at a new corner oak in the back line near the end of the Deer Pond and is also a corner of one other part of said whole tract of the Great Survey ... in the line of land formerly surveyed for Isaac Anderson ... corner stake of land called the Calf Pasture ... 86 1/2 acres. Wit: James Spence (his mark), Isaac Jones. Within deed ackn. 9 Feb 1780.

316. Henry Neill, town of Lewes, yeoman, from Ann Molleston, of the town of Lewes, spinster. 10 Feb 1780. Deed. For £30. Moiety or half part of a lot in the town of Lewes on the corner of Front and Market Streets 60 feet in front (toward bank of Lewes Creek) and back towards and adjoining Mr. Shankland's piece of ground, 100 by 60 feet, described by a deed of gift from Alexander Molleston to his children for the same (of whom the said Ann Molleston is now the only survivor to whom the land descended). Wit: Elizabeth Neill, D. Train. Within deed ackn. 10 Feb 1780.

317. Simon Kollock, Esqr., Sussex Co., merchant, from John Clowes, Esqr., Sussex Co. 10 Feb 1780. Two tracts on the head of Indian River, one called Penny Neck granted by patent by proprietor's warrant of Maryland to William Burton 7 Aug 1732. Beginning on the south side of Sheep Pen Branch ... 40 acres. And William Burton assigned his right of said patent to Ebenezar Jones who assigned his right to Edward Pettet who assigned his right to afsd. John Clowes. The other tract called Cedar Hill was granted by patent dated 27 June 1744 of Maryland to William Powell. Beginning at a

post on the east side of the road, 1 perch from the road nearly where the bridge going over the Branch ... 20 acres. And the said William Powell by his last will devised afsd. 20 acres to his wife Fenby(?) who later married Robert Monroe and they by their deed of sale dated 8 March 1769 conveyed same to afsd. John Clowes. For £67, 60 acres. Wit: Henry Neill, Wm. Kollock. Within deed ackn. 10 Feb 1780.

318. John Jessep and Elenor his wife of Sussex Co., from Patrick Braughan, Dorchester Co., Maryland. Deed. 30 Aug 1779. Part of a tract called Bridge Branch in Northwest Fork Hundred. 8 acres, £150. Wit: Daniel Polk, Margaret Nutter Polk. Within deed ackn. 11 Feb 1780.

319. Hap Hazzard, Sussex Co., yeoman, from William Burton, Broadkiln Hundred, yeoman, and his wife Mary. Deed. 20 Dec 1779. Parcel in Broadkill Hundred called Abrahams Lot originally granted by patent to Abraham Potter which tract after divers conveyances and assurances became vested in afsd. William Burton who by his bond dated 25 Feb 1776 obliged himself to convey to Luke Carpenter the above mentioned Abrahams Lot who died having appointed Joshua Burton exr. of his last will who sold said 62 acres at a publick auction to Hap Hazzard for £77. Beginning at a corner stone of Samuel Rowland's land ... Wit: Samuel Rowland, Matthias Collings. Within deed ackn. 11 Feb 1780.

320. Mary Stillwell from Isaac Brown. Deed. 3 Dec 1779. For £10, all that messuages or tenement in Northwest Fork Hundred, a part of a tract called Poplar Ridge lately resurveyed to the original Poplar Ridge for Isaac Brown. 84 acres. Wit: Daniel Polk, Suffiah Brown (her mark). Within deed ackn. 11 Feb 1780.

321. John Clampitt from Warrick Hattabough, Kent Co., Delaware. Bond for conveyance. Warrick Hattabough is bound to John Clampitt for £300. 11 April 1780. To convey 150 acres now in possession of Joseph Hall belonging to the heirs of Samuel Black and joining the land of Joseph Hall, Samuel Dodd and Robert Homes. Wit: Thomas Berry, Elisha West.

321. William Jordan Hall, Sussex Co., from John Purkins, Worcester Co., Maryland. Deed. 3 May 1779. For £253.50, tract called Friendships Addition (9 1/2 acres); also the tract called Sandy Ridge (9 acres) and also a resurvey by Joshua Hall (151 acres), all of which was conveyed to said Purkins by Levin Dirrickson. Thos. Batson, Stephen Fisher. Within deed ackn. 3 May 1780.

322. John Metcalfe, planter, Sussex Co., from Hannah Johnson, Sussex Co., widow. Deed. 9 Nov 1778. A parcel in Slaughter Neck on the east side of Cedar Creek containing 396 3/4 acres which formerly belonged to Coston Townsend, dec'd., and now the property of the heirs of Ebenezer Spencer adjoining the lands of Stephen Townsend on the one side and the land which formerly belonged to Thomas Lay, dec'd. For £400. Wit: David Wattson, Baker Johnson. Within deed ackn. 3 May 1780.

323. Thomas Grice, Sussex Co., farmer, from Nathaniel Bowman Mariner and wife Jean, Sussex Co.,. Deed. 9 March 1780. For £100, a parcel in Indian River Hundred, granted to Nathaniel Bowman Marriner on 8 Nov 1752 for 100 acres on the east side of the road from St. George's Chappel to Doe Bridge. Beginning at a corner oak of James Davison's 95 acres. Wit: Robert Prettyman, William Prettyman. Within deed ackn. 3 May 1780.

324. Nathaniel Waples, Esqr. from Smith Frame, Sussex Co., and wife Comfort. Deed. 22 Jan 1780. A parcel in Indian River Hundred called Mountjoy which was granted by warrant dated 8 June 1737 to Samuel Johnson who on 9 Dec 1737 assigned his right to said warrant to Robert Lacy who by his last will dated 13 March 1753 devised part of afsd. tract to his son Parker Lacy who by his deed of sale dated 2 Nov 1756 conveyed same Joseph Warrington (book I No. 9, folio 137) who by deed of sale dated 28 Feb 1771 conveyed same to afsd. Smith Frame son of Robert Frame (book L No. 11, folio 134) but George Frame son of afsd. Robert Frame alleging the afsd. parcel to be the right of his father the afsd. Robert Frame dec'd., preferred a petition to the Orphans Court asking for a division of the land among the several heirs of said Robert Frame; appointed freeholders determined that the land would not admit of division and Smith Frame the eldest son accepted the afsd. tract at the valuation made by the freeholders (10 shillings per acre). Beginning at a corner marked oak standing one perch to the westward of the main road leading from Dagsbury to Dover and 2 miles up the said road from Doe Bridge over the head of Indian River ... to a corner oak of land resurveyed to Samuel Cary on 7 July 1741 called The Three Whole Halves ... then by a dividing line along an old Indian Road between the afsd. parcel and lands willed by afsd. Robert Lacy to his son Robert Lacy now also dec'd. and purchased by afsd. Nathaniel Waples of the said Robert Lacy the younger ... to a sapling being the third bounder of a tract called Striff [Strife] surveyed to John Cary 20 April 1717 ... to an oak of the land surveyed to Thomas Walker on 9 Jan 1717 ... 138 acres. For £3500. Wit: Thos. Gray, Rhoads Shankland. Within deed ackn. 3 May 1780.

325. Thomas Battson from Mary McCray, widow and extx. of Robert McCray of Worcester Co. Deed. 22 Nov 1779. Whereas Robert McCray bought a tract from William Gray called Gray's Adventure on the south side of a Gumb Swamp on the head of Indian Town Branch and afsd. Robert McCray left in his will that said tract was to be sold by his wife (afsd. widow of Worcester Co.) For £820, 100 acres. Wit: William Townsend, Racklife Conner. Within deed ackn. 3 May 1780.

326. Elizabeth Oakey, widow of Thomas Oakey, late of Sussex Co., from Hugh and William Stevenson, Sussex Co., yeomen. Deed. 3 May 1780. For £27, a parcel on the northwest side of Hairfields Branch, part of a tract surveyed for William Colter, 106 acres. Wit: Rhoads Shankland, Robert Mariner. Within deed ackn. 3 May 1780.

326. William Hall, Sussex Co., taylor, from George West, Sussex Co. Deed. 22 Sep 1779. Tract in Broadkill Hundred, part of a

tract whereof George West late of the county, dec'd., and father of above named George West, was seized of said land and died intestate leaving several children who were legal heirs and said George West the younger accepted the valuation set on the lands by the Orphans Court. Beginning at a post by the edge of the road from Coolspring to the Drawbridge over the Broadkiln Creek ... along the land belonging to the heirs of David McIlvain ... 10 acres, for £18. Wit: William Peery, James Barry. Within deed ackn. 3 May 1780.

327. Levin Milbey, Sussex Co., from John Clowes, Esqr., Sussex Co., Deed. 3 May 1780. Tract in Indian River Hundred on the Cow Bridge Branch granted by proprietor's warrant to Francis Cornwell who conveyed same by deed to John Clowes dated 4 Nov 1760. Beginning on the southwest side Bever Dam branch ... oak near the line of Gossling land ... northeast side of Morrisses Mill Pond ... 300 acres. Wit: Richard Bassett, Rhoads Shankland. Within deed ackn. 3 May 1780.

328. Adam Black, Sussex Co., blacksmith, from William Bell, Sussex Co., yeoman. Deed. 7 March 1780. For £4000, a tract called Bells Purchase. Beginning at an oak on the south side of Vineses Branch ... 100 acres. Wit: Samuel Jones, Sophia Maddux. Within deed ackn. 3 May 1780.

329. John Holloway of Maryland from Levi Lynch, Sussex Co. Deed. 1780. For £50, 100 acres left to said Levi Lynch by his father Abraham Linch in his last will being part of a tract called Friends Assistance, on the northernmost side of the said tract. Wit: Adam Black, Levi Collins. Within deed ackn. 3 May 1780.

329. Samuel Wiltbank, Sussex Co., from Cornelius Wiltbank, Sussex Co., and wife Rachel. Deed. 3 Nov 1779. A tract called The New Design(?) Trail, on the north side of Broadkiln Creek beginning at a corner post of the old line of Hazzard land and being the corner of Cornwell's land, 60 acres, being part of a patent called Howards Choice and part of a parcel containing 193 acres bought of Daniel Palmer and now the property of afsd. Cornelius Wiltbank; and they also convey another piece of marsh being part of a patent called Ragged Hammock Tract containing 100 acres beginning at Walter Youlin's line containing 22 acres for a total of 82 acres, for £106.7.6. Wit: Rhoads Shankland, Jos. Hall. Within deed ackn. 3 May 1780.

330. John Little from James Thompson, Sussex Co., yeoman, and wife Margaret. Deed. A parcel in Indian River Hundred on the southwest side of Braces Branch adjoining the lands formerly of Isaac Fleming which said parcel was formerly surveyed for Thomas Bates and by sundry means became the property of James and Margaret Thompson, afsd. Beginning at an oak of John Russel's line ... 237 acres; also a parcel of 18 acres surveyed by virtue of a warrant granted to Martha Little, widow. dated 18 April 1754 on the north side of the above recited land adjoining the branch afsd. For £40. Wit: James Martin, Rhoads Shankland. Within deed ackn. 3 May 1780.

332. James Wilkins of the forrest of Broadkill Hundred, from

Newcomb and Benja. White, Sussex Co., sadler and ship carpenter. Deed. 3 May 1780. For £150, a parcel in Broadkill Hundred granted by proprietor's warrant to Jacob White and by him assigned to said Newcomb and Benjamin White afsd. Beginning at a maple standing on the branch of Evans' Mill Pond ... to a white oak of the land of Thomas Marey formerly now Evans's ... 100 acres, surveyed 14 Feb 1757. Wit: Robert Shankland, Rhoads Shankland. Within deed ackn. 3 May 1780.

332. Moses Cox, Sussex Co., and wife Rhoda, from Elias Johnson, Sussex Co., yeoman. Deed. 3 May 1780. For £50, a parcel on the west side of Green Branch, part of a larger tract granted by patent to Simon Johnson for 150 acres dated 29 Sep 1757 being two full shares of 100 acres of the above recited patent at the northwest end thereof ... 66 2/3 acres, surveyed 17 March 1780. Wit: Levin Okey, Rhoads Shankland. Within deed ackn. 3 May 1780.

333. Jonathan Stephenson, Sussex Co., yeoman, from Robert Coulter, Junr. Sussex Co. Deed. 6 May 1779. For £100, a parcel on the south side of Love Long Branch. Beginning at a post at the southeast end of Little Dam in the lane between said Little and this land ... an oak in the line of the heirs of Wm. Allin ... 215 acres, being part of a tract laid out for 1200 acres to Richard Bundick and by sundry means the afsd. land containing 215 acres descended to afsd. Robert Coulter son of John Coulter. Wit: William Matthews, Rhoads Shankland. Within deed ackn. 4 May 1780.

334. Selby Hickman, Sussex Co., from William Millard, Sussex Co., and wife Mary. Deed. 11 Feb 1780. Parcel in Broadkiln Hundred being part of a tract which was conveyed by William Shankland, formerly High Sheriff of said county, to Thomas Staton by deed dated 3 Feb 1746 who by his last will devised part of afsd. land to his son Thomas Staton who by his deed dated 1 Sep 1761 conveyed 100 acres of said tract to John Mustard who by his deed dated 3 May 1769 conveyed same 100 acres to Robert Jones who by his deed dated 28 May 1774 conveyed same to James Gordon, and Thomas Gordon admr. of said James Gordon by virtue of an order from the Orphans Court conveyed same dated 17 Feb 1776 to afsd. William Millard. Beginning at a corner oak on the east side of the Mill Creek near the edge thereof ... to a line belonging to the heirs of David Clowes. Wit: David Thornton, James Rigen (his mark). Within deed ackn. 4 May 1780.

335. Henry Safford, Sussex Co., planter, from Obediah Smith, Sussex Co., planter. Deed. 11 March 1780. For £50, all that part of a tract called Yoark in Northwest Fork Hundred, 16 1/2 acres; also part of a tract called Cow Garden, 3 1/2 acres. Wit: Daniel Polk, Charles Brown. Mary the wife of Obediah Smith releases her dower right. Within deed ackn. 11 March 1780.

336. Obediah Smith, Sussex Co., planter, from Henry Safford, Sussex Co., planter, and wife Stashe. Deed. 11 March 1780. For £60, that part of a tract called Brothers Adventure in Northwest Fork Hundred and near said Obediah Smith's other land. 44 acres. Wit: Daniel Polk, Charles Brown.

337. Obediah Smith, Sussex Co., planter, from Thomas Smith, Sussex Co., planter. Deed. 10 March 1780. For £500, part of tract called Yoark in the Northwest Fork Hundred, 54 acres; also a tract called Cow Garden, beginning at an oak on the west side of the Green Pond that lays on the south side of the Double Fork Branch ... 50 acres; also a tract called Calf Pasture surveyed for Thomas Smith 23 March 1776, 50 1/4 acres; also a tract called Lone Pine surveyed for Thomas Smith on 25 March 1776, beginning at a marked oak on the northwest side of Tilgman Brown's land, 76 1/4 acres. Wit: Daniel Polk, Charles Brown. Within deed ackn. 4 May 1780.

338. Thomas Smith, Sussex Co., planter, from Obediah Smith, Sussex Co., planter, and wife Mary. Deed. 11 March 1780. For £200, a tract called Venture in Broad Creek Hundred, 100 acres according to patent and also a tract called Addition near the other tract surveyed and taken up in 1776 for Obediah Smith. Wit: Daniel Polk, Charles Brown. Within deed ackn. 4 May 1780.

339. Joseph Bradly, Sussex Co., planter, from Jacob Kindred, Sussex Co., planter, and wife Crate. Deed. 22 Oct 1779. For £100, a tract called Jacobs Fancey originally called Cannons Savannah and taken up by Stephen Cannon in Maryland, in the Northwest Fork Hundred, 110 acres, 83 acres of afsd. land to be made over by general warrantee which is patented; the other part is not patented so that the said Joseph Bradley only by the said Jacob Kindred right and was taken up by virtue of a warrant of a resurvey in 1776 and was added to the other land. Wit: Daniel Polk, Zadok Nutter. Within deed ackn. 4 May 1780.

340. John Ange, Sussex Co., planter, from Thomas Ange, Sussex Co., planter. Deed. 11 March 1780. For £40, a tract called Cartery(?) that John Ange, Senr. formerly held which is the only part of the tract on the east side of Mill Branch; the Mill Branch to be a division between said Thomas Ange and John Ange. Wit: Daniel Polk, Zadok Nutter. Within deed ackn. 4 May 1780.

341. Thomas Collings, Sussex Co., yeoman, from Brantson Lofland, Sussex Co., yeoman,. Deed. 15 March 1780. For £100, part of a tract of 600 acres formerly taken up and surveyed for John and Samuel Willson which said part or tract is in Primehook Neck in Cedar Creek Hundred on the north side of the South Branch of Primehook Creek. Boundary runs to the line of land belonging to the heirs of Thos. Till ... to a stone of Nehemiah Davis's land ... edge of Caleb Cirwithin's mill pond ... 100 acres. Wit: Luke Wattson, Isaac Wattson. Within deed ackn. 4 May 1780.

342. Belitha Laws from William Burroughs, both of Sussex Co., yeomen. Deed. March 1780. Whereas Isaac Freeland obtained a proprietor's warrant dated 12 May 1741 for 200 acres in Cedar Neck in Cedar Creek Hundred. Beginning at a corner of land formerly of John Truitt and Magdaline Manlove, widow ... to an oak in Jeremiah Morrises line now belonging to Andrew Collings ... stake in a savanna in Hart's line on the southeast side of a road leading from Hays Tavern to Fork Landing ... 244 acres and 120 perches ... which said warrant on 7 Jan 1752 by Isaac Freeland assigned to John

Burroughs who on 13 April in the year afsd. assigned same to his son William Burroughs who on 28 April 1769 assigned to William Clifton by means of his bond and on 25 July 1771 said Clifton assigned bond to Luke Davis who on 5 Feb 1780 assigned said bond to Belitha Laws afsd. For £60. Wit: Joshua Laws, Samuel Basnett. Within deed ackn. 4 May 1780.

343. Samuel Basnett from Belitha Laws, both of Sussex Co., yeomen. Deed. 1780. A parcel in the forrest of Cedar Creek. Beginning at a stake in Hart's line on the southeast side of a road leading from Capt. Hays's Inn to Fork Landing, 96 acres and 30 square perches, being part of a larger tract called Freelands Adventure which was transferred by sundry means to Belitha Laws. Wit: William Burroughs, Joshua Coston. On 12 May 1741 a proprietor's warrant was granted to Isaac Freeland for 200 acres in Cedar Creek Hundred. There was 245 acres laid off to said Freeland and 7 Jan 1752 assigned by said Freeland to John Burroughs and on 13 April 1765 by him assigned to his son Wm. Burroughs and on 28 April 1769 by him transferred to William Clifton and at the same time gave said Clifton a bond for making over the land 25 July 1771 said Clifton assigned bond to Luke Davis 5 Feb 1780 who assigned same to Belitha Laws, afsd. who obtained a legal conveyance of said 240 acres. Within deed ackn. 4 May 1780. [Plat included]

344. John Morris, Sussex Co., planter, from Joshua Morris, Sussex Co. Deed. 4 May 1780. A tract of 158 acres called Barnards Blumery which was granted to Benoni Barnard by the Proprietor of Maryland confirmed by patent dated 29 Sep 1762 who conveyed same to William Robinson who conveyed same to afsd. Joshua Morris. For £50, 50 acres at the head of Indian River and on the north side of Sheep Pen Branch and on the northern most end of said tract whereon said John Morris now lives. Wit: Joseph Hall, Jonathan Stevenson. Within deed ackn. 4 May 1780.

345. Thomas Prettyman, Sussex Co., farmer, from John Walker, Sussex Co., yeoman. Deed. 1 Dec 1778. For £115, two parcels in the forrest, one of which was taken up by Lazarus Kinny formerly in the Province of Maryland and patented to said Kinny under the commissioners of Maryland in 1716 for 200 acres and the other was taken up by John Calwell and 296 acres part of the said tract was assigned to Thomas Walker grandfather to the afsd. John Walker called Walkers Addition dated 8 Aug 1727 and whereas the first tract called Finnys Lott is said to have been conveyed from said Lazarus Kinny to afsd. Thomas Walker and whereas said Walker grandfather to the afsd. John Walker did devise in his last will to his son James Walker father to the afsd. John walker all the above recited two tracts by his will dated 22 Sep 1731. Beginning at a marked oak on the north side of Tussekey Branch, 200 acres. The bounds of the other tract called Walkers Addition begin at the first bounder of Kinnys Lott ... 296 acres. Wit: Samuel Shankland, Rhoads Shankland. Within deed ackn. 4 May 1780.

346. Simon Edwards, Sussex Co., pilot, from Prettyman Stockley, Sussex Co., weaver. Deed. 3 Feb 1780. For £370, part of a parcel conveyed by deed from Reece Woolf to said Prettyman Stockley for 6

acres dated 6 Feb 1769, the afsd. parcel being 5 acres of afsd. 6 acres, 1 acre excepted which is out at the east corner of said 6 acres which said 5 acres is bounded to the northeast by the land of the heirs of John Hall, to the southeast by the main road to Lewes, to the southwest by the lands of Cales heirs and to the northwest by --- Street. Wit: Jams. Coulter, John Neill. Within deed ackn. 5 May 1780.

346. Robert Mariner's petition for order of the court to Luke Wattson, sheriff, to convey land. 3 May 1780. Whereas James Love late of the county afsd., yeoman, dec'd., was possessed of a parcel in Indian River Hundred containing 75 acres, mortgaged to the Loan Office of Sussex Co., and died without discharging the said mortgage, and the land was sold for £100 by the sheriff, purchased by Nathaniel Bowman Mariner for the use of the petitioner. [He requests that land be conveyed.]

347. Robert Mariner, Sussex Co., yeoman, from Luke Wattson, Sheriff. Deed. 3 May 1780. Whereas James Love late of Sussex Co., yeoman, was possessed of a tract in Indian River Hundred on the north side of Ivey Branch ... in the line of Robert Stephenson ... 75 acres. Wit: Jona. Nottingham, N. Bowman Mariner. Within deed ackn. 4 May 1780.

348. Joseph Warrington's bond to James Stafford, Sussex Co., for conveyance of land. Joseph Warrenton, Sussex Co., planter, is bound to James Stafford, for £76. 13 Dec 1775. To convey a parcel in Indian River Hundred in the forrest of the same being part of a larger tract called Welches Folly. Beginning at a stake on the south side of said tract on a line also of said land and at a stake being a corner of 250 acres laid off to Joseph Hall, farmer, 194 acres. Wit: Hugh Stephenson, David Rankin. Bond assigned to Joseph Hall on 9 Aug 1779. Wit: Windsor Rawlins, John Fleming. Within deed ackn. 3 May 1780.

348. Rhoads Shankland and Alexander Warrington, as exrs. of the last will of Joseph Warrington. That afsd. Joseph Warrington on 13 Dec 1775 entered into a writing obligatory to convey 194 acres to James Stafford who assigned the bond to Joseph Hall for whom the petitioners wish to sign a deed. 3 Nov 1779.

349. Joseph Hall from Rhoads Shankland and Alexander Warrington exrs. of Joseph Warrington. Deed. [See above entries.] Beginning at a corner oak of Robert Holmes's land. Wit: Thomas Robinson, Junr., William Hall. Within deed ackn. 3 May 1780.

350. Robert White and others petition for leave of court to convey lands etc. 4 May 1780. Petition of Robert White, yeoman, Wrixam White, guardian of the person and estate of his son Jacob White, a minor, William Hall, guardian of the persons and estates of Jane Wilkins White and Israel White, minors, children of Isaac White, dec'd. That Jacob White the Elder late of county afsd. purchased of William Prettyman dec'd. a parcel of marsh containing 31 1/4 acres in Lewes and Rehoboth hundred; that William Prettyman passed his bond to convey said marsh to said Jacob White the elder.

William Prettyman died intestate before a conveyance was made. Administration of William Prettyman's estate was granted to Comfort Prettyman, his widow who later died intestate before said marsh was conveyed. Administration of Comfort Prettyman's estate was granted to Peery Prettyman. Afsd. Jacob White the elder hath since died having made his last will wherein he devised said marsh to his two sons, Isaac and above named Robert White and to his grandson Jacob White, to be equally divided. Peery Prettyman by his deed as admr. d.b.n. of William Prettyman conveyed said parcel to said Robert White, Jacob White, Jane Wilkins White and Isaac White which said Jane Wilkins White and Isaac White are the heirs and legal representatives of the first above named Isaac White, dec'd. But there was a mistake in the courses of the deed and another deed is requested from Prudence Prettyman admx. of said Perry Prettyman who was admr. of Comfort Prettyman who was admx. of said William Prettyman, to said Robert White, Jacob White, Jane Wilkins White and Isaac White.

350. Robert White and Jane Wilkins White and Isaac White, heirs of Isaac White, and Jacob White a minor son of Wrixam White, all of Sussex Co., from Prudence Prettyman admx. of Perry Prettyman, Sussex Co. who was admr. of Comfort Prettyman who was admx. of William Prettyman. Deed. 4 May 1780. A parcel of marsh in Lewes and Rehoboth Hundred containing 31 1/4 acres, being part of a larger parcel of marsh formerly granted by patent to one Cornwell which was the property of afsd. William Prettyman. Beginning at a corner post of John Prettyman's marsh ... to Coolspring Creek. William Prettyman on 9 June 1768 bonded himself to convey said parcel to Jacob White at whose death the parcel became the property of Robert White, Jane Wilkins White, Isaac White and Jacob White, minor, but the afsd. William Prettyman died before any conveyance was made and it was conveyed by the action of Perry Prettyman but a mistake was made in the deed which this deed rectifies. For £75. Wit: Sacker Wyatt, Jonathan Stevenson. Within deed ackn. 5 May 1780.

351. Joshua Hall, from John Collins, Sussex Co., Gentleman. Deed of release for 60 acres of land. Whereas Joseph Collins late of Worcester Co., Maryland, planter, was possessed of a parcel then in Worcester Co. but now Sussex Co., on the southeast side of Nanticoke River called Collins's Luck, and by his deed of sale dated 19 April 1759 conveyed to Thomas Coopes and his wife Elizabeth, 160 acres, part of the said tract, and Joseph Collins by his last will devised the residue of this tract to his daughter Margaret but there was a mistake in the description of the land in the deed from said Collins to said Coopes whereas this deed of release rectifies the error. Wit: James Henry, Peter Ftt. Wright. Within deed ackn. 3 Aug 1780.

352. A table of courses for White Brown for part a tract of land called Addition to Four Tracts willed by Abraham Clarkson; as also part of a tract called Clarksons Forrest joining the afsd. tract. [A plat is shown.]

353. William Robins, Sussex Co., carpenter, from Alexander

Parimore, Sussex Co. Deed. 21 Jan 1780. Tract, 160 acres, patented to Elinor Dobson by the Proprietary of Maryland on 20 Dec 1741. Bounded back in the woods on the north side of the eastern most branch of Gravelly Branch. Beginning at the edge of a fresh water marsh and about 6 perches southwest of a small improvement of Abraham Ingram, the first bounder of land of said Ingram called Bair Garden, the same land that Elinor Dobson by her last will devised to her daughter Mary, mother to the afsd. Alexander Parimore, and Mary dying under coverture intestate and the land then being in the province of Maryland the right of property thereof by the laws of that province was vested in her eldest son the afsd. Alexander Parimore party to these presents. For £60. Wit: Dan Dingee, Luke Heaverlo.

354. Stephen Redden, Sussex Co., yeoman, from Aaron McKemmey, Sussex Co., yeoman. Deed. 1 July 1780. A tract in Broadkill forrest on the head of Gravelly Branch containing 200 acres which was patented to Richard Dobson on the 4th of the 8th month 1718 who by his last will devised same to his two daughters Jane and Rachel who made division thereof and said Jane later married Walter McKimmey by whom she had issue, afsd. Aron and two daughters, Elizabeth and Jane. Dying intestate her part of the afsd. land became the property of her said children and said Elizabeth and Jane being at full age on 6 May 1777 by their deed of sale conveyed to afsd. Aron McKimmey their rights to the land. For 120 bushels of corn and one cow and calf. Beginning on the south side of the Bever Dam ... Wit: William Robins, James McNeal. Within deed ackn. 9 Nov 1780.

354. Nathaniel Waples, Sussex Co., from Betty Hill, William Brian and Nanney Brian his wife, John Shaw and Comfort his wife, all of Sussex Co. Deed. 14 Oct 1780. A parcel in Indian River Hundred called Rock Hole which was granted by warrant dated 9 Nov 1714 to Elizabeth Hill and by her ordered to be surveyed to Cornelious Wiltbank which warrant was assigned to Robert Burton and surveyed to him 30 Dec 1723 for 272 acres, and Robert Burton by his last will dated 25 April 1724 devised said tract to his son Samuel Burton who by his deed of sale dated 5 Aug 1752 conveyed same to Thomas Coullour and Asher Mott [Moot], recorded in Book H No. 7, folio 333 and in the same book on folio 382 is recorded Jacob Kollock, High Sheriff, deed dated 11 Dec 1753, the sale of the moiety of Thomas Coullour to said Asher Mott to satisfy a Judgment. Benjamin Stockley, attorney of said Mott, by his deed of sale dated 3 March 1761 conveyed the 272 acres to William Harmonson (Book I No. 9, folio 293) who by his deed dated 2 March 1764 conveyed 170 acres of said land to Absolam Hutson (Book K No. 10, folio 71) and the remaining part of the said tract William Harmonson by his deed dated 6 Sep 1768 conveyed to Solomon Hill (Book K No. 10, folio 335) who by his last will dated 8 Jan 1778 devised same to his wife Betty Hill during her natural life and after her decease to be equally divided between his two daughters, Comfort Shaw who was then married to John Shaw and Nanney Brion who also had married William Brion. For £3500. Wit: Elisha Dickerson, John Sharp (his mark). Within deed ackn. 8 Nov 1780.

356. William Wyatt, Sussex Co., yeoman, from John Black, Junr., Sussex Co., taylor. Deed. 29 Aug 1780. For £75, a parcel in Lewes and Rehoboth Hundred adjoining the lands whereon Nicholas Little now dwells being part of a larger tract granted by patent to Samuel Gray called Grays Inn containing 632 acres, 110 3/4 acres of which by sundry means became the property of James Campbell by deed from George Campbell dated 6 Aug 1733 (Liber G. No. 6, folio 41) and James Campbell died intestate leaving issue one daughter the mother of the above named John Black to whom the land descended and who died intestate leaving issue the above named John Black to whom the parcel descended. Wit: William Peery, Mary Peery. Within deed ackn. 8 Nov 1780.

357. Peter Hubbert from Sarah Dirrickson, Sussex Co., and her son Robt. Minors, Kent Co., planter. Deed. 13 April 1780. For £180, part of the tract called Cannons Regulation on the north side of Nanticoke River near the side of Muddy Creek, 10 acres; and all that tract that lies on the east side of Muddy Creek of 50 acres. Wit: Jeremiah Cannon, Jacob Cannon. Within deed ackn. 8 Nov 1780.

358. Jacob Rogers, Sussex Co., from John Nicolson, Sussex Co. Deed. 19 July 1780. For £750, part of two tracts, one called Dumphrize, the other called Brotherhood, on the sea board side of Assawamon Bay called Rambly Marsh containing 175 acres. Wit: Thos. Batson, William Wordan Hall. Within deed ackn. 8 Nov 1780.

358. Walton Parnall, Worcester Co., Maryland, from Jacob Rogers, Sussex Co. Deed. 4 Aug 1780. For £700, part of a tract called Brotherhood, on the seaboard side on Assawaman Bay called Rumbly Marsh at a point of marsh on the Little Bay. Wit: Thos. Batson, Parker Rogers. Within deed ackn. 8 Nov 1780.

359. Edward Dingle, Sussex Co., from Charles Whorton, Sussex Co., farmer. Deed. 29 Feb 1780. Whereas John Groome was seized of two indefinable estates known as Grooms First Purchase and Poor Chance at whose death the estates revolved to his mother Mary Davidson, there being no nearer heir to the said Groom and the said Mary Davidson dying Charles Worton became seized said estates as being the only child of the said Mary Davidson then alive. For £55 to William Mason, 4 acres of Grooms Purchase, beginning at a stump in Dingle's Garden, about 1 miles from Blackfoot Town on the north side of a county road that leads from Blackfoot to Francis's; and a parcel being part of tract called Poor Chance about 1 1/2 miles from Dagsberry ... to Joseph Houston's line is drawn for the 23 acres that was sold out of the original tract, 77 acres. Wit: John West, Paul Waples. Within deed ackn. 8 Nov 1780.

360. John Waples, son of John, of Sussex Co., from Robert Minors of Kent Co., Delaware, and Levin Dirrickson and his wife Sarah of Sussex Co. Deed. 19 June 1780. For £52, a parcel being part of two tracts called Long Acre and Cumberland. That part called Long Acre was granted to Richard Crocket on 25 Aug 1747 and the part called Cumberland was granted to William Taylor on 3 May 1705. Beginning at the first bounder of the above named Long Acre standing in a field formerly belonging to Solomon Nock in Pyney

Neck on the north side of Peppers Creek and on the south side of Indian River ... to intersect the dividing line between the said John Waples and Elihu Waples ... 51 acres. The two mentioned parcels were conveyed to Sarah Wingate and Charles Minors from afsd. William Johnson and by sundry means became the property of Robert Minors, Levin and Sarah Dirrickson. Wit: Jona. Nottingham, Love Wingate. Within deed ackn. 8 Nov 1780.

361. John Waples, Sussex Co., from Abel Nottingham, yeoman, and wife Hannah, Sussex Co. Deed. 8 Nov 1780. For £90, three parcels in Poiney Neck and on the south side of Indian River, 50 acres being part of a tract called Painters Ignorance on a small creek called Island Creek, 50 acres; also 100 acres being part of a tract called Morriss Purchase containing 500 acres in the same neck and adjoining the above said 50 acres; also 6 acres being part of a tract called Long Acre granted to Richard Crockett on 25 Aug 1747 and conveyed from said Richard Crockett to afsd. Abel Nottingham. Wit: N. Waples, Levin Dirickson. Within deed ackn. 8 Nov 1780.

362. Elihu Waples, Sussex Co., from William Waples of Pyna Neck in Sussex Co. Deed. 8 Nov 1780. For £100, a part of a tract called Morris Purchase, 500 acres on the south side of Indian River in Pyney Neck on Peppers Creek. Whereas Samuel Morris obtained a grant (Maryland) to 500 acres being the original tract and died intestate and William Morris became heir at law to afsd. land and conveyed same to John Smith who on 30 April 1750 for £60 sold to Paul Waples father to the above said William Waples. Wit: Nathl. Waples, Richard Green. Within deed ackn. 8 Nov 1780.

362. Elihu Waples, Sussex Co., from Robert Minors, Kent Co., Delaware, and Levin Dirrikson and Sarah his wife of Sussex Co. Deed. 19 June 1780. For £144, two parcels in Poiney Neck on the south side of Indian River and the north side of Peppers Creek, 88 1/2 acres of a tract called Long Acre granted to Richard Crockett on 25 Aug 1747 and conveyed by him onto William Johnson who conveyed same to Sarah Wingate and Charles Minors, son of the afsd. Sarah Wingate. Beginning at the first bounder of a tract called Comberland standing on the north side of Peppers Creek ... to intersect a piece of land laid out for John Waples brother to the said Elihu being part of the said tract called Long Acre ...; also 51 1/2 acres being part of a tract called Comberland which tract was granted to William Taylord on 3 May 1705 and the said 51 1/2 acres was conveyed to Sarah Wingate and Charles Minors from above said William Johnson - in the whole 140 1/4 acres. Wit: Jona. Nottingham, Love Wingate. Within deed ackn. 8 Nov 1780.

363. Priscilla Waples, Sussex Co., from Robert Minors of Kent Co., Delaware, and Levin Dirrickson and his wife Sarah of Sussex Co. Deed. 19 June 1780. For £130, a part of a tract called Comberland granted to William Taylord on 3 May 1705. Boundary runs to Peter Waple's line of a tract called Aydelotts Neglect ... to intersect John Waple's line ... 137 acres. 70 acres of this land was conveyed to Charles Minors from Thomas Johnson late of said county and 30 acres of the above said land was conveyed to said Charles Minors from Linzey Brother and remainder of the 137 acres was

conveyed to Sarah Wingate and said Charles Minors from William Johnson. Wit: Jona. Nottingham, Love Wingate. Within deed ackn. 8 Nov 1780.

364. Robert Houston, Sussex Co., from Jacob Burton. Deed, Sussex Co. 2 Nov 1780. For £15, part of a tract called Conclusion. Beginning at a marked oak in a small drean issuing out of Indian Town Branch it being the nearest drean to Robert Houston's bounder nearly southeast from John Wingate's house, 13 acres. Wit: Elisha Cottingham, Elihu Waples. Within deed ackn. 8 Nov 1780.

365. Paul Waples, Sussex Co., from Charles Whorton, farmer, Sussex Co. 29 Feb 1780. For £45. Whereas John Groom was seized in an estate of inheritance known as Poor Chance, patented under Maryland, and now lying in Sussex Co., who dying the said estate revolved to his mother, Mary Davidson, there being no nearer heir. And the said Mary Davidson dying Charles Whorton became seized of the said estate being the only child of the said Mary Davidson then alive. Beginning at the bounder of the tract that stands about a mile above Blackfoot between Indian River and the county road, about 7 rods to the sw from house Paul Waples now lives in, bounder of Edward Dingle resurvey. 75 acres. Wit: John West, Edwd. Dingle. 8 Nov 1780.

366. Edward Craig from Mary Davison of the city of Philadelphia, widow, 8 acres, for £48, being 1/3 of a large piece on sw side of Lewes Town being 23 and 3/4 acres, being one moiety whereof John Simonton by his last will devised to his three daughters to wit, Jane, Sarah and Mary (party to these presents), the other moiety of the said land was conveyed by deed of sale to John Simonton, the younger, by a certain John Miers and the said John Simonton the younger being so seized of the other moiety of this land afterwards died intestate and without issue leaving four sisters, to wit, Jane, Sarah, Mary (party to these presents) and Elizabeth to whom the said moiety or half part descended and came as next of kin and coheirs to their said brother John Simonton, the younger afsd. under Act of Assembly for settling intestate estates. And whereas the said Elizabeth afterward married Noble Lewis who by their deed of release, released their right to said Jane, Sarah and Mary who by agreement caused division to be made to the parcel. The middle parcel (divided crossway) was allotted to Mary. 13 Oct 1780. Wit: Phillip Kollock Rusel. 8 Nov 1780.

367. George Walker, planter, Sussex Co., from Gammage Evans Hodgson, planter, Sussex Co. 7 Nov 1780. A tract of land in Sussex Co., 100 acres, called Woodcrafts Venture which was granted to Solomon Rodgers, confirmed to him by patent from the proprietor of Maryland on 3 April 1750 and did by his deed of conveyance dated 1755 make over said 100 acres to William Ezekiel Woodcraft and the said William Ezekiel Woodcraft did by deed of conveyance dated 15 January 1760 make over the said hundred acres to Solomon Rodgers, Junr. who did by his deed of conveyance dated 24 March 1770 make over his right to the land to Thomas Wildgoose and the said Thomas Wildgoose did by deed of conveyance

make over the land to the said Gammage Evans Hodgson. In
consideration of 100 acres called the Vinyard which afsd George
Walker has delivered to Gammage Evans Hodgson. To w. side of
small dreen at the head of Indian Town Creek, n. side of tract
surveyed for Thomas Wildgoose. Wit: William Kollock, William
Reynolds. 8 Nov 1780.

367. Gammage Evans Hodgson from George Walker. [See above.]
Boundary references: Benston's fence, Barker's line. Wit: same
as above. 8 Nov 1780.

368. Confiscated land. William Fisher, cordwinder of Sussex
Co., from Levin Dirrikson, Commissioner appointed by an Act of
Assembly, an Act of Free Pardon and Oblivion and for other
purposes - to make sale and dispose of forfeited estates. 4 Jan
1779. Tract in Rehoboth Hundred about 4 miles from the
courthouse being part of a larger tract of land called Sandyall.
To e. side of road that leads from Lewes Town to mill called
Kollock's Mill and was granted by a commissioners warrant of
Resurvey dated at Philadelphia on 10th day of 6th month 1715 at
the request of Edward Parker in behalf and as guardian unto the
heirs of William Orr, deceast and surveyed by Robert Shankland
and William Orr, miller, one of the heirs of the aforesaid
William Orr deceast, by his deed of sale dated 6 Feb 1721
conveyed the land to Daniel Fling which deed of sale is recorded
in Book E, folio 444 and said Daniel by his deed of sale dated 9
Dec 1747 conveyed 101 acres of the aforesaid land to John Oakey
which was recorded in Book H, number 7, folio 159. And the said
John Oakey and Mary Oakey his wife by their deed of sale dated
1777, conveyed the land to Nehemiah Field, late of this county.
To land of David Shankland, land held by William Holland, Daniel
Fling's Swamp, land of heirs of Jacob Kollock, deceased, called
Sundyall. Seized on 16 May 1778 and Nehemiah Field being one of
the offenders by name described in the Act of Assembly. Sold by
public auction on 2 Oct 1778 to Nathaniel Waples, to be conveyed
to William Fisher upon his paying the purchase money, £250. Wit:
Simon Kollock, N. Waples. 8 Nov 1780.

369. Bond. William Polk from John Polk for conveyance of land.
Know that I John Polk of Worcester Co., planter, am held and
firmly bound unto William Polk of Sussex Co., son of John Polk,
blacksmith, penal sum of £200 to be paid to William Polk. 29
February 1772. That John Polk assigned over his right to tract
that formerly belonged to John Polk, blacksmith, lying in Sussex
Co. For £100. 8 Nov 1780.

370. Deed. William Polk, Sussex Co., Delaware, from John
Stewart of Kent Co., Delaware for £300. 6 November 1780.
Whereas Samuel Stewart, late of Sussex Co., obtained a warrant
from the Commissioners of property at Philadelphia, dated 15
March 1714 for 200 acres of land executed by Robert Shankland,
Deputy Surveyor of Sussex Co., on 17 January 1717 in surveying
420 acres for the said Samuel Stewart and the aforesaid John
Stewart, recourse being had to the records of said Shankland
Surveys situated on the w. side of Delaware Bay and in Cedar

Creek Hundred in the line of the Manner of Wonninghust which said dividend of land was never divided between the said Samuel Stewart and John Stewart and the said John Stewart is the only surviving heir of the said Samuel Stewart. Wit: Samuel Kemp and John Williams. 8 Nov 1780.

371. Deed. Elijah Melson, ship carpenter, Sussex Co., from Levin Dirrikson, Esq., Sussex Co. 9 November 1780. Reference to Act of Assembly of 26 June 1778, An Act of Free Pardons and Oblivion and for other purposes, appointing Levin Dirrikson, Esq. Commissioner of the County of Sussex to sell and convey all the estate both real and personal of several persons in the said Act named. And whereas Levin Dirrikson did sell by virtue of the act the property of Boaz Manlove, Esq., including among other things, a tract of land in Broad Kill Hundred which Boaz Manlove purchased of Solomon Hill. Boundary references: corner of the lands of the heirs of Jonathan Tilney, dec'd., 106 1/2 acres, for £297. Wit: Russel Drain. 9 Nov 1780.

371. Deed. William Burton, Broadkill Hundred, yeoman, from George Walker, Sussex Co., yeoman. 8 Nov 1780. For £100. Grist mill on the Coolspring Branch in Broadkill Hundred, formerly built by said George Walker and those 2 acres of land on the west side and 1/2 acre of land on the east side of Coolspring Branch which was condemned for the use of the mill. Wit: George Conwell, D. Train. 9 Nov. 1780.

372. Deed. Aaron Perry from Aaron Irons, Sussex Co. 4 Aug 1780. Whereas a certain tract or parcel of land lying in Indian River Hundred, being part of the property of Thomas Warrington, late of Sussex Co., deceased, which said Thomas Warrington by his last will devised to his son Joseph Warrington who obliged himself to convey 130 acres thereof to Peter Robinson but the said Joseph Warrington dying before any conveyance was made agreeable to the tenor of the said writing and Sarah Warrington, widow and relict of the said Joseph Warrington having married Elias West the said Elias West and Sarah his wife by deed of sale duly executed having first obtained an order of the court of common pleas for Sussex Co. Peter Robinson by his deed of sale dated 2 Nov 1774, conveyed said 130 acres to aforesaid Aaron Irons. Runs to the edge of Russell's Creek; heirs of Wrixam West; Waller's land. 130 acres of land. £5. Wit: Wm. Kollock, Thomas Godwin, Jacob Irons. 9 Nov 1780.

373. John Russel's petition for order of Court to Rhoads Shankland, Sheriff, to convey lands to him. 9 Nov 1780. Petition shows that whereas John Rodney and David Hall, Esqrs., late trustees of the General Loan Office of Sussex Co., obtained a Judgment at May term in 1775 against John Lewis admr. of the estate of William Atchison, late of the county, Gentleman, deceased, for £60, whereupon 2 acres in the town of Lewes, adjoining on the south east side lotts of land of Rev. Matthew Wilson and on the south west side bound by lands of the heirs of William Piles and Joseph Eldridge, deceased, being the same land which the said William Atchison granted in mortgage to William

Till, Esqr., dec'd. then trustees of the General Loan Office.
The land was sold by the sheriff and the land was purchased for
£15.12.6 by the petitioner.

373. Deed. John Russel, scrivener, from Rhoads Shankland. 9
Nov 1780. [Same land as above.] Wit: John Wiltbank, John Laws.
9 Nov 1780.

374. Bond. William Vaughan and others from James Taylar, Junr.
Know that I James Taylor, Junr., of Caroline Co., Virginia,
Gentleman, am held bound to William Vaughan, Jethro Vaughan and
George Booth, all of Somerset Co., Maryland, in the sum of £200.
12 Oct 1775. Whereas James Taylor hath sold to the above named
William Vaughan, Jethro Vaughan and George Booth his right to
tract called Coxes Discovery in Little Creek in Somerset Co. and
the wife of James Taylor hath not acknowledged her right of dower
in the tract. Should she claim her dower right then the above
to be of full force. Wit: George Dashiell, Wm. Horsey.

375. Bond. Mary Waples from Elihu Waples for possession of
land. I Elihu Waples of Sussex Co. am held firmly bound in the
sum of £400. 19 June 1780. To convey "that 1/3 of the lands
that were willed to me by my father John Waples called Morrises
Purchase and 1/3 part of my right" to the tracts, Long Acre and
Comberland in Piney Neck. Wit: Jona. Nottingham, Levin
Dirrikson.

375. Deed. Nehemiah Messick, yeoman, from Joshua Hall,
blacksmith and wife Comfort, Sussex Co. 8 Feb 1780. Whereas
there are two pieces of land formerly in Worcester Co., Maryland,
but now in Sussex Co., on the southeast side of the Nanticoke
River, the one piece containing 40 acres known as Givens's
Discovery, which Day Given by his deed of sale dated 7 March 1754
conveyed to Elizabeth Hall, mother of the aforesaid Joshua Hall,
the other piece containing 160 acres adjoining thereto and known
as Collins's Luck, which Joseph Collins by his deed of sale dated
19 April 1759 conveyed to Thomas Copes and Elizabeth his wife
(late the above named Elizabeth Hall) and the said Thomas Copes
and Elizabeth his wife being so seized of the said two pieces did
by their deed of sale dated 11 May 1763 convey the same to the
above named Joshua Hall and William Hall with a reserve of the
dower of said Elizabeth during her natural life. And William
Hall by his deed of release dated 23 Aug 1777 released his right
to Joshua Hall. Wit: John Draper Russel. 8 Feb 1781.

376. Deed. Isaac Cooper, Sussex Co., from William Kirkpatrick,
Sussex Co. For £125. 3 Feb 1781. A tract of land in Little
Creek Hundred whereon stands the afsd. Isaac Cooper's mansion
plantation which land was on 18 April 1754 granted by the
Proprietary of Maryland to John Kirkpatrick and John Kirkpatrick
on 6 Feb 1770 passed a bond obligatory on himself to assign the
land to Isaac Cooper and said John Kirkpatrick is since deceased
leaving issue his eldest son the afsd. William Kirkpatrick and
several other children and the said land has not been conveyed.
Runs to the south side of Broad Creek near a line of tract

surveyed for Joseph Marshall called Providence. Wit: John Polk, Luke Huffington. 7 Feb 1781.

377. Deed. Isaac Vaughan, Sussex Co., from Dudson Bacon, Sussex Co. For £15. 25 Jan 1781. Whereas Dudson Bacon by virtue of a deed of general warrantee from Day Scott and Alice his wife dated 2 July 1737 and recorded in the records of Somerset Co. in Liber EJ No. X, folio 187 and 188, became seized and possessed of 100 acres, it being part of a larger tract of land called Cox's Discovery which was on 4 Dec 1694 granted by patent by the Proprietary of Maryland to Edward Day, lying on the west side of Little Creek in Sussex Co. And Dudson Bacon did afterward on 25 Dec 1753 give a bond obligatory on himself conditioned for his conveying to Ephraim Vaughan 50 acres of the above described land, to be taken off the west end. Whereas Ephraim Vaughan devised the afsd 50 acres to his eldest son Wm. Vaughan who by his last will devised the 50 acres to his younger brother Isaac Vaughan, afsd. party to these presents. Wit: William Polk and Isaac Cooper. 7 Feb 1781.

378. Deed. George Booth from Dudson Bacon. 25 Jan 1781. Whereas Dudson Bacon by virtue of a deed of General Warrantee from Day Scott, ... etc. [See above deed] 145 acres. £130. Reference to Caleb Balding's mill pond. Wit: William Polk, Isaac Cooper. 7 Feb 1781.

379. Deed. William Vaughan from Dudson Bacon. 5 Jan 1781. Whereas Dudson Bacon by virtue of a deed ... [See above deed] 100 acres, £15. Whereas Dudson Bacon did on 25 Dec 1753 pass a bond obligatory on himself confirming to Jethro Vaughan his right to 50 acres of the above described 100 acres, that is off the east end and whereas Jethro Vaughan by his last will devised the same to his eldest son William Vaughan. Jethro Vaughan is now dead and the land never was conveyed to him by Dudson Bacon. Wit: William Polk, Isaac Cooper. 7 Feb 1781.

380. Deed. Obediah Smith, Sussex Co., planter, from William Clarkson, Sussex Co., planter. 6 Nov 1779. Whereas Thomas Clarkson had by his Lordship's patent under the great seal of Maryland granted to him on 19 May 1757, 3 acres on the south side of Nanticoke River in Worcester Co., called Mill Landing. And whereas Thomas did afterwards make a resurvey on the said 3 acres and added thereunto 500 acres being called Mill Landing Enlarged, being granted on 29 Sep 1762. William Clarkson is the heir of Thomas Clarkson. Wit: Daniel Polk, Thomas Smith. 7 Feb 1781

381. Deed. Richard Adams, planter, Sussex Co., from Absolam Adams, planter, Sussex Co. 27 July 1780. £20. Part of tract called Sarah's Delight and all of the tract that lyeth to the west side of Harper's Branch. 45 1/4 acres. Wit: Daniel Polk, Joseph Godwin. 7 Feb 1781.

381. Deed. William Jurdon Hall, Sussex Co., from Jacob Rogers, Sussex Co. 5 June 1780. For £100. 43 3/4 acres, being part of a tract called Brotherwood, lying on the sea board side and in

Rumbly Marsh, about 1 mile from Finia's Island. Beginning at a post in Rumbly Marsh on the dividing line between Jacob Rogers and John Rogers, dec'd., heirs ... to a corner post of Thomas Selby's ... place called the Ridge. Wit: Jona. Bell, Jona. Nottingham. 7 Feb 1781.

382. Julius Augustus Jackson petition for order to Rhoads Shankland, Sheriff. 9 Feb 1781. Shows that John Paptist was indebted to petitioner in the sum of 40 shillings and absented himself from his usual place of abode. Petitioner obtained a writ of attachment against said John Paptist. Land of Paptist was sold to petitioner for £71. [During this period the sheriff, John Woodgate died.]

383. Deed. Julius Augustus Jackson, practitioner of physick, from Rhoads Shankland, Sheriff. [See above petition.] Run to an oak between John Cannon's mill pond and Nathaniel Horney's mill pond; near the corner of a tract called Long Lott. 55 1/4 acres. £71. Wit: J. Russel, Jur., Rust Jackson. 9 Feb 1781.

384. Confiscated land. Deed. William Jurdan Hall, Gentleman, from Levin Dirikson, Commissioner. 2 Sep 80. For £11.5. The right of Joshua Hill to a plantation confirmed to him by John Walker by a bound of possession dated 18 June 1776. Joshua Hill was seized of the land on 16 May 1778, being one of the offenders mentioned in the Act of Assembly passed 26 June 1778. Being at the head of a branch called Deep or Millers Mill Branch and on the south side of a country road that leads from Peleg Walter's Tavern to St. Martin's Church and adjoining to the west line that divides the Maryland and Delaware State and the plantation that the above said John Walker lived on. Wit: Edwd. Dingle, Jona. Nottingham. 7 Feb 1781.

385. Deed. Joseph Godwin, Sussex Co., planter, from Absolam Adams, Sussex Co., planter. 27 July 1780. For £20. Part of a tract called Sarah's Delight and all that whole tract that lyeth to the eastward of Harpers Branch now in the possession of Joseph Godwin. 29 3/4 acres. Wit: Daniel Polk, Richard Adams. 7 Feb 1781.

385. Deed. Joseph Waples from William Newbold, Margaret Newbold, Robert Hood and Mary his wife, John Thoroughgood and Esther his wife and Joshua Ingram and Margaret his wife - all of Sussex Co. 6 Feb 1781. Land in Indian River Hundred, 200 acres, part of a larger tract called Holm's Dispatch which was granted to John Holmes by a proprietary warrant and surveyed 14 Jan 1742. And John Holmes by his deed of sale dated 2 March 1747 conveyed the aforesaid 200 acres to Margaret Waples and Margaret Waples by her last will devised the land to her son William Waples but if he should die without issue then she devised the land to her grandson Thomas Newbold and the said William Waples and the said Thomas Newbold both dying without issue the said land descended to the aforesaid William Newbold, Mary Hood, Esther Thoroughgood and Margaret Ingram, wife of Joshua Ingram the brother and sisters of the afsd. Thomas Newbold or to the aforesaid Margaret

Newbold sister to the afsd William Waples. Beginning at the
corner of the 1100 acre tract of Robert Burton; corner of Thomas
Prettyman's land. £255. Wit: John Waples, Rhodah Stephenson.
Mary Hood wife of Robert Hood and Esther Thoroughgood wife of
John Thoroughgood and Margaret Ingram wife of Joshua Ingram,
being examined separate from their husbands, they did say that
they signed the deed of their own free and voluntary will. 7 Feb
1781.

387. James Walker, Sussex Co., yeoman, from John McCullah,
Sussex Co., yeoman. 7 Feb 1781. Two small parcels of land
joining each other in Broadkiln Hundred - one piece of 101 acres
was conveyed by deed of sale dated 3 Aug 1747 from Mary Potter
and others to Alexander McCullah, father of the above named John
McCullah, as shown in Liber H no. 7, folio 146; the other piece
of 35 acres was conveyed by deed of sale dated 13 March 1753 from
Robert Burton and Ann his wife to said Alexander McCullah,
boundaries described in Book H, folio 352. And Alexander
McCullah died intestate, seized of the land. John McCullah after
having had the necessary proceedings in the Orphans Court was
seized of the land and by his bond obligatory, obliged himself to
Jacob Walker, father of the above named James Walker, but Jacob
Walker died intestate before any conveyance of the lands was made
from the said John McCullah. Whereof Thomas Walker, eldest son
of said Jacob Walker, deceased had the land conveyed to him and
then sold the land to above named James Walker. £136. Wit:
Phillips Kollock, Jo. Russel. 7 Feb 1781.

388. Deed. William Bagwell, Sussex Co., yeoman, from John
Bagwell, Sussex Co., yeoman, brother. Indenture of release 5 Feb
1781. Whereas the parties have made a division of land in Indian
River Hundred "which was formerly purchased by our ancestors from
William Burton of Accomack County in Virginia and last owned by
our father Thomas Bagwell, deceased, and by his will devised unto
us and we the said parties do divide as follows": [description
given]. Beginning at the Old Bridge that crossed the ditch
between Bald Eagle Island released to John Bagwell and the main
land of Thomas Bagwell, deceased; Ann Bagwell, widow's thirds;
tract called Bluff Point; Rehoboth Bay near a large cockel shell
bank; Roman T Pond. 62 acres. Wit: William Burton, William
Burton, Junr. 8 Feb 1781.

389. Deed. John Bagwell, Sussex Co., yeoman, from William
Bagwell, Sussex Co., yeoman. [See above.] 8 Feb 1781.

389. Deed. David Hall, Junr., Lewes and Rehoboth Hundred, in
Trust from Richard Little and wife Sarah, of same hundred. 8 Feb
1781. Whereas Joseph Turner, deceased in his lifetime was seized
of a tract in said hundred, 434 acres, on sw side of Lewes Creek
and by his will dated 23 Aug 1750 devised said plantation to his
four daughters, Martha, Elizabeth, Priscilla and Sarah and died
seized thereof. And whereas the said Martha and Priscilla died
intestate and without issue and the same premises descended to
Elizabeth who married William Dodd and afterwards died intestate
leaving issue one son named William and to the afsd. Sarah, party

to these presents, who married with the above mentioned Richard
Little. For the use of said Richard Little and Sarah his wife
during the term of their natural lives and life of the longest
liver and after their decease to William Pope son of Charles and
Jean Pope of Kent Co., Delaware. For £200. Wit: John Wiltbank,
William Ware. 8 Feb 1781.

390. Deed. Elijah West, planter, Sussex Co., from Avory Morgan,
planter, Sussex Co. 8 Feb 1781. For £1500. Part of a tract
called Marsh Point Inlarged on the east side of Black water Creek
and on the south side of Indian River it being all that tract
granted to Avery Morgan deceased father to the present Avery
Morgan son, 20 March 1761, recourse to the patent. Beginning at
the mouth of Cockel Gutt issuing out of Black Water Creek on the
south side of Indian River, Gutt dividing George and Thomas West
deceased pastures usually called Elder Branch; homegoing line of
a tract of land called Wests Recovery. 13 acres. Wit: Rhoad
Shanklin, Jos. Hall. 8 Feb 1781.

391. Deed. Benjamin Black, from John Black, junr., Sussex Co.,
taylor. Whereas two pieces of land containing 106 acres being
part of a larger tract containing 475 acres in Cedar Creek
Hundred granted by proprietary warrant to Robert Hudson, the
other piece containing 30 acres being part of land and marsh
granted by patent to Robert Hart lying in the hundred aforesaid
on the bayside known as Long Acre, the first above mentioned 106
acres James Black father of the above John Black purchased of the
heirs of Charles Coulter dec'd., the other 30 acres and marsh he
the said James Black purchased of his brother John Black and was
a part of the intestate lands of his father George Black,
deceased. And said James Black being so seized and possessed of
the two parcels of land and marsh afterwards died intestate
leaving Elizabeth his widow and issue five children, to wit, John
his eldest son (party to these presents), Mary, Elizabeth, Delila
and Joseph to whom the said lands descended and came as his next
of kin and heirs - 1/3 to Elizabeth his widow for and during her
life, 2/6 to John his eldest son, 1/6 to each of his other
children. George Black appointed guardian of the said John Black
at an Orphans Court held on 13 Feb 1777 obtained an order for the
division of the land. Donovan Spencer, William Bell, John
Chance, William Draper and Thomas Evans were appointed and caused
to be laid off the division of land. Wit: Jos. Hall Russel. 8
Feb 1781.

392. Deed of partition and release between Nathaniel Waples,
Esqr., Sussex Co., and Sam: Waples, Accomack Co. Virginia. 11
Oct 1779. Whereas a tract lying in Indian River Hundred called
Batchelors Lot adjoining the north side of Indian River and a
tract called Warwick which tract was granted by the Court of
Sussex to Edward Southern on 8th day of 1st month 1681 and Mary
Southern, widow and admx of Edward Southern conveyed it to
Griffin Jones which said Griffin Jones obtained a patent for the
said tract on the 4th day of the 6th month 1684 containing 650
acres which patent stands recorded in the Rolls Office for Sussex
Co. in Book A, folio 257. Griffin Jones by his deed of sale

dated 12th day of the 3rd month 1685 conveyed the land to Thomas Loyd and said Thomas Loyd conveyed the tract to Morris Edwards and said Morris Edwards by his deed of sale dated 5 Oct 1689 conveyed the land to Robert Clifton and said Robert Clifton by his deed of sale dated 23 Jan 1693 conveyed 150 acres of the land to Mathew Stevens and said Mathew Stevens by his deed of sale dated 7 Sep 1698 conveyed the 150 acres to John Barker and said John Barker by his deed of sale dated 23 Dec 1698 conveyed the land to William Clark, and Honor Clark, widow and admx of said William Clark, by deed of sale dated 1 Nov 1708 conveyed said land to Job Barker and Mary Barker and Job Barker and Ann his wife and Mary Barker (which Mary married Leonard Johnson) by their deed of sale dated 17 April 1730 conveyed said land to Richard Poltney (Book I, number 9, folio 379-389) who by his deed of sale dated 14 July 1732 conveyed said land to Christopher Topham (recorded in Book G, no. 6, folio 12) who by his deed of sale dated 5 Feb 1733 conveyed the land to William Waples (Book G, folio 55-56) and the above Robert Clifton by his deed of sale dated 7 May 1713 conveyed 500 acres, the remaining part of the above recited 650 acres to the afsd. William Waples (Book I, no. 9, folio 383) whereby the said William Waples became seized of the land and by his last will dated 2 Oct 1744 devised the said tract to his two sons, Peter and Paul Waples and the said Peter Waples and Paul Waples in order to make a division of land between them on 12 Feb 1750 submitted to arbitration of Woolsey Burton and Jacob Phillips, Esqrs. [Their boundary lines are given.] Boundary References: Southern Creek; tract called Warwick. 364 acres laid off to Paul Waples on the north. And whereas there is one other tract of land in Indian River Hundred formerly surveyed for Francis Pope and afterwards resurveyed to John Holms by virtue of a proprietary warrant dated 22 Feb 1739, 372 acres, and the said John Holmes and Ann his wife which Ann was daughter of the afsd. Francis Pope by their deed of sale dated 8 May 1755 conveyed 129 acres to Joseph Hickman (Book I, no. 9, folio 98-99) and the Joseph Hickman being indebted to Abraham Wynkoop who obtained judgment against him for said debt, to satisfy the debt the 129 acres was sold at public auction where it was struck off to the afsd. Paul Waples for £35.1 but the said Paul Waples dying before obtaining a deed, the sheriff conveyed the land to Temperance Waples wife of the afsd. Paul Waples, dec'd. by deed dated 8 Feb 1758. And Paul Waples having become seized of the whole of the above recited 364 acres and above recited 129 acres by his last will dated 8 Jan 1757 devised all his land to be equally divided among his four sons, Dirickson Waples, Paul Waples, Nathaniel Waples and Samuel Waples and if either of his sons should die without issue then their part to be divided among the survivors. And Direckson Waples and Paul Waples dying without leaving lawful issue and the above described land became the property of Nathaniel and Samuel Waples. Runs to a line of land belonging to Matthias Collins; line of land of James Wilkins. Wit: William Perry, Mary Perry, Henry Price. 21 Nov 1780. Wit: Paul White, Wm. Polk, Thomas Snead. 21 Nov 1780. Proved 9 May 1781.

395. Deed. William Matthews, Sussex Co., from Jesse Dean,

yeoman, and wife Jemima, Sussex Co. 11 May 1781. Whereas there is a parcel of land in Slutkill Neck in Broadkiln Hundred, 130 acres, being part of a larger tract formerly belonging to Richard Dobson, late of Sussex Co., deceased, and in that part was laid off pursuant to the directions of the Act of Assembly in such cases made and provided unto Isabella and Ann Dobson, two of the daughters of the said Richard Dobson (recorded by Orphans Court) and is the same which Joseph West late of Sussex Co. by his conveyance bond dated 8 Feb 1762 obliged himself to convey to Samuel Coulter late of the county all the above mentioned 130 acres. Beginning at an oak standing near the mill pond formerly belonging to William Stephenson late of the co. deceased; share of the whole tract allotted to Sarah Dobson another of daughters of Richard Dobson. And whereas Samuel Coulter died intestate and Charles Coulter, his son, admr of the estate of Samuel Coulter did assign the bond to Alexander Stokly late of Sussex Co., deceased, who died intestate and Naomi Stokly, admx of his estate, assigned the bond to aforesaid Charles Coulter who assigned the bond to Jesse Dean the part to these presents. And whereas the aforesaid Joseph West after making the writing obligatory and before conveying the land, died first making his last will and appointed Lewis West executor who died intestate before making any deed or conveyance. And the estate was committed to Benjamin West, late of the county aforesaid who on 9 May 1776 preferred a petition to the court which agreed to order Benjamin West to convey the land to Jesse Dean and his wife who now convey same to said William Matthews for £165. Wit: Thomas Grew (Grue?), Thomas Grue (?), Junr., David Train, Jonathan Woolf. 11 May 1781.

396. Deed. Daniel Morris, Junr., Sussex Co., from Thomas Clifton, Senr., Mispillion Hundred, Kent Co., Delaware. 9 May 1781. For £160. Parcel of land belonging to the tract called Boices Venture that lies on the south side of the main road leading by the above Daniel Morris's, 8 acres and 30 perches. Wit: Jonathan Clifton, Curtis Morris. 9 May 1781.

397. Deed. Eliphaz Morris, yeoman, Sussex Co., from David Thornton, yeoman, and wife Hannah, of Sussex Co. 24 March 1781. £900. Land in Slaughter Neck in Cedar Creek Hundred being part of two larger tracts one called Twillington and the other called Dickinson's Bevery, 217 acres and 32 perches. Beginning on the southeast side of Cedar Creek a short distance above the store house and landing; land of Mary Draper (a minor). Wit: Wm. Hazzard, John Law. 25 March 1781.

398. Confiscated land. Deed. William Jurdan Hall, Gentleman, from Levin Dirrickson, Commissioner. 9 May 1781. £350. Right of Joshua Hill to tract called Dunns Improvement. On the south side of a creek issuing out of Assawamon Sound called Turkey Branch ... Dunn's Old Field ... Millers Road. 200 acres. Surveyed by Joshua Killon 20 May 1776 by virtue of a resurvey warrant on a tract called Friendship's Addition on 334 acres of vacant land. Wit: John Clowes, Marmix Virden. 9 May 1781.

399. Bond for conveyance of land. £100. John Hopkins is bound to Sacker Wyatt. Whereas Sacker Wyatt and John Hopkins are in possession of land granted by patent to Roger Gum as 500 acres of which 102 acres was deeded to the aforesaid John Hopkins by William Pettyjohn on the south east end of said tract and the said Sacker Wyatt having purchased 200 acres part of the aforesaid 500 acres adjoining on the north west side of the afsd. Parties have agreed to make a division line. Near the land of the heirs of Josiah Martin, deceased. Wit: William Perry, James Martin. 9 May 1781.

400. Confiscated land. Deed. Isaac Draper, Kent Co., Delaware, from Levin Dirickson. Parcel of land in Broadkiln Hundred and on the north side of Broadkiln Creek near the head thereof bounded by lands of John Ponder on the west, Samuel Heaverlo on the north and east by lands which Boaz Manlove late of Sussex Co. purchased of Solomon Hill and on the south by the aforesaid creek. 200 acres which was land of Boaz Manlove seized on 16 May 1778. Wit: John Clowes, Marnix Virden. 9 May 1781.

401. Deed Reece Woolf, yeoman, from James and Hugh Hall, Sussex Co., yeomen. 10 March 1781. Whereas a tract being one moiety of a larger tract in Indian River Hundred, called Salsbury Plains which was granted by proprietary warrant to John Hall, father of the above said James and Hugh Hall. And John Hall being seized of the said larger tract made his last will wherein he devised the land to his above named sons, James and Hugh. Runs to the line of Daniel Cooper's land. 112 acres. £75. Wit: John S. Dorman, Andrew Colter. 9 May 1781.

402. Deed of mortgage, Eleaner Hitchcock, widow, from Uriah Hazzard, yeoman, and wife Sarah of town of Lewes. 23 April 1781. Land adjoining the town of Lewes, on north side of Pagan Creek or Branch then along a street known as Middle, Second or Market Street, adjoining land said to be the property of Cornelius Wiltbank, 12 acres. Being the same that formerly belonged to John Simonton, late of the town of Lewes who died intestate leaving four sisters, to wit, Jane, Sarah, Mary and Elizabeth (the wife of Noble Lewis) to whom the land descended. Nathaniel Bailey and the aforesaid Jane his wife, John Shanklin and afsd. Sarah his wife, and James Davison and afsd. Mary his wife by their deed of release did release and confirm the land to Noble Lewis who with wife Elizabeth sold to Phillips Kollock of the town of Lewes who by indenture dated 24 March 1779 did sell to Uriah Hazzard for £50. [Annotation - Be it remembered on 22 Jan 1791 Phillips Kollock, executor of last will of Eleanor Hitchcock acknowledged full payment on the land.] Wit: J. Wiltbank, Dd. Train. 23 April 1781.

403. George Fitzjarral's deposition. Aug 1, 1781. Before Alexr. Laws, Justice of the Peace. George Fitzjarral about 5 years ago charged Matthew Clifton of Sussex Co. of stealing one hogg or sow and killing and eating the same and he the said Jarral says that it was done as follows that he went to said Matthew Clifton one night and that he the sd. Clifton cleaning

said sow on the floor and after gutting her took the offel and hair and went out and burned them in the ground. Then Aug 1 1781 came above George Fitzjarral and made oath who states that the above story is completely false. And that he killed the hoggs himself and carried the burned hair to Clifton's. And that his son was found dead soon thereafter in the woods.

404. Deed. Jesse Smith, farmer, Sussex Co., from Benjamin Black, yeoman, Sussex Co. 6 Aug 1781. Whereas there are two parcels of land in Cedar Creek Neck, one containing 106 acres being part of a larger tract of 475 acres granted by proprietaries warrant to Robert Hudson, the other piece of land and marsh containing 30 acres being part of a larger tract originally granted by patent to Robert Hart on the bayside called Long Acre which James Black purchased of his brother John Black and the afsd 106 acres the said James Black purchased of the heirs of Charles Coulter and James Black being so thereof seized has since died intestate leaving Elizabeth his widow and issue five children, viz., John his eldest son, Mary, Elizabeth, Magdelin and Joseph and after the several proceedings being held for the laying of the widow's thirds and the division and partition of the remainder among the several heirs, five men appointed for that purposes made return that the same would not admit of a division and John Black conveyed on 8 Feb last his right to Benjamin Black and Benjamin Black sold for £120 the land to Jesse Smith. Wit: Wm. Hazzard, Joseph Oliver. 8 Aug 1781.

405. Deed Josiah Mitchel, Worcester Co., from Joshua Rogers, Worcester Co., Maryland. 28 May 1781. For £300, land called Mattapeny formerly in Worcester Co. but not in Sussex Co. near St. Martin's Sound joining Rumbly Marsh. Beginning north of Herron Creek near a corner tree of a tract formerly surveyed for Ambros White called Happ Entrance. Wit: Jos. Dirrickson, Love Wingate. 8 Aug 1781.

405. Deed. James Hickman, Sussex Co., from Thomas Hickman, Sussex Co. 7 Aug 1781. For love and affection of Thomas Hickman for his son James Hickman, and 5 shillings. All that part of a tract called Layton's Fancy that lyeth towards Levin Cliftons to the amount of 21 1/2 acres and all that part of a tract called Saplin Ridge that lyeth towards the afsd Levin Clifton containing 69 1/2 acres. And all that part of a tract called Hickman's Conclusion that lyeth towards the afsd Levin Clifton's containing 81 1/2 acres. All three parcels lying in the Northwest Fork Hundred. Wit: Phillips Kollock, Francis Wright. 6 Aug 1781.

406. Deed. Robert Mariner, mariner, from Constant Mariner, Sussex Co., yeoman. £5. Releases tract in Indian River Hundred, 100 acres being the same land Nathaniel Waples, Esqr., Robert Prettyman and Robert Stevenson, arbitrators, on 13 April 1779 ordered Constant Mariner by his general deed of release to convey to said Robert Mariner. Beginning at Ivy Branch being the place of beginning of the land that Nathaniel Bowman Mariner purchased of Elizabeth Mariner, extx. of Richard Mariner, dec'd. which he hath since conveyed to Constant Mariner; Constant Mariner's

Resurvey; line of the eleven hundred acre tract being that part
which belongs to Robert Prettyman. 1 May 1780. Wit: Moses
Mariner, Martha Sheort(?). 8 Aug 1781.

407. Deed. 9 Aug 1781. Edward Craig, Sussex Co, yeoman and wife
Sarah, John Craig, Sussex Co., yeoman and wife Comfort, Thomas
Walker, Sussex Co., yeoman, and wife Ruth, William Prettyman,
Sussex Co., yeoman, and wife Elizabeth alias Betty to George
Walton (son of George), Sussex Co., yeoman and wife Mary. Parcel
of land in Rehoboth Neck whereof Harmon Harmonson late of the
county aforesaid, died seized, which land descended to his
daughter Mary late Mary Craig late the wife of afsd. Hamilton
Craig late of Sussex Co., deceased which said Mary died leaving
issue by the said Hamilton Craig the afsd Edward Craig, John
Craig, Ruth the wife of afsd Thomas Walker, Elizabeth alias Betty
the wife of afsd William Prettyman, Mary the wife of afsd George
Walton, Robert Craig and Esther Craig to whom the said land
descended. For £5. Southern corner of the whole tract. 30
acres. Wit: Dd. Train, J. Russel.9 Aug 1781.

408. Deed. Edward Craig from John Craig and others. 9 Aug
1781. John Craig and Comfort his wife, William Prettyman and
Elizabeth his wife, Thomas Walker and Ruth his wife, George
Walton and Mary his wife, all of Sussex Co., which John,
Elizabeth, Ruth and Mary were son and daughters of Hamilton Craig
deceased of the one part and Edward Craig of the other part.
Land of which Hamilton Craige in right of his late wife Mary one
of the daughters of Harmon Harmonson being seized afterwards made
his last will "And whereas there is a certain tract or parcel of
land lying and being in Rehoboth Neck in the County afsd and
being now in my possession which descended to my deceast wife by
the death of her father Harmon Harmonson as her maiden dower my
will and desire is that my daughter Mary Craig shall have 31
acres of the said land laid out and surveyed on the south side
... the remainder I give to my son Edward but if said Edward die
without issue then the land to be equally divided among my four
daughters, Elizabeth who married William Prettyman, Ruth Craig,
Mary Craig and Esther Craig. 9 Aug 1781.

410. Deed. Summerset Dickerson, Sussex Co., house carpenter,
from John Clowes, Sussex Co., mariner. 8 Feb 1776. Whereas said
John Clowes has by a deed of sale from Henry Ozburg of Sussex Co.
dated 8 May 1765 title to 82 acres being the most southwesterly
part of Milford Patent and also by sundry assignments and sales
hath right to 85 acres of land surveyed by virtue of a
Proprietary Warrant granted 25 Nov 1717 to Robert Eaton of said
county which 85 acres is adjoining the aforesaid 82 acres. For
£115. Beginning at a corner of Milford Patent ... John Neill's
line ... John Coulter's land; ... oak of James Hall ... corner
post in Jacob Shellman's line; Burton's line. Wit: John Bell,
John Dawson. 8 Aug 1781.

411. Deed. John Collins, Sussex Co., from Day Givan, Somerset
Co., MD, planter. 31 July 1781. Tract called Addition, 384
acres heretofore in Worcester County, now Broad Creek Hundred of

Sussex Co., Delaware, by virtue of Lord Baltimore's grant and whereas Day Given hath since conveyed 136 acres, part of said tract, to Joseph Collins in fee simple and likewise 3 acres to James Hardy, all the remainder called Addition, 245 acres, to said John Collins. For £20. Beginning at the first bounder of a tract called Out Lett. Wit: Jos. Hall, Dd. Proth(?). 9 Aug 1781.

412. Deed. 27 May 1780. Tereau [also Trasa, Terese, Terrese and Terreas] Burk, Baltimore Town, Maryland, to Captain Moses Lynn of the Township of Fairfield, Connecticut. Whereas John Burk, late of Somerset County, Maryland, deceast, on 11 Aug 1760 obtained grant from the proprietor of Maryland for a tract called Lott, 9 acres, in Little Creek Hundred, Sussex Co., on the mouth of Little Creek and the said John Burk by virtue of a grant made by the proprietor on 27 March 1756 to him and James Johnson as joint tenants for a tract called Chance, 12 acres, in said hundred where said John Burk lived at the time of his decease became seized of the tract called Chance on the death of said Johnson and being so seized of said two tracts died intestate having issue four daughters, to wit, Betty, Peggy, the said Terese and Rulany and by the deaths of Betty and Peggy the land descended to Terrese and Rulany. The said Terreas Burk, being the eldest representative of her deceased father, conveys the land to Moses Lynn for £21. Wit: Robt. Houston, Jonathan Bell. 27 May 1780. Proved 9 Aug 1781.

413. Deed. Henry Hooper and others to lead the uses of a Common Recovery. 9 Aug 1781. Between Henry Hooper of Sussex Co., Gent. and John Tennant, Sussex Co., and John Rodney of Sussex Co., Gent. [3 parties] That Henry Hooper for 5 shillings paid by John Tennant whereby Henry Hooper assigns a certain part or western dividend of the tract called Martins Hundred otherwise Hoopers Forrest which was devised to Thomas Hooper (father of the above named Henry Hooper, party hereto) by the last will of Henry Hooper, grandfather of said Henry Hooper party hereto and being the same part which was allotted and laid off to said Thomas Hooper by Mathew Travers and Henry Hooper Gent. on 26 Nov 1726 by virtue of the last will, recorded in the records of Dorchester Co., Maryland, Book P, page 145. Tract is now situate in Northwest Fork Hundred, Sussex Co. And further agreed that it will be lawful to and for the said John Rodney at the costs and charges of said Henry Hooper before the end of the present term to sue forth and prosecute one or more writ or writs of entry ...? before the Justices of the Court of Common Pleas at Lewes. Wit: J. Moore, Wm. Polk. 11 aug 1781.

415. Deed George Collins and Jno. Wiltbank, Esq. To lead the uses of a Common Recovery. 5 Nov 1781. George Collins of Kent Co., Gent. and John Wiltbank, Esq. of Sussex Co., and Phillips Kollock of Sussex Co., Gent. [3 parties] George Collins and John Wiltbank for the barring all estates tail and remainder over of and in the lands ... herein after mentioned and for 5 shillings, paid by David Train, George Collins and John Wiltbank sell to David Train 150 acres, 4-5 miles south of town of Lewes. Beginning at the corner tree of John Carway's land near the

branch of the Low Valley. Also land being part of a tract taken up by Harmanus Wiltbank and binding on the northwest with the land of Abraham Wiltbank and on the south east with the street of Lewes Town. Beginning at the southeast end of the dwelling house of Abraham Wiltbank. Also land in the bounds of town of Lewes called Rye field. Beginning at northwest edge of Market Street; southwest edge of the Block house pond; south east edge of Shipcarpenter's Street; Finwicks Branch that issueth out of Pagan Creek. Wit: J. Russel, Wm. Bradley, Junr. 8 Nov 1781.

416. Deed. Phillips Kollock and others to John Wiltbank, Esq. 10 Nov 1781. Phillips Kollock of the first part, David Train of the second part, John Wiltbank and George Collins of the third part. Whereas the Court of Common Pleas on 7 Nov 1781, Phillips Kollock by a writ of entry Sur Desscisioninle post did demand against afsd David Train all 100 acres, 50 acres of arable land, 40 acres of pasture, 40 acres of wood, 10 acres of swamp and 10 acres of cripple in Sussex Co., about 4-5 miles southward of town of Lewes. Beginning at a corner tree of John Carway's land; Deep Valley. Also 27 acres and 32 square perches, 15 acres of arable land and 15 acres of pasture in Sussex Co., being part of a large tract taken up by Harmanus Wiltbanck. Beginning at the southeast end of the dwelling house of Abraham Wiltbank; street of Lewes Town - and other land - into which the David Train had not entry but after the disccision[?] which Hugh Hunt unjustly and without judgment made to the said Phillips Kollock within 30 years then last past upon which said writ the aforesaid David Train did appear at the same court in his proper person and did vouch to warranty the aforesaid John Wiltbanck and George Collins who also appeared at the same court in their proper persons and entered into the warranty of the same and afterwards did vouch to warranty the common voucher ... and afterward made default whereby a good and perfect common Recovery of the lands, tenements and premises aforesaid was had. 5 shillings paid by John Wiltbanck. Wit: Richard Bassett, James Cooper. Ackn. 8 Nov 1781.

417. William Bradly, Junr., son of William Bradly, Senr., from William Bradly, Senr, Sussex Co., planter. 24 May 1781. For £10. Tract called Johns Folly in Northwest Fork Hundred. Beginning on west side of the Little Branch that issueth out of the east side of Double Creek branch that issueth out of west side of the North East Fork of Nanticoke River. 50 acres. Wit: Daniel Polk, Robert Cannon. 7 Nov 1781.

418. Deed. Nehemiah Bennett, Sussex Co., cordwainer, from Miriam Hodson, Sussex Co. 2 Oct 1781. Whereas a parcel of land in Slaughter Neck being the same which formerly belonged to Robert Hodson, deceased. Beginning at a post on south side of Cedar Creek; near the corner of the orchard being James Beavanses corner; hickory of Joshua Lofland's land; hickory of Thomas Hays; Aaron Oliver's corner. 100 3/4 acres and 23 perches resurveyed 7 May 1771 by Caleb Cirwithin. For £40. Wit: John Metcalf, Hercules Kollock. 7 Nov 1781.

419. Deed. Silvester Webb, Sussex Co., from Mark Davis, Sussex Co. 30 Oct 1781. Tract on the south side of the head of the most northern branch of Prime Hook Creek commonly called Bridge or Beaver Dam Branch in Cedar Creek Hundred which tract by virtue of a proprietary warrant was surveyed for James Jones who by his last will devised to his son Joshua Jones the whole of the tract and said Joshua Jones did by deed make over 90 1/2 acres to afsd Mark Davis. Wit: Nehemiah Davis, Junr., Herculas Kollock. 7 Nov 1781.

419. Deed. Edward Craige from Richard Howard, pilot. Whereas Stephen Green, late of Sussex Co., shipwright, in his lifetime was seized of sundry tracts and parcels of land in Lewes and Rehoboth Hundred did devise that at the death of his wife Naomie Green, all the remainder of his lands should be sold and money equally divided among his children, vizt., Martha Green, Elenor Green, Stephen Green, John Green and Ambros Green. And whereas the said Richard Howard afterwards married the said Martha Green who is since deceased and the said Elenor Green and John Green hath since died intestate and without issue leaving four brothers, to wit, William, Richard, Stephen and Ambros and one sister, to wit, the above named Martha, their next of kin and heir at law. For £100. Wit: J. Russel, Elizabeth Russel. 7 Nov 1781.

420. Deed. Phillips Russel, Sussex Co., house carpenter, from William Welch, Sussex Co., yeoman, and wife Rachel (late Rachel Rust), admx of Jona. Rust, deceased. 13 March 1781. Whereas Jonathan Rust was seized of two parcels of land, one containing 257 acres, by virtue of proprietaries warrant, and the other of 80 acres purchased of Joseph Howard (Liber L No. 11, folio 140) in Indian River Hundred, and Jonathan Rust by his deed of sale dated 3 May 1774 conveyed to his son John Rust, 80 acres, part of the above two parcels (Liber L, folio 414) and afterward died intestate possessed of the remainder of the said two parcels. Wit: J. Russel, Jean Russel. 7 Nov 1781.

421. William Welch, yeoman, from Phillips Russel, house carpenter. 16 March 1781. For £204. Land in Indian River Hundred, 257 acres, being the same land Jonathan Rust lately died intestate seized and possessed which appears in a deed of sale from William Welch and Rachel his wife dated 13 March 1781. [See above entry.] 7 Nov. 1781.

422. Deed Elisha Dickerson from Samuel Hudson and others. 8 Nov 1781. Between Samuel Hudson, Aaron Dodd and wife Hannah, John Stephenson and wife Rhoda, Ann Hill and Walter Hudson, all of Sussex Co. and Elisha Dickerson, Sussex Co., blacksmith. For £120, tract on north side of Indian River near place called the Rock Hole being part of a larger tract taken up by Robert Burton which said land was granted to Elizabeth Hill by a proprietary warrant dated 9 Nov 1714 which said warrant was assigned over to the said Robert Burton and from him by sundry conveyances down to Absolam Hudson, dec'd., father of the same Samuel, Hannah, Rhoda, Ann and Walter, parties to these presents. Absolam died

intestate leaving the above named children together with two
others, to wit, Anderson and Mary. 170 acres. Wit: Phillips
Kollock, J. Russel. 8 Nov 1781.

423. Deed. George Bacon, Sussex Co., from Day Givans, Somerset
Co., Maryland. 27 June 1781. Whereas Day Givans hath contracted
for and sold to Robert Houston, Senr., of Sussex Co. for part of
a tract called Givans His Discovery in Broad Creek Hundred that
lies east of a small branch running through said tract and
whereas all the title the said Houston had for the conveyance of
said land has since become the property of said George Bacon, Day
Givans for £5 conveys said land. Wit: John Polk, Jonathan Bell,
John Collins. 9 Nov 1781.

423. Deed. Assenath Owens, a minor child and daughter of Robert
Owens, late of Sussex Co., from Jonathan Manlove, Sussex Co.,
yeoman. 14 Dec 1781. Whereas Jonathan Manlove on 11 Nov 1779
passed a bond obligatory on himself conditioned for the conveying
title of him and his wife Rachel to tract called Swan Pond, 50
acres, adjoining lands of Robert Owens, dec'd. to John Griffith
of Sussex Co. which bond on 4 March 1780 was assigned by John
Griffith to afsd. Robert Owens who bequeaths the land to Assenath
Owens, his eldest daughter, now party to these presents. £1500.
Surveyed to Wm. Evans, father of Jona. Manlove's late wife, on 23
July 1730. Wit: Alexr. Laws, Jesse Truitt. 6 Feb 1782.

425. Deed. Jacob Walker, Sussex Co., yeoman, from Thomas
Walker, Sussex Co., yeoman. 1 May 1780. Whereas Jacob Walker,
late of Sussex Co., yeoman (father of the parties to these
present) in his lifetime was seized of a parcel of land in Lewes
and Rehoboth Hundred, called Coopers Hall, containing 70 3/4
acres and died intestate leaving Leah his widow and issue six
children, to wit, Thomas one of the parties to these presents,
James, Jacob the other party to these presents, George, Mary and
Leah to whom the said tract and two other tracts descended. And
whereas Thomas Walker being the eldest son offered his petition
on 27 Aug 1774 to make partition of the land or its valuation.
Whereas Leah Walker, the deceased widow's is since dead. £211.10
paid by Jacob Walker. Beginning at the division line with
William Fisher. Wit: Jos.Hall, D. Prothony. 7 Feb 1782.

426. Deed. 10 Nov 1782. Between John Stephenson (son of Hugh
Stephenson) and wife Rhoda, Ann Hill widow of John Hill and
Walter Hudson, all of Sussex Co. to Nathaniel Waples, Esqr. of
Sussex Co. Whereas there is a tract in Indian River Hundred on
the north side of the head of the Indian River called Rock Hole
which was granted by warrant dated 9 Nov 1714 to Elizabeth Hill
and by her was ordered to be surveyed unto Cornelius Wiltbanck;
said warrant was assigned over to Robert Burton and surveyed unto
him 30 Dec 1723 for 272 acres and Robert Burton by his last will
dated 25 Aug 1724 devised the tract to his son Samuel Burton and
said Samuel Burton by his deed dated 5 Aug 1752 conveyed the land
to Thomas Collour and Asher Moot, recorded in Book H no. 7, folio
333 and in the same book, folio 382 stands recorded Jacob Kollock
Esqr. then high Sheriff's deed of sale dated 11 Dec 1753 unto the

above named Asher Moot for Thomas Collours one moiety or half
part of the aforesaid tract being sold by the Sheriff to satisfy
judgment obtained against above named Thomas Collour by the afsd.
Asher Moot. Asher Moot being of the Province of Pennsylvania did
by his letter of attorney impower Benjamin Stockley to make sale
of the 272 acres of land who conveyed the land to William
Harmonson (Book I no. 9, folio 293). William by his deed of sale
dated 2 March 1764 conveyed 170 acres of the land to Absolam
Hudson (Book K, no. 10, folio 71) and Absolam Hudson dying
intestate the lands with others fell among his several heirs
amongst such was the above Rhoda Hudson who had married the above
named John Stephenson and Ann Hill who had married John Hill,
deceased, and Walter Hudson, all parties to the indenture.
Reference to dividing line between this tract and that part of
the original tract held by Nathaniel Waples that he purchased
from the heirs of Solomon Hill, deceased. 170 acres. For £45.
Wit: Hugh Stephenson, William Frame, Hannah Dodd. 22 Nov 1781.
Proved 6 Feb 1782.

427. Deed. Luke Walton from Thomas Collings and others. 11
March 1777. Between Thomas Collings and Purcey his wife, William
Walton, Israel Brown and Mary his wife of the one part and Luke
Walter, Sussex Co. of the other part. Whereas a tract whereon
Luke Walton dwells which land was granted to Anthony Woodward by
warrant dated 6 March 1723. Anthony Woodward sold the land to
John Walton and John Walton by his last will dated 14 Jan 1744
did leave the same to Luke Walton in the following words, "I give
to my son Luke Walton a plantation I bought of Anthony Woodward
the south side my mill dam all the land thereunto, to take
possession after my wife's widowhood." For £5. Wit: Wm.
Hazzard, Dan. Dingee. Proved 6 Feb 1782.

428. Deed. Ebenezer Whaley, Little Creek Hundred, from
Nathaniel Whaley, Little Creek Hundred. 5 Feb 1782. Whereas
George Hearn of Worcester Co. on 18 March 1746 became seized of a
parcel of land called Goshan, 50 acres, by virtue of Lord and
Proprietor of Maryland's grant to him and on 18 April 1748 became
seized in like manner of tract called Goshan's Addition, 97
acres, both of which were in Worcester Co. and George Hearn
conveyed the same to Nathaniel Whaley. For £100. Wit: William
Whaley, Isaac Whaley. 6 Feb 1782.

429. Deed. Philip Marvel from Thomas Marvel. 20 May 1776.
Between Thomas Marvel, Senr. of Worcester Co formerly but now
Sussex Co. and Philip Marvel of said co., planter. Whereas a
parcel of land in Indian River Hundred, 100 acres, granted by
Proprietary of Maryland to afsd. Thomas Marvel by patent dated 16
Sep 1760. Of which land is sold 54 1/2 acres for £10. Wit:
Francis Johnson, Rhoads Shankland, David Rankin. Ackn. 7 Feb
1782.

430. Bond. Edward Vaughan and Ann Vaughan of Sussex Co. are
bound to Elisha Long of Sussex Co., yeoman, for £20,000 to be
paid to said Elisha Long 29 Dec 1779. To convey a tract of 137
acres in Nanticoke Hundred, called Stony Branch or Charles

Tindals Branch. Beginning at Oak on northeast side of Stony Branch; lands of Samuel Tindal; lands of John Smith; joining lands of Elisha Long. Wit: Saml. Laverty, Robt. W. McCalley. Proved 6 Feb 1682.

430. Petition of William Polk, Esqr., exr. of Edward Vaughan, dec'd. 8 Feb 1782. Whereas Edward Vaughan and Ann Vaughan by their writing obligatory dated 29 Dec 1779 were obligated to Elisha Long. Whereas before conveying the land Edward Vaughan and Ann Vaughan died. Granted 8 Feb 1782 to William Polk, executor of Edward Vaughan, authority to convey deed to Elisha Long. Granted 8 Feb 1782.

431. Deed. William Polk, Esqr., Sussex Co. from Elias Veach, Sussex Co., yeoman, and wife Elizabeth. 3 Jan 1782. For £25. Two parcels of marsh called Persimon Island the one moiety conveyed by deed dated 3 Aug 1725 from Elias Fisher to Joshua Hickman which said marsh was granted by warrant dated 1st day of 1st month 1715 to William Fisher in Cedar Creek Hundred in Slaughter Neck between Draper's Inlet and the Flat Inlet in Sussex Co. adjoining marsh of Charles Draper. 85 acres. 25 acres of marsh. Said two parcels of marsh were devised by the last will of Joshua Hickman to Joseph Hickman, deceased of which Elizabeth Veach is the only daughter and surviving heir. Total 110 acres. Wit: James Moore, Jesse Veach. 4 Feb 1782. Ackn. 7 Feb 1782.

432. Deed. Samuel Pavey from Thomas Banning and wife Mary. 5 Jan 1782. For £100. Tract called Double Purchase in Northwest Fork Hundred on the south side of Brights Branch, 65 acres. Also a tract called Bannings Chance surveyed unto Thomas Banning 10 July 1776 by virtue of a warrant granted to said Banning 24 June 1776 for 35 acres. Reference to fourth line of tract called Clarksons Industry. 26 acres. Wit: Daniel Polk, Curtis Jacobs, Thomas Smith. 5 Jan 1782. Proved 7 Feb 1782.

433. Bond. Edmond Dickerson, yeoman, from Samuel Hand, blacksmith, for conveyance of land. Samuel Hand bound to Edmond Dickerson for £200. 12 --- 1778. To convey a tract adjoining lands of Thomas Pettyjohn, lands of Edmond Dickerson and lands of the heirs of James Stevenson and adjoining land of Richard Parimore and Isaac Chase, 83 acres. Wit: Jonathan Cohoon, William Smuling. 8 Feb 1782.

434. 8 Feb 1782. Petition of Thomas, admr. of Samuel Hand, blacksmith, deceased, who died intestate before any deed or conveyance was made to Edmond Dickerson; petitioner requests to make such conveyance. [See below entry.]

435. Deed. Edmond Dickerson from Thos. Hand admr. of Saml. Hand, deceased. Whereas Samuel Hand in his lifetime was seized in fee simple of a certain tract called Stephenson's Forethoughts in Broadkiln Hundred adjoining the lands of Edmond Dickerson, Thomas Pettyjohn, the heirs of James Stephenson, deceased, Richard Parremore, and heirs of Isaac Chace, deceased, originally

granted to aforesaid James Stephenson, deceased in his lifetime by warrant dated 27 Oct 1757 for 200 acres and surveyed 15 Nov next following and found on actual survey to contain but about 83 acres and was afterwards conveyed by the executors of James Stephenson to John Parrimore in discharge of a bond give by said James Stephenson in his lifetime to Richard Parrimore who assigned the same to John Parrimore who by his indenture dated 4 May 1768 conveyed the same to aforesaid Samuel Hand who was so seized by his bond dated 12 March 1778 was bound to Edmond Dickerson in the sum of £200. [See petition above]. Wit: Dd. Train, Jonathan Calhoon. Ackn. 8 Feb 1782.

436. Deed. Jonathan Calhoon, Sussex Co., from Edmond Dickerson, Sussex Co. 10 Feb. 1776. There is a tract in Broadkill Hundred on the east side of Long Bridge Branch being part of a larger tract which Joseph Cord of said county, deceased, devised to his son Joseph Cord and Joseph Cord the younger conveyed 200 acres of said land to Edmond Dickerson. For £75. Wit: John Clowes, Joseph Morris. 8 Feb 1782.

437. Deed. I, Frankey Bucher of Sussex Co in consideration of the sum of £30 ... paid by my son in law William Bucher release possession of 1/3 of lands that my husband William Bucher died seized with being my right of dower. 25 Jan 1782. Wit: John Collings, Littleton Abdil, Selah Collings. Ackn. 8 Feb 1782.

438. Deed. John Marshell from Peter White and wife. 4 Jan 1782. Between Peter White of the town of Lewes, Gentleman, and wife Elizabeth, and John Marshall of the same town, pilot. For £150, messuage and lot in the front street of the town of Lewes 60 feet by 200 feet bounded on the front with the bank of Lewes Town Creek, on the south east with the lott formerly belonging to Jacob Phillips, on the southwest with the Second Street and on the northwest with the lotts formerly belonging to John and Albertus Jacobs. Wit: D. Hally, jr., Simon Kollock. 4 Jan 1782. Ackn. 9 Feb 1782.

439. Deed. Richard Howard of the town of Lewes, pilot, from Edward Craig, yeoman and wife Sarah. 9 Feb 1782. For £50, 8 acres, being 1/3 part of a larger parcel on the south side of Lewes Town by estimation 23 and 3/4 acres being the same land the one moiety whereof John Simonton by his last will devised to his three daughters, to wit, Jane, Sarah and Mary. The other moiety of the said large parcel was conveyed by deed of sale to John Simonton the younger by John Miers and the said John Simonton the younger being seized of this land died intestate and without issue leaving four sisters to wit, Jane, Sarah, Mary and Elizabeth to whom the moiety or half part descended. Elizabeth afterwards married Noble Lewis who by their deed of release released all their right to the large parcel to said Sarah, Jane and Mary who divided the land. Mary conveyed her part to Edward Craig and Sarah his wife, which 8 acres they convey to Richard Howard. Wit: Jno. Wiltbank, J. Russel. Ackn. 9 Feb 1782.

440. Deed. Edward Craig, Sussex Co., and wife Sarah, to Richard

Howard, town of Lewes, pilot. 9 Feb 1782. For £20. Two lotts in town of Lewes on the southwest side of the meeting house lott. Reference to line of David Hall's land. Wit: J. Wiltbank, J. Russel. Ackn. 9 Feb 1782.

441. Deed. John Fleetwood, Sussex Co., planter, from Lemuel Williams, Sussex Co., cordwainer. 21st day of the 4th month 1781. For £100. Land in Broadkiln Neck and south side of Primehook Creek being part of a larger tract taken up by Nathaniel Walker and by several conveyances is now in possession of William Conwel and conveyed by William Conwell to said Lemuel Williams by a deed of sale dated 2nd of 5th month 1776. 1 acre. Wit: Jos. Hall, Rhoads Shankland. Ackn. 8 May 1782.

441. Deed. Albertus Jacobs, Sussex Co., yeoman, from William Jacobs, Sussex Co., yeoman, and wife Sarah. Land which is part of a larger tract in Lewes and Rehoboth Hundred in Kickout Neck whereof Albertus Jacobs the elder (grandfather of the above named Albertus Jacobs) died intestate, seized of the land, leaving issue several children whereupon James Jacobs his eldest son conveyed to Nathaniel Jacobs 85 acres who died intestate leaving issue several children whereupon William Jacobs (party to these presents) his eldest son conveyed the land to above named Albertus Jacobs. For £401. The boundary interesects Pothook Creek. Wit: J. Russel, John Burton, Junr. Ackn. 8 May 1782.

442. Deed. William Jacobs, Sussex Co., yeoman, from Albertus Jacobs, Sussex Co., yeoman and wife Elizabeth. 3 April 1782. Land in the town of Lewes on the bank of Lewes Creek, joining on the southeast side of the house and lott whereon Henry Neill now dwells being part of three lotts originally granted by the court of Sussex Co. to John Kiphaven who by his last will devised the same to his two grandsons John and Albertus Jacobs who both died intestate, seized thereof as tenants in common leaving issue several children whereupon James Jacobs eldest son of the above said Albertus Jacobs and Albertus Jacobs eldest son of said John Jacobs after having had the necessary proceedings in the Orphans Court accepted the said lotts and other lands of their fathers at the valuation pursuant to the Act of Assembly for selling intestate estates. And the said James Jacobs and Albertus Jacobs being seized of the land, James Jacobs died intestate leaving the above Albertus Jacobs his only child and heir at law. And the said Albertus Jacobs son of the said John Jacobs by his last will devised his part of said lotts as part of his estate to his daughter Sarah Jacobs. And the said Albertus Jacobs party to these presents and the Sarah Jacobs being so seized of the lotts as tenants in common whereupon the said Sarah Jacobs by Sarah Jacobs her guardian and Albertus Jacobs entered an amicable action to partition the lotts. The commissioners (Rhoads Shankland, Samuel Paynter and John Russel), informed that John Boyd had sold off from the said lotts the lott whereon the said Henry Neill now dwells and that James Jacobs in his lifetime had sold to Robert Shankland 400 square feet off the northwest corner of said lotts, they did divide the remainder of the lotts. £50. Wit: J. Russel, John Burton, Junr. Ackn. 8 May 1782.

444. Deed. William Fitchet, Sussex Co., from Joseph Cord, Sussex Co. 29 April 1782. Tract in Broadkiln Hundred being part of a larger tract, patented 24 June 1708 and granted to Honor Clark for 560 acres which said Honor Clark afterwards married Thomas Bedwell and which land Thomas Bedwell and Honor his wife conveyed to William Darter and William Darter and Margaret his wife conveyed said tract to Joseph Cord and Joseph Cord by his last will dated 3 April 1738 devised his lands such that the first land being part of the aforesaid 560 acres is now the property of the above named Joseph Cord party to these presents. Reference to Smith's land. 169 acres. Wit: William Pury, William Matthews. Ackn. 8 May 1782.

445. Deed. William Fitchet, Sussex Co. from John Gootee and wife Bridget of Accomack Co., Virginia. 3 Jan 1782. Whereas a tract in Broadkiln Hundred, 300 acres being part of a larger tract formerly the property of Paul Simpler which larger tract was sold by Rhods Shankland, Esqr., High Sheriff, the property of Paul Simpler was conveyed to Benjamin Records who by his deed of sale dated 8 Jan 1775 conveyed it to Moles Patterson and said Moles Patterson by his deed dated 5 Feb 1775 by his attorney William Pury conveyed 300 acres of said tract to Samuel Owens and said Samuel Owens and Esther his wife by their deed of sale dated 7 Aug 1779 conveyed said 300 acres to above named John Gootee party to these presents. Wit: Daniel Rodgers, Major Baily, Mary Brazer. Proved 8 May 1782.

446. Deed. Abel Notingham from Hugh Stephenson. 5 May 1782. Tract in Broadkiln Hundred, 21 acres, being part of a larger tract granted by Proprietaries warrant dated 23 1740 for 50 acres to the above named Hugh Stephenson. Reference to line of land surveyed for William Shelpman. For £10. Wit: William Pury, Levin Okey. Ackn. 8 May 1782.

447. Deed. Joshua Robinson, Senr., from Jos. Robinson, Junr and others. 6 May 1782. Between Joshua Robinson, Junr., Betty Long, Armwell Long, all of Sussex Co. and Joshua Robinson, Senr., planter. Tract in Pine Neck on the south side of Indian River being part of a larger tract called Chance (formerly granted to Southy Witington by patent from Proprietor of Maryland). Beginning in a valley on the eastern most end of Joshua Robinson's plantation. 57 acres for £60. Wit: Azariah Brookfield, Isaac Atkinson. Proved 8 May 1782.

448. Deed. John Hopkins, Junr., Sussex Co., planter, from John Hopkins, Sussex Co., farmer and wife Sophia. For 5 shillings. Parcel of land being a part of a tract granted by warrant to Anderson Parker dated at Philadelphia 24th of 8th month 1715 and by sundry assignments, conveyances and devises became the property of John Hopkins, Senr. Also a small piece of land surveyed at request of Ann Sandress [Sandresson] on 13 April 1734 for 55 acres and by sundry conveyances and devises became the property of aforesaid John Hopkins, Senr. Wit: James Martin, John Martin. Ackn. deed of release 9 May 1782.

449. Deed. Know that we, John Hopkins, Senr. of Sussex Co., farmer, and Sophia his wife, for 5 shillings paid by William Hopkins, planter, release parcel of land being a part of a larger tract granted by warrant to Anderson Parker dated 24th of 8th month 1715 which by sundry assignments, conveyances and devises became the property of John Hopkins, Senr. Beginning at a division line between John Hopkins, Junr. and said William Hopkins. 143 acres. Wit: James Martin, John Martin. Deed of release ackn. 9 May 1782.

449. Defeasible Deed. 13 April 1782 between Joseph Dashiell of Worcester co., Maryland and Josiah Polk of Somerset Co., Maryland to John Mitchell of Sussex Co. John Mitchell on 17 Nov 1768 by deed of bargain and sale from William Allen, Levin Gale and Henry Steel, trustees under the Act of Assembly for granting a compensation to the Nanticoke Indians for the lands in the Act mentioned had conveyed to him 2536 acres lying in Worcester Co. being part of the lands laid off for afsd Indians. Whereas said Joseph Dashiell and Josiah Polk at the request of said John Mitchell became security for said John Mitchell for the payment of the consideration money afsd, he the said John Mitchell by his deed of mortgage conveyed to said Joseph Dashiell and Josiah Polk all the land in the first deed mentioned by way of counter security. This indenture further witnesseth that the said Joseph Dashiell and Josiah Polk in consideration that the said John Mitchell hath paid up the consideration money in the first recited deed mentioned ... and hath taken up the bonds by which the said Joseph Dashiel and Josiah Polk became security for the same the said Joseph Dashiel and Josiah Polk release ... Wit: Isaac Henry, John Collins. Proved 9 May 1782.

450. Deed. John Mitchell from Price Russel and others. 10 Dec 1781. Between Price Russel and wife Ann and Arthur Denwood and wife Rebecca of Somerset Co., Maryland of the one part and John Mitchell of Sussex Co. of the other part. Whereas Col. William Stevens had surveyed and laid out for him on 8 June 1683, 3 tracts, to wit, Batchelors Contrivance of 150 acres, Bachelors Delight of 250 acres and Batchelors Invention, 250 acres - on the south side of Broad Creek in Somerset Co. and on 13 June 1683 the said Col. William Stevens assigned his right to all said lands to James Wyth and Marmaduke Mister of Somerset Co. who had patented from the Lord Proprietor of Maryland on 10 Sep 1684. And they conveyed the same to James McMurray of Somerset Co. by deed of bargain and sale who died intestate leaving male issue one son named John McMurray to whom the lands descended, who died leaving male issue, James McMurray to whom the same lands descended and who died leaving no male issue but two daughters, to wit, the said Ann Russel and Rebecca Denwood to whom the 650 acres descended. For £40. Wit: Joseph Venables, Gillis Polk, John Collins. Proved 10 May 1682.

453. Deed. William Polk from Isaac Kinney. --- 1782. Between Isaac Kinney of Little Creek Hundred and William Polk of same place, yeoman. Isaac Kinney in obedience to a decree of the Court of Chancery of Sussex Co. and for the sum of 5 shillings

releases and grants eastern dividend or part of a tract called
Desert in Little Creek Hundred and is the same which Isaac Kinney
holds by virtue of a deed from Elverton Caldwell and represented
in the plot drawn. 50 acres. Wit: J.Rodney, Caleb Balding. 2
Aug 1782. [Plat is included.]

454. Deed. Foster Donavan from Alexander Paremore. 3 Nov 1779.
Between Alexander Paremore of Sussex Co., yeoman, and Foster
Donavan, Sussex Co. Tract by patent granted by the proprietaries
of Maryland dated 3 Aug 1739, 125 acres, called Troublesome
Ridge, formerly in Somerset County but not Sussex Co. Beginning
about 80 poles to the southeast of upper Beverdam on the
southeast fork of Gravely Branch that makes a neck commonly
called Parkers Neck. That said Richard Dobson being seized died
leaving the afsd Alexander Paremore, heir at law. For £75. Wit:
Wm. Hazzard, George Hazzard. Ackn. 6 Aug 1782.

455. Deed. Know that I Ann Nelms of Somerset Co., Maryland, one
of the surviving heirs of Edward Roberts, Junr., dec'd., as well
for and in consideration of the sum of £18 to me paid by the
admrs. of Francis Roberts, dec'd. as for the further sum of £15
to me paid by Nancey Pollitt who was then widow of Roger Tasker
Polk, dec'd. and is one of the surviving heirs of said Francis
Robert dec'd., release and quit claim to said Nancy Pollitt,
Edward Roberts, William Roberts, Jun. and Sarah Roberts,
surviving heirs of Francis Roberts, dec'd., land in Cedar Creek
Neck on north prong of the Northern Branch of fork of Cedar Creek
commonly called Pole Thicket, 210 acres which land was granted to
Matthew Parker in 1716 which descended to his only daughter Naomi
who married Abraham Wiltbank and they conveyed same to afsd.
Edward Roberts Junr., deceased. Wit: John Laws, Ann Freeny.
Ackn. 6 Aug 1682.

456. Deed. Samuel Spencer from John Mitcalf. 1782. Between
John Mitcalf, Sussex Co., yeoman and Samuel Spencer, Sussex Co.,
yeoman. For £242. formerly belonging to Ebenezer Spencer,
deceased, in Slaughter Neck, Cedar Creek Hundred. Beginning at a
corner post on the south side of Cedar Creek being a corner of
John Mitcalf's land ... to a post in Stephen Townsend's line;
Sikes Island.
Wit: Daniel Sturges, Peter White. Ackn. 7 Aug 1782.

456. Bond. Levin Crapper from Samuel Walton for conveyance of
land. Samuel Walton bound to Levin Crapper, merchant, for £100,
14 May 1772, to convey certain parcel of land. Reference to
corner tree of Sawmill Range; Molton's line; corner of Israel
Brown's land. 22 acres. Wit: Isaac Wattson, Molton Crapper.
Proved 7 Aug 1782.

457. Deed. Jonathan Woolf from David Hall, Esqr. Between David
Hall of the town of Lewes, Sussex Co., Esqr. and Jonathan Woolf
of Lewes and Rehoboth Hundred, hatter. Parcel of land part of a
larger tract called St. Martins in Lewes and Rehoboth Hundred
about 2 miles from Lewes Town in the fork of the Indian River
Road and the Road to Philadelphia adjoining a parcel of land that

said Woolf purchased of the said Hall by deed. 16 acres. Wit: Peter White, Joseph Darby. Ackn. 7 Aug 1782.

458. Deed. William Peery from Archabald Hopkins and wife. 5 Aug 1782. Between Archibald Hopkins of Sussex Co. and wife Prudence and William Perry, Sussex Co. Tract in Broadkiln Hundred, 200 acres, being part of a larger tract granted by patent dated 2nd of 2nd month 1686 to William Clark for 800 acres called Mill Plantation which 200 acres aforesaid the said William Clark by deed of sale conveyed to Mathew Ozburn who conveyed it to Thomas Bedwell and Honer Bedwell his wife which they by deed of sale conveyed to William Clark son of William Clark who conveyed same to John Fisher and he by deed of sale conveyed to Enoch Commings and Enoch Commings and Hannah his wife conveyed the same to Robert Smith who dying indebted to sundry persons the 200 acres was sold for payment of debt and conveyed by Ryves Holt and John Neill, exrs. of Robert Smith to James McIlwain who devised same to his son David McIlvain who died intestate and the above Archibald Hopkins who married his eldest daughter the above named Prudence preferred a petition to the Orphans Court to make partition of the said 200 acres among the several heirs but the five freeholders appointed to divide the land reported that the land would not admit of being divided and a valuation was made. Beginning at a corner oak in Coolspring Branch; County Road leading to the town of Lewes; Scudder's line. 2 parcels of 213 and 18 acres, for £500. Wit: James Vent, Samuel Hudson. Ackn. 7 Aug 1782.

459. Deed. Archibald Hopkins from William Peery. 7 Aug 1782 [Same property as conveyed to above William Perry in above entry]. For £500. Wit: James Vent, Samuel Hudson. Ackn. 7 Aug 1782.

461. Bond. Mills McElvain from Archabald Hopkins. Archibald Hopkins, Sussex Co. bound to Mills McIlvain, minor son of Mill McIlvain, late of Sussex Co., dec'd., in the sum of £100. Bound to pay £50 within the lifetime of Archibald Hopkins or within 6 months after his death. Wit: John Clowes, William Perry. Proved 7 Aug 1782.

461. Deed. Benjamin Johnson from Bevins Morris. 1 June 1782. Between Bibbins Morris of Sussex Co., yeoman and Benjamin Johnson, yeoman, Sussex Co. For £100, part of a tract. Reference to Parsleys Swamp(?). 130 acres. Wit: John Riley, William Morris. 7 Aug 1782.

462. Deed. William Morris from Bevins Morris. 1 June 1782. Between Bibbins Morris of Sussex Co., yeoman, and William Morris, yeoman, Sussex Co. For £95, tract in Broadkiln Hundred. Boundary runs to a corner post of Benjamin Johnson's land. 127 acres. Wit: John Riley, Benjamin Johnson. Ackn. 7 Aug 1782.

462. Deed. Bevins Morris, Sussex Co., yeoman, from Benjamin Riley, Sussex Co., saddler. 1 July 1782. For £200. Tract formerly belonging to Benjamin Riley, deceased, who in his last

will devised same to his son Benjamin Riley, party to these presents. Reference to land in the forrest of Cedar Creek Hundred; a dividing corner of Richard Blocksom's land; old red oak of Wm. Abbott's land. 159 3/4 acres. Wit: John Riley, Benjamin Johnson. Proved 7 Aug 1782.

463. Deed. John Hickman from Nehemiah Bennett. Aug 1782. Between Nehemiah Bennett of Sussex Co., shoemaker and John Hickman, Sussex Co. For £110. Land in Slaughter Neck. Beginning at a post on south side of Cedar Creek, a corner of Jonathan Clark's wife's thirds; post supposed to be in widow's Lofland's line; post of said Lofland and John Young's land; dividing line of Hodson's land; post in Thomas Hayses line; Aaron Oliver's line. 49 acres. Surveyed 17 Feb 1775 by Caleb Cirwithin at the request of Jacob Hodson now deceased. Wit: Benjamin Johnson, William Wilson. Ackn. 7 Aug 1782.

464. Deed. William Owens, Junr. from Abraham Adams. 6 Aug 1782. Between Abraham Adams of Sussex Co., yeoman, and William Owens, junr. of the same place, yeoman. For £30. Parcel of land being a part of a tract called Double Purchase originally granted to William Reynolds. Beginning at a corner of land surveyed for the use of Moses Cox ... near Evanses line. Surveyed 13 April 1779. [blank] acres. Wit: Jno. Wiltbank, J. Russel. Ackn. 7 Aug 1782.

465. Deed. William Evans from Thomas Purnall. 29 June 1782. Between Thomas Purnall of Worcester Co., Maryland and William Evans, Sussex Co. Whereas said Thomas Purnall for a valuable consideration paid by Jaquish Hudson did sell to Jaquish Hudson tract called South Petterton and Evan's part it being the lands purchased by the said Thomas Purnall of John Morris and which lands were conveyed to afsd Thomas Purnall by Joseph Evans containing 205 acres as will be seen in the last will of William Evans, deceased. And Jaquish Hudson has sold his right to the land to afsd William Evans by assignment of the bond of afsd Thomas Purnall for the conveyance of the lands. For 5 shillings. Wit: Thomas Dale, John Evans. Ackn. 1782.

466. Deed. William Evans, Sussex Co., from Elisha Evans, Sussex Co. 7 Aug 1782. Tract left to Elisha Evans by his father, William Evans' last will dated 26 May 1764 to the south of John Evans, Junr.'s plantation, that is, all the remaining part of North Petherinton from the said John Evans Junr., bounds. 80 acres and all the remaining part of South Petherinton containing 125 acres and 60 acres in the wood called Timber Ridge to be holden by him the said William Evans. For 5 shillings. Wit: John Evans, Eli Evans. Proved 7 Aug 1782.

467. Deed. Joshua Rodney, Esqr., from Elizabeth Simpson. 10 June 1782. Between Elizabeth Simpson, spinstress, of Lewes Town and John Rodney, Sussex Co. For supporting her at sundry times, also the sum of 5 shillings, a lott in Lewes Town being the moiety or half part of two lots devised by the last will of James Simpson, her father, to his two daughters, Elizabeth and

Margaret, to be equally divided between them. Beginning at the edge of Front Street about 60 feet southeast of Carpenters Street ... bounds of said Elizabeth and Margaret's lots now belonging to Thomas Martin. Containing 60 feet front and 200 feet back. Wit: Penelope Kollock, J. Russel. Proved 8 Aug 1782.

467. Deed. Levi Collings from John Dagworthy, Esqr. 29 June 1782. Between General John Dagworthy of Sussex Co. and Levi Collings of Sussex Co. For £100, 33 1/3 acres, part of a tract called Timber Land Enlarged surveyed 6 May 1760 for said John Dagworthy for 1946 acres. Reference to Robert McNas home going line ... land where Levi Collings now dwells. Wit: Levin Dirickson, Nathl. Mitchell. Proved 8 Aug 1782.

468. Deed. John Creighton from John Mitchell. 15 July 1782. For £755. Tract on Broad Creek formerly in Worcester Co. now Sussex Co., out of the tract called Indian Land which said Mitchell bought agreeable to an Act of Assembly of Maryland. Reference to The Mill Pond; said Mitchell's new road. 302 acres. Wit: William Peery, Chas. Moore. Ackn. 9 Aug 1782.

469. Bill of sale. Mary and Sussanah Field from John Field. John Fields, Sussex Co., yeoman, for £20, paid by Mary Field of the town of Lewes, transfer to Mary Field and her daughter Susannah Field that undivided moiety or equal half of messuage and lot in town of Lewes whereon said Mary Field now dwells being late part of the estate of Nehemiah Field and the same part which was sold by Levin Dirrickson Esqr., Commissioner for forfeited estates. Wit: J. Moore, D. Train. Proved 9 Aug 1782.

469. Bill of sale. Mary Field from Henry Fisher of the town of Lewes. For £500, 3 lots in town of Lewes, the first adjoins the house and lot on Front or High Street, bounded on the Southeast wherein said Mary Field now lives and on the northwest by a lot now or late of Moses Allen and on the northeast by the bank of Lewes Creek. The second of said lots is bounded on the northwest by above mentioned house and lot wherein said Mary Field now lives, on the northeast by afsd. bank of Lewes Creek, on the southeast by a lot now occupied by Herculas Kollock and on the southwest by the street afsd. The third of said lots is bounded on the northeast by the street afsd, on the southeast by a lot of William West, on the southwest by another lot of said William West and on the northwest by a lot of Francis Cahoon - being the same lots which were lately the property of Nehemiah Field and sold by Levin Dirrickson, Esqr. Commissioner of forfeited estates. Wit: Willm. Davis, Daniel Rodney. Ackn. 9 Aug 1782.

470. Deed. Margaret Kollock, widow, from Mary Field. For £60. 3 lots in town of Lewes. Also the house and lot wherein she now dwells, the first 3 lots purchased by Major Henry Fisher [see above] and sold to Mary Field. Wit: Henry Neill, D. Train. Proved 9 Aug 1782.

471. Deed. Margaret Kollock from Levin Dirrickson, Commissioner for forfeited estates. Whereas Levin on 2 Oct 1778 by virtue of

Act of Assembly made public sale of a moiety or half part of a messuage, tenement and lot in town of Lewes, as part of the estate of Nehemiah Field, did sell to John Field, for £20, he being the highest bidder. And John Field by his deed dated 29 Jan 1779 did convey to Mary Field and Susannah Field daughter of said Mary Field afsd. property who by her deed dated 29 June 1780 conveyed to Margaret Kollock. Wit: Willm. Davis, William Brereton. Ackn. 9 Aug 1782.

472. Deed. Margaret Kollock from Levin Dirrickson, Commissioner for the sale of forfeited estates. Several lots in the town of Lewes, formerly part of the estate of Nehemiah Field, were sold to Henry Fisher of the town of Lewes for £173 who by his deed dated 31 May 1779 conveyed the lots to Mary Field who by her deed dated 29 June 1780 conveyed the lots to Margaret Kollock. Wit: Willm. Davis, William Brereton. Ackn. 9 Aug 1782.

473. Deed. William Kollock from Rhoads Shanklin, Sheriff. 10 Aug 1782. Whereas Margaret Kollock, extx of the will of Jacob Kollock in 1781 by the consideration of the court recovered judgment against Simon Kollock, exr of the last will of Cornelius Kollock, deceased for £92, 15 shillings and 10 pence whereas the property of Cornelius Kollock was ordered to be sold to satisfy the debt to Margaret Kollock. Whereupon the tract whereon William Kollock now dwells containing 100 acres and one lot in Lewes Town and the tract was sold to William Kollock for £60. Wit: Nicholas Little, George Frame. Ackn. 10 Aug 1782.

474. Bill of sale. Jacob Moore, Esqr., Attorney, town of Lewes, from Catharine Wiltbank of Lewes Town. Know that Catharine Wiltbank of Lewes Town, for £80, 80 acres in Lewes Town bounded by Lewes Creek, lands of John Wiltbank, Esqr. and James Thompson, formerly the property of Abraham Wiltbank and lately sold as his property by Levin Dirrickson, Commissioner for forfeited estates. Wit: Henry Neill, D.Train. Proved 9 Aug 1782.

474. Deed. Jacob Moore, Esqr. from Levin Dirrickson, Commissioners for sale of forfeited estates. Property of Abraham Wiltbank, sold to Catharine Wiltbank of town of Lewes for £550 and she conveyed same on 29 June 1780 to Jacob Moore of town of Lewes. 80 acres. Wit: Willm. Davis, William Brereton. Ackn. 9 Aug 1782.

475. Deed. Mitchel Lank from Catharine Starr, spinster. For 5 shillings, parcel being part of a larger tract called Whellers Hall taken up by patent by Richard Patie, dated 14th of 2nd month 1687 on the southeaster most side thereof. Beginning at the edge of Mill Creek; John Holland's line. 100 acres. Wit: James Lank, Thos. Gray. Proved 5 Nov 1782.

476. Deed. Milby Johnston from Alexander Reed. 6 Nov 1782. Between Alexander Reed of Sussex Co., yeoman and Milby Johnston of Sussex Co., mariner. Tract of 100 acres called Patridge Tract which was conveyed to Moses Allen, pilot of this county by above said Alexander Reed. Moses Allen for £100 paid by Milby

Johnston. Reference to west side of the county road leading from
Lewes Town to the saw mill in Indian River Hundred adjoining the
lands of Samuel Lingo and Wm. Grice. Wit: Guning Bedford, Junr.,
Joseph Hall. Ackn. 6 Nov 1782.

476. Bond. Nathaniel Baily to William Baily for conveyance of
land. Nathaniel Baily, yeoman, bound to his son William Baily,
both of Sussex Co., for £500, 10 Sep 1781. That the exrs. of
Nathaniel Baily, after his death, conveyed to William Baily a
tract of 201 acres in Rehoboth Hundred wherein Nathaniel Baily
now lives which Nathaniel Baily purchased from exrs. of Jonathan
Baily, dec'd. and the other six acres thereof he purchased from
Stephen Green, dec'd. If the wife of Nathaniel Baily, Jennet,
shall survive her husband then she shall hold her dowery during
her lifetime. Wit: J. Russel, Joshua Ball. Proved 7 Nov 1782.

477. Deed. James Buchanan, Gent., from Levin Derrickson,
Commissioner of forfeited estates. 23 Oct 1780. For £66.5,
title of Simon Kollock, cooper, had in tract called Thomas Coart
on the east side of Nanticoke River and on the north side of Mill
Branch, 500 acres; also its resurvey dated 11 June 1776. Bought
at public sale in 1778 by James Buchanan. Wit: Enoch Scudder,
Jos. Dirickson. Ackn. 7 Nov 1782.

478. Deed. William Maloney, Sussex Co., yeoman, from John
Hudson, Sussex Co., saddler. For £122, land in Northwest Fork
Hundred, called Batchelors Quarter or Williams's Vexation, which
John Hudson, after necessary proceedings of the Orphans Court,
accepted at valuation. Boundary runs across the land of David
Williams, deceased. 176 acres, excepting 10 1/2 acres taken of
by an older survey of Robert Wallace's land. Wit: John Laws, J.
Wiltbank. Ackn. 7 Nov 1782.

478. Deed. George Walton from George Black and wife. 1 March
1782. Between George Black and Wife Sarah, Sussex Co. and George
Walton, yeoman. Land in Cedar Creek Neck purchased formerly by
Henry Spencer from Robert Hart and sold by him to Mark Gandron
and by him to Gabriel Gandron son and heir of the said Mark
Gandron who for £13 paid by Joseph Spencer assigned the tract to
him and William Spencer, son and heir at law of afsd Henry
Spencer, conveyed the land to above said Joseph Spencer. And
Donovan Spencer, son of said Joseph Spencer, sold said dividend
of land to Nathan Spencer who sold it to Aziael Spencer who by
his deed of sale dated 29 July 1772 conveyed same to George
Black. Beginning at the corner hickory of Robert Hart's. 40
acres surveyed and laid out on 16 March 1713. Wit: Wm. Hazzard,
Jno. Wiltbank. Ackn. 7 Nov 1782.

479. Deed. George Walton, Junr., Sussex Co., yeoman, from
George Black, Sussex Co., yeoman, and wife Sary. Tract in Cedar
Creek Neck purchased by Abraham Wynkoop, Esqr. from the heirs of
Robert Hart the original patentee which land is called Long Acre
and Abraham Wynkoop conveyed same to George Black the elder,
dec'd. who died intestate leaving several heirs and widow. Land
was allotted to John Black, eldest son of deceased George Black,

party of these presents. 30 acres, for £15. Wit: Wm. Hazzard, J. Wiltbank. Ackn. 7 Nov 1782.

480. Deed. George Walton, yeoman, from George Black and wife Sary. Tract in Cedar Creek Neck purchased by Abraham Wynkoop from the heirs of Robert Hart and by Abraham Wynkoop devised to his son Benjamin Wynkoop who sold the same to Azeail Spencer per deed 2 Feb 1763 and said Spencer conveyed same to afsd George Black by deed dated 27 July 1772. 11 acres and 115 square perches. For £50. Wit: Wm. Hazzard, J. Wiltbank. Ackn. 7 Nov 1782.

481. Deed. Charles Whitely, Dorchester Co., planter, from John Anderton and wife Amelia of Dorchester Co., merchant. 6 Sep 1782. For £504.7.9. Tract in Northwest Fork Hundred called Lees First Purchase. 306 1/2 acres. Wit: Thos. White, Wm. Polk. Proved 7 Nov 1782.

482. Deed. Daniel Dingee, Sussex Co., from Peter Rea, Sussex Co. 1 Nov 1782. For £200. Tract called Tory or Troy in Northwest Fork Hundred on Herring Branch. 56 acres. Also a part of another parcel called Ringsend of which land was also taken up authority aforesaid and the warrant granted to Isaac Bradley of Northwest fork but surveyed for Peter Rea by reason of a purchase made by Peter Rea from said Bradley, 140 acres. Wit: Andrew Fountain, Samuel Fountain. Proved 7 Nov 1782.

483. Deed. Thomas Ludenam from Levin Hickman. 19 Aug 1782. Between Levin Hickman of Sussex Co. admr. of Nehemiah Hickman, deceased, and Thomas Ludenam, Sussex Co., yeoman. Levin Hickman preferred a petition to the Orphans Court for the sale of the lands of Nehemiah Hickman as would allow the discharge of the remainder of his debts. And whereas Nehemiah Hickman died intestate seized of two parcels in Northwest Fork Hundred, one parcel containing 50 acres granted by patent dated 10 Dec 1740 from the proprietaries of Maryland to Timothy Carsey called Kilkanny, the other containing 70 acres adjoining the aforesaid tract granted by a warrant of resurvey, whereupon Levin Hickman exposed to sale these two tracts and they were purchased by Thomas Ludenam for £101.5. Wit: John Laws, Mary Turner. Proved 9 Nov 1782.

484. Deed. Daniel Murphey Thompson, Sussex Co., infant, from Hezekiah Gray, Sussex Co., blacksmith, and wife Sarah. 8 Nov 1782. Tract in Lewes and Rehoboth Hundred called Society Hall, the same tract whereof Thomas Gray, father of aforesaid Hezekiah Gray lately died seized and possessed which said Thomas Gray devised one moiety to Hezekiah Gray party to these presents. For £10 paid by Daniel Murphey in behalf of Daniel Murphey Thompson. Wit: Jno. Wiltbank, Wm. Short. Ackn. 8 Nov 1782.

485. Deed of mortgage. Josiah Polk, Somerset Co., Maryland, from Uriah Hazzard, Sussex Co. 23 Jan 1782. For £100, land which Uriah Hazzard purchased of Phillips Kollock, 12 1/2 acres being part of a tract which other part is in possession of Edward

Craige and Richard Howard, situate near the bounds of the town of
Lewes, also 4 feather beds and furniture, 1 yoke of oxen, 1 cow,
1 small gelding, 1 mare, sorrell, 7 head of sheep. Full payment
to be made before 15 February next. Wit: James Polk, Thomas
Martin Secundus. Ackn. 8 Nov 1782. Annotation: Be it remembered
that on 29 Oct 1785 Isaac Henry, attorney in fact of the exrs. of
Josiah Polk, the mortgagee in this recorded deed informed that he
in behalf of the said exrs. had received full satisfaction from
Uriah Hazzard, mortgagor, and he released and quit claim for and
behalf of the said exrs.

485. Deed. Aaron Marshall, town of Lewes, cordwainer, from Ann
Westly, town of Lewes, widow and admr. of Richd. Westly, pilot,
dec'd. 9 Nov 1782. Sale of two lots in the town of Lewes to
discharge debts of deceased. For £30. Reference to a lot of
Thomas Martin. Which lots James Simpson by his last will dated
27 Jan 1730 devised to his wife Margaret Simpson who by her last
will dated 28 June 1753 after bequeathing sundry small legacies
to her other children did bequeath to her daughter Elizabeth
Simpson all the remainder of her estate who by deed of sale dated
3 May 1768 conveyed the two lotts to said Richard Westly. Wit:
George Parker, William Brereton. 9 Nov 1782.

486. Deed. John Sheldon Dormon, Sussex Co., yeoman, from Selby
Hickman, Sussex Co., taylor, and wife Ann. 30 May 1782.
Whereas William Shankland, Sheriff conveyed to Thomas Staton a
tract in Broadkiln Hundred which said Thomas Staton by his last
will dated 11 April 1751 devised part to his son Thomas Staton
who by his deed dated 1 Sep 1761 conveyed 100 acres of the land
to John Mustard. Beginning at the East side of the Mill Creek.
100 acres which John Mustard by his deed dated 3 May 1769
conveyed to Robert Jones who by his deed dated 28 May 1774
conveyed same to James Gordon who died intestate and Thomas
Gordon admr. of said James Gordon by virtue of an order from the
Orphans Court conveyed the 100 acres by deed of sale dated 17 Feb
1766 [sic] to William Millard who by his deed of sale dated 11
Feb 1780 conveyed said land to Silby Hickman, party to these
presents. Wit: John Clowes, Rebeka Glover. Ackn. 5 Feb 1783.

487. Deed. 20 Sep 1782. Between John Waters of Somerset Co.,
Maryland to Humphries Brown of Dorchester Co., Maryland. For
£100, tract called Wailes in the Northwest Fork Hundred.
Reference to a tract called Double Purchase. Also 13 acres
called Timber Tree Neck Addition, adjoining tract called Wales
afsd.; also part of a tract called Double Purchase, 85 acres.
Wit: Daniel Polk, White Brown. Ackn. 5 Feb 1783.

488. Deed. Richard Tull, Sussex Co., planter, from Jeremiah
Warwick, Sussex Co., planter. 8 June 1782. For £50, that part
of tract Curtisy in the Northwest Fork Hundred on the northwest
side of Nanticoke River beginning at a division line between
Henry King and said Warwick, containing 36 acres. Wit: Daniel
Polk, Francis Wright. Ackn. 5 Feb 1783.

489. Deed. Curtis Morriss from Daniel Morriss, Senr. 7 Nov

1782. Tract called Rogers Deffected, all to the eastern side from a bounder called Morrisses Pleasure. Wit: Daniel Clifton, Matthew Clifton, Thos. Clifton, Brinkley Morris.

489. Deed. Daniel Morris, Junr. from his father Daniel Morriss, Senr. 7 Nov 1782. A resurvey made upon a tract called Morrisses Pleasure. Wit: Daniel Clifton, Matthew Clifton, Jonathan Arnott, Thomas Clifton. Proved 5 Feb 1783.

489. Deed. 13 Dec 1777. Jean Wallace of the town of Lewes, widow, to Hap Hazzard, yeoman, a parcel in Broadkiln Hundred on the north side of a branch of Broad Creek proceeding from Cold Spring Creek, 800 acres formerly granted by patent from Francis Lovelace, Governor of New York, dated 8th of 5th month 1672 to Harmanus Frederick Wiltbank who conveyed same to John Kirk and was resurveyed on 11th of 10th month 1684 and said John Kirk with 800 acres confirmed and obtained a patent dated 19th of 3rd month 1686. John Kirk son and sole heir of above named John Kirk by his deed of sale sold the land to William Piles who by his last will gave the land to his four sons, Joseph, William, Isaac and John Piles to be equally divided. Joseph Piles, one of the sons of William Piles conveyed his part, being 268 acres to Robert Shankland who died intestate whereof the 268 acres descended to his four children, to wit: William Shankland, Elizabeth Neill late Elizabeth Shankland, Robert Shankland and Alexander Shankland who by their several and respective deeds conveyed the land to Samuel Gray who by his will devised the same to his son David Gray who married Jean Wallace party to these presents which David Gray by his last will devised the same to Jean Wallace (by the name of Jean Gray). 5 acres of this parcel for £30. Reference to County road leading from the drawbridge to Parkers Mill; Craig's line. Wit: Thos. Paremore, William Anderson Parker, Ann King. Proved 6 Feb 1783.

490. Hap Hazard, Sussex Co., yeoman, from James Fisher and wife Alice of Sussex Co. 15 Feb 1782. Tract of land and marsh in Slutkill Neck formerly surveyed for Baptists Newcomb the elder containing 100 acres conveyed to William Burton (son of Richard) who sold the above James Fisher 10 aces and 108 perches for £19. Beginning at a dividing line between afsd. tract and Jacob Hazzard; stake on James Fisher's Old Marsh line near the head of Fork Gut; corner stake in the marsh in Samuel Rowlan's line; Trumpertys Island. Wit: John Wiltbank, John Abbot Warrington. Ackn. 6 Feb 1783.

491. Deed. Joseph Hazzard, gives to his son Cord Hazzard a parcel part of which he bought of Edward and Finwick Fisher by deed retaining use in his lifetime and right of dower of his wife Mary Hazzard, 120 acres. Reference to Knight Howards; dividing line of Cornelious Wiltbank.
Also another parcel of land and marsh in the Island Track, 24 acres and 12 perches; Town woods; corner post on the beach at the end of Long Point; the great pond. Wit: Nathaniel Bradford, John Lerrek, Samuel Williams. Ackn. 6 Feb 1783.

492. Joseph Hazzard confirms to his son John Hazzard a parcel of land in Broadkiln Neck, part of a tract that he purchased of Edward and Finex Fisher retaining use in his lifetime and wife Mary's right of dower. 181 acres. Also 24 acres of woodland. Wit: Nathaniel Bradford, John Lerrick, Lemuel Williams. Ackn. 6 Feb 1783.

493. Joseph Hazzard for 5 shillings gives to his son William Hazzard, farmer, a tract in Broadkiln Hundred, 230 acres, and also 18 acres of woodland. Retaining use in his lifetime and wife Mary's right of dower. Wit: Nathaniel Bradford, John Lerrick, Lemuel Williams. Ackn. 6 Feb 1783.

494. Deed. John Conwell, Junr., Sussex Co., from John Conwell, Senr., Sussex Co. 23 April 1782. A tract of land and marsh in Broadkill Neck, containing 1275 acres granted by patent 9 Sep 1702 to William Dyer the younger which by sundry transferances became the property of afsd. John Conwell the elder. For £100. 107 acres. Boundary runs to a stone of William Conwell's land; corner in Joseph Hazzard's line. 111 acres reserving 4 acres for his granddaughter Hannah Conwell, daughter of his son David Conwell, dec'd. Wit: Abraham Conwell, Wm. Hazzard. Ackn. 6 Feb 1783.

494. Deed. Ezekiel Brown, Sussex Co., from Daniel Dingee, Sussex Co. 4 Jan 1783. £150. Tract called Tory or Troy taken up by Peter Rea of Sussex Co., schoolmaster, situate in Northwest Fork Hundred near the head of a branch joining the lands of Henry Hooper and Joseph Cannon, containing 50 acres; also another parcel being part of a tract called Ringsend taken up by Isaac Bradley of Northwest Fork, both tracts taken up by virtue of the proprietaries warrant in 1776 and said land called Ringsend purchased by said Peter Rea from said Bradley after which said Rea sold to divers persons before the sale to Daniel Dingee, joining the lands of divers persons at Herring Gut, 100 acres. Wit: Daniel Rogers, George Hazzard. Ackn. 6 Feb 1783.

495. Deed. John Dazey, Sussex Co., from Moses Dazey, Sussex Co. 6 Feb 1783. For £72, messuage and tract called Addition in Mudey Neck. Reference to a tract called Betty's Lott owned by Wattson Whorton; Massy's blacksmith shop; Solomon Evans; Betty's lott. 72 acres. Wit: Jos. Hall, Watson Wharton. Ackn. 6 Feb 1783.

496. Wattson Wharton, Sussex Co., from Gammage Evans Hodgson, Sussex Co. 6 Feb 1783. For £53. Messuage and parcel of land called Betty's Lot. Beginning at a flat ridge near a swamp called Elbs Swamp, about 3/4 of a mile from a tract now in possession of Thomas Dazey. 50 acres, which was granted to Margaret Hodge by a patent dated 26 Feb 1747 at Annapolis, Maryland. Messuage and tract called Addition in Muddy Neck. Reference to Betty's Lott; parcel deeded out of tract called Addition from Moses Dazey to Hinman Wharton deceased now in the possession of Watson Wharton. 17 acres which land was granted to Moses Dazey in 1760. Wit: Jos. Hall, John Dazey. Ackn. 6 Feb 1783.

497. Deed. Gamage Evans Hodgson, Sussex Co., planter, from Moses Dazey, Sussex Co., planter. 6 Feb 1780. 37 acres called Addition, taken up by Moses Cazey and Gamedge Evans Hodson. Boundary references: Elbow Swamp; Edmond Taylor's line; Bucks Ridge. Wit: Jos. Hall, Watson Wharton. Ackn. 6 Feb 1783.

497. Deed. 22 Dec 1781. John Ponder, planter, to Joseph Morris of Somerset Co., Maryland, for £40, tract in Broadkill Hundred now in possession of William Thorp bounding on land of John Hand, Edmond Reed, heirs of Bena. Riley, William Thorp, William Carpenter, John Riley, Joseph Morris, Senr, Denis Morris and Zadock Lindal. Wit: John W. Dean, James Ponder. Proved and ackn. 6 Feb 1783.

498. Deed. Joseph Morris, Junr., Sussex Co., yeoman, from William Thorpe of Broadkiln Hundred, yeoman, and wife Mary. 55 and 3/8 acres. Beginning at a post on the south side of road that leads from Lawrence Rileys to John Clowes's; land where William Thorpe now lives. The same land that Lawrence Riley, the elder, sold to said William Thorpe without having executed a deed and Lawrence Riley and John Riley, exrs. of Lawrence Riley, the elder, by their deed dated 6 Dec 1774 did convey same to William Thorpe. And another tract in the hundred aforesaid adjoining lands of William Carpenter, John Riley, Joseph Morris, Senr., Dennis Morris and Zadock Lindal being the same whereon William Thorpe now dwells containing 250 acres, for £270. Wit: John Clowes, William Passwaters. Proved 6 Feb 1783.

500. Deed to lead the uses of a Common Recovery. Wm. Matthews from Thomas Deal. 4 Feb 1783. Between Thomas Deal of Worcester Co., Maryland, yeoman and William Coffin of Sussex Co., yeoman. Aforesaid Thomas Deal and William Coffin for 5 shillings paid by William Matthews land in Baltimore Hundred called Scottish Plotts alias Scottish Plott containing 400 acres. Wit: Elijah Cannon, Richard Bassett. Ackn. 4 Feb 1783.

501. Deed. 16 Nov 1782. Mary Burroughs of the City of Philadelphia, widow, Benjamin Smith and wife Sarah, Hill Smith and wife Ann - all in the township of Manington (Warrington?), county of Salem, New Jersey to Thomas Evans of Cedar Creek Hundred. Whereas James Thomas of Sussex Co., was possessed of a tract of 500 acres on the south side of Cypress Branch of Prime Hook and after James Thomas died intestate and without issue, the tract descended to the heirs of Micha Thomas who is supposed a brother of said James Thomas, and Micha Thomas died intestate leaving four daughters, to wit, Ann Thomas, Mary Thomas, Elizabeth Thomas and Grace Thomas to whom the land descended. Ann Thomas, afterwards Ann Hacket conveyed her portion to John Powel who died intestate leaving two daughters, to wit, Mary and Sarah Powel and Mary died with no issue with her part descending to her sister Sarah Powel who died leaving issue three daughters, to wit, Mary, Sarah and Ann Nicholson now Burroughs and Smith, parties to these presents. Wit: Robert Johnson, Elijah Cattell(?), Edward Stapleford. Prove 7 Feb 1783.

223

502. Deed. John Clowes, Esqr., Sussex Co., from William
Millard, Sussex Co., shipwright. 1 April 1783. Tract in
Broadkill Hundred, 60 acres, being part of the estate of John
Clowes, Esqr., deceased, in dividing of which estate agreeable to
the last will of John Clowes, Lot number 7 became the right and
property of his daughter Catharine who married John Young and by
their deed dated 23 April 1774 conveyed same to William Millard 9
acres of afsd. lot and also by their deed dated 23 April 1776
conveyed to aforesaid William Millard all the remainder of Not.
No. 7, supposed to containing 50 acres in security for the
payment of £70. Wit: John Ingram, Thos.Thompson. Ackn. 1 April
1783.

503. Deed. John Ingram (Ingraham), Sussex Co., yeoman, from
William Millard, shipwright, and wife Mary of Sussex Co. 1 April
1783. Whereas Issabella Anett by division of her deceased father
William Stephenson's land became seized of 90 acres thereof and
by virtue of a purchase of lands formerly belonging to Mary Barry
became seized of 10 acres of land adjoining to the aforesaid 90
acres and being so possessed of the 100 acres, died intestate
leaving issue several daughters and Mary Annett being the oldest
of said daughters sold the land by deed of sale dated 7 Feb 1776
to William Bownass who by his deed of sale dated 3 Feb 1779
conveyed same to William Millard, party to these presents. Wit:
John Clowes, Thos. Thompson. Ackn. 1 April 1783.

504. Bond. George and Saml. Walton to Levin Crapper for
conveyance of land. George Walton, Junr. and Samuel Walton, both
of Sussex Co., yeomen, are bound to Levin Crapper, Sussex Co.,
merchant, for £200. 10 Feb 1772. To convey 80 acres and 154
perches being part of the land left to George and Samuel Walton
by the last will of their father John Walton, adjoining the land
bought by Levin Crapper from Wynkoop, Esqr., land sold said
Crapper last May, and also adjoining land of Israel Brown. Wit:
Bethuel Walton, Junr., Molton Crapper. Proved 7 May 1783.

504. Deed. Isaac Wootton, Sussex Co., planter, from John
Wootton, Sussex Co., planter. 26 March 1783. Whereas John
Wootton obtained a grant from the Lord Proprietor of Maryland for
a tract called Sandown in Worcester Co., now Little Creek Hundred
of Sussex Co., for £5 paid by his son Isaac Wootton. 256 acres,
now the dwelling plantation of said Isaac Wootton. Wit: Arthur
Hosea, Jonathan Wootton. Proved 7 May 1783.

505. Deed. 26 March 1783. John Wootton of Sussex Co. to his
son Elijah Wootton of the same place, planter. John Wootton is
seized of 148 acres part of a tract Houns Ditch in Little Creek
Hundred. Reference to corner of a parcel of land heretofore
conveyed to Jean Hugg. Wit: Arthur Hosea, Jonathan Wootton.
Proved 7 May 1783.

506. Deed. 7 Jan 1783. Matthias Collins of Sussex Co. and wife
Tabitha to Samuel Waples of Accomack Co., Virginia. A tract in
Indian River Hundred which is part of a larger tract surveyed
unto Francis Pope on 19 April 1722 and afterwards resurveyed unto

John Holmes by virtue of a warrant of Resurvey from Honourable Thomas Penn, dated 22 Feb 1739 and surveyed for 372 acres on 12 Jan 1742 for the aforesaid John Holmes. And the said Holmes and Ann his wife by their deed of sale dated 5 Feb 1756 conveyed 143 acres of the afsd. 372 acres to Jonathan Jacobs and said Jacobs by his deed of sale dated 30 Nov 1757 conveyed same to William Collins then of the Province of Maryland in Worcester Co., and said William Collins by his last will dated 3 March 1775 devised the land to his son Matthias Collins, party to these presents and his daughter Sarah Collins. Beginning at an oak in the Old Field in a small sink in the line of land wherein Dirickson Waples, dec'd., held a dividend and now is held by Samuel Waples; survey of Francis Copes and John Holmes Resurvey on the east side of the road lately laid out from Dagsbury to St. George's Chapel called the Ferry Road; line of land formerly surveyed to Peter and Paul Waples; land laid off to James Wilkins; corner post of several dividends of land sold by afsd. John Holmes to William Vaughan, Joseph Hickman and Jonathan Jacobs, deceased. 127 acres, for £225. Wit: Burton Johnson, Wm. Bagwell, Bethshaba Burton, N. Waples. Ackn. 7 May 1783.

507. Deed. 5 May 1783. John Richards of Sussex Co., planter, to Edward Ross, Sussex Co., planter. For £180. That part of a tract called Poplar Levil Improved in Sussex Co. in Northwest Fork Hundred, 54 acres. Wit: Daniel Polk, David Richards. Proved 7 May 1783.

508. Deed Thomas Dawson, Sussex Co., yeoman, from Joseph Godwin, Sussex Co., admr. of Zachariah Nicolls, yeoman, deceased, Sussex Co. 7 May 1783. Joseph Godwin sold a piece of the land of the deceased lying in Northwest Fork Hundred being part of a tract taken up by Marmaduke Storey, Senr. surveyed by William Killen Esqr., on 6 Feb 1752 by a Proprietary order of Pennsylvania dated 30 Nov 1750 and bought by the said Zachariah Nicolls as will appear on a bond of conveyance dated 11 April 1758. Land near Marshahope Bridge - sold at public auction for £50.5. 53 acres. Wit: Wm. Polk, John Laws. Ackn. 7 May 1783.

509. Deed. 1 Feb 1783. Nathaniel Whaley of Little Creek Hundred, Sussex Co. to William Whalley of the same place. For £40, tract called Maidenhead, 50 acres formerly taken up and patented by George Herne then in Worcester Co., granted 11 May 1749. Beginning at the head of a gulley or drain issuing out of the head of Broad Creek; east side of an old cart road called Caldwells Road. Wit: Samuel Hearn, Benjamin Vinson, Lowder Hearn. Ackn. 7 May 1783.

509. Deed. 1 Feb 1783. Nathaniel Whalley, Senr and Ebenezer Whalley, both of Little Creek Hundred to Luther Hearne of the same place. Whereas George Hearn of Worcester Co. on 18 April 1746 became seized of a tract called Goshams Addition, containing 26 acres in Sussex Co. but formerly in Worcester Co. who conveyed the land to said Nathaniel Whalley. Wit: Samuel Hern, Benjamin Vinson, Clem Hearn. Proved 7 May 1783.

510. Bond. John Nutter of Dorchester Co., is bound to William Macknat of Dorchester Co. in the sum of £40, on 20 Jan 1746/7. To convey a tract called Cow Pasture on the head of the Northwest fork of the Nanticoke River to be conveyed to William Macknat. Wit: William Nutter, Charles Brown. Moses Ratledge and Ann Ratledge assign right to bond to Thomas Dawson. Wit: John Pierce, Daniel Benson. Thomas Dawson assigned his right to bond to Zabdiel Dawson, 7 March 1783. Wit: Oliver Jump, Sarah Jump. Proved 7 May 1783.

511. James Brown, Junr. petition for leave of Court to convey lands to Zabdiel Dawson. 7 May 1783. Petition of James Brown, Junr. admr of property of Tilghman Brown, Sussex Co., yeoman, which said Tilghman Brown was exr. of Charles Brown, late of Dorchester co. dec'd. which Charles Brown was exr. of John Nutter late of Dorchester Co. Whereas a tract of 60 acres granted by patent from the Proprietor of Maryland dated 18 Feb 1724 to Charles Nutter which land was situate in Dorchester Co. and called Calf Pasture. Charles Nutter afterwards died intestate whereof his eldest son, John Nutter acknowledged himself to be firmly bound to William Macknat. William McNat died intestate before a conveyance of the land was made leaving issue one daughter, Ann Macknat to whom the land descended; said Ann married Moses Ratledge which Ann and Moses Ratledge for a consideration assigned the bond to Thomas Dawson who assigned it to Zabdiel Dawson. Petition granted 7 May 1783.

512. Deed Zabdiel Dawson from James Brown, Junr., admr. 7 May 1783. [See above.] Wit: John Laws, Wm. Polk.

513. Deed. 28 April 1783. John Rodney of the town of Lewes, yeoman, and Sarah Biggs of the City of Philadelphia to Henry Fisher of the town of Lewes, pilot. Whereas James Simpson, late of the town aforesaid was seized of a parcel of land and devised same to his two daughters Elizabeth and Margaret Simpson. The two lots were divided, the part of Margaret now belonging to Thomas Martin, whereas Margaret died leaving issue the afsd Sarah, the party to these presents by her first husband James Holland deceased. Whereas the aforesaid Elizabeth Simpson by indenture dated 10 June 1782 did convey her interest to aforesaid John Rodney. For £16.10. Wit: Phillips Kollock, Caleb Rodney. Ackn. 7 May 1783.

514. Deed. 4 March 1783. John Russel of Caroline Co., Maryland and wife Sarah to Shadrach Liden of Caroline Co. For £1625 and 150 bushels of corn, tract called Loyds Forrest in Sussex Co. Beginning at an oak standing in the province line where the northern most line of Jarvey Safford's part of said land crosses the same ... 166 acres. Wit: Joseph Godwin, Wm. Morgan. Proved 7 May 1783.

515. Deed. 1 May 1783. Joseph Godwin of Sussex Co. and wife Mary Ann to James Harris of Caroline Co., Maryland. For £140, tract called Salleys Plains, in Sussex Co. Reference to Loyd's Forrest to the stone line that divides Delaware and Maryland, 139

3/4 acres. Wit: Thomas Dawson, Sarah Godwin. Ackn. 7 May 1783.

516. Deed. 8 May 1783. Obadiah Eldridge of Sussex Co., yeoman, to John Rowland of Sussex Co., tanner. Land in Lewes and Rehoboth Hundred on Pagan Branch or Head of Pagan Creek adjoining to the eastward, westward and southward, lands of Jabez Fisher and to the northward, lands of Peter Fretwell Wright (being part of a larger tract), devised by Joseph Eldredge late of the county afsd. yeoman and Mary Eldridge his wife to their two grandsons to wit, Thomas Moore and the above named Obadiah Eldridge [divided as described]. For £97.10, 27 acres. Wit: John Laws, Joseh(?) Hall. Ackn. 8 May 1783.

517. Deed. Samuel Johnston from Dan: Clifton, bond for conveyance.

INDEX

Single names
Charles, 158
Comly, 104
Dick, 110
Essex, 89
Florah, 130
Hannah, 174
Isaac, 89
Jeanny, 126
Leah, 126
Mess, 158
Moses, 126
Nance, 130
Patty, 158
Pheabe, 18
Robin, 126
Sary, 126
Sofier, 126
Zacker, 153

-A-
ABBOTT, William, 214
ABDIL, Littleton, 208
ABRAHAM(S) BRANCH, 14, 116
ABRAHAMS LOT, 107, 126, 178
ACCOMACK County, Virginia, 3, 5, 29, 39, 45, 49, 55, 57, 78, 95, 149, 166, 174, 195, 196, 210
ACKWORTHS SAVANNAH, 124
ADAMS, Abraham, 135, 214
    Absolam, 193, 194
    Alexander, 124
    Cornilea, 48
    Elijah, 43
    Elinor, 142
    George, 124
    James, 141
    John, 8, 45, 48, 49, 57, 140
    Mary, 52, 53, 55
    Nathan, 142
    Peter, 52, 53, 55
    Richard, 193, 194
    Roger, 141, 142
    Thomas, 141
ADAMS FOLLEY, 11
ADDITION, 182, 201, 202, 221, 222
ADDITION TO FELLOWSHIP, 30
ADDITION TO FOUR TRACTS, 185
ALIF, Parker, 18
ALLEGOOD, William, 131
ALLEN, Elizabeth, 2, 161
    John, 1, 2
    Joseph, 1
    Mary, 2
    Moses, 1, 161, 215, 216
    William, 1, 2, 211
ALLIGOOG, William, 113
ALLIN, Andrew, 113
    John, 1
    Joseph, 1
    Moses, 1, 50, 55, 83, 90
    Robert, 166
    William, 1, 181
ALLISON, James, 12
ANDERSON, Isaac, 177
    J., 17
    Jonathan, 141
ANDERTON, Amelia, 218
    John, 218
ANDREWS, Thomas, 149
ANDROS, Edmund, 19
ANDROSS, Edmond, 4
ANGE, John, 164, 182
    Thomas, 164, 182
ANGOLA HUNDRED, 4, 12, 30, 36, 42, 103, 125, 146, 174, 175
ANGOLA NECK, 28, 39, 105, 106, 107, 112, 118, 156, 175
ANNAPOLIS, Maryland, 167
ANNET, Esabella, 82
    Isabell, 46
    Issabella, 223
    John, 82
    Mary, 82
ANNETT, Essabella, 47
    Isabella, 46, 159
    John, 46
    Mary, 120, 159, 223
ANNITT, Isabella, 120
ARCADA, 1, 4
ARCADIA, 2, 26, 103
AREY, William, 40
ARGO, Alexander, 121
ARGOE, Alexander, 33
ARGU, Alexander, 33
ARGUE, Moses, 33
ARNAL, Samuel, 42
    William, 17, 42, 48
ARNOTT, Jonathan, 220
ARTHUR'S BRANCH, 135
ASSAWAMMON BAY, 166
ASSAWAMON BAY, 161, 187
ASSAWAMON CREEK, 161, 174
ASSAWAMON SOUND, 198
ATCHINSON, William, 191
ATCHISON, William, 191

ATKENS, Elijah, 103
Hannah, 103
Joseph, 10
Mary, 10
ATKINS, Joseph, 151, 172
William, 111
ATKINSON,
Benjamin, 94
Isaac, 210
Samuel, 166
AUGUSTY (AUGUSTA) County, Virginia, 150
AYDELOTT, Frances, 140
George Howard, 135
John, 135
Joseph, 135, 140
Mary, 135
AYUDELOTTS NEGLECT, 188

-B-
BACKELOSS, 142
BACON, Dudson, 129, 193
George, 205
BAGWEL, William, 49
BAGWELL, Ann, 51, 70, 195
Elizabeth, 63
Francis, 5
John, 61, 63, 70, 195
Mary, 63
Thomas, 5, 48, 70, 195
William, 5, 44, 45, 48, 51, 57, 63, 70, 148, 195, 224
BAGWELL CREEK, 49
BAGWELLS CREEK, 45
BAILEY, Jane, 199
Jean, 82
Jennet, 60
John, 26
Jonathan, 16, 17, 33, 90
Joseph, 16, 90,
118
Nathaniel, 60, 82, 113, 199
BAILIS, James, 133
BAILY, Jane, 165
Jennet, 217
John, 26
Jonathan, 113, 217
Major, 210
Nathaniel, 165, 217
William, 217
BAINUM,
Batholomew, 117
Elinor, 117
BAIR GARDEN, 186
BAKER, John, 162
Solomon, 93
BALD CYPRUS SWAMP, 125
BALD EAGLE ISLAND, 195
BALDING, Caleb, 127, 193, 212
BALEY, Daniel, 33
BALL, Joshua, 217
BALTIMORE, Lord, 120, 122, 127, 145, 202
BALTIMORE County, Maryland, 39
BALTIMORE HUNDRED, 135, 222
BANK, 51
BANNING, Mary, 207
Thomas, 207
BANNINGS CHANCE, 207
BAR, Cloe, 148
James, 109, 133, 148
Pherabah, 104
BARCROFT, Joseph, 19
BARE SWAMP, 81
BARKER, Abigail, 132
Ann, 197
Job, 13, 133, 134, 197
John, 95, 197
Leath., 17
Leatherberry,
13, 114, 133, 134
Leatherbery, 154
Leatherbury, 132
Mary, 197
Peery, 133
Perry, 13, 134
William, 13, 134
BARKER'S BRANCH, 137
BARKERT,
Leatherberry, 112
BARKSTEAD, Joshua, 26
BARN, James, 119
BARNARD, Benoni, 183
BARNARDS BLUMERY, 183
BARNS' BRANCH, 21
BARR, James, 96
BARRATT, William, 46
BARREN CREEK, 12
BARRET KIRK'S LAND, 121
BARRETT, Mary, 82
William, 82
BARRY, James, 180
Mary, 120, 159, 223
BARTON, Robert, 125
BASHAM, 140
BASHAN, 79, 84, 89
BASHEM, 117
BASNETT, Samuel, 183
BASSETT, Richard, 68, 180, 203, 222
BATCHELORS CONTRIVANCE, 211
BATCHELORS FOLLY, 136
BATCHELORS INTERVENTION, 211
BATCHELORS LOT, 10, 196
BATCHELORS QUARTER, 142,

INDEX

217
BATSON, Thomas, 178, 187
BATTSON, Thomas, 179
BAYLES, James, 124
  James Francis, 105
BAYLY, Clement, 144
BAYSIDE, 158
BEACHAMP, Edmond, 144
BEAR SWELL, 31
BEAVAN, James, 158
BEAVANS,
  Cornelius, 138
  James, 203
  Rowland, 110, 172
BEAVER DAM, 12
BEAVER DAM BRANCH, 204
BEAVINS,
  Cornelius, 138
BEBENS, Cornelius, 128
BECKET, Elizabeth, 39
  Susannah, 39
  William, 39, 105
BEDFORD, Guning, 217
BEDFORD County, Pennsylvania, 58, 69
BEDWELL, Honer, 213
  Honor, 210
  Thomas, 210, 213
BELL, John, 71, 72, 201
  Jonathan, 113, 176, 194, 202, 205
  Mary, 90
  William, 1, 57, 77, 101, 180, 196
BELLAMY'S CORNER, 76, 78
BELLEMY, John, 25, 49
BELLS PURCHASE, 180
BENEM, George, 95
BENN, 145
BENNET, Purnal, 81
  Stephen, 81
BENNET LINE, 81
BENNETT, Nehemiah, 203, 214
BENNIT, Joshua, 43
  William, 21
BENSON, Daniel, 225
  George, 142
BENSTON'S FENCE, 190
BETTY'S LOTT, 221
BETTYS PURCHASE, 166
BEVANS, Rowland, 67
BEVER DAM, 19, 34, 38, 52, 81, 103, 212
BEVER DAM BRANCH, 31, 67, 79, 97, 104, 125, 128, 129, 143, 180
BEVINS, William, 125, 157
BIGGS, Peter, 115
  Sarah, 116, 225
BIGNAL, John, 90
  Rhoda, 90
  William, 90
BITE THE BITER, 121
BIVINS, William, 125, 127
BLACK, Adam, 167, 168, 180
  Ann, 57
  Benjamin, 45, 196, 200
  Delila, 196
  Elizabeth, 153, 196, 200
  George, 11, 50, 56, 57, 62, 63, 96, 101, 135, 153, 217, 218
  James, 10, 34, 50, 62, 78, 80, 154, 196, 200
  John, 55, 56, 57, 62, 63, 96, 150, 187, 196, 200, 217
  Joseph, 196, 200
  Magdelin, 200
  Mary, 196, 200
  Mitchel, 123
  Mitchell, 123
  Naomi, 55
  Samuel, 150, 178
  Sarah, 50, 217
  Sary, 217, 218
  William, 150, 161
BLACK SWAMP, 150
BLACK WALNUT ISLAND, 111
BLACK WATER CREEK, 196
BLACKFOOT, 189
BLACKFOOT TOWN, 187
BLACKFORD,
  Richard, 82
BLACKS BRIDGE, 77
BLACKSMITH'S HALL, 13, 88
BLACKWATER BRANCH, 169
BLACKWATER CREEK, 160
BLIZARD, Thomas, 160
  William, 67, 69, 114
BLOCKSAM, Richard, 143
BLOCKSOM, Richard, 31, 169, 214
  William, 3, 169
BLOXSOM, Richard, 18, 103
BLUFF POINT, 195
BLUNDEL, James, 91, 92
  Samuel, 91, 92
BOICES VENTURE, 198
BONASS, William, 102
BONNEM, George, 94
BOOTH, George, 192, 193
  Joseph, 10

BOROUGH, Mary, 4
BORROUGH, Boaz, 70
BORROUGHS,
 William, 60
BOUCHER, William,
 132, 156
BOUND, Isaac, 27
BOUNDS, Leaven,
 117
 Levin, 35
 Thomas, 35, 117
BOWLER, Joshua, 10
BOWMAN, Caleb, 124
 Henry, 10, 23,
 24, 35, 37, 44,
 56, 61, 81, 134
 John, 23, 24,
 35, 56, 163
 Mary, 163
 Nathaniel, 76,
 142
BOWMAN'S BRANCH,
 9, 24, 33, 69,
 121, 136
BOWMANS FARM, 144
BOWNASS, William,
 223
BOWNDES PLACE, 148
BOWNESS, William,
 102, 107, 120,
 159, 160
BOWSTOCK, Thomas,
 62, 88
BOYCE, Jonathan,
 135
 William, 176
BOYD, Ada, 42
 Adah, 161
 John, 39, 209
BOYER, Elizabeth,
 115, 162, 163
 Thomas, 114,
 115, 162, 163
BOZMAN, Sarah, 131
 William, 131
BRABASON STREET,
 26
BRACES BRANCH,
 112, 180
BRACEY, Robert,
 123
BRACEY'S [Bracy's]
 BRANCH, 25, 26,
 65, 106, 123

BRADFORD, Comfort,
 135
 Nathaniel, 97,
 135, 220, 221
 Sarah, 135
BRADLEY, Isaac,
 130, 131, 147,
 218, 221
 Joseph, 182
 Thomas, 168
 William, 154
BRADLY, Isaac,
 145, 156, 171
 Joseph, 182
 William, 203
BRANDYWINE, 159
BRATTIN, Hugh, 102
BRATTON
 (Braughton),
 Elisha, 167,
 102
 Isbal, 167
 John, 118
BRAUGHAN, Patrick,
 178
BRAZER, Mary, 210
BRERETON, Henry,
 92
 John, 87
 William, 101,
 216, 219
BRETON, Elisha,
 102
 Esabel, 102
BRIAN, Nanney, 186
 William, 186
BRICE, John, 107,
 126
BRIDELL, Elihu,
 137
BRIDGE BRANCH, 22,
 132, 178
BRIDGE DAM BRANCH,
 204
BRIDGE PLACE, 66
BRIDGE PLANTATION,
 88
BRIERRY BRANCH, 69
BRIGHT, Charles,
 40
BRIGHTS BEAVER
 DAM, 40
BRIGHTS BEVER DAM,
 109

BRIGHTS BRANCH,
 207
BRION, Nanney, 186
 William, 186
BRITTINGHAM,
 Isaac, 151
 Nathan, 66
 William, 66
BRITTINGHAM HILL,
 83
BROAD CREEK, 12,
 124, 125, 127,
 176, 192, 211,
 215, 220, 224
BROAD CREEK
 HUNDRED, 123,
 157, 170, 201,
 205
BROAD KILL, 14
BROAD KILL
 HUNDRED, 191
BROAD KILN CREEK,
 2
BROAD WATER, 115
BROADIE, Robert,
 173
BROADKILL, 15
BROADKILL CREEK,
 5, 40, 48, 58,
 78, 92, 97,
 109, 126, 145,
 172
BROADKILL FORREST,
 12, 16, 19, 20,
 30, 32, 35, 38,
 63, 65, 78, 86,
 99, 132, 133,
 137, 138, 149,
 153, 156, 159,
 163, 186
BROADKILL HUNDRED,
 7, 8, 9, 10,
 11, 12, 13, 18,
 19, 31, 34, 39,
 40, 43, 46, 47,
 49, 50, 51, 54,
 57, 62, 67, 69,
 72, 73, 81, 82,
 83, 84, 85, 90,
 91, 93, 94, 96,
 100, 101, 102,
 103, 104, 106,
 107, 110, 112,
 113, 114, 118,

120, 121, 125,
126, 127, 129,
131, 133, 137,
138, 139, 141,
143, 145, 146,
147, 148, 150,
153, 154, 161,
172, 174, 178,
179, 181, 208,
222, 223
BROADKILL NECK, 97
BROADKILN CREEK,
   40, 119, 199
BROADKILN FORREST,
   25, 162
BROADKILN HUNDRED,
   71, 96, 119,
   164, 165, 167,
   170, 175, 178,
   181, 195, 198,
   199, 207, 210,
   213, 219, 220,
   221
BROADKILN NECK,
   209, 221
BROCK, Tabitha, 98
BROOK BRANCH, 25
BROOKFIELD,
   Azariah, 210
BROOKS, James, 98
BROTHER, Linzey,
   188
BROTHERHOOD, 166,
   187
BROTHERN, Joseph,
   117
BROTHERS PORTION,
   THE 55
BROTHERWOOD, 193
BROWN, Ann, 144
   Charles, 43,
   128, 147, 148,
   149, 171, 181,
   182, 225
   Curtis, 147,
   148, 149
   Daniel, 52
   Elinor, 125, 147
   Elizabeth, 23
   Ezekiel, 141,
   144, 221
   Humphries, 219
   Isaac, 144, 178
   Israel, 23, 24,
   61, 134, 206,
   223
   James, 139, 149,
   163, 164, 171,
   225
   Jane, 23
   John, 23, 24,
   44, 147, 148,
   149
   Joseph, 149
   Mary, 23, 206
   Rachel, 23
   Rebecca, 147,
   148
   Sarah, 23, 24,
   128, 147, 149,
   171
   Suffiah, 178
   Tilghman, 131,
   147, 182, 225
   White, 139, 185,
   219
   William, 23
BROWN'S SECURITY,
   147
BRUCE, Alexander,
   27
BRYAN, Ann
   Elizabeth, 45,
   105
   Arthur, 168
   Jonathan, 45,
   105, 149
   Lydia, 45
   Mary, 45, 105
   Thomas, 82, 85,
   92, 114
   William, 45, 105
BRYANT, Jonathan,
   149
BRYER AND THISTLE,
   16
BRYON, Thomas, 67
BUCHANAN, James,
   47, 217
   William, 39
BUCHER, Frankey,
   208
   William, 208
BUCKS RIDGE, 222
BUNDELIN FOLLY,
   166
BUNDICK, Richard,
   1, 2, 4, 181
BUNDOCK, Richard,
   26
BUNKERS HILL, 144
BURBYGE, Thomas,
   92
BURDEN TOWN, 157
BURK, John, 202
   Tereau, 202
   Terese, 202
   Terreas, 202
   Terrese, 202
   Trasa, 202
BURNS, Elizabeth,
   109, 143
BUROGHBUNG BRANCH,
   166
BURROBUNG BRANCH,
   157
BURROUGHS, Ann,
   222
   John, 183
   Mary, 222
   Warren, 84, 89,
   140, 141
   Warron, 33
   William, 182,
   183
BURROW, Patent, 77
BURTON, Ann, 28,
   45, 195
   Benjamin, 65,
   67, 70, 90,
   105, 113
   Bethshaba, 224
   Elizabeth, 21,
   113, 166
   Jacob, 28, 55,
   87, 172, 189
   John, 120, 175,
   209
   John Stratton,
   51
   Joseph, 95
   Joshua, 27, 28,
   87, 104, 112,
   118, 178
   Luke, 174
   Mary, 178
   Richard, 21, 48,
   113, 220
   Robert, 9, 12,
   14, 17, 53,
   101, 113, 174,

175, 186, 195, 204, 205
Samuel, 65, 186, 205
Sarah, 28, 87
William, 5, 20, 21, 27, 28, 45, 48, 49, 51, 54, 55, 57, 66, 74, 75, 87, 94, 95, 100, 119, 120, 126, 141, 157, 175, 177, 178, 191, 195, 220
Woolsey, 51, 70, 197
BURTON'S OLD MILL DAM, 172
BUSHY, Thicket, 19
BUTCHER, William, 76, 165
BUTLER, Samuel, 117
BYONS GRAVE, 125

-C-
CADE, Charles, 107, 126
John, 141, 167
Richard, 31
Richardson, 32, 62, 84, 90, 91, 92
Robert, 10, 80, 107, 108, 126
Thomas, 126
CADWALDER, Thomas, 113
CADY, John, 126
CAHOON, Frances, 1
Francis, 50, 215
William, 164
CAID, John, 16
CALDWELL,
Elverton, 212
James, 101
Mary, 101
CALDWELLS ROAD, 224
CALE, Margret, 81
Robert, 30
Thomas, 1, 60, 82
CALF PASTURE, 177, 225
CALHOON, Francis, 161
Jonathan, 208
CALLAWAY, Edward, 166
CALLAWAYS NEGLECT, 125
CALWELL, John, 183
CAMBLE, Dorthia, 85
James, 49
CAMBRIDGE BRANCH, 140
CAMPBELL, Dorthia, 8
George, 187
James, 8, 170, 187
CAMPBLE, Ann, 85
Dorthea, 85
Esther, 85, 86
James, 11, 85
John, 55
Margret, 85
Mary, 85
Nathan, 11, 85, 86
Rebeckah, 11
Samuel, 71
CAMPLE, John, 55, 168
CAMRON, Andrew, 48
CANARIKILL CREEK, 60
CANNAAN, 149
CANNAN, Matthew, 158
CANNON, Abraham, 171
Constantine, 139, 142, 155
Elijah, 222
Jacob, 187
Jeremiah, 113, 158, 187
John, 194
Joseph, 221
Levin, 142
Robert, 203
Sarah, 171
Starling, 139
Stephen, 182
Thomas, 171

CANNONS REGULATION, 187
CANNONS SAVANNAH, 182
CAPE CHANNEL, 157
CAPT HAYS'S INN, 183
CARES NECK, 12
CAREY, Edward, 25, 30
Samuel, 29
Thomas, 19, 20
William, 29, 86
CARHART, Rosanna, 69
William, 69
CARLILE, John, 15, 67, 121
Pemberton, 33, 68, 89, 108
CARLISLE'S MILL TRACT, 81
CAROLINE County, Maryland, 133, 144, 163, 167
CAROLINE County, Virginia, 192
CARPENTER,
Benjamin, 8, 30, 42, 48, 53, 54, 98
Comfort, 30
George, 93
Henry, 98
Jacob, 93
James, 21, 25, 58, 80, 98, 114, 140
Joseph, 14
Luke, 80
Mary, 98
Naphtaly, 22, 25, 98
Napthaly, 21
William, 15, 85, 222
CARPENTERS STREET, 215
CARREL, Elizabeth, 150
Joseph, 25
Margaret, 150
Margret, 150
Sarah, 150

CARSEY, Timothy, 218
CARTER, Geroge, 133
  Joseph, 46
CARTERY, 182
CARWAY, John, 202, 203
CARY, Ebenezar, 44
  Ebenezer, 127
  Edward, 31
  Eli, 49
  Elias, 29
  Frances, 106, 112
  John, 83, 112, 123, 174, 179
  Joseph, 29
  Martha, 106, 107
  Marthew, 112
  Naomi, 83
  Samuel, 13, 29, 49, 125, 133, 166, 174, 179
  Thomas, 15, 20, 30, 50, 62, 64, 88, 106, 107, 125, 127
  William, 29, 125
CATTAIL BRANCH, 76
CATTELL, Elijah, 222
CAULK, Lambeth, 153
CAVE NECK, 54
CAVENDER, James, 166
CAW BRIDGE, 92
CEDAR CREEK, 3, 4, 9, 27, 29, 31, 38, 41, 43, 55, 56, 63, 71, 77, 80, 81, 87, 103, 114, 123, 157, 158, 166, 173, 178, 198, 212, 214
CEDAR CREEK BRANCH, 72, 124
CEDAR CREEK FORREST, 18, 20, 33, 59, 81
CEDAR CREEK HUNDRED, 2, 3, 8, 9, 10, 15, 20, 22, 23, 24, 28, 31, 33, 34, 35, 37, 38, 41, 42, 43, 46, 47, 50, 53, 55, 57, 60, 61, 62, 64, 68, 69, 70, 72, 73, 78, 79, 80, 81, 84, 86, 87, 88, 89, 96, 99, 101, 102, 108, 110, 111, 116, 117, 121, 123, 124, 140, 144, 152, 157, 163, 169, 173, 176, 182, 183, 191, 196, 198, 204, 207, 212, 214, 222
CEDAR CREEK NECK, 9, 10, 11, 27, 31, 38, 50, 57, 62, 63, 67, 69, 79, 89, 99, 101, 103, 170, 200, 217, 218
CEDAR HILL, 177
CHACE, Isaac, 10
CHADDS, Francis, 46
CHADWICK, Benjamin, 22
CHAISE, Isaac, 94
CHAMBERS, Ben., 176
  George, 92
CHANCE, 162, 202, 210
  John, 94, 140, 159, 196
  Spencer, 9
  William, 9, 23, 24, 25, 150, 152
CHANCES FOLLEY, 43
CHARLES TINDAL'S BRANCH, 123, 207
CHASE, Isaac, 207
CHEET, 10, 95
CHESTER County, Pennsylvania, 28, 77
CHEW, Benjamin, 113
CHIPMAN, Margaret, 101
  Parez, 107
  Paris, 101, 162, 163
CHRISTOPHER, Agothey, 15
  Wrixam, 7
CHURCH BRANCH, 157
CIRWITHIN, Caleb, 24, 25, 43, 49, 71, 73, 78, 106, 116, 117, 133, 145, 182, 203
  John, 24, 25, 28, 49, 63, 110, 116, 119
  Martha, 110
CIRWITHIN'S MILL CREEK, 28
CLAMPET, John, 138, 170
  Sophia, 170
CLAMPIT, John, 43
  Richard, 43
  Suffier, 43
CLAMPITT, John, 178
CLANDANIEL, Ahab, 20
  John, 11, 50, 56
  Prudence, 56
CLARK, Charles, 15
  Elizabeth, 20, 61, 62, 88, 115, 134
  Honor, 210
  Honour, 71, 197
  Jonathan, 214
  Rebecca, 134
  Rhodes, 135
  William, 2, 3, 20, 25, 38, 40, 61, 63, 71, 95, 101, 105, 117, 119, 123, 134, 148, 170, 197, 213
CLARKSON, Abraham, 185

234 INDEX

Elizabeth, 105, 139
Mary, 164
Richard, 138, 164
Robert, 171
Starling, 139
Thomas, 193
William, 193
CLARKSONS FORREST, 185
CLARKSONS INDUSTRY, 207
CLARRANCE, 149
CLAY, Ann, 135
CLAY SWAMP, 161, 163
CLAYPOOLE, James, 16
Jehu, 136, 141
CLERK, William, 133
CLIFTON, Dan, 226
Jehu, 84, 119
Jehue, 119
Jonathan, 198
Levi, 132
Levin, 69, 122, 128
Matthew, 200, 220
Robert, 197
Thomas, 1, 27, 198, 220
William, 183
CLIFTONS, Levin, 200
CLIFTONS DELIGHT, 142
CLINDANIEL, George, 11
John, 101
Luke, 81
CLOWES, Catharine, 66, 88, 223
David, 66, 75, 88, 92, 145, 151
Gerhardus, 75, 88, 145, 151
Gurhardus, 66
John, 165, 6, 9, 15, 16, 19, 20, 22, 25, 35, 38,
39, 40, 45, 46, 47, 48, 50, 58, 59, 62, 63, 64, 65, 66, 75, 81, 82, 84, 86, 87, 88, 89, 90, 91, 93, 94, 107, 113, 114, 120, 127, 130, 132, 133, 141, 145, 146, 151, 153, 156, 159, 162, 163, 166, 177, 178, 180, 198, 199, 201, 208, 213, 219, 222, 223
Lydia, 165, 66, 88, 151
Mary, 66, 88, 151
Sophia, 92
William, 66, 88, 151
COART, Thomas, 217
COCKREL GUTT, 196
COD, John, 144
CODD, Berkley, 73
Berkly, 77
Mary, 73, 77
COFFAN, Nehemiah, 109
COFFIN, John, 161
Nehemiah, 151, 172
William, 161, 222
COHOON, Jonathan, 93, 207
COLD SPRING BRANCH, 126, 136, 168
COLD SPRING CREEK, 220
COLDWELL, Samuel, 6
COLLINGS, Andrew, 14, 15, 19, 34, 35, 40, 86, 102, 103, 157, 159, 166, 182
Charles, 81
Darby, 132
Elijah, 153
Elizabeth, 117
Ezekiel, 96
George, 7
Hester, 96
John, 46, 102, 103, 125, 132, 159, 162, 166, 208
Joseph, 49, 117
Levi, 215
Levin, 52
Mary, 7
Matthias, 178
Purcey, 206
Selah, 208
Thomas, 182, 206
Truitt, 166
William, 96, 132
COLLINS, Andrew, 46, 133
George, 7, 202, 203
John, 34, 37, 46, 185, 201, 202, 205, 211
Joseph, 185, 192, 202
Joshua, 151
Levi, 180
Margaret, 185
Mathias, 224
Matthias, 197, 223
Sarah, 224
Tabitha, 223
William, 224
COLLINS LUCK, 192
COLLOUR, Thomas, 205
COLLOURS, Thomas, 206
COLTER, Andrew, 199
COMBERLAND, 192
COMMINGS, Enoch, 213
Hannah, 213
COMMON RECOVERY, 202, 222
CONCLUSION TO FRIENDS DESIRE, 177
CONNAWAY, John, 123

INDEX 235

Levin, 123, 124, 137
CONNER, Racklife, 179
CONNINGHAM, Jester, 125
CONSELL, Lydia, 145
CONWAY, John, 127
Philip, 125
CONWEL, William, 209
CONWELL, Abraham, 221
David, 13, 43
Elias, 18, 38
Francis, 133
George, 191
Hannah, 221
Jacob, 18
James, 156
Jeremiah, 66, 151
Jery, 66
John, 18, 27, 55, 114, 221
Joseph, 17, 18, 104
Lydia, 66, 88, 145
Rachel, 18
William, 78, 88, 99, 113, 117, 127, 133, 138, 143, 144, 221
COOKS CHANCE, 12
COOL SPRING ROAD, 34
COOLSPRING, 4, 5, 109, 170, 180
COOLSPRING BRANCH, 11, 43, 51, 54, 105, 107, 162, 191, 213
COOLSPRING CREEK, 8, 48, 52, 54, 74, 185
COOLSPRING TRACT, 8, 43, 85
COOPER, Daniel, 199
Isaac, 157, 158, 192, 193
James, 136, 142, 143, 203

COOPERS HALL, 51, 52, 205
COOPES, Daniel, 172
Elizabeth, 185
Thomas, 185
COOPS, Daniel, 151
COPES, Daniel, 10
Elizabeth, 192
Francis, 224
Mary, 10
Thomas, 162, 192
CORBET, Rodger, 19
CORBIN, Coventon, 39
CORD, Ann, 165
Hannah, 8, 71
Jane, 13, 94
John, 8, 16, 19, 46, 71, 114, 165
Joseph, 2, 13, 71, 93, 94, 101, 126, 208, 210
Mary, 165
William, 137
CORD HAZZARD, 29
CORD TRACT, 15
CORDERY, Noble, 60
CORDREY, Noble, 9
CORDRY, Noble, 9
CORKE, City of 19
CORNWALL, Rebeckah, 26
William, 26
CORNWELL, Francis, 2, 161, 180
John, 27, 172
CORNWILL, Francis, 105
COSSEY, Philip, 46, 72
Sary, 72
COSTON, Benton, 72, 125
Ezekial, 72
Joshua, 72, 125, 183
COTLAND LAND, 9
COTTINGHAM, Elisha, 189
COULLOR, Thomas, 186

COULTER, Andrew, 109
Charles, 134, 137, 143, 167, 196, 198, 200
James, 134, 148, 184
John, 1, 109, 129, 181, 201
Joseph, 134
Robert, 134, 181
Samuel, 137, 167, 198
William, 96
COVE NECK, 32
COVERDAL, Israel, 117
Jacob, 141
John, 58
COVERDALE, John, 15, 47, 86, 87, 121
Mary, 86
Richard, 20, 121
COVERDALL, Israel, 84, 87, 141
John, 34
Mary, 87
Richard, 84, 87, 141
Susanna, 34
COVINGTON, Robert, 130
COW BRIDGE BRANCH, 7, 17, 29, 94, 108, 174, 180
COW GARDEN, 181, 182
COW PASTURE, 225
COW QUARTER, 165
COW VALLEY, 51
COWAN, George, 88
COWARD, Penelope Holt, 41
COWDREY, Josias, 56
William, 56
COWEN, George, 71
COX, Moses, 181, 214
Rhoda, 181
COXES DISCOVERY, 192, 129, 193
COXES PERFORMANCE,

175
CRABS POND, 146
CRAIG, Alexander,
  107, 154
  Comfort, 201
  Edward, 97, 189,
    201, 208
  Esther, 201
  Hamilton, 107,
    201
  John, 3, 107,
    201
  Mary, 3, 201
  Robert, 107,
    126, 154
  Ruth, 201
  Sarah, 201, 208
CRAIGE, Edward,
  50, 64, 169,
  204, 219
  Hamilton, 64
  John, 39, 149
  Robert, 126
  Sarah, 169
  William, 75
CRAIGS LAND, 4
CRAPPER, Betty,
  152, 158
  John, 42
  Levi, 23
  Levin, 18, 21,
    25, 35, 37, 41,
    42, 43, 52, 55,
    57, 61, 68, 86,
    90, 99, 101,
    113, 134, 136,
    150, 152, 158,
    212, 223
  Molton, 61, 134,
    150, 152, 158,
    212
  Sarah, 42
  Zadock, 158
CRAVINS, Robert, 5
CRAWLEY, John, 30
CRAWLY, John, 36
CREIGHTON, John,
  215
CREW, John, 97
CRIPPEN,
  Catharine, 9
  John, 9
  Joseph, 9
  Mary, 9

Thomas, 9
CROCKET, Richard,
  187
CROCKETT, Richard,
  188
CROLLY, John, 146
CROTHERS, John, 29
CROUCH, John, 116
  Robert, 150
  Thomas, 163, 169
CROUTCH, Thomas,
  140
CROW, Ann, 92
CRUTHERS, John, 30
CUMBERLAND, 187
CUNNINGHAM,
  Arther, 125
  Jester, 127
CURRIER, Caleb, 20
CURTISY, 219
CUTT, Pheby
  Liping, 45
CYPRESS BRANCH,
  222
CYPRUS BRANCH, 46,
  47, 116, 140
CYPRUS HALL, 62,
  70, 88

-D-
DAGG, Andrew, 141
DAGSBERRY, 187
DAGSBURY, 179, 224
DAGWORTHY, John,
  113, 215
DALE, Thomas, 214
DAN, John, 127
DANELS, William,
  166
DANIELLY, William,
  85
DANIELS, William,
  116
DANIELS VENTURE,
  168
DANIELY, Kesiah,
  21
  William, 21
DANLEY, William,
  163
DARBY, Elizabeth,
  17, 33, 97
  Ephraim, 1, 16,
    97, 113, 131

Hannah, 97, 98,
  111
John, 17
Joseph, 93, 102,
  141, 213
Samuel, 7, 9,
  14, 17, 33,
  105, 114
Sanders, 97
Simon, 17, 33
DARTER, Margaret,
  210
  William, 12,
    138, 210
DASHIELL, George,
  192
  John, 211
  Joseph, 211
DAUGHTER, William,
  164
DAUGHTERS,
  William, 40
DAUGHTER'S TRACT,
  40
DAVID FLING'S
  SWAMP, 190
DAVIDSON, James,
  53, 91
  Mary, 187
DAVIS, Ann, 111
  Isaac, 85
  John, 81, 87
  Luke, 183
  Mark, 73, 76,
    78, 111, 114,
    204
  Mary, 37, 111
  Nehemiah, 23,
    24, 28, 37, 39,
    43, 69, 74, 79,
    85, 89, 106,
    111, 113, 114,
    115, 116, 118,
    125, 142, 144,
    172, 182, 204
  Robert, 65
  Samuel, 1, 33
  Sarah, 76, 111
  Thomas, 21, 27,
    30, 52, 80, 81,
    85, 115
  William, 49, 51,
    58, 74, 85, 99,
    101, 106, 128,

INDEX 237

139, 154, 215, 216
Zerubbabel, 151
DAVIS FARM, 144
DAVISON, James, 60, 82, 165, 179, 199
 Lewis, 58
 Mary, 60, 82, 165, 189, 199
DAVOCK, Mary, 65
 Naomy, 65
 Thomas, 62, 65, 71
DAWSON, Elizabeth, 149
 John, 142, 201
 Joseph, 139, 145, 149
 Leah, 142
 Thomas, 224, 225, 226
 Zabdiel, 225
DAY, Edward, 193
 George, 44
 Hannah, 148
 John, 115, 148
 Prittyman, 66, 86
 William, 115
DAZEY, John, 221
 Moses, 221, 222
 Thomas, 221
DEAL, Peter, 160
 Thomas, 222
DEAN, Jemima, 198
 Jesse, 137, 197, 198
 John, 102, 103
 John W., 103, 104, 118, 120, 125, 166, 167, 168, 170, 222
 John Wilson, 39, 75, 81
 Joshua, 79
 Wilson, 28
DEATH BED, 108
DEATH BED TRACT, 110
DEEP BRANCH, 194
DEEP CREEK, 11, 12, 124, 125, 132, 135

DEEP CREEK FORREST, 139
DEEP CREEK HUNDRED, 120
DEEP VALLEY, 96, 203
DEER POND, 177
DELANY, William, 7
DELLANEY, William, 94, 150
DENNIS, J., 162, 174
 Jane, 36
 Robert, 174
DENWOOD, Arthur, 211
 Rebecca, 211
DEPRAY, John, 24
DEPREY, Andrew, 4
 John, 4, 97
 Mary, 97
DEPUTY, Betsy, 176
 Nunez, 176
 Silvester, 176
 Solomon, 176
 William, 176
DERRICKSON, Levin, 217
DERVAL, William, 121
DESERT, 150
DESIRE, 144
DEVILS WOOD YARD, 67
DEWESE, Elizabeth, 52
DEWESSE,
 Cornelius, 52
 Elizabeth, 52
DEWSON, Jacob, 9
DIBETY, Silvester, 167
DICHERS HILL, 36
DICKERSON,
 Catharine, 151
 Catherine, 151
 Edmond, 101, 207, 208
 Elisha, 186, 204
 John, 41
 Peter, 151
 Sumerset, 159
 Summerset, 201
DICKINSON, Edmond,

94
DICKINSON'S BEVERY, 198
DICKOSON, Edmund, 93
 Jonathan, 59
 Mary, 93
DICKSON, Edmon, 13
 John, 58
 Jonathan, 59
DICKSON BEVEY, 58
DINGE, Daniel, 113
 Obediah, 6
DINGEE, Charles, 4
 Dan., 186, 206
 Daniel, 106, 218, 221
DINGLE, Edward, 187, 189, 194
DINGLE GARDEN, 187
DIRICKSON, Joseph, 156, 217
 Levin, 158, 188, 199, 215
 Samuel, 118
DIRIKSON, Levin, 194
DIRRICKSON,
 Benjamin, 173
 George, 168, 170
 Joseph, 118, 200
 Levi, 192
 Levin, 118, 170, 177, 187, 188, 191, 198, 215, 216
 Sarah, 187, 188
DIRRIKSON, Levin, 190
DITCHERS HALL, 25
DITCHERS HILL, 19
DIXON, John, 98
DOBBS County, North Carolina, 22
DOBSON, Ann, 137, 198
 Elinor, 153, 186
 Isabella, 198
 Isable, 137
 Jane, 186
 Rachel, 186
 Richard, 38, 64, 137, 186, 198,

212
Sarah, 198
DOBSON'S MARSH, 63
DOD, Thomas, 110
DODD, Aaron, 148,
  161, 168, 169,
  204
  Agness, 168
  Elizabeth, 196
  Hannah, 204, 206
  Joseph, 159,
    168, 169
  Manuel, 168, 169
  Manuel
    (Manlove), 168
  Meriam, 168
  Moses, 159, 161,
    168
  Samuel, 85, 160,
    178
  Sarah, 159
  Solomon, 71, 99
  Thomas, 99
  William, 196
DODDS BRANCH, 26
DOE BRIDGE, 17,
  179
DOLBE, Jonathan,
  120
DONAVAN, Foster,
  15, 38, 64, 212
DONE, Robert, 37,
  38
DONELY, Casiah,
  119
  Jemima, 119
  Kezia, 119
  Mapp, 119
  Mary, 119
  William, 119
DONOAHO, Thomas,
  102
DORCHESTER County,
  Maryland, 11,
  12, 31, 46, 68,
  104, 121, 122,
  125, 132, 141,
  148, 149, 161,
  164, 178, 218,
  219, 225
DORMAN, John S.,
  199
  John Sheldon, 88
  Mary, 88

DORMON, John
  Sheldon, 66,
  87, 145, 146,
  151, 219
  Mary, 66, 87,
  146
DORSET
  (DORCHESTER)
  County,
  Maryland, 11,
  12, 46
DOSSET
  (DORCHESTER)
  County,
  Maryland, 31
DOUBLE BRANCH, 207
DOUBLE CREEK
  BRANCH, 203
DOUBLE FORK
  BRANCH, 122,
  168, 182
DOUBLE PURCHASE,
  135, 149, 207,
  219
DOUGHOTY, James,
  154
DOUGLASS, William,
  144
DOVER, Kent
  County,
  Delaware, 61,
  88, 179
DOWNAM, Jonathan,
  99
DRAIN, Elizabeth,
  34
  John, 34, 153
  Russel, 191
DRAKES NECK, 13,
  90, 105, 172
DRANES GREEN, 16
DRAPER, Alexander,
  3, 47, 55, 63,
  71, 81, 87, 89,
  106, 114, 144,
  162, 163
  Avery, 21, 49,
  78, 89, 98, 130
  Charles, 6, 9,
  29, 45, 55, 71,
  73, 76, 78, 81,
  144, 166, 167,
  168, 170, 207
  Esther, 144

  Henry, 21, 27,
  30, 43, 52, 81,
  89, 114, 130,
  132
  Isaac, 15, 16,
  19, 30, 58, 59,
  85, 89, 114,
  199
  James, 99, 100
  John, 27, 31,
  46, 55, 72, 88,
  114, 119, 162,
  163
  Joseph, 55, 111,
  144
  Mary, 198
  Nehemiah, 63, 99
  Rachel, 106
  Samuel, 115,
  162, 163
  Sarah, 63
  Thomas, 28
  William, 55, 78,
  81, 149, 153,
  196
DRAPER'S INLET,
  207
DRAPER'S MILL, 27
DRAPERS QUARTER,
  144
DRAPERS SAWMILL,
  125
DRAWBRIDGE, 4, 38,
  66, 75, 97,
  109, 113, 145,
  180
DRISKELL, William,
  157
DUBLIN, IRELAND,
  City of, 19,
  26, 61
DUCK CREEK, 77
DUCK CREEK
  HUNDRED, 39
DULAVAN, Foster,
  40
  William, 143
DUMFRIES, 165, 166
DUMPHRIZE, 187
DUNKIN, Mathew,
  122
  Thomas, 122
DUNNAVAN, John,
  143

Mary, 143
Timothy, 143
DUNNS IMPROVEMENT, 198
DUNN'S OLD FIELD, 198
DURHAM, Richard, 59
DUTCHMAN'S BRANCH, 37, 110
DUTTON, John, 137
  Thomas, 137, 151
DYER, James, 105
  Major William, 105
  William, 91, 221
DYOR, Major William, 105

-E-
EARL, Joseph, 39
EARLE, Joseph, 13
EATON, Robert, 201
EAVAN, Thomas, 9
EAVANS, Edward, 61
  Rebecca, 61
  Thomas, 39, 45
ECCLESTON,
  Elizabeth, 134
  Hugh, 134
EDWARDS, Morris, 197
  Samuel, 60, 89, 124
  Simon, 60, 183
ELBOW SWAMP, 222
ELBS SWAMP, 221
ELDER BRANCH, 196
ELDREDGE, Joseph, 226
ELDRIDGE, Joseph, 45, 157, 191
  Mary, 157, 226
  Obadiah, 226
  Obediah, 157
ELLEGOOD, John, 38
  Thomas, 38
  William, 142, 152
ELLETT, Elisha, 152
ELLIS, George, 19
  William, 19
ELON ROADS, 4

EMMET, William, 132
EMOTS BRANCH, 64
ENGLAND, Mary, 25
ENGLISH, Joseph, 9, 128
  Robert, 32
ENNALLS, William, 135
ENNALS, Joseph, 134
  Mary, 134
ENNALS BRANCH, 106
ENNELS, Henry, 141
ENNES, William
  Brittingham, 163
ENNIS, John, 50, 113, 163
  Levin, 67
  William B., 163
  William Brittingham, 62, 65, 67, 149
EVANS, Caleb, 156
  Edward, 20, 61, 62, 88, 115, 134
  Eli, 214
  Elisha, 214
  Elizabeth, 166
  John, 28, 39, 57, 160, 214
  Joseph, 214
  Rebecca, 20, 88
  Rebeckah, 62, 88, 115
  Riley, 174
  Solomon, 221
  Thomas, 28, 132, 150, 158, 166, 172, 196, 222
  William, 160, 205, 214
  William Riley, 161
EVANS' MILL, 181
EVANS' SAW MILL, 67, 106
EVANSES LINE, 214
EVEANS, John, 28
  Thomas, 28
EVENS, John, 28
EVERSON,

Garthwright, 130

-F-
FAIRFIELD, CT, 202
FANCEY, Jacobs, 182
FARMERS DELIGHT, 88
FARNAL, Thomas, 132
FASSET, John, 14
FASSETT, Elijah, 166
  James, 177
FASSIT, Elizabeth, 95
  John, 14
  Smith, 35
  William, 95
FAX HALL, 147
FEDDEMAN, Joseph, 38
FENWICK, James, 32
  Mary, 32
  Thomas, 32
  William, 32
FIDDEMAN, Joseph, 40
FIELD, Henry, 216
  John, 16, 215, 216
  Mary, 68, 215, 216
  Mills, 31
  Nehemiah, 1, 68, 73, 74, 77, 83, 190, 215, 216
  Susannah, 215, 216
FIELDS, John, 215
FINCH, John, 47, 101, 175
FINCH HALL, 47, 101
FINIA'S ISLAND, 194
FINNYS LOTT, 183
FINWICK, William, 78
FINWICKS BRANCH, 203
FINWICK'S STREET, 99
FIRMAN, David, 85

INDEX

Richard, 132
FIRST CHOICE, 163
FIRST STREET, 10, 51
FISHER, Alice, 220
  Edward, 220, 221
  Elias, 26, 207
  Finex, 221
  Finwick, 220
  Hannah, 51, 59, 97
  Henry, 1, 30, 37, 38, 41, 49, 51, 53, 56, 83, 215, 216, 225
  Jabez, 157, 226
  James, 51, 67, 75, 94, 97, 98, 100, 101, 113, 146, 220
  John, 8, 48, 98, 100, 129, 141, 154, 167, 173, 213
  Joshua, 2, 10, 25, 60, 62, 77, 88, 101, 115, 119, 126, 154
  Margret, 51
  Mary, 221
  Miers, 2, 20, 62, 70, 77, 88
  Samuel, 129
  Sarah, 129, 154
  Stephen, 178
  Thomas, 2, 5, 44, 63, 68, 100, 101, 119, 129, 146, 154
  William, 27, 52, 53, 55, 97, 98, 114, 151, 154, 170, 190, 205
FISHERS GUTT, 14
FISHING BRANCH, 116
FISHING CREEK, 134
FITCHET, William, 210
FITSJARREL, Elizabeth, 177
FITZJARRAL, George, 200
FIVE KNATCH'D SURVEY, 86
FLEETWOOD, John, 127, 135, 209
  Nehemiah, 127
FLEMING, Ann, 133
  John, 159, 184
  Margaret, 43, 85, 170
  Margret, 86
  Robert, 43, 85, 86, 170
FLING, Daniel, 53, 55, 190
FLOWER, John, 164
FLOWERS, John, 164
FOLLEY, Stone, 71
FORGESON, Charles, 69
  Mary, 69
  Rosanna, 69
  Sarah, 69
  Violinda, 69
FORK GUT, 220
FORK LANDING, 182, 183
FORK ROADS, 84
FORKED POPLAR, 31, 163
FORMAN, David, 14, 176
  Joseph, 176
FORREST, Loyds, 168
FORTEN, 162
FOSSET, John, 53
FOSTER, Arthur, 30
  Shepard, 150
  William, 26
FOUNTAIN, Andrew, 218
  Major, 142
  Samuel, 142, 218
FOWLAR, Arthur, 35
  John, 35
FOWLER, Arther, 35
  Arthur, 20, 117, 170, 171
  Jessee, 170, 171
  John, 15, 99, 164
  Jonathan, 35
  William, 6, 164
FOWLERS, John, 35
FOWLERS ADVENTURE, 170
FOWLERS CHANCE, 170
FOWLER'S FANCEY, 171
FOWLERS FANCY, 170
FRAME, Elizabeth, 121
  George, 17, 34, 76, 84, 96, 115, 151, 161, 179, 216
  Nathan, 17, 34, 109, 121
  Robert, 17, 34, 109, 179
  Smith, 34, 36, 109, 124, 179
  William, 121, 129, 206
FRAME'S SAWMILL, 49
FRANKLAND, Walter, 11
FRANKLIN, Samuel, 11
  Walter, 11
FREELAND, Isaac, 182
FREELANDS ADVENTURE, 183
FREENY, Ann, 212
FRIENDS ASSISTANCE, 180
FRIENDS DISCOVERY, 174
FRIENDSHIP, 168
FRIENDSHIP ADDITION, 170
FRIENDSHIP'S ADDITION, 178, 198
FRONT STREET, 215
FRUITFUL PLAIN, 140
FULLERTON, 16
  Andrew, 16, 57, 174
FURLONG, Edward, 115, 144
  Nehemiah, 144
FURLONGS, 85
FURMAN, David, 85
FUSHAM, James, 174

Maron, 174
FUTCHER, John, 9, 19, 102, 116
William, 19

-G-
GALE, Levi, 141
  Levin, 211
GANDRON, Gabriel, 57, 217
  Mark, 57, 217
GARDEN, Mark, 57
GASKINS, William, 152
GAULT, Angelita, 28
  John, 28
  John Turvel, 28
GAWDY, Ann, 128
  Moses, 128
GAWDY'S DELIGHT, 128
GEORGE DODD'S PLANTATION, 66
GETTERS RUN, 40
GILBERT NECK, 82
GILL, Elizabeth, 98
  Robert, 32, 98, 115
  William, 14, 47, 60, 155
GITTERS BRANCH, 143
GITTIA RUN, 49
GIVAN, Day, 201
GIVANS, Day, 205
GIVANS HIS DISCOVERY, 205
GIVENS' DISCOVERY, 192
GLADES, THE, 65
GLADSTOWER, 149
GLOVER, Rebeka, 219
GODDARD, Elizabeth, 128
GODWARD, Elizabeth, 98
GODWIN, Elizabeth, 84
  Joseph, 193, 194, 224, 225
  Mary Ann, 225

Michael, 65, 83, 112
Naomi, 65, 112
Neomie, 62
Sarah, 226
Thomas, 191
William, 45, 65, 139, 164
GOFORTH, Zachariah, 5
GOLDEN GROVE, 61
GOLDEN QUARTER, 105
GOLDS SMITH HALL, 56
GOLDSMITH, Jemima, 56
  Thomas, 56
  William, 56
GOLDSMITH'S LAND, 56
GOOD LUCK, 9
GOOD LUCK AT LAST, 129, 136
GOOD NEIGHBORHOOD, 132
GOOD NEIGHBOURHOOD, 150
GOODSON, John, 25
GOOTEE, Bridget, 210
  John, 210
GORDAN, James, 137
GORDAY, Moses, 128
GORDEN, James, 7, 17, 89, 93
  Nathaniel, 89, 90, 114
  Thomas, 89
GORDON, James, 7, 29, 138, 181, 219
  John, 7
  Mary, 90
  Nathaniel, 9
  Thomas, 90, 138, 155, 219
GORDON'S MILL, 7
GORDY, Moses, 128
GORHANS ADDITION, 169
GOSHAMS ADDITION, 224
GOSHAN, 206

GOSHAN'S ADDITION, 206
GOSLEN, Wateman, 143
GOSSLING, 180
GOYLE, Mary, 10
  Peter, 10
GRACE, Solomon, 173
GRATTIN, Joseph, 113
GRAVELLY BRANCH, 12, 35, 61, 177, 186
GRAVELLY LANDING, 9
GRAVELY BRANCH, 212
GRAY, David, 34, 48, 74, 93, 104, 105, 113, 220
  Hezekiah, 218
  James, 120, 161
  Jean, 220
  Jessee, 162
  John, 66
  Joseph, 162
  Samuel, 105, 187, 220
  Sarah, 89, 218
  Sophia, 52, 137
  Thomas, 11, 17, 22, 26, 45, 52, 64, 83, 114, 123, 125, 136, 137, 138, 144, 149, 179, 216, 218
  William, 179
GRAY'S ADVENTURE, 179
GRAYS INN, 187
GRAYS SHINGLE ROAD, 157
GREAT BRANCH, 43, 114
GREAT NECK, 15, 34, 79, 84, 89, 117, 121, 140, 141
GREAT SURVEY, 177
GREEN, Ambros, 204
  Amrose, 128

INDEX

David, 31, 105
Elenor, 204
Ezekiel, 47,
  110, 138
George, 94
John, 128, 204
Marth, 113
Martha, 204
Naomi, 128, 204
Nelley, 128
Patty, 128
Prettyman, 8
Richard, 121,
  128, 188, 204
Samuel Johnson,
  92
Stephen, 8, 18,
  22, 113, 128,
  130, 204, 217
William, 204
GREEN BRANCH, 39,
  59, 67, 106,
  117, 181
GREEN DRAINS, 19
GREEN DRANES, 15,
  59
GREEN POND, 122,
  182
GREENALL, Robert,
  55
GREENFIELD, 136
GREENWAY, Robert,
  24
  Sarah, 24
GREW (GRUE),
  Thomas, 198
GRICE, Thomas, 53,
  179
  William, 217
GRIFFIN, Jerom,
  119
GRIFFITH, John,
  205
  Joseph, 64, 104
  Salathiel, 151
GROOM, John, 189
GROOME, John, 187
GROOMS FIRST
  PURCHASE, 187
GROVE, Samuel, 12,
  13, 141
  Susanna, 12, 141
  Thomas, 12, 13,
  30, 32, 82, 89,
  90, 99, 105,
  130, 133, 141,
  145, 167
GROVES, Thomas,
  28, 106, 126
GRUBBY BRANCH, 43
GRUBBY NECK, 135,
  152
GRUBBY NECK
  BRANCH, 152,
  166
GRUBBY PLAIN, 80
GRUMBLES, Nellay,
  156
GULLET, George,
  143
  Mary, 143
GUM, Jacob, 138,
  167
  Roger, 199
GUM BRANCH, 28,
  69, 157
GUMB SWAMP, 179
GUMLY, John, 98
GUNBY, James, 139
GUTT, Joyce, 42

-H-

HACKET, Ann, 222
HAIRFIELDS BRANCH,
  179
HALBERT, Sarah,
  110
HALL, Adam, 169
  Asa, 167
  Asey, 167
  Comfort, 192
  David, 6, 7, 8,
  10, 13, 22, 33,
  37, 44, 47, 59,
  68, 75, 99,
  100, 101, 104,
  108, 111, 118,
  127, 138, 140,
  191, 195, 209,
  212
  Elizabeth, 192
  Hannah, 30
  Hugh, 109, 119,
  199
  J., 152
  James, 15, 67,
  109, 121, 199,
  201
  Jenney, 44
  John, 1, 29, 41,
  71, 94, 95,
  184, 199
  Jordan, 165
  Joseph, 8, 45,
  75, 108, 133,
  153, 159, 161,
  180, 183, 184,
  202, 205, 209,
  217, 221, 226
  Joshua, 98, 170,
  185, 192
  Mary, 111
  Peter, 8, 56
  Sidah, 163
  Sophia, 167
  Thomas, 14, 18,
  114
  William, 114,
  129, 160, 169,
  170, 173, 179,
  184, 192
  William Jordan,
  178, 187
  William Jurdan,
  194, 198
  William Jurdon,
  165, 193
HALLY, D., 208
HAMBLETON, John,
  107
HAMILTON, James,
  113
HAMMILTON, John,
  126
HAMMOND, Bowden,
  140
  Jonathan, 79
  Mary, 77
HAMMONS, Jonathan,
  93
  Mary, 93
  Thomas, 67
HAMPSHIRE CO, 16
HAMPSHIRE,
  Massachussetts
  Bay, 57
HAND, John, 42,
  222
  Samuel, 47, 48,
  90, 91, 132,

156, 161, 162,
207, 208
Thomas, 207
William, 134
HANDCOCK,
Mycakiah, 104
HANDSWORTH,
Nancey, 155
HANDY, Benjamin,
41
George, 136
HANDZER, Thomas,
76
William, 76
HANSER, Aminadab,
142
HANZER, Aminadab,
93
Amindat, 53
Arrunadab, 76
HAPHOOTS FORTUNE,
167
HAPP ENTRANCE, 200
HARDEY, Thomas,
44, 53
HARDUM, Thomas,
123
HARDY, James, 202
HAREFIELD BRANCH,
82, 95
HARMON, Henry,
108, 113
HARMONSON, Harmon,
201
John, 8, 17, 64,
105, 167
William, 186,
206
HARNEY, John, 156
HARPER, Henry, 112
James, 27, 47
HARPER'S BRANCH,
193, 194
HARRIS, Abraham,
15, 66, 94
James, 225
Mary, 94
HARRISON, John, 33
HARRISS, Charles,
94
Mary, 94
HARRISSON, Thomas,
153
HART, Absalom, 1

John, 109
Richard, 113
Robert, 11, 38,
50, 57, 62, 63,
77, 79, 80, 89,
96, 196, 200,
217, 218
HARTS CHOICE, 38
HARTS TRACT, 101,
28
HASHOLD, George,
16, 57
HASHOLD'S FORTUNE,
16, 57, 95
HASTINGS, John,
160
HATFIELD, Elijah,
121, 122
Whitelay
(Wheatly), 143
Whitely, 143
HAVELO, Frances,
56
James, 56
HAWKES NEXT, 74
HAWKS NEST GUTT,
2, 3
HAWS ISLAND, 114
HAY, Richard, 136
HAYNES, Charles,
116
John, 126
HAYS, Nathan, 108
Richard, 18, 68
Thomas, 203
Unicy, 68
HAYS TAVERN, 182
HAYSES, Thomas,
214
HAZARD, William,
118
HAZZARD, Arther,
123, 130
Arthur, 30, 42,
127, 130
Cord, 1, 37,
110, 112, 123,
220
David, 111, 112,
137
Elihu, 153
George, 212, 221
Hap, 20, 43, 82,
89, 91, 101,

103, 108, 109,
113, 136, 178,
220
Jacob, 28, 51,
63, 89, 94,
100, 153, 167,
169, 220
John, 29, 66,
92, 126, 131,
221
Joseph, 2, 37,
135, 167, 220,
221
Mary, 2, 220
Sally, 137
Sarah, 166, 199
Uriah, 160, 165,
166, 199, 218,
219
William, 10, 21,
25, 35, 38, 39,
44, 50, 57, 61,
62, 63, 64, 68,
72, 79, 80, 88,
96, 104, 108,
121, 198, 200,
206, 212, 217,
218, 221
HAZZARD'S LAND,
145
HEARN, Clem, 224
George, 206, 224
Lowder, 224
Samuel, 224
HEARNE, Comfort,
12
George, 12
Luther, 224
HEART, Robert, 67
HEAVELO, Andrew,
38, 63, 64
Anthony, 172
Hannah, 19
James, 172
John, 8, 12, 13,
94, 160
Jonathan, 172
Luke, 115
Margaret, 172
Sarah, 172
William, 172
HEAVELOE, James,
153
HEAVERLO, Andrew,

106
Hannah, 8
James, 156
John, 7
Luke, 186
Samuel, 135,
    159, 199
HELLINGS, Jacob,
    11
    Mary, 11, 85, 86
HEMMONS, James,
    22, 80
    John, 14, 95,
    108
    Jonathan, 121
    Sealea (Celia),
    121
    Thomas, 121
HEMOND, Thomas, 84
HENDERSON, Alice,
    6, 7
    John, 6
HENMON, Richard, 4
HENRY, Isaac, 136,
    169, 211, 219
    James, 185
    Jonathan, 104
    William, 18, 95
HERN, Samuel, 224
HERNE, George, 224
HERRING BRANCH,
    41, 62, 142,
    218
HERRING CREEK, 105
HERRING RUN, 142
HERRON CREEK, 200
HEVELO, Samuel,
    82, 120
HEVERLO, Hannah,
    71
    John, 7, 71
    Samuel, 97
HICKMAN, Ann, 219
    Elizabeth, 111
    Jacob, 102
    James, 148, 200
    John, 79, 111,
    114, 115, 214
    Joseph, 101,
    102, 197, 207,
    224
    Joshua, 148, 207
    Levi, 148
    Levin, 147, 218

Nathaniel, 108,
    112
Nehemiah, 218
Phebe, 112
Sarah, 111
Selby, 156, 181,
    219
Silby, 219
Thomas, 122,
    128, 147, 148,
    200
William, 79,
    111, 167
HICKMAN'S
    CONCLUSION,
    200, 201
HICKMAN'S FIELDS,
    102
HICKORY RIDGE, 139
HIGGENS, Philip,
    15
HIGGNOTT, Thomas,
    173
HILL, Absolom, 12
    Ann, 204, 205
    Betty, 186
    Brittingham, 112
    Comfort, 30, 42
    Elizabeth, 65,
    186, 204
    George, 44, 49
    John, 12, 30,
    40, 42, 135,
    146, 147, 205
    Joshua, 113,
    135, 150, 163,
    168, 170, 174,
    177, 194, 198
    Margaret, 42
    Margret, 30, 42
    Richard, 80
    Robert, 30, 42,
    103, 130
    Solomon, 186,
    199, 206
    William, 103
HILL BRANCH, 58
HILLS BRANCH, 106
HILLS CONTENT, 44
HILYARD, Rachel,
    70
HINDES NECK, 104
HINDS, 89
    Barbaray, 89

Sarah, 89
Thomas, 11, 21,
    50, 79, 89, 162
HITCHCOCK,
    Eleaner, 199
    Elenor, 166
    John, 115
HODGE, Margaret,
    221
HODGES LINE, 102
HODGSON, Gamage
    Evans, 222
    Gammage Evans,
    189, 190, 221
HODSON, ---, 214
    Jacob, 158, 214
    Miriam, 203
    Robert, 158
HOFF, Rachel, 70
    Richard, 70
HOG ISLAND, 111
HOG RANGE, 125
HOGG QUARTER, 157
HOGG RANGE, 142
HOGGS QUARTER, 139
HOLCAGER, Ephraim,
    6
HOLLAND, Hannah,
    104
    Isaac, 150
    Israel, 137
    James, 33, 104,
    116, 225
    Margaret, 116
    Sarah, 116
    William, 84,
    113, 150, 151,
    154, 190
HOLLAWAY, John,
    45, 57
HOLLEAGER,
    Ephraim, 9
HOLLOWAY, John,
    45, 49, 180
HOLMES, Ann, 224
    John, 14, 149,
    153, 194, 224
    Robert, 184
HOLMS, Ann, 197
    John, 64, 197
HOLM'S DISPATCH,
    194
HOLT, Catharine,
    41

Richard, 14
Rives, 25, 41, 50
Ryves, 42, 152, 213
HOMES, John, 31, 78
Robert, 178
Thomas, 29
HONEY COMB TRACT, 20
HOOD, James, 5, 37, 153
Mary, 37, 153, 194, 195
Robert, 11, 37, 153, 194, 195
HOOKS NORTON, 102
HOOPER, Henry, 152, 202, 221
John, 152
Thomas, 202
HOOPERS FORREST, 202
HOPKINS,
Archabald, 213
Archibald, 213
Daniel, 34, 46
Ezekiel, 160
John, 5, 129, 154, 199, 210, 211
Josiah, 160
Prudence, 213
Richard, 34
Samuel, 16, 34, 57, 95
Sarah, 160
Sophia, 211
William, 211
HOPKINS DISCOVERY, 160
HORNEY, Nathaniel, 194
HORSE HEAD, 123
HORSE POND BRANCH, 122
HORSE POUND, 117
HORSE POUND TRACT, 35
HORSEY, Isaac, 113, 128, 132, 176
William, 176, 192

HOSEA, Arthur, 223
HOSMAN, Comfort, 99
Daniel, 98
Elizabeth, 98, 99
Jane, 99
Joseph, 26, 98, 99, 103
Stockley, 98, 99
HOSSMAN, Daniel, 175
Elizabeth, 175
HOUNDS HATCH, 131
HOUNS DITCH, 222
HOUSTON, James, 158
John, 157, 158, 176
Joseph, 12, 175, 187
Leonard, 158
Micajah, 103, 116
Robert, 158, 172, 175, 176, 189, 202, 205
HOW, John, 26, 36
HOWARD, Joseph, 204
Knight, 220
Richard, 204, 208, 209, 219
HOWARDS CHOICE, 180
HUBBERT, Anatasia, 158
Catharine, 158
Edward, 158
Jeremiah, 158
Joseph, 158
Kezia, 158
Michael, 158
Peter, 158, 187
Sarah, 158
Thomas, 158
HUCKLEBERRY SWAMP, 76, 77
HUCKLEBURY SWAMP, 73
HUDSON, Absolam, 204, 206
Ananias, 68, 69
Ann, 204

Annanias, 18
Benjamin, 166, 167, 176
Betsy, 176
Hannah, 204
Henry, 68, 69
Jaquish, 214
John, 68, 69, 119, 166, 167, 176, 217
Joshua, 68, 69
Major, 68, 72
Miles, 162
Polly, 176
Rhoda, 204, 206
Richard, 176
Robert, 10, 196, 200, 203
Samuel, 130, 131, 204, 213
Thomas, 155
Walter, 204, 205, 206
William, 68, 69, 70, 72, 166, 176
HUDSONS ADDITION, 173
HUFFINGTON, Luke, 193
HUGG, Elias, 17, 27, 34, 37, 44, 91
Jean, 222
HUGGENS, Philip, 15
HUGH, Elias, 48
HUMPHRIES, Thomas, 62
HUNT, Hugh, 203
HURLEY, Edmond, 117
HURST, James, 12
HUTSON, Absolam, 186

-I-
INDIAN ASSAWAMON CREEK, 161
INDIAN CREEK, 165
INDIAN LAND, 215
INDIAN RIVER, 7, 16, 17, 21, 26, 29, 31, 45, 49,

86, 95, 108,
110, 118, 133,
140, 173, 174,
177, 183, 188,
189, 196, 204,
210
INDIAN RIVER
FORREST, 82
INDIAN RIVER
HUNDRED, 1, 2,
4, 5, 9, 10,
13, 14, 17, 20,
27, 29, 32, 36,
37, 42, 44, 45,
46, 48, 53, 54,
55, 64, 75, 76,
83, 85, 86, 87,
91, 92, 95,
100, 102, 103,
105, 108, 111,
112, 114, 115,
123, 124, 125,
127, 131, 134,
142, 149, 160,
161, 171, 172,
174, 175, 179,
180, 184, 186,
191, 194, 195,
196, 199, 200,
204, 206, 217,
223
INDIAN RIVER ROAD,
26, 212
INDIAN TOWN
BRANCH, 189
INDIAN TOWN CREEK,
190
INGLISH, Ann, 63
INGRAM, Abraham,
177, 186
Ann, 112
Isaac, 176, 177
Issac, 69
Jacob, 176
James, 86
Job, 21, 113,
121, 176
John, 20, 48,
50, 94, 106, 223
Joshua, 194, 195
Margaret, 194,
195
Thomas, 112
INGRAM (INGRAHAM),
John, 223
INKLEY, Elnathan,
107
INKLY, Anna, 107
Mary, 107
Sarah, 107
IRELAND, 12, 19,
36, 61
IRON VALLEY, 28,
38
IRONS, Aaron, 68,
100, 191
Jacob, 191
Jane, 31, 68
IVEY BRANCH, 76,
160
IVEY ISLAND, 23
IVY BRANCH, 53,
200

-J-
JACK, French, 44
JACKSON, Ezekiel,
67, 85, 114
Julius Augustus,
194
Mitchel, 86
Rust, 194
JACOBS, Albert,
92, 161
Albertus, 155,
156, 208, 209
Alburtus, 95,
116, 161
Alertus, 161
Arbertus, 162
Benjamin, 25, 36
Constantine, 149
Curtis, 207
Elizabeth, 209
Hannah, 27, 155
James, 209
John, 27, 155,
208, 209
Jonathan, 56,
224
Joseph, 19, 26,
36
Martha, 155
Mary, 27
Mrs., 161
Nathaniel, 14,
18, 76, 92, 209
Nottingham, 56
Patience, 14,
18, 76
Richard, 56
Sarah, 56, 95,
209
William, 209
JEFFERS, Ann, 58
William, 58
JEFFERSON,
Richard, 110,
173
JEFFERY, William,
149
JENKENS, Comfort,
6
JENKINS, Comfort,
50
JERSEY TRACT, 82
JESSEP, Elenor, 178
John, 148, 149,
166, 178
JESSOP, Elenor,
147
Eloner, 125
James, 125
John, 125
JESSUP, James, 142
John, 147
JEWET, William,
152
JEWETT, William,
142
JOANS, Thomas, 55
JOHN MAY'S
PASTURE, 56
JOHNS BRANCH, 30,
35
JOHNS FOLLY, 203
JOHNS NECK, 169
JOHNSON, Agness,
107
Arthur, 107, 126
Baker, 11, 43,
178
Benjamin, 47,
93, 102, 114,
162, 213, 214
Betty, 202
Burton, 224
Cornelius, 133
David, 154
Elias, 181
Francis, 206
Hannah, 154, 178

Isaiah, 47
James, 133, 202
John, 41, 86, 87
Joseph, 154
Leonard, 197
Margret, 11
Mary, 197
Peggy, 202
Purnal, 1, 8,
    48, 54, 61, 62,
    84, 95, 164
Robert, 222
Rulany, 202
Samuel, 29, 36,
    111, 179
Sarah, 48
Simon, 181
Sneed, 120
Terese, 202
Thomas, 188
William, 29, 82,
    108, 110, 120,
    188
JOHNSTON, Francis,
    159
John, 153
Milby, 216, 217
Samuel, 226
JONES, Ann, 1
Anne, 1
Burrel, 138
Ebenezar, 177
Edward, 168
Ezekiel, 38
Griffin, 196
Griffith, 36, 69
Isaac, 2, 36,
    82, 92, 112,
    177
James, 204
John, 1, 15, 19,
    55, 86, 92, 107
Joshua, 204
Mary, 112
Naomi, 153
Robert, 8, 42,
    93, 114, 138,
    143, 150, 159,
    181, 219
Samuel, 180
Thomas, 55, 118,
    153
William, 75, 76,
    83

JONES'S ADVENTURE,
    33, 121
JOSEPH, Jeremiah,
    91, 92
JOUNS, James, 3
    Susanna, 3
JOYCE, Samuel, 42
JOYND MEADOW, 135
JOYNE, Ezekiel, 40
JOYNES, Ezekiel,
    38
JOYNS, Ezekiel,
    40, 63, 64
JUMP, Jemima, 92
    John Bound, 92
    Oliver, 225
    Samuel, 82
    Sarah, 225
JUSTICE, James,
    116

-K-
KANNING, William,
    27, 175
KEARY, Pherabah,
    104
KELLET, William,
    26
KEMP, Samuel, 191
KENDRICK, James,
    102
KENEYS BRANCH, 9
KENMAN, John, 138
KENNEY'S BRANCH,
    43, 110
KENNING, William,
    146
KENNY'S BRANCH,
    114
KENNY'S SAVANNA,
    65
KENNY'S SAVANNAH,
    139
KENT County,
    Delaware, 5, 8,
    9, 11, 18, 20,
    21, 22, 24, 39,
    52, 57, 62, 70,
    77, 80, 88,
    106, 114, 118,
    196, 199
KENT SHORE, 23
KICK IN, 155
KICK OUT, 155

KICKIN, 162
KICKINN, 155
KILIAMS TRACT, 71
KILKANNY, 218
KILLAMB, Elijah,
    71
    Jane, 71
KILLEM, Elijah, 71
KILLEN, Henry, 22
    Mark, 61
    William, 224
KILLIN, 19
    Henry, 80
KILLING, Henry, 80
KILLINGSWORTH,
    Esther, 117
    John, 74
    Joseph, 117
KILLINGWORTH,
    John, 73
KILLO, Isaac, 101,
    102, 158
    Sarah, 158
KILLON, Joshua,
    198
KIMBALL'S NECK,
    118
KINDRED, Crate,
    182
    Jacob, 163, 182
KING, Ann, 220
    Caldwell, 157
    Elias, 37
    Henry, 156, 219
    Hugh, 65, 130,
    131
    James, 130, 131
    John, 19, 130
    William, 130,
    131
KING STREET, 45
KINGS CREEK, 19
KINGS ROAD, 44,
    54, 66, 108,
    135, 143
KINNEY, Isaac,
    211, 212
    Joseph, 150
    William, 150
KINNEY'S CHANCE,
    150
KINNING, William,
    27
KINNY, Lazarus,

INDEX

183
KIPHAVEN, John, 5,
  209
  William, 7
KIPSHAVEN, John,
  155
KIRK, John, 48,
  54, 220
KIRKPATRICK, John,
  192
  William, 192
KNE GUM, 110
KNEE GUM, 53
KNIGHT, George, 34
KNIGHT HOWARD, 106
KNOCK, Comfort,
  101
  Elisha, 31, 78
  Joseph, 132, 133
  Margaret, 78
  Solomon, 16, 31,
  101
KNOTT, Ann, 156
KOLLOCK, Comfort,
  93, 101
  Cornelius, 118,
  216
  George, 6, 7,
  22, 59, 86, 105
  Herculas, 204,
  215
  Hercules, 4, 5,
  7, 203
  Herculous, 22,
  66
  Hester, 30, 68
  Jacob, 1, 3, 5,
  6, 8, 17, 22,
  29, 33, 41, 47,
  50, 51, 52, 53,
  60, 61, 66, 68,
  74, 91, 96, 97,
  104, 113, 115,
  118, 143, 147,
  149, 161, 186,
  190, 205, 216
  Margaret, 101,
  143, 161, 215,
  216
  Margret, 68, 96,
  97, 115
  Mary, 5, 14, 18,
  22, 59, 65, 68,
  143

Penelope, 165,
  215
Philips, 13, 47,
  55, 66, 68, 83,
  93, 94, 101
Phillips, 76,
  136, 164, 165,
  166, 167, 195,
  199, 200, 202,
  203, 205, 218,
  225
Shepard, 5, 6,
  7, 22, 54, 59,
  66
Simon, 3, 4, 6,
  7, 22, 31, 53,
  54, 55, 60,
  129, 177, 208,
  216, 217
William, 178,
  190, 191, 216
KOLLOCK'S MILL,
  190
KOLLOCKS STREET,
  10

-L-
LACEY, Jemima, 7
  John, 92
  Mary, 174
  Robert, 29, 40,
  174
LACY, John, 110
  Parker, 36, 179
  Robert, 36, 179
LAFFERTY, Thomas,
  156
LAMB, Abner, 136
LANDING ROAD, 55,
  152
LANE, John, 121,
  177
  Joseph, 33, 34
LANK, James, 216
  Mitchel, 216
LATON, Alexander,
  43, 127
LAUGHERTY, Thomas,
  89
LAVERTY, Samuel,
  141, 167, 207
  Thomas, 84, 117,
  140, 142
LAW, James, 120

John, 198
LAWS, Alexander,
  30, 35, 171,
  176, 200, 205
  Anne, 176
  Belitha, 182,
  183
  John, 30, 35,
  113, 142, 143,
  169, 170, 171,
  175, 176, 192,
  212, 217, 218,
  224, 225, 226
  Joshua, 183
  Thomas, 145, 148
  William, 35
LAWS POND, 65
LAY, Baptis, 78
  Thomas, 9, 43,
  73, 127, 178
LAYFIELD, George,
  131, 140, 141
  Isaac, 140, 141
  Thomas, 100,
  126, 140, 141
LAYTON, Alexander,
  43
  Robert, 122,
  128, 132
  William, 148
LAYTON'S FANCY,
  200
LEAH, Daniel, 88
LEAK, Daniel, 62
LEATHERBERRY,
  Elizabeth, 42
  Thomas, 42
  William, 42
LEBANON, 2, 111
LEBANUN PATENT,
  111
LEE, Robert, 2,
  80, 140
  Wilson, 10, 11,
  19
LEES FIRST
  PURCHASE, 218
LERREK, John, 220
LERRICK, John, 221
LEWES, Port of, 29
LEWES, Town of, 1,
  3, 4, 5, 6, 10,
  14, 18, 22, 26,

INDEX   249

31, 36, 37, 41,
42, 44, 45, 46,
47, 48, 50, 51,
52, 54, 60, 60,
64, 66, 67, 68,
73, 74, 82, 82,
89, 92, 93, 95,
96, 98, 98, 99,
100, 104, 104,
105, 108, 110,
111, 115, 116,
118, 126, 130,
135, 139, 143,
149, 154, 161,
165, 166, 169,
170, 177, 184,
185, 187, 190,
191, 199, 203,
204, 205, 208,
209, 209, 214,
215, 216, 217,
218, 219, 220,
225, 226
LEWES, Elizabeth,
 35
 Simeon, 35
LEWES CREEK, 8,
 16, 68, 74, 90,
 128, 156, 196,
 209, 215
LEWES HUNDRED, 34
LEWES TOWN BANK,
 208
LEWES TOWN CREEK,
 74
LEWIS, Elizabeth,
 60, 83, 95,
 165, 189, 199,
 208
 Fairn, 109
 John, 4, 50, 66,
 92, 93, 104,
 109, 128, 191
 Mary, 50, 163
 Noble, 60, 82,
 83, 165, 189,
 199, 208
 Thomas, 161, 163
 William, 16, 75
 Wrixam (Wr.,
 Wrx.), 3, 18,
 36, 45, 48, 50,
 51, 83, 97,
 105, 109, 113,

115
LEWIS BRANCH, 12
LEWIS CREEK, 17
LEWIS TOWN, 26
LIBERTY OF THOMAS
 COURT, 26
LIDEN, Shadrach,
 225
LIGHT, Elizabeth,
 40
 John, 40
 Lacey, 40
 Mary, 40
 William, 40
LIGHTFOOT, Thomas,
 11, 12
 William, 11, 12
LINCH, Abraham,
 180
 John, 156, 159
 Reuben, 144
LINDAL, Joseph, 89
 Peter, 110
 Zadock, 140, 222
LINDALL, Joseph,
 15
 Thomas, 15
LINDEL, Joseph,
 117
LINDELL, Peter, 53
LINDLE, Joseph,
 79, 84
LINGO, Bettey, 14
 Elizabeth, 53,
 143
 Elizabeth
 (Betty), 53
 Henry, 143
 John, 14, 53
 Samuel, 91, 217
 William, 109
LINKORN, 142
LINNING, 14
LITTLE, Absolom,
 2, 11, 64, 69,
 92, 120, 126
 Adonijah, 95
 John, 4, 14, 25,
 96, 98, 103,
 180
 Martha, 180
 Nicholas, 187,
 216
 Richard, 4, 46,

74, 93, 111,
 195, 196
 Sarah, 196
 William, 1, 2
LITTLE BOLTON, 64
LITTLE BRANCH, 59,
 203
LITTLE BRIDGE
 BRANCH, 80
LITTLE BRITTEN, 6
LITTLE BROADWATER,
 115
LITTLE BUTTIN, 106
LITTLE BUTTON, 9,
 43
LITTLE CREEK, 12,
 99, 127, 150,
 193, 202
LITTLE CREEK
 HUNDRED, 129,
 157, 192, 202,
 206, 211, 212,
 223, 224
LITTLE PASTURE
 NECK, 47
LLOYD, Edward,
 167, 168
 Elizabeth, 167
LOCKWOOD, John, 4
LODGE, Robert, 105
LOFFLAND, Comfort,
 111
 Dorman, 111
LOFFLEY, John, 15
LOFLAND, ---, 214
 Avis, 87
 Branson, 114
 Branston, 119
 Brantson, 116,
 144, 182
 Brantston, 162
 Danilly, 80
 Dorman, 44, 87,
 100, 112, 127,
 128
 Dormon, 3, 28,
 29, 80, 81,
 111, 118, 166
 Dornon, 11
 Elizabeth, 81
 Gabriel, 81
 Isaac, 87
 John, 53, 73,
 87, 110, 127

Joshua, 167, 203
Littleton, 90
Purnal, 87
Sarah, 87
William, 28, 53, 80, 84, 87, 110
LOFLANDS FORK, 156
LOFLANDS FORK ROAD, 28
LOFLEY, Daniel, 22
  Danielly, 22
  Dormon, 22
  William, 15
LOFTLAND,
  Brantson, 163
  John, 141
  Johnson, 163
LOFTLANDS FORK ROADS, 38
LOFTON, Joseph, 37
LOGAN, Charles, 88
  William, 113
LOGHOUSE BRANCH, 85
LONG, Armwell, 210
  Betty, 210
  Elisha, 206
LONG ACRE, 62, 63, 96, 156, 187, 188, 192, 200
LONG BRANCH, 72, 107
LONG BRANCH BRIDGE, 71
LONG BRIDGE BRANCH, 13, 46, 65, 93, 94, 208
LONG LOTT, 156, 194
LONG LOVE BRANCH, 1, 2, 14, 58, 103
LONG NECK, 5, 29, 42, 45, 48, 49, 55, 57, 94
LONG POINT GUT, 89, 175
LONG SAVANNAH, 140
LOUGHLAND,
  Danielly, 22
  Dormon, 22
  Elizabeth, 11
  Gabriel, 96
  John, 61, 84, 96

Littleton, 91
  Sarah, 84
  Weightman, 87
  William, 58
LOVE, James, 149, 184
LOVE CREEK, 39
LOVE LONG BRANCH, 181
LOVELACE, Francis, 220
LOVE'S BRANCH, 93
LOWBRIDGE BRANCH, 80
LOYD, Thomas, 197
LOYDS FORREST, 225
LUCAS, Peter, 41
  Sarah, 41
LUCK BY CHANCE, 32, 118
LUDENAM, Thomas, 218
LUFTON, Joseph, 35
  Mary, 35
LYNCH, Levi, 180
LYNN, Moses, 202
LYON, John, 71, 73, 77, 78

-M-
M--- Nathan, 138
MCCALL, Mark, 26, 79
MCCALLEY, Robert W., 207
  Robert Watson, 73, 117
MACCARREL, James, 107
MCCARREL, James, 126
MACCARREL, Robert, 107
MCCARREL, Robert, 126
MCCAY, Alexander, 69, 72
  Elizabeth, 79
  John, 68, 79, 99
  Naomie, 72
  Patience, 67
  William, 67, 68, 72, 79
MCCRAY, Mary, 179

Robert, 179
MCCREA, Robert, 140
MCCREAS LOT, 140
MCCULLAH,
  Alexander, 195
  John, 136, 195
MCDOWEL, Andrew, 28
MCDOWELL, Andrew, 38
  Isaac, 115
MCELVAIN, Mills, 213
MCGILL, Andrew, 42
MCILVAIN, Andrew, 37, 94, 108, 112, 124
  David, 133, 180
  Mills, 213
MCILWAIN, James, 213
MCIVAIN, James, 32
  Robert, 1
MCKEAN, Thomas, 70
MCKEMMEY, Aaron, 186
MCKIMMEY, Aron, 186
  Elizabeth, 186
  Jane, 186
  Walter, 186
MACKLIN, Charles, 69
MACKNAT, Ann, 225
  William, 225
MCKNETT, Magdalin, 153
MCLANE, Thomas, 153
MCMURRAY, James, 211
  John, 211
MCNAS, Robert, 215
MCNEAL, James, 186
MCNEEL, Neil, 32
  Sarah, 32
MACOLLY, Robert Watson, 117
MADDUX, Sophia, 180
MAGGS, Francis, 146
MAIDEN PLANTATION,

121
MAIDENHEAD, 224
MAIDENHEAD
  THICKET, 126
MALCOLM, Henry, 70
MALONEY, William,
  217
MANLOVE, Boaz, 3,
  4, 6, 8, 9, 13,
  16, 25, 26, 28,
  30, 31, 32, 38,
  39, 40, 41, 42,
  45, 47, 48, 53,
  58, 66, 71, 84,
  88, 107, 113,
  115, 138, 191,
  199
  Elizabeth, 37
  John, 66, 101
  Jonathan, 9, 68,
  99, 101, 205
  Magdalane, 41
  Magdaline, 20,
  182
  Magdalon, 4
  Manual, 68
  Manuel, 4, 41,
  104
  Margaret, 101
  Mark, 35, 37, 81
  Mary, 37, 101
  Nathan, 80, 81
  Rachel, 205
  Sarah, 56
  Thomas, 37, 56
  William, 101
MANLOVE'S BRANCH,
  99
MANLOVE'S GROVE,
  160
MANNER OF
  WONNINGHURST,
  191
MAPLE BRANCH, 177
MAREY, Thomas, 181
MARINE, Constant,
  142
MARINER, Bowman,
  149
  Constant, 149,
  160, 200
  Elizabeth, 142,
  200
  Gilbert, 7

Moses, 171, 201
Nathaniel
  Bowman, 200
Nathl. B., 160
Nathniel Bowman,
  184
Richard, 142,
  200
Robert, 149,
  160, 179, 184,
  200
MARK, Jane, 77
MARKAM, William,
  25
MARKET STREET, 17,
  60, 83, 99
MARKS SAVANAH, 169
MARRICK, Sarah,
  104
  William, 104
MARRIER, Nathaniel
  Bowman, 53
MARRINE, William,
  108
MARRINER, Bowmans,
  171
  Constant, 14,
  53, 93, 95
  Elizabeth, 66
  Gilbert, 5, 54,
  62, 66, 84
  Jacob, 53, 171
  Jean, 179
  John, 10, 17, 53
  Joshua, 53
  Moses, 14, 172
  Nathaniel
    Bowman, 179
  Nathaniel Brown,
    93
  Richard, 53
  Robert, 95
  Thomas, 14, 95,
  110
  William, 26, 108
MARROW BONE LANE,
  26
MARSH, Peter, 4,
  34, 51, 90
  Polly, 34
MARSH PASTURE, 6
MARSH PATENT, 21,
  30, 52
MARSH POINT, 196

MARSHAHOPE BRIDGE,
  142, 224
MARSHALL, Aaron,
  219
  John, 208
  Joseph, 193
MARSHEHOPE BRIDGE,
  177
MARSHELL, John,
  208
MARSHES CREEK, 52
MARSHIHOPE BRIDGE,
  139
MARTAINS VINEYARD,
  114
MARTIN, Elizabeth,
  156
  George, 154
  Henry, 47
  James, 5, 52,
  105, 150, 170,
  174, 180, 199,
  210, 211
  John, 210, 211
  Josiah, 4, 156,
  199
  Josias, 5, 11
  Rebeckah, 47
  Sarah, 225
  Thomas, 115,
  116, 149, 215,
  219, 225
MARTIN' VINEYARD,
  89
MARTINS HUNDRED,
  142, 152, 155,
  202
MARTON, James, 5
MARVEL, Philip,
  206
  Thomas, 73, 106,
  206
MASON, Elia, 87
  John, 26
  William, 187
MASONS LINE, 31
MASSACHUSETT BAY,
  New England, 16
MASSEY, Robert,
  161
MATHEWS, William,
  107, 119, 126
MATTAPENY, 200
MATTHEWS, William,

181, 197, 198, 210, 222
MAUGHAN, John, 123
MAULL, James, 15, 16
  Jane, 15
  John, 15, 16, 26, 89, 90
  Mary, 15, 16
  Nehemiah, 15, 16
  William, 16, 90
MAURICE, Theodore, 77, 78
MAXFIELD, Jane, 9
MAY, Ann, 29, 37, 56, 69
  Draper, 27, 28, 37, 42, 69, 72, 146, 148
  John, 77
  Jonathan, 21, 27, 30, 39, 42, 52, 69, 72
  Margret, 77
  Mary, 69
  Sarah, 42
  Thomas, 21, 27, 30, 34, 35, 37, 42, 52, 56, 69, 72, 77
MAYS POND, 77
MEADES, Francis, 42
MEADS, Francis, 30, 36
MEARS, Robert, 61
MECAY, John, 72
  William, 69
MELSON, Elijah, 191
MERIDETH, Samuel, 9
MERIDITH, Rees, 16
MERIDTH, Rees, 16
MERRY BRANCH, 121
MERSHALL, Thomas, 1
MESSECK, George, 157
MESSICK, George, 176
  Levin, 94
  Nehemiah, 94, 192
  Obediah, 19, 35, 37
METCALF, John, 203
  Richard, 17
METCALFE, John, 178
MIDDLE CREEK, 13, 90, 112, 132
MIDDLE SECOND, 83
MIDDLE STREET, 60
MIDDLEBOROUGH, 22, 128
MIDDLESEX, 137
MIERS, John, 60, 74, 189, 208
  Margery, 16
MIERY BRANCH, 125
MIFFLEN, Benjamin, 19
MIFFLIN, Benjamin, 14, 15, 16, 114, 137, 151, 156
  John, 16
MIFLIN, Benjamin, 7, 85, 86, 132
MILBEY, Levin, 154, 180
  Nathaniel, 172
MILBEY'S LAND, 172
MILBY, Levin, 42, 105
  Nathaniel, 13, 105, 135
MILES END, 12
MILEY, Elizabeth, 13
MILFORD, 120
MILFORD PATENT, 201
MILL BRANCH, 18, 103, 143, 182, 217
MILL CREEK, 9, 93, 118, 133, 138, 181, 216, 219
MILL CREEK BRANCH, 49, 96, 167
MILL DAM, 25, 105, 118
MILL LANDING, 193
MILL PLANTATION, 148, 213
MILL POND, 25, 54, 215
MILL RANGE, 61
MILL ROAD, 123
MILLARD, Joseph, 74, 83
  Marget, 74
  Mary, 66, 181
  William, 78, 94, 106, 117, 138, 159, 181, 219, 223
MILLER, John, 34, 101, 102
  Joseph, 168, 170
  Nanny, 118
  Robert, 102
MILLERS MILL BRANCH, 194
MILLERS ROAD, 198
MILLIARD, Mary, 223
MILLMAN, Jonathan, 173
  Mary, 173
  Peter, 173
MILLS, Edmond, 3
MILMAN, Jonathan, 63
  Michael, 173
MINORS, Charles, 188, 189
  Robert, 187, 188
MIRE BRANCH, 15
MISPILLION CREEK, 9, 23, 24, 27, 29, 30, 31, 33, 38, 41, 42, 44, 61, 62, 63, 69, 72, 78, 121, 134
MISPILLION HUNDRED, 43, 139, 198
MISTER, Marmaduke, 211
MITCALF, John, 212
MITCHEL, Abraham, 12
  John, 157
  Josiah, 200
  Stephan, 119
  Stephen, 72
MITCHELL, Abraham, 11
  John, 128, 158, 160, 211, 215

Nathaniel, 215
MITTEN, William,
    40, 41
MITTON, James, 72
MOLINEX, Jane, 33
MOLLESTON,
    Alexander, 5,
    7, 22, 177
    Ann, 177
    Henry, 67
    John, 155
    William, 3
MOLLINEX, William,
    33
MOLLISON, John, 155
MOLLISTON,
    William, 161
MOLTON'S LINE, 212
MONKEY'S BRANCH,
    76, 92
MONROE, Robert,
    178
MONTIUS BRANCH,
    58, 98
MOONE, County of
    Kildare
    (Ireland), 26
MOOR, Charles,
    158, 161, 176
    Shiles, 156
    Thomas, 157
    William, 84, 157
MOORE, Charles,
    157, 215
    Hester, 143
    J., 30, 38, 42,
    45, 48, 55, 74,
    83, 95, 97,
    115, 135, 202,
    215
    Jacob, 37, 68,
    157, 216
    James, 207
    Thomas, 157, 226
MOOT, Asher, 205,
    206
MORGAN, Avory, 196
    David, 41
    Elijah, 41
    Evan, 14
    George, 155
    Jacobs, 162
    Jonathan, 141,
    142

Joseph, 41
Manlove, 95
Martha, 162
Robert, 162
William, 225
MORGINS, Joseph,
    35
MORRAN, John, 121
MORRIS, Ann, 19
    Anna, 36
    Anne, 26, 36
    Bevins, 137, 213
    Bibbins, 213
    Brinkley, 220
    Catharine, 21
    Curtis, 198
    Daniel, 198, 220
    Denis, 222
    Dennis, 29, 87,
    96, 137
    Eliphaz, 198
    Elisha, 24
    Eunice, 81
    George, 81
    Jacob, 113, 137
    James, 26
    John, 33, 183,
    214
    Jonas, 19, 26,
    36
    Joseph, 29, 208,
    222
    Joshua, 183
    Josiah, 31
    Mary, 19, 26, 36
    Robert, 24
    Samuel, 26, 188
    Theodore, 73
    Thomas, 26
    William, 137,
    188, 213
MORRIS LAND, 19
MORRISES PURCHASE,
    192
MORRISS, Curtis,
    219
    Daniel, 139,
    219, 220
MORRISS PURCHASE,
    188
MORRISSES,
    Jeremiah, 182
MORRISSES
    PLEASURE, 220

MORRISSES VENTURE,
    122, 168
MORTON,
    Allexander, 141
MOSLEY, Absolum,
    73
MOTHERKILL
    HUNDRED, 23
MOTT, Asher, 186
    Gersham, 119,
    126
    Gershom, 101
MOUMFORD, William,
    133
MOUNT JOY, 174
MOUNT MELICK, 26
MOUNT PLEASANT
    TOWNSHIP, 171
MOUNTFORD, John,
    133
    Samuel, 78
    William, 133
MOUNTJOY, 179
MOUSLEY, Absolom,
    127
MUDDY CREEK, 187
MUDDY NECK, 57,
    221
MUIR, James, 161
MULBERRY STREET,
    26, 42, 99
MULLINEX, Jane,
    121
    Richard, 120
    William, 121
MUMFORD, William,
    133
MURPHEY, Ann, 18
    Daniel, 26, 218
    Hannah, 26
    John, 24, 60
    William, 18
MURPHY, Daniel,
    27, 161
    John, 9
MURRAY, Francis, 3
    James, 168
MURROW, James, 168
MUSMILLION CREEK,
    149, 153
MUSTARD, John, 9,
    138, 181, 219
MUSTERD, John, 8
MUSTERT, John, 93

INDEX

MY FORTUNE, 144

-N-
NANTICOKE RIVER, 132, 141, 143
NANTICOKE HUNDRED, 206
NANTICOKE INDIANS, 211
NANTICOKE RIVER, 12, 28, 118, 121, 122, 123, 125, 128, 134, 136, 140, 142, 147, 152, 173, 176, 185, 187, 192, 193, 203, 217, 219, 225
NATHANIEL HORNEY'S MILL, 194
NAWS, Hannah, 8
  Nathaniel, 8
NEAL, John, 138
  William, 138
NEALS FOLLY, 138
NEAR PLANTATION, 66, 88
NECK ROAD, 123
NECKS ROAD, 158
NEEDHAM, John, 153
NEEL, John, 134
NEIL, Bathiah, 154
  John, 154
NEILL, Elizabeth, 177, 220
  Henry, 100, 105, 177, 178, 209, 215, 216
  John, 151, 167, 171, 184, 201, 213
  Margret, 154
  Robert, 154
NEILLE, Henry, 102
NELMS, Ann, 212
NEVE, Samuel, 17
NEW CASTLE County, Delaware, 11, 61, 73, 76, 77, 78, 88, 108, 109, 119
NEW DESIGN TRAIL, THE 180
NEW MARLBOROUGH, 212
NEW YORK, City of 11, 45, 49, 52
NEWBOLD, Francis, 100, 140
  James, 4, 100, 126
  John, 100
  Margaret, 194, 195
  Rachel, 100
  Thomas, 194
  William, 194
NEWCASTLE, Town of, 78
NEWCOMB, Baptis, 82
  Baptist, 75, 94, 220
  Elizabeth, 40
  Thomas, 40, 109, 110
NEWPORT, 92
NICHOLAS BRANCH, 56
NICHOLAS TURNER'S LINE, 58
NICHOLSON, Ann, 222
  Mary, 222
  Sarah, 222
NICKSON, John, 87
NICOLLS, Zachariah, 224
NICOLSON, John, 187
NIEL, Elizabeth, 7
  John, 7, 120
NOCK, Elisha, 130
  Joseph, 123
  Sollomon, 119
  Solomon, 57, 58, 59, 126, 187
NOCKS, Elisha, 16
NORMAN, John, 166
NORTH PETHERNTON, 160
NORTHAMPTON County, Virginia, 44, 53, 107
NORTHEAST BRANCH, 152
NORTHERN BRANCH, 212
NORTHWEST FORK HUNDRED, 12, 122, 131, 142, 144, 145, 147, 148, 149, 152, 156, 163, 168, 171, 173, 177, 178, 181, 182, 200, 203, 207, 217, 218, 219, 221, 224, 225
NORTHWEST FORK RIVER, 143
NOTINGHAM, Abel, 210
NOTTINGHAM, Abel, 188
  Able, 138
  Clark, 109
  Hannah, 188
  Jacob, 57
  John, 161
  Jonathan, 153, 184, 189, 192, 194
NUNEZ, Daniel, 1, 3, 5, 10, 13, 14, 17, 30, 32, 36, 37, 38, 42, 47, 51, 53, 54, 60, 65, 66, 67, 69, 72, 91, 95, 96, 98, 101, 113, 115, 143, 162
  Hannah, 36, 60
  Mr., 34
NUTTER, Charles, 225
  Christopher, 114, 148, 156, 162
  David, 152
  John, 79, 111, 125, 225
  Robert, 147, 156
  Sarah, 147, 156
  William, 225
  Zadok, 182
NUTTERS ADVENTURE, 155
NUTTERS FARM, 79
NUTTERS LOTT, 148,

156
NUTTERS NECK, 121, 122
NUTTERS NEGLECT, 121

-O-
OAKEY, Elizabeth, 179
John, 17, 190
Mary, 190
Robert, 42
Thomas, 95
OAKLEY, Thomas, 179
OKEY, Levi, 210
Levin, 181
OLAVER, George, 108
Jean, 23
Levi, 23, 24
OLD BRIDGE, 195
OLD BRIDGE NECK, 173
OLD MARSH LINE, 220
OLD MILL ROAD, 115
OLD POINT, 146
OLD SCHOOL HOUSE, 175
OLIVER, Aaron, 158, 203, 214
Esther, 80
Joseph, 61, 80, 200
Samuel, 127
O'NEAL, James, 124
Thomas, 124
ONLEY, Elizabeth, 78
John, 78
Smith, 78
Tabitha, 78
ORPHANS CHOICE, 130
ORPHANS PORTION, THE 2
ORR, John, 169
William, 53, 59, 190
OTTEN, John, 81
OTWELL, Curtis, 152
Naomie, 112

William, 112
OUTTEN, Obed, 132
OWENS, Ann, 152
Assenath, 205
David, 152
Esther, 210
James, 35, 169
John, 20, 30
Robert, 205
Samuel, 30, 35, 119, 129, 169, 210
William, 30, 139, 152, 155, 169, 214
OWEN'S FANCY, 152
OWINGIES BRIDGE, 139
OZBON, Henry, 120
Jonathan, 120
Mathew, 97
Matthew, 120
Thomas, 91, 96, 99
OZBUN, Matthew, 91
Thomas, 48, 79
OZBURG, Henry, 201
OZBURN, Matthew, 213

-P-
PAGAN BRANCH, 165, 199, 226
PAGAN CREEK, 1, 8, 36, 44, 60, 75, 83, 104, 118, 165, 166, 199, 203, 226
PAGAN NECK, 166
PAGE, William, 63
PAGES PATENT, 111
PAINTERS IGNORANCE, 188
PALLEN, Thomas, 26
PALMER, Daniel, 180
PAPTIST, John, 194
PAREMORE,
Alexander, 212
John, 164
Mary, 164, 165
Mathew, 164
Matthew, 165
Thomas, 220

PARIMORE,
Alexander, 186
Mary, 186
Richard, 207
Solomon, 65
PARISH OF ST. MARY SHANDON, 26
PARKER, Anderson, 27, 54, 64, 65, 71, 104, 113, 115, 118, 120, 126, 128, 129, 136, 153, 154, 210, 211
Ann, 149
Betty, 149
Edward, 190
Eli, 79, 86, 87
George, 12, 219
Gilb., 100
Gilbelcher, 6, 113
Gilbilsher, 22
Gilbs., 55
Gillb., 154
Gillbn., 44
John, 55, 61, 125, 134, 137
Matthew, 212
Peter, 22, 27, 31, 36, 54, 55, 66, 71, 114, 115
Thomas, 176
Thomas Hall, 166
William, 19, 33, 40, 75, 76, 92, 121
William Parker, 220
PARKERS MILL, 4, 220
PARMER, Joseph, 106
PARNALL, Walton, 187
PARREMORE, Joseph, 136
Richard, 207
PARRIMER, Job, 135
Matthew, 107
Richard, 10
PARRIMORE, John, 208

Joseph, 125
Richard, 208
Solomon, 65, 99
PARSLEY, Abraham, 34, 56, 61, 151
Anthony, 56
Frances, 56
Prudence, 56
PARSLEYS SWAMP, 213
PARSONS, John, 44, 124
PARTNERSHIP, 148
PARTRIDGE TRACT, 91
PASINOUS WARD, 131
PASSWATERS, William, 222
PASWATERS, William, 86
PATHALIA, 62, 70, 88
PATIE, Richard, 216
PATRIDGE TRACT, 216
PATTERSON, Moles, 108, 109, 119, 129
Moses, 210
PAVEY, Samuel, 207
PAYNTER, Andrew, 39
Elizabeth, 51
John, 6, 7, 26, 68, 114
Lemuel Collison, 115
Samuel, 6, 7, 12, 26, 109, 118, 156, 209
PAYNTERS GUTT, 9
PAYNTERS NECK, 115
PAYNTOR, Richard, 19
PAYTNER, Lemuel Collison, 130
PEACH BLOSSOM, 19, 115, 130
PEARSON, John, 116
Thomas, 116
PEERY, Elizabeth, 153
Magdalin, 153
Mary, 8, 37, 148, 153, 187
William, 4, 7, 8, 9, 10, 11, 17, 34, 36, 37, 52, 67, 85, 96, 103, 105, 109, 118, 119, 129, 130, 131, 132, 136, 153, 180, 187, 213, 215
PEERYS MILL POND, 5
PELEG WALTER'S TAVERN, 194
PEMBERTON, Elizabeth, 5
Thomas, 5
PEMBERTON BRANCH, 40
PEMBERTONS BRANCH, 5, 30, 62, 84
PENN, John, 12
Richard, 113
Thomas, 224
PENNINGTON, 69, 72
Henry, 27, 28, 69, 72, 166
Rachel, 77
PENNINGTON PATENT, 81
PENNY NECK, 177
PEPPERS CREEK, 188
PERCUSSION BRANCH, 136
PERROT, Richard, 73, 77
PERROTT, Richard, 78
PERRY, Aaron, 191
Cathrine, 4
Charles, 4, 81, 118
James, 90
Mary, 197
William, 86, 100, 134, 138, 170, 197, 199, 213
PERRYMAN, Perry, 23
PERSIMON ISLAND, 207
PESSIMON (PERSIMMON)
BOTTOM, 143
PETERKIN, James, 52, 116
Thomas, 52
PETERS, Richard, 113
PETERS GUTT, 14, 146
PETTET, Edward, 177
PETTYJOHN, James, 15, 16
Samuel, 16
Thomas, 19
William, 129, 133
PHENIX, William, 168
PHILADELPHIA, City of 1, 2, 5, 6, 11, 16, 17, 19, 24, 26, 36, 42, 44, 61, 70, 77, 82, 85, 88, 112, 116, 135
PHILADELPHIA County, Pennsylvania, 25, 36, 43
PHILIPS, Jacob, 47, 48
PHILLIPS, Jacob, 47, 197, 208
PHINIX, Darcus, 168
William, 168
PHIPPS, Absolum, 132
PHIPS, Absolom, 19
PIERCE, John, 225
Sarah, 99
William, 38, 99
PILES, Isaac, 48, 220
Jacob, 48
James, 54
John, 54, 220
Joseph, 220
William, 25, 48, 49, 54, 191, 220
PILES NECK, 113
PILES PATENT, 48
PILSONS LOTT, 12

INDEX 257

PINE GROVE
  FURNACE, 11
PINE NECK, 210
PINEY BRANCH, 90
PINEY NECK, 93,
  192
PINEY RUN, 90
PINYARD, Rachel,
  23
PIPER, Joseph, 121
PLOOKHEY,
  Cornelius, 74
PLOWMAN, John, 50,
  89, 99, 101,
  150
PLUCKOO,
  Cornelius, 83
  Judith, 83
PLUCKOY,
  Cornelius, 73
  Judith, 73
PLUCKOY (PLOOKER),
  Cornelius, 73
PLUMSTEAD,
  William, 17
POINEY NECK, 188
POINT, THE, 106
POINTER, William,
  24, 55
POINTERS FIELD, 55
POLE THICKET, 212
POLK, Charles, 84,
  117, 140, 177
  Daniel, 128,
  142, 147, 148,
  149, 166, 168,
  171, 178, 181,
  182, 193, 194,
  203, 207, 219, 224
  Daniell, 156
  Ephraim, 140
  George, 117,
  125, 127
  Gillis, 211
  James, 157, 219
  John, 3, 33,
  125, 127, 141,
  157, 158, 175,
  190, 193, 205
  Josiah, 176,
  211, 218, 219
  Leonard, 157
  Levin, 150
  Lydia, 122

  Margaret Nutter,
  178
  Mary, 157, 158,
  175
  Robert, 157
  Roger Tasker,
  212
  William, 113,
  150, 157, 163,
  171, 176, 190,
  193, 197, 202,
  207, 211, 218,
  224, 225
  Zephaniah, 122,
  123
POLLET, Richard,
  23
POLLITT, Nancy,
  212
POLLOCK, James,
  118
POLTNEY, Richard,
  197
PONDER, Elizabeth,
  53
  James, 222
  John, 30, 53,
  82, 120, 159,
  199, 222
POOL, John, 108
POOR, Comfort, 1
  Mary, 21
  Nehemiah, 21
POOR CHANCE, 187,
  189
POORE, Major, 84
  Mary, 85
POPE, Charles, 196
  Francis, 197,
  223
  Jean, 196
  William, 196
POPLAR HILL, 148,
  171
POPLAR LEVIL
  IMPROVED, 224
POPLAR RIDGE, 145,
  178
POSELS, Thomas,
  116
POSTEL, John, 166
POSTELS, John, 116
POTHOOKS GUTT, 128
POTTER, Abraham,

  2, 33, 77, 107,
  126, 178
  Edmond, 149, 153
  Enoch, 39, 77
  John, 28, 33,
  39, 105, 125,
  141, 149
  Mary, 77
POWEL, Gabriel,
  143
  John, 222
  Mary, 222
  Sarah, 222
POWELL, Fenby, 178
  Gabriel, 143
  Mary, 143
  William, 129,
  177, 178
POWER, Mary, 84
  Nehemiah, 84
POYNTER,
  Nathaniel, 25
  Rosley, 121
  Susanna, 18
  Thomas, 18
  William, 120
PRAT, Charles, 1
PRESTON, Samuel,
  36, 52
PRETTYJOHN, Ann,
  110
  Hannah, 67
  James, 46, 50,
  110, 114, 140,
  151, 165
  John, 41, 67,
  73, 106
  Richard, 67, 106
  Samuel, 41, 50,
  110
  Thomas, 114,
  139, 207
  William, 154,
  199
PRETTYMAN, Barton,
  44
  Betty, 201
  Comfort, 22,
  136, 139, 185
  Elizabeth, 21,
  51, 201
  John, 2, 3, 9,
  14, 44, 52, 185
  Peery, 185

Perry, 135, 136, 139, 154, 157
Prudence, 185
Robert, 7, 9, 179, 200, 201
Thomas, 9, 10, 17, 154, 183, 195
William, 6, 22, 136, 139, 179, 184, 185, 201
PRICE, Henry, 197
Thomas, 21, 167
William, 75
PRIDE, John, 7
William, 91, 97
PRIDOW, Rachel, 155
PRIME CREEK NECK, 77
PRIME HOOK, 222
PRIME HOOK CREEK, 12, 16, 25, 28, 46, 57, 99, 105, 133, 141, 167, 182, 204, 209
PRIME HOOK NECK, 24, 49, 73, 76, 77, 78, 116, 133, 153, 182
PRIMEHOOK CREEK BRANCH, 80
PRIMEHOOK GREAT MARSHES, 25
PRIMEHOOK PONDS, 127
PRITTIMAN, Thomas, 14
PRITTYMAN, Burton, 47, 83, 105
Comfort, 74
Honesty, 95
Isaac, 42, 95
John, 52, 53, 91, 102, 104
Perry, 45, 74
Robert, 53
Sarah, 42
Thomas, 53, 102
William, 45, 51, 52, 74, 83, 92, 95, 96
PROVIDENCE

TOWNSHIP, 25, 36
PURKINS, John, 166, 168, 170, 178
PURNAL, Thomas, 77
PURNALL, Thomas, 214
William, 55
PURY, William, 210
PUZZLE, 143
PYLES, Joseph, 143
PYNEY NECK, 188

-Q-
Quaker Meeting House, 8
QUEENS County, Ireland, 26

-R-
RACKLIFF, Charles, 170
Nathaniel, 168
RACKOON SAVANNAH, 117
RAGGED HAMMOCK TRACT, 180
RALPH, George, 129
RAMBLY MARSH, 187
RANGE TRACT, 61
RANKEN, Aby, 133
David, 27, 120, 132
RANKENS, David, 18, 26
Mary, 26
RANKIN, Aby, 133
David, 103, 133, 171, 184, 206
RATLEDGE, Ann, 225
Moses, 225
RATLIFF, William, 121
RAWLINS, Charles, 5, 17
Windsor, 184
REA, Peter, 142, 152, 218, 221
READ, Abraham, 91
Alexander, 64, 91
Allin, 91
Edmond, 90

Edmund, 78, 90, 91
George, 73, 76, 77, 78, 97, 153
Gertrude, 78
James, 33, 84, 89
John, 31, 33, 37, 38, 78, 90, 91
Martha, 78
Matthew, 85
READY, Aaron, 125, 127
Aron, 125
Isaac, 127
John, 125, 127
READYS CHOICE, 127
RECORDS, Benjamin, 210
John, 153
Naomi, 153
REDDEN, Stephen, 186
REED, Alexander, 216
Edmond, 222
Elizabeth, 78
Ezekiel, 164
George, 73
Gertrude, 73
James, 15, 64, 151
John, 31, 64, 65, 124
Littleton, 78
Nehemiah, 7, 29, 30, 67, 106, 151
REHOBOTH, 6, 204
REHOBOTH BAY, 4, 13, 19, 45, 49, 90, 105, 123, 132, 175, 195
REHOBOTH HUNDRED, 4, 5, 7, 14, 18, 25, 37, 45, 47, 51, 52, 53, 58, 65, 66, 74, 89, 92, 97, 98, 100, 104, 108, 113, 115, 119, 126, 130, 139,

151, 154, 157,
161, 184, 185,
187, 190, 205,
209, 212, 217,
218, 226
REHOBOTH NECK, 22,
201
REHOBOTH ROAD, 22
RELPH, W., 136
William, 129,
136
RENCH, James, 38
RENNALS BRANCH, 15
REVEL, Steven, 71
REYLEY, Benjamin,
119
REYNOLDS, Elinor,
110
Henry, 110
James, 67, 73,
106, 110
John, 117
Richard, 15, 19,
117, 123
Thomas, 62
William, 46, 99,
135, 190, 214
RHOADS, Henman,
127
Hinman, 100
John, 50
RICH NECK, 24, 116
RICHARDS, David,
156, 224
James, 147, 148,
149
John, 103, 224
Joseph, 103
Joshua, 20, 95,
96
Robert, 102
William, 103,
143
RICHARDS STRUGGLE,
140
RICHARDSON,
Azariah, 25
Azariat, 21
Elizabeth, 25
James, 9, 25
John, 167
Joseph, 135
RICKARDS, Ann, 124
Benjamin, 48,

54, 108, 109,
119
Charity, 124
Charles, 124
Elizabeth, 124
Esther, 54
George, 3, 21,
84
John, 3, 24, 43,
173
Jones, 174
Joseph, 148
Joshua, 21, 46
William, 69,
123, 124, 166,
167
RICKARDS DELIGHT,
124
RICKARDS PLACE, 88
RICKETS, George,
119
RICKETTS, James,
150
RICORDS, Benjamin,
138
RIDER, George,
108, 110, 114
RIGEN, James, 181
RIGGEN, James, 107
RIGGS, Peter, 4
RIGGS LAND, 4
RIGS, Ann, 18
John, 18
Levi, 18
Peter, 18
Rachel, 18
Susanna, 18
William, 18
RIGUA, John, 53
RILEY, Benjamin,
22, 30, 78,
103, 163, 214,
222
Grace, 121
John, 213, 214,
222
Larance, 113
Larrance, 29, 30
Laurance, 78
Laurence, 121
Lawrence, 118,
222
William, 32
RINGSEND, 218, 221

ROADS, Elon, 4
John, 4
ROBENS, Levi, 8
ROBERTS, Edward,
20, 212
Francis, 18, 69,
212
Hugh, 43, 44
Sarah, 212
William, 212
ROBERTS MILL POND,
119
ROBINS, Levi, 104,
108, 112, 113,
126
Phebe, 108, 112
William, 153,
185, 186
ROBINSON, Ada, 42
Burton, 83, 94,
175
John, 44, 150
Joseph, 49, 175,
210
Joshua, 133,
174, 210
Martha, 133
Parker, 19, 55,
70, 76, 86, 93,
104, 107, 113,
122, 126, 146
Peter, 6, 13,
27, 39, 41, 45,
49, 50, 51, 53,
55, 59, 60, 69,
70, 80, 82, 85,
86, 87, 88, 89,
90, 98, 100,
104, 105, 112,
125, 135, 175,
191
Ruth, 107, 126
Thomas, 6, 13,
21, 27, 28, 39,
42, 47, 49, 51,
53, 55, 64, 69,
76, 83, 84, 86,
87, 93, 105,
107, 113, 124,
125, 146, 147,
153, 175, 184
William, 65,

118, 183
ROBINSONS BRANCH, 45
ROCK HOLE, 186, 204
RODGERS, Daniel, 158, 210
  Solomon, 189
RODNEY, Caleb, 225
  Ceasar, 62
  Daniel, 215
  Hannah, 146
  J., 61, 89, 98, 135, 136, 166, 212
  John, 6, 14, 18, 32, 41, 67, 78, 90, 98, 113, 118, 128, 147, 154, 167, 171, 191, 202, 225
  Joshua, 214
  Penelope, 136
  Ruth, 146
ROGERS, Daniel, 169, 221
  Jacob, 187, 193, 194
  John, 194
  Joshua, 200
  Parker, 187
ROGERS DEFFECTED, 220
ROLAND, Elizabeth, 112
ROLLS, Bryant, 2
ROLPHS LINE, 32
RORTON, David, 39
  Joseph, 39
ROSEMERRY NECK, 82, 92
ROSMERY NECK, 7
ROSS, Edward, 224
  James, 122
  Mathew, 121
  Robert, 121, 122
  William, 122, 142
ROSSES VENTURE, 121, 122
ROST, Jane, 146
ROTEN, Josiah, 31
ROTON, Josiah, 163
ROTTEN, David, 7

Joseph, 7
Josiah, 31
ROUND POLE BRANCH, 120
ROUND POOL BRANCH, 47, 48, 96
ROUNDS, James, 133
ROUSE, John, 109, 112, 119
ROWANS County, North Carolina, 33
ROWL, Bryan, 92
ROWLAN, Samuel, 126, 220
  Widow, 143
ROWLAND,
  Elizabeth, 104
  John, 39, 226
  Samuel, 17, 19, 39, 75, 77, 90, 101, 107, 120, 178
  Thomas, 17, 75, 116
  William, 17, 75
ROYAL, Samuel, 20
RUKSAN, James, 138
RUMBLY MARSH, 187, 194, 200
RUNNELS, William, 173
RUSSEL, Ann, 211
  Catharine, 17
  Elizabeth, 129, 204
  Emanuel, 112, 129
  Ephraim, 17, 19
  Esther, 129
  J., 33, 41, 53, 81, 104, 113, 118, 123, 128, 129, 137, 146, 147, 152, 153, 154, 157, 161, 162, 163, 164, 165, 167, 170, 176, 177, 194, 201, 203, 204, 205, 208, 209, 214, 215, 217
  Jane, 99
  Jean, 129, 170

Jo., 195
John, 5, 6, 13, 17, 22, 45, 50, 51, 52, 71, 78, 82, 87, 92, 93, 97, 103, 111, 114, 120, 128, 131, 133, 163, 180, 191, 192, 209, 225
John Draper, 192
Joseph, 14, 19, 77
Joseph Hall, 196
Levi, 38, 40, 159
Manlove, 38, 40
Mary, 40, 129
Phil., 14
Philip, 5, 19, 99
Phillip, 104
Phillips, 204
Price, 211
Ruth, 129
Samuel, 19, 40
Sarah, 225
Tabitha, 129, 154
William, 38, 40, 99, 109, 154
RUSSELL, Jane, 95
  John, 3, 50, 68, 74, 99, 167
  Mary, 62
  Phillip Kollock, 189
  William, 95
RUSSELL'S CREEK, 191
RUSSUL, Mary, 149
RUST, John, 97, 149, 204
  Jonathan, 37, 97, 161, 204
  Peter, 118
  Rachel, 204
RYE FIELD, 203
RYLEY, Benjamin, 90, 91
  John, 103
  Laurence, 103
RYLY, Lawrence, 20
RYVES HALL, 147

INDEX

-S-

SADLER, Michael, 26
SAFFORD, Henry, 145, 168, 181
  Jarvey, 225
  Nathan, 145
  Sarah, 145
  Stashe, 181
ST. GEORGE'S, 224
ST. GEORGE'S CHAPPEL, 91, 123, 179
ST. MARTAINS, 36
ST. MARTINS, 108, 212
ST. MARTIN'S CHURCH, 194
SAINT MARTINS RIVER, 162
ST. MARTIN'S SOUND, 200
ST. MATHEW'S CHURCH, 99
SALLEYS PLAINS, 225
SALMAN, James, 139
SALMON, James, 139
SALMONDS, Benjamin, 102
SALMONS, Benjamin, 102
SALSBURY PLAINS, 199
SALTERAGES BRANCH, 69
SAMMON, Solomon, 132
SAMPLES, Elias, 172
  Sarah, 172
SAMUELS, Richard, 46
SANDOWN, 223
SANDRESS (SANDRESSON), Ann, 210
SANDY BRANCH, 168
SANDY NECK, 134
SANDY RIDGE, 170
SANDYALL, 190
SAPLIN RIDGE, 200
SAPLING RIDGE, 122, 128

SARAH'S DELIGHT, 193, 194
SAVAGE, Robinson, 174
SAWMILL RANGE, 23, 24, 44, 212
SAWMILL RANGE TRACT, 134
SCARBOROUGH, Mathew, 160
  William, 160
SCHOLFIELD, Benjamin, 153
SCIDMORE, Thomas, 91
SCOOT, Michel, 117
SCOTT, Alice, 193
  Day, 193
  Gustavus, 176
  Jeremiah, 26, 36
SCOTTISH PLOTT, 222
SCOTTISH PLOTTS, 222
SCUDDER, David, 143
  Enoch, 217
  Jonathan, 148
  Rachel, 148
SCUDDER'S LINE, 213
SCUDER, Aby, 133
  David, 118, 133
  Hannah, 133
  Jonathan, 133
  Ruth, 133
SEALE, 145
SECOND ADDITION, 149
SECOND CHOICE, 125
SECOND STREET, 51, 99, 116, 118, 161
SECUNDUS, Thomas Martin, 219
SELBY, Thomas, 194
SHADLY, William, 67
SHADRICK STURGIS'S LAND, 152
SHALTMAN, Jacob, 159
SHANKLAND, Alexander, 4,

6, 7, 17, 60, 76, 220
  Ann, 82, 97, 106
  David, 18, 51, 52, 53, 55, 93, 154, 190
  Elizabeth, 220
  Hester, 34
  James, 36
  John, 1, 2, 8, 13, 27, 34, 40, 49, 57, 60, 64, 75, 82, 165
  Jonathan, 27
  Joseph, 8, 28, 34, 36, 38, 59
  Moses, 43, 156
  Rhoads, 1, 2, 8, 9, 10, 14, 15, 17, 18, 31, 34, 36, 37, 38, 39, 40, 44, 46, 48, 58, 64, 65, 67, 69, 72, 82, 87, 97, 106, 108, 110, 113, 114, 115, 117, 121, 124, 125, 128, 138, 139, 140, 146, 148, 149, 151, 154, 156, 157, 159, 160, 161, 163, 164, 168, 169, 172, 173, 177, 179, 180, 181, 183, 184, 191, 192, 194, 206, 209
  Rhodes, 84
  Rhods, 35, 210
  Roads, 29, 31, 34, 109
  Robert, 7, 34, 48, 128, 153, 173, 181, 190, 220
  Sam., 34
  Samuel, 10, 28, 34, 36, 38, 39, 84, 110, 140, 156, 183
  Sarah, 34, 57, 60, 97, 119,

165, 169
William, 4, 5, 7, 8, 22, 27, 36, 61, 93, 119, 126, 138, 140, 155, 181, 219, 220
SHANKLANDS DISCOVERY, 38, 39
SHANKLANDS ISLAND, 156
SHANKLIN, John, 199
Rhoads, 196, 216
Sarah, 199
SHARP, James, 112, 123, 131
John, 114, 138, 164, 186
William, 112
SHARPE, James, 107
William, 106, 107
SHAVER, Ann, 152
Isaac, 150, 152
John, 152
SHAW, Comfort, 186
John, 186
SHEARMON, Thomas, 110
SHELDON, Mary, 145
SHELLMAN, Jacob, 201
SHELPMAN, Isaac, 85
William, 210
SHELTMAN, William, 117
SHEORT, Martha, 201
SHERMAN, George, 110
John, 108
SHETKILL NECK, 54
SHIELD, Luke, 17, 48, 86, 113
SHIELDS, Luke, 54
SHIP CARPENTER'S STREET, 60, 203
SHIPPEN, Edward, 113
SHOCKLEY, Richard, 21, 31, 162,
163
William, 31, 71, 80, 140, 158, 167
SHORT, Adam, 162
William, 218
SIKES ISLAND, 212
SILVER PLAINS, 15
SIMMONS, William, 146
SIMONTON, Comfort, 60
Elizabeth, 60, 83, 189, 199, 208
Jane, 189, 199, 208
Jean, 83
Jennet, 60
John, 60, 82, 83, 165, 166, 189, 199, 208
Mary, 60, 83, 189, 199, 208
Sarah, 60, 83, 189, 199, 208
SIMPLER, Andrew, 94, 108, 110
Andrus, 82
Paul, 108, 109, 119, 210
Paull, 108, 109
SIMPSON,
Elizabeth, 214, 219, 225
James, 161, 214, 219, 225
Margaret, 215, 219, 225
Rachel, 18
Robert, 18
SIMSON, Elizabeth, 18, 116
James, 50, 116
Margaret, 116
William, 18
SIRMAN, Thomas, 114
SKIDMORE, Elijah, 32
Mary, 32, 34
Thomas, 96
SLAUGHS, Samuel Shelton, 164
SLAUGHTER BRANCH, 76, 78
SLAUGHTER CREEK, 21, 25, 49, 76, 77, 79, 114, 162
SLAUGHTER NECK, 3, 6, 9, 21, 22, 41, 43, 70, 73, 80, 85, 87, 89, 101, 102, 130, 144, 158, 162, 167, 178, 198, 203, 207, 212, 214
SLAUGHTER NECK FORREST, 2, 139
SLUTKILL NECK, 75, 94, 137, 198, 220
SMITH, Ann, 222
Benjamin, 222
Comfort, 179
David, 3, 20, 27, 31, 71, 111, 123, 124, 167
Elizabeth, 166
Henry, 13, 28, 41, 71, 75, 78, 80, 110, 114, 116, 118, 145, 149, 165
Hezekiah, 168
Hill, 222
Isaac, 4, 14, 28, 29, 39, 45, 48, 63, 72, 79, 84, 90, 101, 104, 108, 109, 120, 126, 133, 161, 170, 172, 176, 177
James, 136
Jesse, 200
Job, 124
John, 80, 111, 123, 124, 132, 188
Lova Mitchell, 155
Mary, 71, 92, 170, 181, 182
Matthews, 12

INDEX

Mitchel, 46
Mitchell, 34
Nehemiah, 60
Nutter, 111
Obediah, 181, 182, 193
Priscilla, 118
Rebeckah, 30, 42
Robert, 213
Sarah, 111, 222
Thomas, 32, 79, 80, 182, 193, 207
William, 30, 42, 111, 123, 124
SMITH'S DELIGHT, 124
SMITHS FOLLY, 166
SMITHS NECK, 140
SMITH'S SURVEY, 71
SMULING, William, 207
SMYTHERS, Mary, 8
  Serjeant, 8
SNEAD, Thomas, 197
SNOWDEN, John, 85
  Sarah, 85
SOCKAROCKAH, 29
SOCKAROCKETS BRANCH, 91
SOCKEROCKETT, 94
SOCKROCKAT, 29
SOCKROCKET BRANCH, 10, 151
SOMERSET County, Maryland, 11, 12, 29, 31, 72, 117, 129, 135, 136, 152, 161, 175, 192, 193, 202, 205, 212, 219, 222
SOULSTERS INHERITANCE, 30, 36, 42
SOUTH BRANCH, 182
SOUTH HAMPTON, 89
SOUTH PETTERTON, 214
SOUTHERN, Edward, 44, 196
  Mary, 196
SOUTHERN CREEK, 197

SOUTHERON, Edward, 36
  Mary, 36
SOUTHRENS CREEK, 95
SOW BRIDGE BRANCH, 58, 85, 94, 106
SPENCE, Ann, 177
  James, 123, 177
  John, 177
SPENCER, Azael, 57
  Azeail, 218
  Aziael, 217
  Azl., 79
  Donavan, 217
  Donovan, 57, 80, 96, 196
  Ebenezar, 9, 43
  Ebenezer, 3, 6, 29, 103, 178, 212
  Elizabeth, 63
  Esther, 80
  Henry, 56, 57, 63, 217
  John, 3, 15, 40, 71, 80, 91, 96, 107
  Joseph, 57, 217
  Joshua, 44, 63
  Levi, 44
  Louisa, 44
  Nathan, 3, 57, 94, 217
  Samuel, 9, 63, 103, 212
  William, 57, 63, 129, 154, 217
SPENCER CHANCE, 38, 42, 43, 44, 63
SPENCER'S BRANCH, 44, 63
SPENCER'S HALL, 77
SPITTLE FIELD, 68
SPOONER, Charles, 5
SPRING GARDEN, 120
SPRINGFORD PATENT, 154
STAFFORD, Henry, 123, 181
  Jacob, 58
  James, 184

Jarvey, 168
Levi, 145
Nathan, 122, 123, 142
Rosanna, 58
STAFFORDS ADVENTURE, 122, 123
STAFFORDS LOT, 122
STALLION HEAD NECK, 69
STANFORD, James, 46, 82
STAPLEFORD, David, 118
  Edward, 118, 222
  Mary, 118
STAR, Bethiah, 54, 65
  Bethial, 54
  James, 54, 65
  Jonathan, 54, 65
  Nathaniel, 54, 65
  Richard, 54
  Sarah, 54, 65, 129
STARR, Catharine, 216
  Jonathan, 129
  Nathaniel, 137
STATON, Hill, 19
  Mary, 143
  Thomas, 8, 9, 35, 64, 93, 109, 129, 138, 143, 181, 219
STAYTON, Nehemiah, 136
  William, 142, 152, 155, 170, 171
STAYTON'S ADVENTURE, 170
STEAL (STEEL), James, 131
  Prisgrave, 15
  William, 131
STEEL, Benjamin, 138
  Daniel, 47, 138
  Henry, 211
  James, 20, 138
  Nathaniel, 138

Prisgrave, 139
Prisgrove, 47
  William, 20, 25,
    47, 128, 138
STEPHENS, Avory,
    173
  William, 37
STEPHENSON,
  Edward, 151,
    167, 174
  Hugh, 10, 69,
    95, 138, 151,
    167, 172, 184,
    205, 206, 210
  James, 10, 94,
    95, 208
  John, 75, 76,
    95, 204, 205,
    206
  Jonathan, 66,
    181
  Margaret, 130,
    149, 174
  Mary, 69
  Rhoda, 204, 205
  Rhodah, 195
  Robert, 6, 82,
    94, 120, 147,
    159, 184
  Samuel, 91
  William, 16, 82,
    94, 120, 147,
    198, 223
STEPHENSON'S
  FORETHOUGHTS,
    207
STEPHENSON'S LAND,
    31
STEVENS, Mathew,
    197
  William, 44, 211
STEVENS CREEK, 95
STEVENSON, Elinor,
    106
  Hugh, 179
  James, 90, 207
  John, 44, 83,
    113
  Jonathan, 183,
    185
  Robert, 102,
    106, 153, 160,
    200
  Samuel, 96, 97

William, 65,
    118, 179
STEWARD, William,
    71
STEWART, Catty,
    159
  David, 33, 91,
    141
  John, 190, 191
  Mary, 41, 118
  Samuel, 190, 191
  Sophia, 91
  William, 41, 64,
    118
STILLWELL, Mary,
    178
STOCKLEY,
  Alexander, 137,
    146
  Benjamin, 8, 10,
    45, 46, 151,
    172, 175, 186,
    206
  Cornelius, 2, 8,
    140
  Elizabeth, 51,
    53, 97
  Jacob, 45, 46,
    58, 97, 134,
    151, 164, 165
  John, 12, 36,
    88, 90, 118,
    147, 160
  Mary, 65, 118,
    147
  Naomi, 137
  Nehemiah, 144
  Olaver, 36, 52
  Oliver, 146
  Patience, 134
  Paynter, 1, 103
  Peter, 160
  Prettyman, 1,
    36, 146, 147,
    156, 183
  Sarah, 149
  Solomon, 5, 65,
    70
  Thomas, 104,
    118, 146, 147
  William, 51, 53,
    58, 97, 112
  Woodman, 32, 87,
    106, 107, 115,

    123, 131, 175
STOCKLY, Nehemiah,
    143
  William, 69
STOKLEY, Solomon,
    26
  Woodman, 104
STOKLY, Alexander,
    198
  Namomi, 198
STONES FOLLEY, 46
STONEY BRANCH, 12
STONY BRANCH, 206
STOREY, Marmaduke,
    224
STORY, Joseph, 177
  Lucreasey, 177
  Marmaduke, 177
STRATON, Ann, 8
  Dorthea, 8
  Isaac, 8
STRECHER, Betty,
    85
  Edward, 85
  Finwick, 98
  Henry, 46
STRECHERS HALL, 47
STREET, John, 2,
    101, 119, 126
STRETCHER, Henry,
    82
STRETCHERS HALL,
    46, 82
STRIFE, 9
STRIFF, 179
STUART, David, 141
  John, 132, 156
  Nancey, 159
  Nancy, 159
  Samuel, 5
  Sofiah, 141
  William, 91, 159
STURGES, Daniel,
    212
STURGIS, Laban,
    102
SULIVAN, Dan, 161
SUR DESSCISIONILE,
    203
SURMAN, Lowder,
    127
SUSAN'S PALACE,
    144
SWAN CREEK BRANCH,

INDEX

44
SWAN HILL, 101,
  119, 126
SWAN POINT, 2
SWAN POND, 205
SYLAVAN, John, 141
SYLVESTER,
  Benjamin, 161

-T-
TALBERT, 81
  Elizabeth, 5
  Robert, 5, 66
  Sarah, 5
TALOR, Marget, 113
TAM, Samuel, 6, 32
  Sarah, 154
TAMPLEN, James, 91
  Richard, 91
TAMPLIN, Isaac, 67
  James, 67, 85,
    92, 167
  John, 67, 92
  Mary, 67
  Moses, 67
  Richard, 67, 85,
    92, 114, 167
  Thomas, 67, 85,
    114
TANNERS HALL, 13,
  132, 134
TATMAN, Lowder, 69
  Lower, 69
  William, 69
TAYLAR, James, 192
TAYLER, John, 104
TAYLER'S HILL, 108
TAYLERS HILLS, 113
TAYLOR, Edmond,
  222
  James, 192
  John, 96, 103
  Thomas, 165
  William, 187
TAYLORD, William,
  188
TAYLORS CHANCE,
  139
TEMPLIN, Richard, 12
TENNANT, John, 202
TENNENT, John, 164
TENNET, John, 144
THARP, Comfort,
  41, 58

Nathan, 41, 58
William, 78, 90,
  91, 103
THISTLEWOOD,
  James, 21
  Sarah, 21
THOMAS, Ann, 46,
  82, 222
  Dodd, 16
  Elizabeth, 46,
    82, 222
  Grace, 46, 82,
    222
  James, 46, 82,
    222
  John, 49
  Luke, 139
  Mary, 46, 82,
    222
  Micah, 46, 82
  Micha, 222
  Rodger, 160
THOMPSON, Bridget,
  112
  Daniel Murphey,
    218
  George, 112
  James, 7, 37,
    77, 88, 93,
    156, 174, 180,
    216
  Margaret, 180
  Mary, 149
  Thomas, 223
  William, 100,
    126, 127
THOMPSON'S RIDGE,
  3, 81
THORN, Betty, 152
  Sydenham, 152
THORNE, Betty,
  151, 158
  Sydenham, 158
THORNTON, David,
  57, 58, 63, 87,
  99, 147, 181,
  198
  Hannah, 198
THOROUGHGOOD,
  Esther, 194,
    195
  John, 194, 195
THORP, William,
  222

THORPE, Mary, 222
THREE WHOLE
  HALVES, THE 179
TILGHMAN, James,
  113
  Tinch, 71
TILL, Gertrude,
  73, 77
  Thomas, 73, 77,
    130
  William, 22, 47,
    73, 77, 167,
    192
TILLS LINE, 49
TILNEY, Jonathan,
  2, 191
  Nehemiah, 60
  Stringer, 39,
    49, 106
TILTON, Ann, 70
  Anne, 70
  Comfort, 60
  James, 70
  John, 60, 70
  Joseph, 70
  Mary, 70
  Miah, 70
  Rachel, 70
  Sarah, 70
  Thomas, 65, 70
TIMBER HILL, 148
TIMBER LAND
  ENLARGED, 215
TIMBER NECK, 4
TIMBER RIDGE, 214
TIMBER TREE NECK,
  219
TINDAL, Samuel,
  207
TINDLEY, Bridget,
  9
  Mary, 9
  Nehemiah, 9
  Thamer, 9
TINGLE, Hugh, 161
  John, 168
TOLBERT, Robert,
  156
  Sarah, 6
TOM, William, 26
TOMALIN, County of
  Kildare
  (Ireland) 26
TOMPLIN, Richard,

TOMPLIN, Richard, 7
Robert, 7
TOPHAM, Christopher, 32, 107, 113, 126, 138, 197
TORBERT, Robert, 139
TORY, 218, 221
TOW BRIDGE BRANCH, 15
TOWER HILL, 52
TOWN OF WARWICK, 16
TOWN WOODS, 220
TOWNSEND, Barkley, 127, 157, 158
Benjamin, 40
Berkley, 157
Charles, 81, 87, 96
Costen, 29
Costin, 9, 43
Coston, 3, 6, 178
Elias, 64, 80, 81, 85, 96
Isaac, 3, 6, 9, 29, 43, 56
Jacob, 80, 81, 123, 124
Jesse, 87
Jessy, 44
Leah, 64
Littleton, 24, 28, 43, 113, 114
Luke, 58, 80, 123, 124
Mary, 157
Solomon, 81, 84, 87
Stephen, 64, 106, 130, 178, 212
William, 29, 64, 80, 81, 106, 179
TRAIN, D., 139, 143, 151, 166, 172, 173, 177, 191, 199, 201, 208, 215
David, 42, 43, 53, 78, 89, 92, 101, 104, 110, 112, 123, 124, 125, 128, 129, 130, 131, 132, 134, 135, 136, 137, 150, 198, 202, 203, 216
Mary, 151
TRAVERS, Mathew, 202
TREE, Daniel, 128
TRIPPE, John, 134
TRIPPETT, William, 40
TROTTER, William, 105, 136
TROUBLESOME RIDGE, 212
TROY, 218, 221
TRUIT, Benjamin, 64, 68, 71, 72, 93
Draper, 88
John, 72
Joseph, 68, 72, 89
Joshua, 69
Mary, 50
Micajah, 82, 97
Samuel, 87
Sarah, 97
Solomon, 18, 72
TRUITT, Benjamin, 18, 20, 88, 99, 134, 144
Collings, 158
Hezekiah, 166
Jesse, 205
John, 50, 69, 85, 182
Joseph, 18, 85
Micajah, 120, 159, 160
Samuel, 173
Solomon, 50
TRUITT'S CHOICE, 50
TRUMERTERS ISLAND, 51
TRUMPERTYS ISLAND, 220
TRUMPETER'S ISLAND, 94
TRYALS, Many, 64
TUCHBURY, John, 102
TULL, Jesse, 164
Richard, 140, 164, 219
William, 134
TULLY, William, 169
TULLYS ADDITION, 169
TURK, Robert, 27
TURKEY BRANCH, 168, 170, 176, 198
TURNER, Charity, 3, 51
Cornelius, 3, 45, 105
Elizabeth, 51, 196
Ephraim, 3, 51, 53
Humphrey, 3, 53, 55
John, 51, 52, 53
Joseph, 113, 196
Joshua, 73
Martha, 196
Mary, 51, 218
Nathan, 51, 53
Priscilla, 196
Samuel, 151
Sarah, 196
Thomas, 156
William, 51
TURPIN, John, 134, 164
Joseph, 41, 164
William, 169
TURSSEWONDOCK, 147
TUSKEY BRANCH, 124
TUSSE WONDOKE, 128
TUSSEKEY BRANCH, 183
TWELLEY, Robert, 67
TWIFORD, John, 134
TWILLEY, ---, 101
Robert, 63, 79, 87
TWILLEY'S LANE, 102

INDEX

TWILLINGTON, 63, 198
TWO LITTLE NECKS, 47
TWO STRINGS TO A BOW, 16

-U-
UNITY FORGE, 38, 140

-V-
VALLEY OF WARRINGS BRANCH, 115
VANDYKE, Nicholas, 63
VANKERK, Barnet, 34
  John, 28
  Thomas, 28
VANKIRK, Art, 56
  Barnet, 61, 89
VAUGHAN, Ann, 206, 207
  Edward, 206, 207
  Ephraim, 129, 193
  Isaac, 193
  Jathro, 129
  Jethro, 192, 193
  Jonathan, 102
  Levin, 129, 157, 158, 176
  Mary, 129
  William, 129, 192, 193, 224
VEACH, Elisha, 207
  Elizabeth, 207
  Jesse, 207
VENABLES, Joseph, 169, 211
VENNEBLS,
  Benjamin, 12
  Joseph, 12
VENT, James, 86, 213
  John, 86
VENTURE, 182
VERKERK, Art, 77
VERKIRK, Art, 56
VINES, John, 133, 148
VINING, John, 3, 19, 20, 21

Phebe, 3, 19, 20, 21, 61, 70, 88
VINSON, Benjamin, 224
VINYARD, 190
VIRDEN, Elizabeth, 154
  John, 117
  Marnix, 52, 129, 134, 154, 199
  Mary, 154
  Ruth, 154
  Tabitha, 154
VIRDIN, Hugh, 132
  Marnix, 29
VIRGINIA, Colony of, 48, 63
VUGHTE, Nicholas, 136

-W-
WAILES, 219
WALKER, Comfort, 163
  Dennis Comfort, 161
  Esther, 136
  George, 40, 51, 105, 127, 136, 189, 190, 191, 205
  Hester, 136
  Jacob, 51, 113, 118, 120, 133, 195, 205
  James, 43, 146, 157, 183, 195, 205
  John, 44, 150, 159, 183, 194
  Leah, 205
  Mary, 205
  Nathaniel, 105, 133, 209
  Ruth, 201
  Thomas, 29, 94, 105, 108, 168, 169, 179, 183, 201, 205
WALKERS ADDITION, 183
WALKERS CHOICE, 105

WALKER'S NECK, 97
WALLACE,
  Elizabeth, 70
  James, 70
  Jean, 220
  Robert, 217
WALLER, Charles, 91
  George, 135, 160, 173
  John, 45, 48, 62, 65, 66, 71, 72, 135, 173
  Monica, 107
  Nelson, 160, 173
WALLER'S CHOICE, 173
WALLER'S LAND, 191
WALLS, Jacob, 108
  Levin, 108, 110
  Samuel, 59
  Sarah, 69
  Thomas, 59, 149
  William, 69, 149
WALTER, Luke, 206
  Peleg, 150, 163, 170
WALTON, Bethuel, 223
  George, 38, 39, 44, 56, 57, 63, 96, 101, 201, 217, 218, 223
  John, 3, 8, 27, 31, 39, 44, 55, 71, 97, 135, 206, 223
  Luke, 32, 46, 206
  Mary, 44, 201
  Namoy, 44
  Samuel, 44, 212, 223
  Tegle, 108
  Tekel, 172
  William, 8, 206
WALTON'S GUTT, 78
WAPLES, Abigail, 46
  Betty, 119
  Burton, 10, 16, 20, 21, 51, 86
  Cornelius, 119, 120
  Dirickson, 10,

106, 197, 224
Elihu, 188, 189, 192
John, 34, 187, 188, 192, 195
Joseph, 154, 156, 174, 194
Margaret, 194
Mary, 192
N., 188
Nathaniel, 146, 174, 179, 186, 188, 190, 196, 197, 200, 205
Paul, 146, 155, 187, 188, 189, 197
Peter, 146, 197
Priscilla, 188
Samuel, 196, 197, 222, 224
Stockley, 95
Temperance, 197
Thomas, 96
William, 10, 16, 46, 76, 146, 154, 174, 188, 194, 195, 197
WARDER, Jeremiah, 5
WARE, William, 17, 116, 196
WARING, Robert, 80
WARMINGHURST, 24
WARRANT, Majour, 31
WARREN, David, 20
Jacob, 126
Jane, 121
Major, 7
Majour, 31
Robert, 16, 67
William, 18
WARRENS CHOICE, 18, 45, 105
WARRENS CREEK, 19, 130
WARRENS NECK, 104
WARRENTON, Joseph, 184
WARRICK
HATTABOUGH, 177
WARRING, 14
Absolom, 84

David, 33
Jacob, 14
Levi, 58, 59
Lodawick, 32
Robert, 58, 59
Wrixam, 58, 84, 87
WARRINGTON,
Alexander, 184
David, 34
Jacob, 123
James, 35
John, 32, 115, 123
John Abbot, 123, 131, 175, 220
Joseph, 13, 32, 36, 100, 124, 148, 161, 179, 184, 191
Lodowick, 32
Rachel, 124, 161
Sarah, 191
Thomas, 13, 100, 112, 123, 191
William, 108, 110
WARRINTON,
William, 108
WARTON, Thomas, 133
WARWICK, 20, 146, 196, 197
Jeremiah, 219
WASTCOAT, Philip, 82
WATER HOLE, 165
WATERS, George, 149
John, 219
Spencer, 164
WATSON, Ann, 37
Bethual, 8, 33
Bethuel, 33, 64, 119, 121
David, 6, 43
Elizabeth, 37
George, 35
Isaac, 2, 11, 22, 44, 69, 87
John, 24, 25, 58, 106, 110, 116
Luke, 25, 26,

31, 37, 78, 117, 123, 124
Mary, 37
Purnal, 37
Samuel, 24, 25, 116, 117
Sarah, 110
Smothers, 155
Thomas, 37, 64
William, 78, 110
WATSONS CHOICE, 4
WATSONS ISLAND, 173
WATSON'S MARSH, 117
WATSONS PATENT, 4, 14
WATTSON, Bethual, 8
Bethuel, 38, 39, 166, 173
David, 6, 9, 29, 43, 178
George, 37
Isaac, 29, 35, 37, 64, 72, 124, 140, 153, 182, 212
John, 24
Luke, 25, 49, 153, 166, 171, 182, 184
Mary, 155, 166
Parnal, 35
Purnal, 37
Samuel, 24
Smothers, 155
Thomas, 35, 37
WATTSON'S CHOICE, 26
WATTSONS MARSHES, 25
WEBB, Benjamin, 72, 166, 169
Dorman, 58, 59, 116
John, 33, 43, 72
Jonas, 72
Silvester, 204
WEBLEY, 123
WELBORNE, Thomas, 95
WELCH, Daniel, 23, 31, 64
Ebenezer, 31

Jacob, 30, 31
John, 31, 64
Rachel, 204
Sarah, 31
William, 204
WELCHES CHANCE, 31
WELCHES FOLLY, 184
WELLS, Richard,
  47, 48
WESLEY, John, 98
  Richard, 116
  William, 18
WEST, Benjamin,
  88, 198
  Bridge, 107
  Bridget, 112
  Elias, 13, 36,
    191
  Elijah, 196
  Ezekiel, 30, 39,
    65, 70
  Gabriel, 24
  George, 107,
    179, 180, 196
  Jane, 38
  Jehu, 106, 107
  John, 95, 112,
    187, 189
  Joseph, 95, 137,
    172, 198
  Lewes, 51
  Lewis, 1, 46,
    95, 198
  Mary, 35, 37
  Peter, 21
  Robert, 7, 18,
    106, 107, 112
  Sarah, 13, 30,
    191
  Solomon, 92
  Thomas, 106,
    107, 112, 196
  William, 1, 26,
    33, 50, 95, 215
  Wrixam, 191
WEST INDIA FORTY,
  104
WESTCHESTER
  County, New
  York, 102
WESTLY, Ann, 219
  John, 92
  Richard, 219
WESTMORELAND
County,
  Pennsylvania,
  143, 146, 171
WESTMORELAND
County,
  Virginia, 149
WESTS RECOVERY,
  196
WHALEY, Ebenezer,
  206
  Isaac, 206
  Nathaniel, 206,
    224
WHALLEY, Ebenezer,
  224
  Nathaniel, 224
WHARTON, Hinman,
  221
  Jonathan, 160
  Thomas, 40
  Watson, 221
WHEALER, John, 50,
  101
  Jonathan, 101
  Kissiah, 101
WHEELER, John, 11
  Kesiah, 101
  William, 10, 11
WHELLERS HALL, 216
WHITE, Alice, 62
  Ambrose, 200
  Benjamin, 181
  Elizabeth, 169,
    208
  George, 84, 89,
    117, 140
  Isaac, 139, 185
  Isbel, 167
  Israel, 184
  Jacob, 52, 55,
    74, 105, 107,
    139, 184, 185
  James, 102, 167
  Jane Wilkins,
    184, 185
  John, 6, 30, 79,
    84, 117, 140
  Kame Wilkins,
    139
  Margaret, 102
  Margett, 161
  Mary, 107
  Newcom, 28, 105
  Newcomb, 76, 181
Paul, 197
Peter, 60, 99,
  111, 139, 169,
  208, 212, 213
Robert, 96, 119,
  139, 185
Sarah, 31
Sophia, 102, 167
Thomas, 161,
  167, 168, 218
William, 58
Wrixam (Wrx.),
  2, 3, 51, 74,
  119, 136, 185
WHITE LEVEL, 168
WHITE MARSH, 136
WHITE OAK NECK,
  108, 113
WHITE OAK SWAMP,
  128
WHITES INDUSTRY,
  163
WHITESIDES,
  Arthur, 171
  Margaret, 171
  Thomas, 171, 172
WHITLEY, Charles,
  218
WHITMAN, Stephen,
  25, 26
WHORTON, Charles,
  187, 189
  Thomas, 169
  Wattson, 221
WICOMICO RIVER,
  125
WIDOW STEVEN'S
  PLANTATION, 13
WIGTON, 141
WILD OAT PATCH, 23
WILDGOOS, Thomas
  Blaids, 96
WILDGOOSE, Thomas,
  189, 190
WILDREDGE, Leah,
  165
WILKINS, James,
  180, 197, 224
WILLEN, Thomas,
  173
WILLETT, John, 141
WILLEY, T., 102
  William, 60, 141
WILLIAMS, Ann, 99,

107
Aram, 89
Charles, 81
Christopher, 164
David, 121, 122, 128, 136
Davis, 132
Ezekiel, 165
Francis, 133
Isaac, 142, 152, 155
John, 75, 128, 191
Jonathan, 41, 58
Joseph, 41
Joshua, 142, 155
Lemmuel, 209
Lemuel, 133, 209, 221
Morgan, 101, 102, 136
Nathaniel, 20, 131
Peter, 10
Reynalds, 37
Reyner, 50, 55
Reyner, 58
Ruth, 10
Rynear, 99, 100
Samuel, 142, 220
Spencer, 155
Thomas, 152
WILLIAMS CHANCE, 152
WILLIAMS SECURITY, 30
WILLIAMS'S VEXATION, 217
WILLING, Thomas, 102
WILLINGS CHANCE, 102
WILLSON, Anna, 32
John, 147, 182
Samuel, 182
Thomas, 163
William, 32
WILMINGTON, Borough of, 109, 129
WILSON, Betsey, 34
James, 141
John, 59, 139
Mathew, 34

Matthew, 9, 34
Moses, 18, 96, 103
Polley, 34
Reuben, 139
Rev. Matthew, 191
Thomas, 22, 39, 64, 158, 163
William, 43, 81, 139, 151, 214
WILSON'S FOLLEY, 22, 80
WILSONS SWAMP, 122
WILSONS SWAMP LANDING, 122
WILTBANCK, Cornelius, 205
Harmanus, 203
Jacob, 8
John, 7, 203
WILTBANK, Abraham, 1, 36, 51, 203, 212, 216
Catharine, 216
Cornelius, 5, 27, 32, 60, 73, 74, 78, 83, 87, 123, 135, 165, 180, 199
Harmanus, 203
Harmanus Frederick, 220
Hermanus, 32
Hermanus Frederick, 48, 54
Isaac, 31, 44, 74, 83
J., 199, 209, 217, 218
Jacob, 36
Jane, 27
John, 1, 2, 3, 18, 19, 22, 36, 44, 47, 51, 52, 60, 70, 96, 99, 104, 113, 122, 123, 125, 163, 192, 196, 202, 203, 208, 214, 216, 217, 218, 220
Marget, 74

Mr., 34
Naomi, 212
Rachel, 73, 83, 180
Samuel, 180
WINDER, William, 169
WINDSOR, John, 175
Mary, 175
WINDSOR BRANCH, 139
WINE, John, 156
WINGATE, John, 28, 189
Love, 119, 188, 189, 200
Philips, 123
Phillip, 139
Sarah, 188, 189
WINGET, John, 87
WINSLEY, William, 73, 127
WINSOR, Lidy, 172
WINWRIGHT, John, 169
WITINGTON, Southy, 210
WITTINGTON, William, 135
WOLF, John, 136
Jonathan, 198
WOLF PIT GUTT, 126
WOLF PIT POND, 175
WOLFE, Ruth, 135
WOOD, Robert, 121
WOODCRAFT, William, 165
William Ezekiel, 189
WOODCRAFTS VENTURE, 189
WOODDROP, Sarah, 1
WOODGATE, John, 118, 147, 194
WOODLAND GROVE, 105
WOODLAND RANGE, 168
WOODS, John, 49, 60, 88, 91, 118
WOODWARD, Anthony, 206
WOOLEN, Edward, 125

INDEX

WOOLF, Francis, 98
  John, 44
  Jonathan, 108,
    198, 212
  Mary, 18
  Rece, 1, 118
  Reece, 13, 14,
    18, 47, 92, 98,
    136, 183, 199
  Rees, 18, 35
  Warrington, 51
WOOLF BRANCH, 2
WOOLF DEN, 33, 110
WOOLF DENN SWAMP,
  121
WOOLF PIT, 2
WOOLF PIT GUTT,
  120
WOOLFE, Jonathan,
  135
WOOLGAST, Otto,
  104
WOOTEN, Benjamin,
  131
  Edward, 131
  John, 131
  Jonathan, 223
WOOTON, Elijah,
  223
  Isaac, 223
  Jemmy, 174
  John, 223
  Nancey, 174
  Peter, 174
WOOTTON, Benjamin,
  174
  Maron, 174
WORCESTER County,
  Maryland, 4,
    11, 13, 15, 20,
    27, 29, 30, 34,
    35, 36, 37, 38,
    39, 46, 49, 55,
    57, 65, 67, 68,
    71, 77, 83, 84,
    84, 86, 87, 92,
    94, 100, 106,
    112, 120, 124,
    125, 128, 131,
    135, 140, 144,
    156, 162, 170,
    185, 190, 192,
    200, 206, 215,
    222, 224

WORMINGHURST, 20,
  24, 50, 68, 166
WORMINGHUST, 173
WORTON, Charles,
  187
WRIGHT, Comfort,
  97
  Edward, 16, 97
  Francis, 121,
    122, 128, 132,
    152, 200
  Fretwell, 29
  John, 15, 16,
    110
  Peter F., 36
  Peter Fretwell,
    8, 39, 97, 98,
    157, 226
  Peter Ft., 47,
    48, 52, 54,
    100, 101, 109,
    112, 118, 147,
    185
  Robert, 30
  Solomon, 16
WROE, William, 160
WYATT, Caleb, 162
  Elijah, 168
  John, 144
  Sacker, 4, 109,
    129, 146, 154,
    185, 199
  William, 18,
    109, 143, 144,
    148, 187
WYNKOOP, Abraham,
  3, 11, 19, 20,
  21, 38, 50, 57,
  61, 62, 63, 70,
  77, 96, 115,
  197, 217, 218
  Abram, 20
  Benjamin, 1, 3,
    19, 20, 38, 44,
    57, 61, 62, 70,
    77, 79, 88, 99,
    218
  Mary, 3, 19, 20,
    21, 61, 70, 71,
    88
  Sarah, 77
  Thomas, 3, 20,
    38, 62, 88
WYNKOOPS ISLAND,

55
WYTH, James, 211

-Y-
YEATS, Joseph, 24
YOSEPH, Joseph, 29
YOULIN, Walter,
  180
YOUNG, Catharine,
  66, 87, 88, 94,
  145, 223
  Esther, 144
  George, 27, 87,
    127
  John, 43, 66,
    75, 87, 88, 94,
    145, 151, 158,
    167, 214, 223
  Nathan, 3
  Nathaniel, 73,
    76, 77, 78,
    132, 144
  Robert, 59, 73,
    76, 77, 78
  Thomas Cary, 31
YOUNG'S ADDITION,
  132

Other books by F. Edward Wright:

Abstracts of Bucks County, Pennsylvania Wills, 1685-1785
Abstracts of Cumberland County, Pennsylvania Wills, 1750-1785
Abstracts of Cumberland County, Pennsylvania Wills, 1785-1825
Abstracts of Philadelphia County Wills, 1726-1747
Abstracts of Philadelphia County Wills, 1748-1763
Abstracts of Philadelphia County Wills, 1763-1784
Abstracts of Philadelphia County Wills, 1777-1790
Abstracts of Philadelphia County Wills, 1790-1802
Abstracts of Philadelphia County Wills, 1802-1809
Abstracts of Philadelphia County Wills, 1810-1815
Abstracts of Philadelphia County Wills, 1815-1819
Abstracts of Philadelphia County Wills, 1820-1825
Abstracts of Philadelphia County, Pennsylvania Wills, 1682-1726
Abstracts of South Central Pennsylvania Newspapers, Volume 1, 1785-1790
Abstracts of South Central Pennsylvania Newspapers, Volume 3, 1796-1800
Abstracts of the Newspapers of Georgetown and the Federal City, 1789-99
Abstracts of York County, Pennsylvania Wills, 1749-1819
Bucks County, Pennsylvania Church Records of the 17th and 18th Centuries Volume 2: Quaker Records: Falls and Middletown Monthly Meetings
Anna Miller Watring and F. Edward Wright
Caroline County, Maryland Marriages, Births and Deaths, 1850-1880
Citizens of the Eastern Shore of Maryland, 1659-1750
Cumberland County, Pennsylvania Church Records of the 18th Century
Delaware Newspaper Abstracts, Volume 1: 1786-1795
Early Charles County, Maryland Settlers, 1658-1745
Marlene Strawser Bates and F. Edward Wright
Early Church Records of Alexandria City and Fairfax County, Virginia
F. Edward Wright and Wesley E. Pippenger
Early Church Records of New Castle County, Delaware, Volume 1, 1701-1800
Frederick County Militia in the War of 1812
Sallie A. Mallick and F. Edward Wright
Inhabitants of Baltimore County, 1692-1763
Land Records of Sussex County, Delaware, 1769-1782
Land Records of Sussex County, Delaware, 1782-1789
Elaine Hastings Mason and F. Edward Wright
Marriage Licenses of Washington, District of Columbia, 1811-1830
Marriages and Deaths from the Newspapers of Allegany and Washington Counties, Maryland, 1820-1830
Marriages and Deaths from The York Recorder, 1821-1830
Marriages and Deaths in the Newspapers of Frederick and Montgomery Counties, Maryland, 1820-1830

Marriages and Deaths in the Newspapers of Lancaster County, Pennsylvania, 1821-1830
Marriages and Deaths in the Newspapers of Lancaster County, Pennsylvania, 1831-1840
Marriages and Deaths of Cumberland County, [Pennsylvania], 1821-1830
Maryland Calendar of Wills Volume 9: 1744-1749
Maryland Calendar of Wills Volume 10: 1748-1753
Maryland Calendar of Wills Volume 11: 1753-1760
Maryland Calendar of Wills Volume 12: 1759-1764
Maryland Calendar of Wills Volume 13: 1764-1767
Maryland Calendar of Wills Volume 14: 1767-1772
Maryland Calendar of Wills Volume 15: 1772-1774
Maryland Calendar of Wills Volume 16: 1774-1777
Maryland Eastern Shore Newspaper Abstracts, Volume 1: 1790-1805
Maryland Eastern Shore Newspaper Abstracts, Volume 2: 1806-1812
Maryland Eastern Shore Newspaper Abstracts, Volume 3: 1813-1818
Maryland Eastern Shore Newspaper Abstracts, Volume 4: 1819-1824
Maryland Eastern Shore Newspaper Abstracts, Volume 5: Northern Counties, 1825-1829
F. Edward Wright and Irma Harper
Maryland Eastern Shore Newspaper Abstracts, Volume 6: Southern Counties, 1825-1829
Maryland Eastern Shore Newspaper Abstracts, Volume 7: Northern Counties, 1830-1834
Irma Harper and F. Edward Wright
Maryland Eastern Shore Newspaper Abstracts, Volume 8: Southern Counties, 1830-1834
Maryland Militia in the Revolutionary War
S. Eugene Clements and F. Edward Wright
Newspaper Abstracts of Allegany and Washington Counties, Maryland, 1811-1815
Newspaper Abstracts of Cecil and Harford Counties, Maryland, 1822-1830
Newspaper Abstracts of Frederick County, Maryland, 1816-1819
Newspaper Abstracts of Frederick County, Maryland, 1811-1815
Sketches of Maryland Eastern Shoremen
Tax List of Chester County, Pennsylvania 1768
Tax List of York County, Pennsylvania 1779
Washington County Church Records of the 18th Century, 1768-1800
Western Maryland Newspaper Abstracts, Volume 1: 1786-1798
Western Maryland Newspaper Abstracts, Volume 2: 1799-1805
Western Maryland Newspaper Abstracts, Volume 3: 1806-1810
Wills of Chester County, Pennsylvania, 1766-1778

www.ingramcontent.com/pod-product-compliance
Lightning Source LLC
Chambersburg PA
CBHW071701160426
43195CB00012B/1537